CONTENTS

VOLUME 450

JULY 1980

THE ANNALS

of The American Academy *of* Political
and Social Science

(ISSN 0002-7162)

RICHARD D. LAMBERT, *Editor*

ALAN W. HESTON, *Assistant Editor*

REFLECTIONS ON THE HOLOCAUST:
Historical, Philosophical, and Educational Dimensions

Special Editors of This Volume

IRENE G. SHUR
Director
Ethnic Studies Institute
Professor of History
West Chester State College
West Chester, Pennsylvania

FRANKLIN H. LITTELL
Chairman
National Institute on the Holocaust
Professor of Religion
Temple University
Philadelphia, Pennsylvania

MARVIN E. WOLFGANG
President
American Academy of Political and Social Science
Professor of Sociology
University of Pennsylvania
Philadelphia, Pennsylvania

PHILADELPHIA

Copy Editor

PRISCILLA A. ESTES

International Standard Book Numbers (ISBN)

ISBN 0-87761-253-6, vol. 450, 1980; paper
ISBN 0-87761-252-8, vol. 450, 1980; cloth

A STATEMENT FROM THE PRESIDENT

The July issue of THE ANNALS is ordinarily the publication of papers at the Annual Meeting. For reasons announced in the September, 1979, issue, we have deferred the 1980 Annual Meeting. The July issue is devoted to an examination of the attempt of national socialism to annihilate European Jewry. The Holocaust, a unique historical phenomenon, has been described as a burnt sacrifice, a burning and a complete annihilation, and it continues to perplex many scholars who ponder over the many unanswered questions. On the other hand, some of my colleagues ask, What can be said new about the Holocaust? This volume is designed to answer that question.

Dr. Franklin H. Littell and Dr. Irene G. Shur, two of the Editors of this volume, believe that much which resembles the denigration of the individual and humanity at large depicted in the subject is still to be learned. Dr. Franklin H. Littell, a Methodist minister and professor of religious studies, is one of the more respected proponents urging revival of scholarly interest in the Holocaust. He sees a scientific, professional insensitivity in Western Civilization today which resembles the denigration of the individual and humanity at large manifested by the Holocaust. Dr. Irene G. Shur, a professor of history, has had personal experience with the Holocaust, having lost most of her family in Poland, and knows that anecdotes become statistics which become aggregate sufferings. She believes that an intimate knowledge of the Holocaust and the historical development which made it possible could provide a bulwark against future "holocausts," regardless of where they might occur or against whom they might be directed.

Appearing after the television Holocaust drama, this volume presages a rising interest in the event and the lessons to be derived from it. The historic memory of the Holocaust must be preserved. The premeditated plan to annihilate a people whose history stretches from Abraham to Martin Buber must not be consigned to the dustbins of history or be permitted to escape investigation.

The annihilation of any ethnic group and especially the brutal murder of artists, scientists, philosophers, and musicians who contributed so much to our culture is a horrendous crime and an inestimable loss. The Holocaust demands continued examination in order to assure that the lessons which it teaches shall not be lost.

MARVIN E. WOLFGANG
PRESIDENT

PREFACE

Since the first confirmed reports were circulated 35 years ago, scholars, theologians, statesmen, and survivors, as well as many others, have asked, Why? Why did a heinous crime of the mass of the Holocaust take place in this, the most civilized century, and in Germany, the most advanced country in Europe? Others have queried, How? How was it possible for Nazis, in less than 12 years to isolate, dehumanize, expropriate, enslave, and murder six million Jews? Some have also asked, What? What did happen? Are accounts of inhumane acts perpetrated by the Nazis and their followers against men, women, and children true? And some have wondered, Why did not various world organizations and nations, appraised of the barbarous acts, attempt to stop them? Why did they deny the helpless a place of refuge?

Since 1945, a worldwide community of scholars has attempted to answer these questions. Especially since 1975, the interest in the Holocaust and its results has stimulated increased research and questions. Scholars representing a wide variety of professions and disciplines continue to examine the Holocaust and to seek to comprehend the historical forces which provoked it as well as to interpret its impact upon contemporary civilization.

In an attempt to answer these questions, we have invited authors from Canada, West Germany, Israel, and the United States and from a cross section of disciplines. This company of scholars addresses itself to the perplexing and often painful questions associated with the Holocaust and deals with both the preceding questions and the new ones that have presented themselves. Among the latter are: What did—or did not—the churches do? How has the German nation attempted to rehabilitate itself? What are the implications for public and professional morality? And how should the Holocaust be taught?

This volume, divided by sections exploring the antecedents, the Holocaust, the meanings, and the lessons, confronts these questions. All sections receive fresh treatment. For now, after three decades, new views of the Holocaust and its impact, as well as new sources, supplement earlier scholarship.

In the antecedents section, the authors seek to reveal the multiple and deep-rooted causes of antisemitism. It is their view that the political, economic, and social crises in the late nineteenth century and the first part of the twentieth century created the conditions. The selection of the Jews as the scapegoat for the ills of Europe was relatively easy because of the latent antisemitism that existed in every part of Christendom. The Holocaust section presents the what, why, and how of the event. The defense used by Ohlendorf, leader of the *Einsatzgruppen*—the first stage of the "murder machine"—at the Nuremberg trials provides insight into the way the Nazis regarded their mission. The use of Jews in the factories and on the experimentation tables is described. The failure of Great Britain and the United States, especially the British Foreign Office and the American State Department, to aid the Jews in Hitler's Europe is analyzed. Papers describing those organizations and individuals that aided Jews reveal new and important data. German, Israeli, and American papers describe persons and organizations and their work. The section concerning the meanings reflects on the aftermath and includes some new insights of theologians, philosophers, historians, and public leaders. New perspectives are developed, and interesting conclusions are drawn. Under the lessons section, current educational developments, as well as the need for more widespread education, better-prepared teachers, and more extensive teaching resources, are explored.

We, the Editors, wish to thank the contributors who agreed to share their expertise and insights with the readers. This unique event has a present and a future as well as a past; to ignore its meanings and lessons is to invite similar incidents of genocide in times to come. With all due respect to the educated reader, we remind him and ourselves once more that the Holocaust was planned, supervised, and executed by a diversified population, including men and women of the modern university. Hence this issue of THE ANNALS appeals to the reader's mind—and also to his active conscience.

IRENE G. SHUR
FRANKLIN H. LITTELL
MARVIN E. WOLFGANG

ANNALS, AAPSS, **450**, July 1980

Historical Antecedents: Why the Holocaust?

By Claude R. Foster, Jr.

ABSTRACT: There are many antecedents to the Holocaust. Antisemitism, the necessary precursor to the Holocaust, has a long history and was usually based on political, economic, religious, or social prejudice. Throughout the nineteenth century, the Jew sought desparately to identify himself with the European Christian community. Many Jews accepted assimilation and conversion in order to gain admission into European society. In the latter part of the nineteenth century, however, a violent racial antisemitism appeared that rejected assimilation as a solution to the "Jewish problem." The tensions among the Jews themselves—liberals versus orthodox and Zionists versus assimilationists—the economic crises, the need to find a scapegoat for national humiliation, the identification of Jews with Marxists and the swing to the political right helped prepare for the outbreak of violent racial antisemitism which led to the Holocaust. With Hitler ideological antisemitism captured a state. Given the monopoly of political power which Hitler quickly acquired, the deep antisemitic roots in every European state, the indifference with which the world witnessed the increasing persecution in Germany, and the intimidation which the Nazis so successfully employed against the German people, the Holocaust in hindsight seemed inevitable.

Claude R. Foster, Jr. is professor of history at West Chester State College and received his Ph.D. in history from the University of Pennsylvania. He was a Fulbright Grantee at the University of Freiburg and studied at Basel and at the Friedrich Schiller University in Jena. He has taught in Germany and has lectured at international symposia on reformation studies convoked in the German Democratic Republic. His publications include many major articles on religion, revolution, and religious liberty in the Mennonite Quarterly Review, Worldview, *and the* Christian Century.

1

IN ROLF Hochuth's play, *The Deputy*, Kurt Gerstein, the Lutheran Christian spy in the SS (*Schutzstaffel*) who seeks to sabotage the gas shipments to concentration camps, speaks sobering words to Father Ricardo Fontana, a Jesuit: "I shall not survive my mission. A Christian in this time cannot survive if his life is consequential."[1]

What a terrible indictment of his generation, a generation which had been the heir of a Christian and Enlightenment tradition. How could it happen that such a culture could become barbaric? How could the nation which brought forth Gotthold Ephraim Lessing (1729–81), the author of *Nathan the Wise*, one of the greater expressions of tolerance in all of literature, engage in mass murder? How could a society in which a prominent Jewish scholar and an influential Christian theologian cultivated a beautiful friendship become infected with a fatal bigotry? The same humane essence, to employ Lessing, which made Moses Mendelssohn a Christian to Johann Gottfried Herder, made Herder a Jew to Mendelssohn.[2] In a letter dated Berlin, 18 May 1781, Mendelssohn (1729–86) wrote to Herder (1744–1803), "Moses, the human being, writes to Herder, the human being; not the Jew to the Superintendent."[3] A few months later, Mendelssohn wrote to Herder, the Lutheran pastor and superintendent in Weimar:

I have held you in esteem for many years, but your essay concerning Lessing

has caused me to be bound ever closer to you, to love you and to earnestly desire to be loved by you, and to be called your friend. Because friendship with such a person as you are can compensate me in my remaining days for the loss of Lessing.[4]

How then could this nation become mankind's executioner?–a nation whose most revered poets wrote such lines as

Let man be noble
helpful and good
for that alone
distinguishes him
from all creatures
which we know[5]

And again, Friedrich Schiller (1759–1805) in *Don Carlos* has the Marquis of Posa address Philipp II:

All the kings of Europe
pay homage to the Spanish name.
Lead the way for Europe's monarchs.
One pen-stroke from this royal hand
and the world will be recreated.
Sire, grant liberty of thought.[6]

EARLY HISTORY OF ANTISEMITISM

Antisemitism has a long history. From the pharaoh who knew not Joseph, to Haman, to Antiochus Epiphanes, to the case against Alfred Dreyfus, to the Final Solution, this strange historical phenomenon has plagued every age. Throughout their history, Jews living in the Diaspora were forced to adjust to the society in which they found themselves. They were called upon either to surrender their unique religious heritage or to face the furnace or the lion's den. In the second century

1. Rolf Hochhuth, *Der Stellvertreter* (Hamburg: Rowohlt Verlag, 1963), p. 65.
2. Gotthold Ephraim Lessing, *Nathan der Weise: Gesammelte Werke* (Munich: Carl Hanser Verlag, 1959), p. 739.
3. Lutz Richter, ed., *Johann Gottfried Herder im Spiegel seiner Zeitgenossen* (East Berlin: Union Verlag, 1978), p. 211.

4. Ibid., p. 213.
5. Goethe, *Das Göttliche; see* Jürgen Moltmann, "Theological Perspectives on the Future," in *Lutheran Brotherhood Colloquium on the Church*, Jan. 29–Feb. 2, 1979.
6. Friedrich Schiller, *Don Carlos*, in *Schiller, Dramen und Gedichte* (Stuttgart: Deutsche Schiller Gesellschaft, 1955), p. 343.

B.C., they were forced to indentify themselves with Hellenistic culture in order that the Seleucid goal of *Homonoia* could be achieved. Their fierce love of independence and their political zeal made them poor subjects under Rome's hegemony and ultimately led to the destruction of Jerusalem. Nor did they fare any better in the *Corpus Christianum*. The Christian European civilization resented the uniqueness of the Jew and his resistance to conversion.

It was not until the French Revolution that persecution of and discrimination against the Jew relented. Liberal reforms in the nineteenth century granted the Jews civil rights. However, many states suspended these rights in the reaction which followed the Congress of Vienna. The emancipation of the Jew did not meet with opposition in the legislative bodies of the second German Empire or in the legislatures of the several German states in 1871, but popular prejudice against the Jew remained very strong.

European society in the liberal nineteenth century continued to place heavy burdens upon the sons of Israel. Many Jews were driven to despair and accepted Christian baptism, the price of admission to European society. Many Jews as well as Christians abandoned religious beliefs under the onslaught of science, secularism, and liberalism. The enemies of faith, according to Johann Hinrich Wichern (1808–81), the Lutheran sociologist of the nineteenth century, are those Jews who have liberated themselves from Judaism and those Christians who have liberated themselves from Christianity. Pagan Jews and pagan Christians have formed an alliance in order to destroy that which is holy.[7]

ASSIMILATION

Heschel Marx (1782–1838), the grandson of a rabbi, the son of a rabbi, the brother of a rabbi, and the son-in-law of a rabbi, was baptized into the Prussian state church in 1817. Heinrich Marx, as he was called after his baptism, no doubt took this step because, as a Jew, he was prohibited from practicing his legal profession in Prussia. After the Congress of Vienna, Trier, where Heschel Marx lived, came under the rule of Prussia. Because of his apparent liberalism, such a "conversion" may have been easier for Heinrich Marx than it would have been for many of his fellow Jews. His son Karl, who almost certainly would have been destined for the rabbinical profession, became an antisemite and the father of an ideology alien to Judiasm. According to Karl Marx: "The worldly cult of the Jew is haggling and his worldly god is money. The social emancipation of the Jew is the emancipation of society from Judaism."[8] Although Marx considered Judaism an evil, reactionary force, one must remember that he was writing within the context of scientific socialism, which posits a Promethean, materialistic society, liberated from all religious belief. It is easy to imagine, however, how such words could be exploited for antisemitic purposes.

Ludwig Börne (1786–1837), years after his baptism and the official renunciation of his Jewish heritage, cried out in despair:

It is like a miracle. A thousand times have I experienced it and yet is eternally new to me. Some reproach me because I am a Jew; others excuse me for it; a

7. Peter Meinhold, ed., *Johann Hinrich Wichern, Sämtliche Werke*, vol. III, pt. 2

(Berlin and Hamburg: Lutherisches Verlagshaus, 1969), pp. 59–60.

8. *Marx-Engels Werke: Zur Judenfrage*, vol. I (East Berlin: Dietz Verlag, 1970), pp. 372–73.

third praises me for it. But all of them think of it. They are as though they were fixed by the spell of this magic Jewish circle and no one can get out. I also know quite well where this evil charm comes from. The poor Germans! Living in the lowest floor, oppressed by the seven floors of the upper classes, their anxiety is made lighter by speaking of people who are still lower than they are and who live in the cellar. Not being a Jew provides them with consolation at not being a state councillor. No, the fact that I was born a Jew has not embittered me against the Germans and has never deluded me. I would indeed not be worthy to enjoy the light of the sun if I paid with scornful grumbling for the great act of grace that God has shown me of letting me both a German and a Jew. . . . Yes because I have known slavery, I understand freedom more than you. Yes, because I was born without a fatherland my desire for a fatherland is more passionate than yours, and because my birthplace was not bigger than the Judengasse and everything behind the locked gates was a foreign country to me, therefore for me now the fatherland is more than the city, more than a territory, more than a province.[9]

Heinrich Heine (1797–1856), of whom Friedrich Nietzsche wrote, "I search vainly through the kingdoms of all ages to find anything equal to his sweet and passionate music"[10] embraced Christianity in 1825. Such a step, according to Heine, was necessary for him in order to be accepted in European society. Heine, like Börne, lived in exile in France. "My marriage with my dear Frau Germania, the blond, bearskin savage," Heine wrote, "has never been happy . . . but it never came to an actual breach. I could never bring myself to renounce by domestic cross."[11] Heine therefore rejected all

suggestions that he become a naturalized French citizen: "Naturalization may be for others . . . but is not fitting for a German poet, who has written the most beautiful German poems. It would be a horrible, insane idea for me to say that I am a German poet and at the same time a naturalized Frenchman."[12]

Both Börne and Heine belonged to the movement "Young Germany," designed to promote liberalism and democracy. Since important figures in this group were Jews, their reactionary opponents sought to discredit the movement by renaming it "Young Palestine."

Ferdinand Lassalle (1825–64), the youthful Maccabean, wanted to lead the new Israel, the proletariat, in its struggle for social and economic equality. The discrimination against his people in the various German states no doubt played a major role in stimulating his revolutionary fervor. However, Lassalle soon came to resent the limitations which his Jewish heritage imposed upon his revolutionary spirit.[13] He, as many other Jews in the nineteenth century, indulged in self-hate. Two things he hated: Jews and litterateurs. "I have the misfortune to be both," he said.

European Jews would have gladly exchanged the nostalgic longing "See you next year in Jerusalem" for integration into European society. Their self-denigration, born out of their desperate attempt to find a home in European culture, recalls the crisis of Job, who could find no meaning in unmerited suffering; a crisis, which for them, reached its acme in the concentration camps:

Let the day perish wherein I was born,

---

9. Køppel Pinson, *Modern Germany: Its History and Civilization* (New York: Macmillan Press, 1967), pp. 67–68.

10. Ibid., p. 68.

11. Ibid., p. 69.

12. Ibid.

13. Ibid., p. 197.

And the night which said,
There is a man-child conceived. . . .
Let that night be barren;
Let no joyful voice come
therein.[14]

RACIAL ANTISEMITISM: ASSIMILATION REJECTED

Early in the nineteenth century, Grattenauer, the commissioner of justice in Berlin, wrote a pamphlet entitled *Against the Jews (Wider die Juden)* in which he demanded that the Jews be forced to wear a yellow insignia, like the "Jew Badge" of thirteenth-century England, in order that everyone could avoid them like the plague.[15] As early as 1819, the cry by which the Nazis were to terrorize the Jews could be heard in many German cities, "Jude Verrecke." About the same time a pamphlet appeared, a *Judenspiegel*, in which the most draconian measures were suggested for suppressing the Jew and his influence in the society.

As the forces of liberalism and democracy grew stronger in the nineteenth century, the emancipation of the Jew and his assimilation into German society advanced. Intermarriage between Jews and Gentiles increased substantially in the late nineteenth century, although it was repugnant to most Germans not only for religious reasons, but also because "good German blood was thereby polluted."[16]

14. Job 3: 3, 7.
15. Arnold Künzli, *Karl Marx: Eine Psychographie* (Vienna: Europa Verlag, 1966), p. 66.
16. Despite the increased intermarriages between Jews and Gentiles in the nineteenth century, membership in German synagogues increased from 300,000 to 403,000 in the period 1816–1871; see Hajo Holborn, *A History of Modern Germany 1840–1945* (New York: Alfred A. Knopf, 1969), p. 280. For the warnings concerning the polluting of German blood, see Karl Dietrich Bracher, *The German Dictatorship*, trans. Jean Steinberg, (New York and Washington: Praeger Publishers, 1973), p. 37.

Heinrich Treitschke (1834–96), the very influential history professor in Berlin whose lectures were attended by William II, wrote concerning the Jews:

The Jews at one time played a necessary role in German history, because of their ability in the management of money. But now that the Aryans have become accustomed to the idiosyncrasies of finance, the Jews are no longer necessary. The international Jew, hidden in the mask of different nationalities, is a disintegrating influence; he can be of no further use to the world. It is necessary to speak openly about the Jews, undisturbed by the fact that the Jewish press befouls what is purely historical truth.[17]

As the influence of the Enlightenment faded and the economic problems of the industrial revolution became more acute, assimilation of the Jew into German society became less attractive to antisemites. An antisemitism based on what was believed to be a Jewish capitalistic monopoly became very pronounced during the first economic crisis of the Second Empire (1871–1918). As the forces of *völkisch* nationalism gained in popularity, German antisemitism also took a violent turn toward racial and enthnic segregation. For the champions of Aryan purity, submitting to Christian baptism and seeking to identify with Christian civilization was no longer an acceptable solution to the Jewish problem.

The first economic crisis: 1873–95

There appears to be a relationship between economic instability and antisemitic hysteria. In the same year (1873) in which the first eco-

17. Louis L. Snyder, ed., *Documents of German History* (New Brunswick: Rutgers University Press, 1958), p. 262.

nomic crisis of the Second Reich began, Wilhelm Marr, who was probably the first to employ the word "antisemite," published a pamphlet, *The Victory of Judaism Over Teutonism (Der Sieg des Judentums über das Gemanentum).* The pamphlet appeared in twelve editions within a six-year period. Marr denied that antisemitism in Germany was based on religious intolerance. "The Jews," he wrote, "had survived eighteen hundred years [that is, in a Christian civilization]. In the nineteenth century, they had become a world power and had transformed Germany into New Palestine by their influence on the government and their control of the press."[18]

In 1874, Otto Glagau picked up Marr's theme. In a series of articles published in widely read weeklies, Glagau indentified the Jews as the leading capitalists. He was convinced that an alien race was sucking the marrow out the bones of the German people.[19]

POLITICAL ANTISEMITISM

Bismarck, in preparing Prussia for the wars against Austria and France by which he hoped to gain German unification, entered into liaison with the National Liberal party, the champion of economic laissez-faire. Gerson Bleichröder, Bismarck's financial agent and advisor for more than 30 years, was a Prussian Jew. Bleichröder was the first Prussian Jew to become a "von" without submitting to baptism. Fritz Stern points out that it was finances made available by Bleichröder which made Prussia's mobilization against Austria possible. For supervising the French indemnity at the conclusion of the Franco-

18. Holborn, p. 281.
19. Ibid.

Prussian War, Bleichröder was awarded the iron cross.

Bismarck's association with Bleichröder as well as William II's friendship with Albert Ballin, the Jewish shipping magnate, and Walter Rathenau, a leading Jewish economist, cannot be satisfactorily explained under the concept of *Hausjude.*[20] In 1873, when the economic crisis began, it was easy for the antisemites to conclude that the Jewish capitalists and the National Liberals, who advocated a liberal, bourgeois, economic program, were to blame. The fact that the National Liberals were also the champions of Jewish emancipation did not escape the conservative forces in the Reischstag, which tended to be antisemitic and which opposed Bismarck's alliance with the National Liberals. In the *Kulturkampf* of the early 1870s, Bismarck relied upon the support of the National Liberals, who also resented the Roman church's political authority in Germany.

Marr's description of the Reich as a "New Palestine" and the conservative resistance in the *Kulturkampf* incensed Bismarck. The Catholic historian Constantin Frantz in his work *National Liberalism and the Jewish Hegemony (Nationalliberalismus und die Judenherrschaft, 1874),* criticized Bismarck's alliance with the National Liberals and described it as an attempt to place

20. Fritz Stern, *Gold and Iron: Bismarck, Bleichröder and the Building of the German Empire* (New York: Alfred A. Knopf, 1976); *see also* Werner E. Mosse and Arnold Paucker, eds., *Juden im Wilhelminischen Deutschland 1890–1914,* Leo Baeck Institute Publication, vol. 33 (Tübingen: J. C. B. Mohr, 1976), where it is pointed out that William II told Sir Edward Grey in 1907 that there were too many Jews in Germany. They should be eliminated. But William had a Jewish adjutant and two of his best friends were Albert Ballin and Walter Rathenau.

Germany under Jewish hegemony. After 1875, even the *Kreuzzeitung*, which usually supported the government, and the Catholic Center party's *Germania* published antisemitic propaganda. The fact that the conservative forces in the Reichstag did not hesitate to enlist the most radical antisemitic allies to bring pressure to bear upon the government did not bode well for the future of Germany's Jews.[21] At this stage in his career, Bismarck concluded that antisemitism was a form of subversion.

As a result of the economic crisis of 1873, Bismarck was finally forced to abandon the liberal economic program and to introduce protective tariffs. The transition from economic laissez-faire to economic nationalism was a gradual one. In a speech on 2 May 1879, Bismarck officially requested the Reichstag to abandon economic liberalism: "In my opinion, since we have placed our tariffs at too low a rate (and I blame myself for that, too), we have been slowly bleeding to death because of insufficient protection."[22] The decision to abandon laissez-faire capitalism, to declare a truce in the *Kulturkampf*, and to seek the support of the more conservative parties could only alienate his former allies, the National Liberals. In his struggle against

Marxism and socialism, the chancellor also was forced to seek rapprochement with those political forces which were most influenced by antisemitic sentiments.

From about 1880 the tide of antisemitism continued to rise in Europe, especially in Germany and Austria. In 1879, Marr founded the League of Antisemites. In 1880, the German Reform party and the Social Reich party were founded. Both these parties employed antisemitism as a rallying point, describing the Jewish question as the most acute national and political problem.[23] In 1881, the League of German Students was founded. The purpose of this league was to propagate antisemitism and nationalism in German universities. The year 1881 also saw the establishment of the German People's League, at about the same time the German Antisemitic League came into existence. The latter organization demanded that Germany adopt immigration laws to restrict Jewish immigration. These laws could be modeled after the American immigration laws, which restricted Chinese immigration. Both the German People's League and the German Antisemitic League rejected assimilation as a solution to the Jewish problem.[24]

Adolf Stöcker, the Prussian court chaplain, founded the Christian Social Worker's party in 1879. Stöcker insisted that he did not want a culture that was not German culture. He therefore was an antisemite. Unlike the more radical racial antisemites, Stöcker would have accepted assimilation. He regarded the Second Reich as the logical historical expression of the Reformation. The German Empire and the Protestant

21. Bracher, p. 38; *see also* Charles Bloch, "Die Französischen Revolutionen von 1789, 1830, 1848 und 1871 Als Meinensteine Auf Dem Weg Zur Demokratie," in *Revolution Und Demokratie in Geschichte und Literatur: Zum 60. Geburtstag von Walter Grab*, eds. Julius H. Schoeps and Imanuel Geiss (Duisburg: Walter Braun Verlag, 1979), pp. 337–53. Bloch points out that the greatest danger to French democracy from 1870 to 1940 also came from the ultra conservative forces of the clergy monarchists, nationalists and antisemites for whom the Dreyfus case, *communi consensu*, provided the rallying point for the counterrevolution.

22. Synder, p. 241.

23. Bracher, p. 40.

24. Ibid.

faith had formed an alliance of throne and altar. Jews were a contradiction to this new historical synthesis. Assimilation or emigration were the only choices left to them.[25]

Helmut von Gerlach, who at one time espoused these views, wrote that antisemitism made its greatest gains in the latter part of the nineteenth century as it was increasingly incorporated into the policies of the conservative parties. What earlier had been represented only by extremists in splinter parties was gaining influence and support in the highest circles.[26]

In 1884, 11 years before the Dreyfus case, Paris hosted an international antisemitic congress. In Germany, Otto Boeckel, the first independent antisemite elected to the Reichstag, published a pamphlet in the same year of his election (1887) entitled *The Jews—The Kings of Our Time (Die Juden—Die Könige unserer Zeit)*. Boeckel won his election in an impoverished district near Marburg by depicting the exploitive Jew as the cause of economic misery. He insisted that Germany's salvation lay in being "Jew-free."[27] Jews were not to be assimilated, but treated as foreigners in Germany, a view which is later repeated in the Twenty-Five Points of the German Worker's Party (25 February 1920) and in the Reich Citizenship Law (Nuremberg Laws, 1935).

When Adolf Hitler was in the first year of his life, Hermann Ahlwardt published, *The Desparate Battle of the Aryan Peoples With Jewry (Der Verzweiflungskampf der arischen Völker mit dem Judentum*, 1890). In 1891, the Universal German League was founded. In 1893, the name was changed to the Pan-German

League (*Alldeutscher Verein*). It called for a sense of racial and cultural kinship among all Germans. It also called for the prohibition of immigration of less worthy elements into the Reich. In 1895, a bill in the Reichstag to prohibit Jewish immigration into the Reich was defeated 165 to 51. Racial antisemitism, however, was striking deeper roots among the German people. In 1887, there was one antisemitic delegate in the Reichstag; in 1890, 5; in 1893, 16; in 1898, 13; in 1903, 11; in 1907, 16; and in 1912, 3.[28]

The economic crisis: 1918–23

The second economic crisis in German history since 1871 came at the end of World War I and seriously taxed the new Weimar Republic. The Versailles treaty was considered by most Germans to be an instrument of the allies to reduce Germany to economic slavery. Those who were blamed for Germany's defeat, the Marxists, Jews, and socialists, and those who sought to comply with the terms of the Versailles treaty were subjected to scurrilous attacks from the radical right. The judicial murder on 15 January 1919 of the Spartacus leaders, Rosa Luxemburg and Karl Liebknecht; the assassination on 26 August 1921 of Mathias Erzberger, who had negotiated the armistice at Compiègne and who had promoted a policy of seeking to honor the terms of the Versailles treaty; and the assassination on 24 June 1922 of Walter Rathenau, the Jewish Foreign Minister who also espoused the policy of fulfilling the terms of the Versailles treaty, made it clear that the republic was veering to the right; and on the right were the most radical antisemitic forces.

After 1923, however, the economic

25. Pinson, p. 158.
26. Ibid., pp. 167–68.
27. Bracher, pp. 40–41.
28. Pinson, pp. 602–3.

fortunes of the Weimar Republic began to improve. In May 1924, in the wake of the Ruhr crisis, the National Socialist party, which had become the chief organ for antisemitism in Germany, was able to win 6.5 percent of the vote and to send 32 delegates to the Reichstag. But in December of that year, as the economy continued to improve, the National Socialists received only 3 percent of the vote and captured fourteen seats in the Reichstag. In the election of 20 May 1928, the Nazis gained only 2.6 percent of the vote and 12 seats in a Reichstag with 491 delegates.[29]

The economic crisis: 1930–33

After the world economic crisis began in 1929, the popularity of the Nazi party increased dramatically. In 1930, for example, the Nazi party won 18.3 percent of the vote, and the party's strength had increased from 12 to 107 seats in the Reichstag. As he saw the economic havoc wrought by Black Friday (24 October 1929), Hitler remarked, "Never in my life have I been so well disposed and inwardly contented as in these days."[30]

Adolf Hitler, 1889–1945

As a schoolboy in Linz, Hitler would no doubt have seen the antisemitic sheets Das Alldeutsche Tageblatt and the Südmark Kalendar.[31] The strange "theozoology" of the former monk Lanz von Liebenfels in the pseudoscientific pamphlet Ostara

certainly did not escape his attention. The Protocols of Zion, purportedly drawn up by Jewish leaders in Berne in 1897, were also read by Hitler. The Protocols supposedly set forth the conspiracy of Jewish leaders to dominate the world. They were accepted by many as authenic.[32] Earlier in the nineteenth century, the French Count Joseph Arthur de Gobineau had published his work Inequality of the Human Races, 1853–55 (Essai sur l'inégalité des races humaines), which depicts the Aryan race as superior and as the ultimate source of culture. Houston Stewart Chamberlain, the son-in-law of Richard Wagner, supplied Hitler with additional material for Aryan superiority in his book Foundations of the Nineteenth Century (Grundlagen des 19. Jahrhunderts, 1899). Richard Wagner, of whom Hitler said, "At every stage in my life, I come back to Richard Wagner," wrote: "The Jew is the plastic demon of the decline of mankind. I consider the Jewish race the sworn enemy of man and all that is noble in him. That we Germans in particular will be ruined by them is beyond dispute."[33]

Adolf Hitler spent the years from 1907 to 1913 in Vienna. In his most formative years (ages 18–24) he said that this city became, "the most thorough school of my life."[34] Georg Ritter von Schönerer (1842–1921), an Austrian politician, called for Anschluss with Bismarck's Reich and for

29. Ibid., pp. 603–4.

30. Joachim C. Fest, Hitler, trans. Richard and Clara Winston, (New York: Harcourt Brace Jovanovich, 1974), p. 270.

31. Harald Steffahn, "Adolf Hitlers Lebensgeschichte: Teil II: Wiener Einflüsse," in Ein Volk, Ein Reich, Ein Führer, vol. I, ed. Christian Zentner (Hamburg: Jahn Verlag, 1975), p. 287; see also Holborn, p. 716.

32. Baldur von Schirach, the leader of the Hitler Youth, claimed that his reading of Henry Ford's book, The International Jew, had converted him to antisemitism. Ford's book assumes that the Protocols of Zion are authentic. See Pinson, p. 487.

33. Richard Wagner, cited in Das Dritte Reich in Bildern und Dokumenten, vol. IV, eds. Heinz Huber and Artur Müller (Munich: Kurt Desch Verlag, 1969), p. 85.

34. Adolf Hitler, Mein Kampf, trans. Ralph Manheim, (Boston: Houghton-Mifflin, 1943), p. 125.

stern antisemitic legislation. At that time in Vienna, Austrian parlimentarians could, with impunity, make public statements such as, "The Jews are a rabble and must be exterminated."[35] Karl Lueger (1844–1910), the mayor of Vienna, whom Hitler called the greatest mayor of all time, remarked concerning the Jews, "It makes no difference whether one hangs them or decapitates them."[36] Theodor Herzl (1860–1904) probably had Lueger in mind when, observing the degredation of Dreyfus in Paris, he came to the conclusion that antisemitism, which could become a major political issue in the two most enlightened cities of Europe, could no longer be regarded as a passing phenomenon. Lueger was elected for his first term in 1895, just five months after the condemnation of Dreyfus.[37] At one time, Herzl, like Marx, had expressed antisemitic sentiments that included even assimilation and conversion as a solution to the Jewish problem. The intense antisemitism which he observed in European society in the late nineteenth century forced him to the conclusion that Jews could not be assimilated into a Christian society. They must have a land of their own. In 1897, the first Zionist Congress was convoked in Basel at Herzl's urging.[38]

The antisemitic malaise oppressing Europe deposited its virus in the young Hitler. Later, through his agency, this antisemitic fever would torment Germany. While all European nations suffered from the contagion, it was Nazi Germany which made antisemitism an official doctrine of the totalitarian state. The long history of antisemitism had ultimately led to the institutionalizing of bigotry.[39]

Antisemitism and European Jewry

In his recent study, *Emanzipation und Anti-Semitismus*, Reinhard Rürup presents the thesis that Jewish emancipation in Germany from 1780 to 1870 was closely associated with the democratic achievements of bourgeois liberalism. The great depression of the 1870s marked the end of bourgeois liberalism.[40] Protective tariffs, a swing to the political right, and the marked increase of racial antisemitism resulted from the new reactionary course. Rürup contends that in Germany in a society which in many respects remained unemancipated, the pace of Jewish emancipation provoked resentment.

This period from 1780 to 1870 was a time of severe identity crisis for European Jews. Many sought entrance into the Christian European society by renouncing their Jewish heritage. As some of their forefathers in the Seleucid Empire, who submitted to painful surgery in order to conceal the sight of circumcision,[41] so many European Jews in the nineteenth century subjected themselves to deep psychological scars by accepting assimilation. Assimilation for

35. Steffahn, p. 286.
36. Ibid.
37. *Encyclopedia Judaica*, vol. III, p. 126.
38. Carl E. Schorske, *Fin-de-Siecle Vienna: Politics and Culture* (New York: Alfred A. Knopf, 1979).

39. Alfred Grosser, "Die Frage nach der deutschen Vergangenheit," in *Wie War Es Möglich: Die Wirklichkeit des Nationalsozialismus*, ed. Alfred Grosser (Munich and Vienna: Carl Hanser Verlag, 1977), p. 15; *see also* Carlo Schmid, *Erinnerungen* (Bern, Munchen, Wien: Scherz Verlag, 1979), pp. 12–14.
40. Reinhard Rurup, *Emanzipation und Antisemitismus* (Göttingen: Vandenhoeck and Ruprecht, 1976).
41. I *Maccabees* I: 11–15; *see also* Gerhard Lisowsky, *Kultur und Geistesgeschichte des jüdischen Volkes* (Stuttgart, Berlin, Köln, Mainz: W. Kohlhammer Verlag, 1968), p. 44.

liberal Jews, as in the case of Heinrich Marx, may have been relatively easy. Liberalism had eroded faith both in traditional Judaism and Christianity. As has been noted, Wichern saw the greatest danger in liberalism. He would have preferred Jews to be converted to Christianity but, failing that, he preferred traditional Judaism to liberalism.[42]

With the sharp increase of racial antisemitism after 1870 and the founding of the Zionist movement in 1897, European Jews found themselves in a new crisis and divided. One group still yearned for assimilation, while the Zionists demanded of all Jews that they be prepared to emigrate to Palestine or at least, until emigration was possible, be prepared to support the founding of a Jewish state. But even the Zionists, despite all the antisemitic propaganda in Germany, were prepared to fight for emperor and Fatherland on the eve of World War I. Some Zionist fraternities were even modeled after the Prussian Turnvereine, and a Zionist pamphlet of 1897 declared that love for the German Fatherland should never abate.[43] As early as 1911, one German Jew foresaw dark days ahead. The time was coming when the son would be without a German Fatherland, although he would continue to yearn for it.[44]

The spiritual and intellectual schism among Germany's Jews was particularly pronounced in the debate between Zionists and those Jews who regarded assimilation as better than an unknown promised land. Hermann Cohen complained that loyal Jews who wished to remain in Germany and to wait patiently for free-

dom of consciousness and mutual respect, which were bound to come in accordance with the fundamental principle of modern culture, were despised and scorned by the Zionists. Such a dreamer, according to the Zionist, is a coward and hypocrite, for he only exploits his patriotism. Deep in his heart, the only Fatherland he recognizes is the Promised Land.[45] Cohen concluded in 1916, "All of non-Zionist Jewry is thus accused of inner duplicity, to the malicious glee of every antisemite."[46]

It was certainly a cruel irony for German Jews that a major argument in Nazi antisemitic propaganda could be found in Zionist writings. Franz Oppenheimer insisted that he was a good Zionist even though he rejected the Zionist Posen Resolution of 1912, which called for *Aliyah*, emigration to Zion (Palestine):

I am not an assimilationist, but I am assimilated. I am a German and (at the same time) I am proud of being a Jew. . . . I am just as proud, however, to have grown up in the land of Walther and Wolfram, of Goethe, Kant and Fichte, and to have absorbed their culture in myself. . . . My Germanness is something sacred to me. But whoever doubts my Jewish clan consciousness, against him I must defend myself as against a murderer. . . . (I do not regard Germany) merely as a place of abode (Wohnland). Germany is . . . my home. . . . I have Jewish clan consciousness, German cultural consciousness, [and] Brandenburgian home consciousness.[47]

Perhaps Hermann Cohen best expressed the attitude of many German Jews. No Aryan German could

42. *See* ftn. 7.
43. Mosse and Paucker, eds., *Juden im Wilhelminischen Deutschland.*
44. Ibid.

45. Stephen M. Poppel, *Zionism in Germany 1897–1933,* (Philadelphia: The Jewish Publication Society in America, 1976), pp. 115–16.
46. Ibid., p. 116.
47. Ibid., p. 61.

have composed a more patriotic or panegyrical creed:

We love our Germanness Deutschtum, not only because we love our homeland as a bird loves its nest, but because . . . we have drawn our intellectual culture . . . from the treasures and mines of the German spirit, . . . the spirit of classical humanity and of true cosmopolitanism. What other people has a Kant? . . . And what people has this spiritual unity of poetic heroes such as have enlivened our spiritual history through Lessing and Herder, through Schiller and Goethe? What people has ever had this unity of classical poetry and philosophy! The German intellectual are all of them prophets of humanity. It is really natural that we German Jews feel ourselves integrated as Jews and as Germans. . . . I read Faust not only as a beautiful poem, but my love goes out to it as to a German epiphany. I feel the same way about Luther . . . Mozart and Beethoven and . . . Freiherr von Stein and Bismarck.[48]

Germany's Jews, divided between assimilationists and Zionists, approached the greatest crisis in the history of their people.

ON THE THRESHOLD OF HOLOCAUST

The influx of Eastern European Jews into Germany and Austria in the period 1910–25 caused antisemitic sentiment to increase. Liberal Jews in Austria and Germany also resented the immigration of Eastern Jews, who were overwhelmingly orthodox and who came at a time when the society was least able to absorb them.[49] Herzl traced antisemitism to Jewish emancipation, when the Jews turned their attention from banking to other professions which previously had been forbidden to them and caused a terrible pressure in European bourgeios competition.[50] Max Domarus also sees economic crisis as a prime cause for antisemitism. In the nineteenth and twentieth centuries the Jews gained access to the academic professions. The legal, medical, and journalistic professions were especially inundated by eager and ambitious newcomers. So long as the economy was sound, such an influx might have been acceptable. As the economic crises of the 1920s and the 1930s created great pressures, the academic circles in Germany demanded the expulsion of the Jews or at least a reduction of their number in proportion to their representation in the entire population.[51] Joachim Fest regards Hitler's antisemitism to be related to the expenditure of his inheritance and his anxiety about his economic future. Hitler's attitude toward the Jews was determined by the fact that he had no secure existence.[52]

Stefan Zweig wrote that in the nineteenth century, Austrian aristocracy had abandoned its former role as patron of the arts in Vienna. This responsibility was assumed by Jews. This role of patron of the arts compensated them for their homelessness, imparted to them a sense of belonging, and testified to their emancipation. Their influence in the press and in the sciences became great.[53]

48. Ibid., pp. 105–6.
49. Walter A. Frank, "Geschichte der Juden in Deutschland Bis Zu Den Nürnberger Gesetzen," in Ein Volk, pp. 312–18. According to Frank, in the period 1910–1925, 390,000 Aryan Germans emigrated and 80,000 Jews immigrated into Germany.

50. Encyclopedia Judaica, p. 126.
51. Max Domarus, Hitler: Reden 1932 Bis 1945, Kommentiert von einem Deutschen Zeitgenossen, 2 vols. (Wiesbaden: R. Löwit, 1973), p. 26.
52. Fest, p. 41.
53. Steffahn, p. 286.

The Jew as scapegoat

The long history of antisemitism, provoked by religious, ethnic, political, and economic intolerance, was often accompanied in the pre–Nazi Era by obscene depiction of the Jew in art and literature, a depiction so obscene that the antisemitic pornography of Julius Streicher in *Der Stürmer* hardly exceeds it.

Given the traditional view of the Jew in European society and given that the Jew constituted a minority in each state, it was easy to make him the scapegoat for the ills which befell those states between 1919 and 1933. National socialism realized that neither Judaism nor Christianity could be made to harmonize with the Nazi *Weltanschauung*. The Jews, because of the long-standing anti-semitic attitudes and because of their minority status, could be dealt with immediately. The reckoning with the Christian faith, according to the secret protocol of Martin Bormann, would come as soon as political conditions permitted.[54]

According to the National Socialist propaganda, the Jews and the Marxists were to blame for Germany's defeat in World War I. The Jews were

to blame for the Versailles treaty, a *Diktat*, designed to humiliate the German people and to reduce them to slavery. The Jews were to blame for the economic collapse of Germany. Overwhelmed by insecurity, inflation, unemployment, and political chaos, the German people were very vulnerable to Nazi propaganda. A scapegoat for the ills of the nation was sought and found. At the same time Jews were persecuted in Nazi Germany and were accused of being Bolshevists, they were persecuted by Stalin and accused of being counterrevolutionaries. Lenin, although not an antisemite per se, made it plain in a published statement in *Iskra* in 1903 that any form of Jewish association or feeling was a form of particularly obnoxious reaction.[55] The position of the unassimilated Jew in the Soviet Union and of all Jews, assimilated or not, in Nazi Germany was one of "damned if you are and damned if you are not."

At the end of November 1935, Hitler gave an interview to Mr. Baillie, the president of United Press. In this interview, Hitler claimed that one of the main reasons for the Nuremberg Laws was to fight bolshevism in Germany and that the laws were not anti-Jewish, but pro-German, and were designed to protect Germans from destructive Jewish influences. Hitler then added that all Bolshevist agitators in Germany had been Jews, and since German borders were not too far from Soviet borders, Germany must constantly defend herself against subversion by Bolshevist agents who were mostly Jews.[56] Hitler never

54. Geheimerlass Martin Bormans vom Juni 1941 an alle Gauleiter, in *Grundriss der Geschichte*, ed. E. Dittrich-Gallmeister et al. (Stuttgart: Ernst Klett Verlag, no date), p. 161. According to Reinhard Heydrich (September 1941), the immediate goal is to prevent churches from regaining lost ground; the long-range goal is complete destruction of churches by accusing them of traitorous activity during war; see Jacques Nobécourt, "Die Enzyklika, Mit brennender Sorge," in *Wie War Es Möglich*, ed. Alfred Grosser, p. 123. As early as December 1933, in its newspaper, *Rote Fahne*, the German Communist Party offered to form an alliance with the churches against the common enemy, National Socialism; see *Rote Fahne*, in *Standpunkt: Evangelische Monatsschrift*, Heft 5, ed. Günter Wirth (reprint, ed., East Berlin: 1975), p. 4.

55. *Encyclopedia Judaica*, pp. 126–128.

56. Domarus, p. 558. Dietrich Eckart wrote the little book *Bolshevism from Moses to Lenin*. During his stay in Landsberg prison, Hitler developed the ideas found in this book; he considered Moses to have been the first Bolshevik; the Apostle Paul, with a

tired of reminding the Western capitalistic democracies that Germany was the only bulwark between them and Jewish bolshevism. In 1937, he compared the impact of bolshevism upon world history with the impact which Christianity, Islam, and the Reformation, respectively, had had upon history. Hitler continued that the world was in a state of revolutionary turmoil; this turmoil was designed and executed by the leaders of Jewish bolshevism in Moscow.[57]

World indifference

In 1936, despite the fact that many liberals in America and England wished to boycott the Berlin Olympics in protest of Nazi ideology and practice, the International Olympic Committee voted to hold the games. The International Olympic Committee was certainly aware of the Nazi-directed boycott of Jewish businesses on 1 April 1933, of the draconian measures taken against Jews even before the enactment of the Nuremberg Laws, and of the Night of the Long Knives (30 June 1934), which saw not only the liquidating of the SA leadership but also the brutal murder of troublesome opponents. Two prominent people ordered murdered among others who had no connection with the SA were Erich Klausener, the leader of the German Catholic Association, and Adalbert Probst, the leader of the Catholic Athletic Association (*Deutsche Jugendkraft*).

The Nuremberg Laws had been in

force for almost a year (November, 1935) when the Olympic Games took place in Berlin in August, 1936. "All the world looks to Berlin" was the daily slogan in the German press. That the National Socialist regime planned to gain a tremendous propaganda coup by hosting the games and, in fact, did, is a matter of history. Lewald, the half-Jewish National Olympic Committee president, was not interested in National Socialist politics. Hitler was anxious to have the games staged in Berlin because he believed that since he had come to power, Germany had been in a difficult foreign policy position. He wanted to gain world approval of his new state at the Olympics. Although Hitler had violated the Versailles treaty and had angered the French by militarizing the Rhineland, the French Olympic team presented the fuehrer with the Nazi salute as it paraded past his box in the Berlin stadium. The propaganda against the Jew, which usually could be seen on every street corner, and Julius Streicher's antisemitic sheet, *Der Stürmer*, vanished from Berlin during the games. Even a few token Jews were permitted to represent Germany. The boycotting of the Berlin Olympics would no doubt have damaged Hitler's regime both domestically and around the world. The American Ernest L. Jahncke, who had voted for the boycott or transfer of the games from Berlin, had to relinquish his position on the International Olympic Committee. His place was taken by Avery Brundage, who had insisted, "The games must go on."[58]

---

disguised Judaism—Christianity—infiltrated the Roman Empire and eroded it from within; *see Mein Kampf*, p. XV; Norman Cameron and R. H. Stevens, trans., *Hitler's Secret Conversations* (New York: Octagon Books, 1972), pp. 62, 586; John Toland, *Adolf Hitler* (Garden City, NY: Doubleday and Co., 1976), p. 83.

57. Domarus, p. 728.

58. Arnd Krüger, "Die Welt Blickt auf Berlin," in *Ein Volk*, pp. 445–60. Krüger contends that Brundage at first delayed the vote of the AAU and then manipulated that vote in order to gain a 58 to 56 vote for participation in the Berlin Olympics.

Emigration, Evian, and Kristallnacht

The Nazi claim that Germany was being "judaized" can hardly be substantiated. In 1933, excluding the Sarrland, Germany had a population of 65 million. Of this number, 500,000 were Jews, or .80 percent of the total population. In 1933, the year that Hitler was appointed chancellor, 63,400 Jews emigrated from Germany.[59] Between 1934 and 1937, about 20,000 to 25,000 Jews emigrated annually from Germany. Most of them settled in France. Only 27 percent emigrated to Palestine. Although the United States immigration authorities agreed to admit 130,000 German Jews a year, the total number of those who came from 1933 to 1937 is placed at 27,000.[60] German Jews obviously preferred to emigrate to countries near Germany so that they might return to their homes as soon as circumstances permitted.

At Evian (6–15 July 1938) 32 states met to discuss resettlement for those Jews seeking to leave Germany and other European states where they were not welcome. The New York Herald Tribune reported on 8 July 1938 that 650,000 European Jewish refugees had been rejected by the nations assembled at Evian. Der Reichswart on 14 July sarcastically exalted, "Jews available, cheap. Who wants them? No one!"[61] The Danziger Vorposten interpreted the results of the Evian Conference as confirmation of Hitler's antisemitic

policy.[62] According to the Danzig Gauleiter, when Forster asked Churchill in July, 1938, if Germany's Jewish policy hindered an English–German agreement, Churchill responded no.[63] When Switzerland complained to the German authorities of the number of German Jews pressing into Switzerland, the German government withdrew German-Jewish passports and issued special identification with a three-centimeter-high J. Thus German Jews could more easily be turned away at the border.[64]

Finally, in October 1938, a memorandum was formulated by the Evian Committee and sent to the German Foreign Office. The memorandum stated that none of the states assembled at Evian challenged the right of the German government to legislate measures pertaining to certain of its citizens because such a right fell within the province of state sovereignty.[65] Emboldened by such a carte blanche, Hitler, was to release the fury of his antisemitism in the Kristallnacht within days on 9 November 1938.

Intimidation and fear

But why did the German people permit the Holocaust to happen? One of the answers must be fear: fear for one's life and for the security of one's family. The warning heard throughout Germany was "keep quiet or else you too will end up in a concentration camp." Johannes R. Becher described the plight of many who were sent to concentration camps:

Say, why were you brought here?
Suspicious, he who told the truth

59. Joachim Fest and Christian Herrendoerfer, Hitler, Eine Karriere, (Frankfurt/Main, Berlin, Vienna: Ulstein Verlag, 1977), p. 72.

60. Paul Stehlin, "Das Münchner Abkommen vom September 1938, "in Wie War Es Möglich, pp. 153–54.

61. Ibid., p. 155.

62. Ibid., pp. 155–56.

63. Ibid., p. 156.

64. Ibid.

65. Ibid.

Judged, whoever perceived the mass deception.

Outlawed, whoever asked, what comes later
Condemned was he to life imprisonment.
And many there were who, nevertheless could not be broken.
Behold, what human beings! What human strength![66]

Even the Jewish population, intimidated and pathetically hoping that a demonstration of solidarity with the Nazis might meliorate National Socialist antisemitism, voted in support of Adolf Hitler in the plebiscite of November 1933.[67] Hans Joachim Schoeps founded and led the German Vanguard, German Jewish Followers of Hitler (Deutscher Vortrupp: Gefolgschaft deutscher Juden).[68] Gerhart Hauptmann, the Noble Prize winner for literature, who also voted yes in November 1933 and who described a brief handshake with Hitler as "the greatest moment in my life," has perhaps given the most blunt and denigrating reason for silence. When Hauptmann was vacationing in Rapallo in 1938, the Hungarian author, Ference Körmendi, asked him about his silence in the light of events in Germany. Hauptmann replied, "Do you know why I am silent? Because I am a coward, I am a coward, I am a coward."[69]

66. Johannes R. Becher: Zum Gedenken, 22 Mai 1891–11 Oktober 1958, (East Berlin: Deutscher Kultur Burd, no date), p. 111. The creative power of the human spirit, even in concentration camps, which Becher here praises is the subject of a recent study; see Mariam Novitch, Spiritual Resistance: 120 Drawings From Concentration Camps and Ghettos 1940–1945 (Milan, Italy: Commune of Milan, 1979).
67. "Alle Juden für Hitler," in Neuer Vorwärts, SPD Emigrantenzeitung, Nov. 1933.
68. Joseph Rovan, "Der Aufbau der Hitlerjugend," in Wie War Es Möglich, pp. 92–93.
69. Jochen R. Klicker, "Der Feige Zeilenschreiber," in Ein Volk, p. 122.

Klaus Scholder, the Tübingen theologian, has recently published excerpts from the diary of a Wehrmacht chaplain. In the experience of the chaplain, the tragic dilemma of many Germans during the Hitler years is reflected. In 1941, H. Wilhelmy, a Wehrmacht chaplain, served in the eleventh armored division. At Berditschew in the Soviet Union he witnessed the execution of hundreds of Jewish men, women, and children by SS execution squads. Wilhelmy describes how the German soldiers turned away in revulsion from this scene of mass murder. The chaplain reported what he had witnessed to a general. The general was greatly shocked by the chaplain's report but when the chaplain demanded that general do something, the general replied, "What do you propose that I should do? You have too great an estimate of my authority. Don't you think what you have told me has caused me grave concern? But what shall I do?" A little later, the general repeated, "What shall I do? I cannot give orders to the SS squads, which are not under my command, to suspend their criminal acts. I cannot wage a private war against commands which originate at the highest source.[70] Scholder comments that the general and the chaplain, despite this experience, served loyally in the Wehrmacht for the duration of the war. Their attempt to prevent the SS execution squads from carrying out their order could have only resulted in martyrdom for the general and the chaplain. They are therefore not guilty in the sense that one could accuse them of murder before the bar

70. H. Wilhelmy, Aus Meinem Leben, Ebernburg, 1977 (vervielfältiges Manuskrupt), in Klaus Scholder, Über den Umgang mit unserer jüngsten Geschiechte (München: Bayerische Landeszentral für politische Bildungsarbeit, 1979), p. 21.

of justice. One could not measure the conduct of the SS execution squads and the conduct of the Wehrmacht soldiers by the same ruler. The silent spectators were innocent and revolted by what they had witnessed. They were, however, not without guilt.[71]

The response of the church

Even the churches in Germany, identifying Christianty with nationalism, permitted themselves to become coordinated. By the time the Final Solution was implemented, they were too spiritually moribund to offer resistance. In July, 1933, the Vatican had signed a concordat with Hitler[72] and many Protestant Christians supported the Nazi-sponsored German Christian church.

But there was a remnant who refused to bow the knee to Baal. Kurt Gerstein did not survive his mission and Father Fontana identified himself with a Jewish family even unto death. The U-boat commander of World War I, Martin Niemöller, who had become a Lutheran minister, was sentenced to solitary confinement because he denounced the National Socialists. Niemöller, along with Dietrich Bonhoeffer and Karl Barth, was the spiritual father of the Barmen Confession (May 1934),

which rejected National Socialist ideology and appealed to German Christians not to embrace the new paganism.[73] The Confessing church and the Barmen Confession group rejected the coordinated Reich Lutheran church, led by Reichs-Bishop Ludwig Müller, and the absurdities of the SA Christi.[74] In conforming to Nazi antisemitic ideology, Christian clergy of Jewish descent were expelled from their pulpits. Niemöller criticized this practice whereby Christian baptism is replaced by geneology.[75] Niemöller was arrested on 1 July 1937 and remained in a concentration camp until the end of the war. In his prison cell he was visited by the prison chaplain who was astonished to see a fellow clergyman in jail. "Brother, why are you in here?" asked the chaplain. Niemöller responded, "Brother, why are you not in here?"[76]

71. Scholder, pp. 21–22. Karl Jaspers in *Die Schuldfrage* (Heidelberg, 1946) lists four categories of guilt: criminal, political, moral and metaphysical; *see also* Jack Kroll, "The Hitler Within Us," *Newsweek*, 28 Jan. 1980, p. 54.

72. This concordat is still in force in West Germany. By this instrument (article 20), the Vatican can appeal to the West German government to remove Hans Küng, the controversial Jesuit theologian, from his teaching position at Tübingen University. According to the concordat, Catholic religious instruction in German schools and universities is under the supervision of church authorities.

73. Martin Niemöller, "Zum Gedenken an Barmen 1934," in *Standpunkt, Evangelische Monatsschrift*, Heft 5 (Mai, 1974), pp. 128–29; in this same number, *see Beilage*, "Vierzig Jahre Barmen," eds. K. H. Bernhardt et al.

74. Walther Hofer and Herbert Michaelis, *Deutsche Geschichte der neuesten Zeit von Bismarcks Entlassung bis zur Gegenwart*, Teil II: 1933–1945: *Handbuch der Deutschen Geschichte*, 4 vols. Akademische Verlagsgesellschaft Athenaion (Konstanz, 1965), 4(II):73. The German Christians understood under the concept "Reichskirche" a church of Aryan Christians. They sought nothing less than a coordinated state church and a synthesis between the National Socialist *Weltanschauung* and the Christian faith. They wanted to be Christ's *Sturm Abteilung*.

75. Carl Ordnung, *Martin Niemöller*, (Berlin: Union Verlag, 1967), p. 12; *see also* Wolfgang Gerlach, "Kirche und Antisemitismus," in *Lutherische Monatshefte*, no. 8, 1979, pp. 463–66.

76. Ibid., p. 14. For a recent survey and bibliography of theological and (or) New Testament roots of antisemitism, *see* Michael B. McGarry, *Christology After Auschwitz*, (New York: Paulist Press, 1977); *see also* Cameron and Stevens, pp. 6, 586–87; Claire Nix, ed., *Heinrich Brüning: Briefe und*

Dietrich Bonhoeffer was hanged at Flossenbürg because of his conspiracy with those who planned to assassinate Hitler. The Soviet philosopher Dmitri Modestovich Ugrinovic claims that Bonhoeffer's theology calls not for resignation in the face of evil, but resistance. He believed that Christian love carried with it a responsibility for all that occurs in the world, in the society, and in the state.[77]

Paul Schneider, the preacher of Buchenwald, was tortured and finally given a lethal injection because he would not be silent. The anniversary of Schneider's martyrdom is marked each year at Buchenwald and in the Herder Church in Weimar.[78]

Father Maximillan Kolbe, a Franciscan, translated the teaching of his Lord into the deed by taking the place of the inmate Gajowniczek, condemned to death by starvation at Auschwitz: "Greater love hath no man than this; that a man lay down his life for his friend." At Buchenwald, a Jewish child, smuggled into the camp when his parents were arrested, was hidden and nourished by the inmates for months. The SS knew that the child was somewhere in the camp. Stefan Jerzy Zweig is alive in his native Poland today because Christians and Communists died under SS torture rather than reveal his hiding place.[79]

ADMONITION

In the summer of 1976, students, colleagues, and I were touring the German Democratic Republic. We lived in Weimar. One morning we took the bus for the short trip to Buchenwald, which is now a museum and a monument dedicated to those who were murdered by the Third Reich. I came into conversation with a gentleman from Poland, who sat in the seat next to me. He had been an inmate at Buchenwald and now, for the first time, was leading a delegation of his countrymen to visit the site. As we approached Buchenwald, he became silent. He began to perspire. His whole body trembled. As we got off the bus at the Buchenwald parking lot, he gave me his hand. There were tears in his eyes. "Forgive me," he said, "for not continuing our conversation, but as we approached the camp, I was seized with dread. It has been thirty-one years since I was liberated from this

Gespräche 1934–1945 (Stuttgart: Deutsche Verlags Anstalt, 1974); Corrie Ten Boom, *Hiding Place* (New York: Bantam Books, 1974); Helmut Gollwitzer, *Dying We Live*, trans. Reinhard C. Kuhn, (New York: The Seabury Press, 1968); Aleksander Rogalski, *Jan Dobraczyński* (East Berlin: Union Verlag, 1970); Gisela Reller, *Maksymilian Kolbe*, (East Berlin: Union Verlag, 1968); Elenore Lester and Frederick E. Werbell, "The Lost Hero of the Holocaust: The Search for Sweden's Raoul Wallenberg," *New York Times Magazine*, 30 March 1980.

77. Dmitri M. Ugrinovic, "Dietrich Bonhoeffer," in *Nauka i Religja*, no. 8, 1973; *see* Carl-Jürgen Kaltenborn, *Dietrich Bonhoeffer* (East Berlin: Union Verlag, 1969). Rabbi Leo Baeck of Berlin stated that it was a great disappointment to him that the Christian churches in Germany did not protest the Nazi boycott of Jewish businesses on 1 April 1933; *see Heinrich Brüning* p. 164, note 6.

78. Walter Feurich, *Paul Schneider* (East Berlin: Union Verlag, 1967). I had the privilege of attending the memorial service (18 July 1979) in the Peter and Paul (Herder) Church in Weimar on the fortieth anniversary of Paul Schneider's martyrdom. Buchenwald is only a few miles from Weimar. The Reverend Werner Leich, Bishop of Thuringia, preached the sermon. Many state authorities attended, including the Minister for Church Affairs in the GDR, Hans Seigewasser, deceased 18 October 1979.

79. Bruno Apitz, *Nackt Unter Wölfen* (Halle/Saale: Mitteldeutscher Verlag, 1958).

camp, but the horror of this place has never left me."

The song of the Buchenwald inmates may still serve as the expression of hope. It should remind us that the most appropriate and permanent monument we can erect to the victims of the Holocaust is the cultivation of a humane conscience that will no longer tolerate tyranny over the minds and bodies of fellow human beings:

O Buchenwald, we whimper not nor repine
And no matter what our future should be
We affirm life, we do not resign

For the day is coming in which we shall be free.[80]

The Holocaust revealed the depths of human depravity. But it also revealed the angels of man's better nature. Charles de Gaulle expressed this truth most succinctly upon a visit to Auschwitz:

What endless sorrow and what limitless horror.
And, nevertheless, here also consoling hope and humaneness.[81]

80. Ibid., p. 350.
81. Aimé Bonifas, *Häftling 20 801* (East Berlin: Union Verlag, 1968), p. 217.

ANNALS, AAPSS, **450**, July 1980

Racism and German Protestant Theology: A Prelude to the Holocaust

By ALAN DAVIES

ABSTRACT: The success of racism in modern Europe had a great deal to do with the experience of military defeat and political collapse; France after 1870 and Germany after 1918 were similar in this respect. As a modern ideology, racism begins in the nineteenth century but older modes of race thinking are rooted in European ethnocentrism stretching backward in time to classical antiquity and the Christian ages. Race thinking was greatly accelerated during the great age of discovery, and even the Enlightenment suffered from white ethnocentric prejudice. When the old Christian universe was replaced by modern secular ideas, racism emerged as a secular myth, the Aryan myth, that soon became a rationale for anti-Jewish feelings in Europe. The alienated European found in this myth a form of spiritual reassurance during an age that seemed disappointing and decadent. German Protestant theology during the nineteenth century was slowly colored by romantic nationalistic ideas that eventually would open the door to racism. The nation, rather than the state, became an "order of creation," and in this way racist doctrines swept into Protestant theology.

Alan Davies is an associate professor of religious studies at Victoria College, University of Toronto. He is a graduate of McGill University, Montreal, and Union Theological Seminary, New York, and has been an Interfaith Fellow at Hebrew Union College, Cincinnati. He is the author of Anti-semitism and the Christian Mind *and is the editor of* Antisemitism and the Foundations of Christianity.

THE FACT has not always been noticed, but Germany after 1918 bore a certain resemblance to France after 1870. In either case, a proud nation was unexpectedly humiliated in war and was then subjected to an even more humiliating peace. In either case, an emperor fell and national trauma ensued, during which vengeful and xenophobic feelings simmered and boiled, spilling over against the new political institutions established to replace the fallen order. In either case, the church, or much of it, found itself in a countercultural situation, longing for the restoration of a lost past. French Catholicism, disestablished since the 1789 revolution, nursed its resentment of the secular republic, which, in turn, equally disliked and distrusted the church and its pretensions. German Protestantism, especially its conservative element, shared a popular disdain for the Weimar Republic as a decadent and illegitimate institution imposed on a defeated Germany by its alien conquerors. Into the disturbed postwar ethos of both nations blew the deadly winds of racist and antisemitic ideas, threatening the fragile democratic structures that had arisen, on the ruins of the former autocracies.

RACISM

Antisemitism in the form of Christian anti-Judaism is far older in time than is racism, a product, in its developed sense, of the nineteenth century, but antisemitism as the racial metamorphosis of the anti-Jewish sentiments of the age was a sinister new doctrine. French Catholics who had hated the Third Republic since its foundations and German Protestants who had hated the Weimar Republic since its foundations were highly susceptible to racial myths that

offered the vision of a more satisfactory social order. It did not matter that these myths drew their substance from the poisonous wells of a Europe deeply troubled at its spiritual center and increasingly less informed by a religious view of human existence with each succeeding generation.

French political extremism was unable to overturn the Third Republic; although during the Boulanger episode (1889) it came close; German political extremism was able to overturn the Weimar Republic, establishing in its place a state with an official racist ideology—the only great European power ever to do so.[1] This was accomplished by means of the Aryan legislation from 1933–35. But the race doctrines that emerged publicly in post-1870 France and victoriously in post-1918 Germany were late arrivals in history, and, even at their peak of popularity, were never more than a minority's viewpoint, at least in their pristine form. "Racism," a term coined in the 1930s, is not the same as "race thinking"; the former implies a fully developed ideology in the sense of a total world view or *Weltanschauung;*[2] the latter merely implies the play of racial images as part of the natural ethnocentrism of the various peoples of the earth.

Beginnings: ethnocentrism

In European history, ethnocentrism is extremely ancient, arising in

1. Not even fascist Italy was really a racist state, despite the presence in Mussolini of contradictory ideas, including the "rudiments of anti-Semitism and a political race doctrine"; see Ernst Nolte, *Three Faces of Fascism*, trans. Leila Vennewitz (New York: Mentor Books, 1969), p. 295.
2. Cf. Karl Mannheim, *Ideology and Utopia*, (New York: Harcourt, Brace & World), 1936, ch. two.

a quasi-racial fashion among the Greeks for whom, in the celebrated case of Aristotle, all non-Hellenes were intrinsically inferior.[3] Greek ethnocentrism broke down somewhat when Aristotle's pupil Alexander conquered the Persians and discovered that his new subjects were not his tutor's barbarian slaves by nature, but members of a different, highly developed culture. Consequently, "the practical demands of imperial statecraft, . . . persuaded Alexander to abandon . . . the parochialism of his distinguished tutor and to adopt some of the teachings of the Stoic philosopher Zeno" in order to construct a new and "wider *homonoia* than hitherto had been envisaged."[4] Nevertheless, the parochial element with its feeling of Greek superiority remained at the core of even the universal society that Alexander sought to establish, so that the Hellenistic Greek still regarded himself as the bearer of enlightenment to the subject peoples in terms only slightly less narrow than Aristotle's. When the Seleucid king Antiochus IV Epiphanes placed a statue of the god Zeus in the Holy of Holies of the temple in Jerusalem (167 B.C.E.), his intention was to emancipate the Jews ˋ from their tribal barbarism by granting them the benefits of Greek religion! It was this proud religious and cultural ethnocentrism that seems to have been the main source of pagan antisemitism in antiquity.[5]

When Europe became Christian, European ethnocentrism was baptized and re-expressed in Christian

symbols or in more ancient religious symbols that had been Christianized, notably, the association of light and darkness (white and black) with good and evil. The link between darkness and evil is certainly old, and not confined to the Christian imagination alone. But early Christian asceticism intensified this association by attaching bestial and demonic qualities to the skin color of Africans. An edifying tale from the desert fathers of the eastern church portrays the spirit of sexual lust, the devil's snare, as a *negro*:[6] an image obviously suggested by the proximity of Egypt to black Africa. This proximity must have inspired the form of an inscription on a pillar erected by the Egyptian pharaoh Sesostris III at the second cataract of the Nile about two millennia before the birth of Jesus, the earliest antiblack racial utterance in recorded history.[7]

In medieval Christian art, the devil was sometimes featured with a black skin and a bestial countenance. More generally, to the medieval mind, white Christian civilization was surrounded by menacing pagan realms that were both literally and figuratively darker, that is, by a universe in which the "children of light" were encircled by the "children of darkness." Even in Renaissance times, white and black "connoted purity and filthiness, virginity and sin, virtue and baseness, beauty and ugliness, beneficence and evil, God and the devil."[8] In its Christian expression,

3. *Politics*, book I, ch. 6.

4. Reinhold Niebuhr, *The Structure of Nations and Empires* (New York: Charles Scribner's Sons), 1959, p. 75.

5. Cf. J. N. Sevenster, *The Roots of Pagan Anti-semitism in the Ancient World* (Leiden: Brill, 1975), *passim*.

6. Cf. Owen Chadwick, ed. *Western Asceticism*, Library of Christian Classics, vol. XII (Philadelphia: Westminster Press, 1958), pp. 61 ff.

7. Juan Comas, "Les Mythes Raciaux," in *Le Racisme devant la Science*, UNESCO (Paris: Gallimard, 1960), pps. 14–15.

8. Winthrop D. Jordan, *White over Black* (Baltimore: Penguin Books, 1973), p. 7.

therefore, ethnocentrism assumed more ominous racial overtones, but it was still far removed from modern racism.

The European encounter with unfamiliar types of men in unprecedented numbers in remote corners of the earth during the great age of discovery (fifteenth–eighteenth centuries) stimulated racial speculation enormously. One result was the notion that the different types of men were simply too different to be reduced to a common denominator; hence, for the first time, biblical monogenesis—the common parentage of humankind in Adam and Eve—came under attack.

This drift to polygenesis, assisted by the Enlightenment passion for classifying data, ignited the fires of race thinking with a more vibrant glow. Could not the various species of humanity be graded on a scale in a manner similar to every other species, with, of course, the white European, who would be doing the grading, at the top? Once the stress fell on difference and grade, nominalism triumphed over realism,[9] or the particular over the general, so that universal man or humankind ceased to exist except as a bare abstraction. Only particular types of men were real, and these were unequal. Thus in one mighty step, the essential thread of human unity was broken.

Nominalism, however, should not be blamed solely for the disaster. Realism also was at fault, for the Great Chain of Being of medieval and classical metaphysics with its element of hierarchy supplied a convenient model for placing the newly discovered types of men on a sliding scale. "If all other created beings were ranked upon a grand scale, why not man? Could it be that the Creator has graded mankind from its noblest specimens to its most brutal savages? The possibilities were there for any European who paused to consider to compare his own society with the newly discovered ones overseas."[10]

The acceleration of race thinking in Europe following the age of discovery is illustrated in the degree to which even the best minds of the Enlightenment compromised their universalist principles by succumbing to unmitigated racial ideas. Most striking was David Hume:

I am apt to suspect the negroes and in general all the other species of men (for there are four or five different kinds) to be naturally inferior to the white. There never was a civilized nation of any other complexion than white, nor even any individual eminent either in action or speculation. No ingenious manufactures amongst them, no arts, no sciences. On the other hand, the most rude and barbarous of the whites, such as the ancient *Germans*, the present *Tartars*, have still something eminent about them, in their valour, form of government, or some other particular. Such a uniform and constant difference could not happen in so many countries and ages, if nature had not made an original distinction betwixt these breeds of men.[11]

Why did Hume allow his critical powers to sink to this dismal level?

9. Théophile Simar, *Étude critique sur la formation de la doctrine des races au XVIIIe siècle et son expansion au XIXe siècle*, Academie Royale de Belgique, classes des lettres et des sciences morales et politiques, Mémoires, deuxième série, Tome XVI (Bruxelles: Martin Lamertin, 1922), p. 10 ff.

10. Jordan, p. 223.
11. "Of National Characters," in *The Philosophical Works*, eds. T. H. Green and T. H. Grose, vol. III (London: 1882), 252 n; Hume is cited by Richard H. Popkin, "The Philosophical Basis of Eighteenth-Century Racism," in *Racism in the Eighteenth Century*, ed. Harold E. Pagliaro (Cleveland: Case Western University Press, 1973), p. 245.

Not, we are told, because of an idiosyncratic prejudice that had nothing to do with his philosophy, although this also may have been true.[12] Rather, the Enlightenment itself was flawed, suffering from the same ethnocentric bias as an older Christendom and a still older Greek civilization and never suspecting this bias in its own lofty vision of itself. The philosophers persuaded themselves (1) that the mentality of nonwhites was inferior to that of white men; (2) that being nonwhite meant either sickness or degeneracy (caused by the physical environment?) because the natural, proper condition of humanity was one of whiteness; (3) that not everyone who looked human really was human, but actually belonged lower down on the scale, somewhere between *homo sapiens* and the apes; and (4) that different types of men were created on separate occasions, and some types, prior to Adam, "never contained the stuff of genuine men."[13] The last view—polygenesis—was supported by the Enlightenment scorn for the Bible as a source of fable and superstition. Christian orthodoxy, on the other hand, whatever its defects, remained wedded to biblical monogenesis as a true account of the common origins of a single humanity.

Development of race thinking

Race thinking, as a vague body of racial ideas connected with ethnocentrism, preceded the birth of racism in its modern ideological sense; the latter, obviously, could not have been born in a vacuum. Racism is always more than mere ethnocentrism, representing a synthesis of older racial ideas into a

world view that at once becomes the true science, the true philosophy, and the true religion. Like all genuine world views, as soon as its initial premises are granted, racism supplies a point of departure for thought at large, unraveling the secret of human existence with guiding principles for the preservation and betterment of life. Like all "isms," racism, because of its cosmic overtones, always appears in the guise of a myth, for only myths can effectively invoke symbols of ultimacy, especially ultimate goodness and evil.

As Paul Tillich knew so well,[14] modern postscientific myths, such as the racist myth, are no less cosmic and religious than are archaic, prescientific myths rooted in the infancy of the human consciousness. While mythic elements were certainly present in the older modes of race thinking, they were never integrated into an autonomous racial myth until the nineteenth century. Instead, they formed parts of other myths, notably, the Christian universe with its own integrated patterns of meaning and value. The great myth of the European racists—the Aryan myth —arose, on the other hand, from the intellectual soil of a secularized European culture.

The Aryan

Who was the Aryan? He was the idealized European, modeled, incidentally, on the aesthetic ideals of Greek sculpture that, during the Renaissance, had been glorified as the highest canons of physical beauty ever conceived.[15] It was

12. Ibid., pp. 246 ff.
13. Ibid., p. 247.

14. Tillich, *The Socialist Decision*, trans. Franklin Sherman (New York: Harper & Row, 1977), pt. I.
15. George L. Mosse, *Toward the Final Solution* (New York: Howard Fertig, 1978), p. 2.

easy and tempting for Europeans to measure their own classical bodily proportions against inferior, that is, aesthetically less pleasing, non-European types. Such comparisons confirmed for them the conviction that they were the children of the gods, the descendants of an original white race, or *Urvolk*, which "in columns of masterful men had marched down ages ago from the roof of the world [Himalayas], founding empires and civilizing the West."[16] Count Gobineau, the "father of racist ideology,"[17] rhapsodized in a majestic vein of Aryan splendor:

Human history is like an immense tapestry. The earth is the frame over which it is stretched. The successive centuries are the tireless weavers. As soon as they are born they immediately seize the shuttle and operate it on the frame, working at it until they die. The broad fabric thus goes on growing beneath their busy fingers. The two most inferior varieties of the human species, the black and yellow races, are the crude foundation, the cotton and wool, which the secondary families of the white group make supple by adding their silk; while the Aryan group, circling its finer threads through the noble generations, designs on its surface a dazzling masterpiece of arabesques in silver and gold.[18]

The Jew

Gobineau was not especially anti-semitic. He thought that the Jews, or Semites, represented a debased form of Aryan racial stock through an in-

fusion of black blood,[19] but still the lowest kind of white man was higher than the highest kind of yellow or black man. As long as the racial philosophers concentrated their vision outside of Europe, denigration of orientals or blacks rather than antisemitism was paramount. As soon as racist eyes were focused inside Europe, where few orientals or blacks were resident, the silhouette of the Semite appeared in sharper contour.

By its very nature, a race myth requires inferior as well as superior races, and, depending on its historical context, moves inexorably in a dualistic direction as time proceeds. Later Gobinists in both France and Germany, affected by the independent rise of political antisemitism as the nineteenth century drew to a close, transformed the master's philosophy into what Léon Poliakov has called a "racial Manichaeism,"[20] or a system in which Aryan and Semite became the countersymbols of goodness and evil in a spiritual and social struggle for control of Europe. The political potency of these racial symbols is significant. Racism, in any case, always contains a strong political dimension, and, as Gobineau's own French background illustrates,[21] racial classifications are often emblems of deep social tensions in a given society.

If the Aryan was the idealized European, the Semite was the demonized non-European—the alien intruder whose presence was deemed

16. Leon Poliakov, *The Aryan Myth*, trans. Edmund Howard (London: Sussex University Press, 1974), p. 191.

17. Cf. Michael D. Biddiss, *Father of Racist Ideology: The Social and Political Thought of Count Gobineau* (London: Weidenfeld & Nicolson), 1970.

18. Count Arthur de Gobineau, *Essai sur l'inégalité des races humaines*, cited in translation by Michael D. Biddiss, ed., *Gobineau: Selected Political Writings* (London: Jonathan Cape, 1970), pp. 162–63.

19. Biddiss, *Father of Racist Ideology*, p. 124.

20. Poliakov, pp. 272 ff.

21. As a pseudo-aristocrat, Gobineau idealized his own social class as France's natural rulers, while projecting the characteristics of the violence-prone lower class mob onto the Negroes and the Philistine bourgeoisie onto the orientals; *see* Mosse, p. 53.

responsible for all the ills and malevolent forces of the age. While Jews were real enough, Semites were largely invented, but this fiction does not detract from the religious power of racist mythology. It only reveals its spurious character.

The myth

France after 1870 and Germany after 1918 were profoundly troubled nations. Spiritual reintegration and revitalization on a national scale was in either case the overwhelming need of the hour. In the maelstrom of French and German personal and political alienation during these two critical periods there arose a powerful myth of renewal calculated to heal a shattered national self-esteem. Beneath the Aryan myth, Mircea Eliade tells us, there beats a "passion for noble origin."[22] To the racist, the Aryan "represents at once the 'primordial' Ancestor and the noble 'hero.' . . . The 'Aryan' was the exemplary model that must be imitated in order to recover racial 'purity,' physical strength, nobility, the heroic 'ethics' of the glorious and creative 'beginnings.' "[23]

The Semite, on the other hand, was associated with the decadence of the present age, particularly the corrupt and inefficient political institutions that had replaced the former empires. Edouard Drumont regarded the Third French Republic as Jew-ridden; Adolf Hitler embraced a similar view of the Weimar Republic in Germany. How could such houses of straw stand against the mighty winds of a new secular religion? How indeed?—especially

when the new religion was able to deck itself in the imposing robes of science, drawing its proof from the fashionable findings of contemporary biologists, geneticists, and anthropologists.

The Aryan myth, then, was a healing myth. Its success demonstrated the perennial need for the sacred on the part of even post-religious ex-Christians, a need that never disappears but intensifies as the old religious symbols fade away. However, the Aryan myth also failed. Lacking genuine transcendence, it could not perform its healing function in an adequate and healthy manner. Aryan symbolism is grounded in the narcissistic instincts of the human ego, the self's own glorification of itself, or self-love. Narcissus in the old Greek fable was punished when the gods permitted his infatuation with his own image to eventually consume and destroy him. The same fate awaits the racist for whom self-love is a snare that can only end in self-destruction.

In speaking of fascism, the first cousin of racism, Ernst Nolte has declared that the great folly of the fascist mind is to locate beauty, truth, and goodness, not in the eternal order of things—the realm of genuine transcendence— but in "a random chance of being" where the "world's primeval brutality" is always in danger of turning against it.[24] Therefore the fascist lives in constant fear.

Racism likewise locates beauty in a random chance of being: the inexplicable appearance in the kaleidoscope of nature of a perfect human race. The higher type of man, however, is constantly threatened by lower types, and civilization is in deadly peril. Hence, vigilant defenders must guard the higher

22. Eliade, *Myth and Reality*, trans. Willard R. Trask (New York: Harper Torchbooks, 1963). p. 183.

23. Ibid.

24. Nolte, p. 102.

against the lower, fearing that those who hate beauty in social existence will, if given an opportunity, destroy it. But the price of such vigilance is very great, consuming the energies and finally the basic humanity of the devotees of race, whose nemesis is the loss of the object of their devotion: their own selves.

GERMAN PROTESTANT THEOLOGY

Much pre-Holocaust German Protestant theology was deeply embedded in German cultural ethnocentrism. Even Martin Luther, although he shared and voiced the popular sentiments of his German contemporaries against an oppressive Italian papacy,[25] cannot be called a German nationalist. Nationalism in its modern sense did not exist in the sixteenth century, nor is there any trace in Luther's writings of a tribal or racist ideology;[26] his antisemitism was religious, not racial. Later Lutheran theologians, however, engulfed by the rising tides of late eighteenth century romanticism, sank under the spell of a subtle new mood of Germanism; a mood, as Albert Schweitzer once remarked, that changed even New Testament criticism into a "secret struggle to reconcile the Germanic religious spirit with the Spirit of Jesus of Nazareth."[27]

Beginnings: redefinition of Luther

Protestant theology became a quest for the proper synthesis be-

tween the Christian faith and the "German soul."[28] In light of this redefinition, Luther was reinterpreted by the Lutherans as a German religious hero whose response to the spiritual crisis of his day arose from the unique properties of his German nature. How can a profound synthesis take place except "in a person whose individual life is at the same time a significant expression of his nationality"?[29] One could go further. How can a great religious movement arise on the cultural soil of any nation except Germany? Do not the Germans, and the Germans alone, possess a special earnestness of soul? This tuning fork was struck with ringing clarity by Johann Gottlieb Fichte:

But it was impossible for the existing state of things (ie., the empty religiosity of pre-Reformation Christendom) to continue once this light (ie., the renaissance of classical learning) had fallen upon a soul whose religion was truly earnest and concerned about life, when this soul was surrounded by a people to whom it could easily impart its more earnest view, and when this people found leaders who cared about its urgent needs. . . . It was in this way that the light fell upon the soul of the German man, Luther.[30]

Fichte, a protégé of Immanuel Kant, uttered these words publicly in French-occupied Berlin in 1807.

Concept of "the Fatherland": Fichte

A fear of national destruction— the humiliation of Prussia by Napo-

25. Cf. Hans Kohn, *The Idea of Nationalism* (New York: Collier Books, 1967). pp. 142–43.

26. Cf. Paul Tillich, *A History of Christian Thought* (New York: Harper & Row, 1968), p. 256.

27. Schweitzer, *The Quest of the Historical Jesus*, trans. W. Montgomery (London: Adam & Charles Black, 1952), p. 310.

28. Cf. Otto Piper, *Recent Developments in German Protestantism* (London: SCM Press, 1934).

29. Ibid., p. 10.

30. Johann Gottlieb Fichte, *Addresses to the German Nation*, trans. R. F. Jones and G. H. Turnbull (Chicago: Open Court Publishing Co., 1922), pp. 93–94.

leon—explains both Fichte's exaltation of the Germans and his depreciation of their neo-Latin conquerors. His chauvinism was real enough, but less extreme than a careless reading of his *Addresses to the German Nation* would suggest, since Fichte was also a universalist who regarded the German spirit as the sanctum for all general values of which the universal one was for the moment enshrined. Germany in his view was the last true culture in Europe and thus the avenue of present and future moral progress: the torchbearer of civilization.

Unfortunately, this universal dimension was weakened by the other side of Fichte's argument that stressed a mystical connection between the Divine Life of God and the mysterious inner life that Fichte located in the spiritual depths of the German nation. It was this connection, lost by other nations, that caused Fichte to exalt the German genius, that "eagle whose mighty body thrusts itself on high and soars on strong and well-practiced wings into the empyrean,"[31] while the foreign genius, like a hummingbird, hovers close to the earth! It was also this connection that caused him to doubt the Jewishness of Jesus, since the religious spirit of Jesus—which, in Fichte's opinion, only the fourth gospel portrays faithfully[32]—so obviously in tune with this Divine Life, had nothing in common with the dead religiosity of Judaism.[33] Per-

haps Jesus, like Luther, possessed a German soul! Not since Marcion had a Christian philosopher so openly denied the Jewish foundations of Christianity. Even the idea of creation was repudiated in gnostic fashion by Fichte as a Jewish, not a Christian, idea, and without support in the fourth gospel.[34]

As the only original people (*Urvolk*), that is, as the only Europeans still in touch with their spiritual origins, the Germans spoke the only original language (*Ursprache*). To Fichte, more than anything else, even more than the occupation of a common territory, the possession of a common language defined the reality of a common people, or of the presence of a nation. Speech arises out of nature, the dwelling place of divinity, and that language is most authentic that most closely nourishes its roots in life itself. Languages are either living or dead, but a dead language, although it can still be spoken, has severed its roots in nature, and can therefore only produce a dead culture. Like dried flowers such a culture can seem beautiful, but its beauty is fragile and superficial. Because the Germans alone had not betrayed their Teutonic birthright, as had their neo-Latin foes, but had still preserved the original European tongue, their culture alone had remained in communion with the hidden currents of God, the underground springs of Spirit. Their knowledge of this truth—as Fichte remarked—should create a special bond of unity and love: "the Fatherland."

From this conception, modern German nationalism rose. Through it, racism, initially a French concoction, was able to lay seige to the

---

31. Ibid., p. 86.
32. Fichte, *The Way towards the Blessed Life*, trans. William Smith, (London: John Chapman, 1849), pp. 95–96. Fichte describes John as the "only teacher of true Christianity" and his gospel as the "purest and most excellent record" of Christianity.
33. Fichte, *The Characteristics of the Present Age* (*The Popular Works of Johann Gottlieb Fichte*), vol. II, trans. William Smith (London: Trübner & Co., 1889), p. 108.

34. Fichte, *The Way towards the Blessed Life*, pp. 101–3.

German romantic imagination, including its Christian center. Since Germany during the Napoleonic Era was not a political entity, it could only be meaningful as a spiritual entity, symbolized by the only available national symbol, the German language. "Aryan" and "Semite" began as linguistic terms, coined by eighteenth-century philologists who were as "innocent as innocent can be" of racism.[35] However, time and the tides of European romanticism soon worked a subtle change in these terms, making them racial as well as linguistic categories on the premise that language and life are joined organically.

Moreover, because the German *literati* were then searching for their own identity through an exploration of German folklore in the lost, twilight world of the pre-Christian Teutons—a search, incidentally, that reflected the fashionable Rousseauistic admiration for the noble savage —it was a simple step for the romantic lovers of antiquity to graft the old Teutons onto the first Aryans who had presumably swept over the earth, colonizing and civilizing. The remoteness of the tribal age made it easy to idealize, and the men of letters could also cite Tacitus, who, in his *Germania*, in order to make a point about Roman decadence, had compared the Romans unfavorably to the virile, freedom-loving, and uncorrupted tribesmen of the Rhine frontier.[36] This polemical and passing comparison from Latin literature, rediscovered by German humanists during the Renaissance, became grist for the mills of the nineteenth-century nationalists.

Religious reforms

Pietism in religion has frequently been linked to romanticism in literature. While the fathers of German pietism, P. J. Spener and August Francke, can hardly be described as German nationalists, their movement of religious reform has been identified as one of the sources of later German nationalism.[37] Not only did the pietists rebel against the Enlightenment understanding of religion as merely another aspect of universal man, that is, the concept of a universal "natural religion" as the underlying basis of every particular religion and therefore the real religion of humanity, regarding it as an "abomination,"[38] but they emphasized the particularity of each expression of the Christian faith. Christianity, in other words, was individualized, becoming an aspect of each separate national identity, or part of the living organism of the nation itself.

In the many political sermons of the great theologian Friedrich Schleiermacher, an ardent Prussian patriot, Protestantism began to acquire a subtle German flavor, for the Christian who lacks loyalty to the Fatherland "always remains an alien in the house of God."[39] Schleiermacher, whose roots in pietism are famous, and who once said that only Germans were deep enough to appreciate his ideas,[40] was a firm believer

35. Hannah Arendt, *The Origins of Totalitarianism* (New York: Meridian Books, 1958), fn. 6, p. 100.

36. "Thus with their virtue protected they live uncorrupted by the allurements of public shows or the stimulant of feastings. . . . No one in Germany laughs at vice, nor do they call it the fashion to corrupt and be corrupted." *Germania* (98), ch. 19.

37. Koppel S. Pinson, *Pietism as a Factor in the Rise of German Nationalism* (New York: Columbia University Press), 1934.

38. Ibid., p. 71.

39. Cited in Pinson, p. 98.

40. John Oman, trans., *On Religion: Speeches to Its Cultured Despisers* (New York: Harper & Brothers), 1958, pp. 9–11.

in the *Volksstaat*, or a type of state built strictly on *völkisch* or national principles. How different in such a system was the "God-conscious" church from the national consciousness, or religious feeling from patriotic feeling? At one point, Schleiermacher even hinted that a single racial origin was the original basis of the *Volk*, although this remark was later qualified.[41] Furthermore, the favorite pietist doctrine of the *Wiedergeburt* was easily transposed into the idea of a national rebirth once the nation also became an individual with its own unique personality.

When Bismarck, through "blood and iron," finally forged a political Germany in 1871, he did not win the approval of the *völkisch* romantics; the new bourgeois empire was not the spiritual nation they desired, nor was it deemed a worthy vessel of this nation. Only after the chancellor's later *Kulturkampf* against the churches had substituted a state founded on "historical national principles" for a state founded on "universal rational principles,"[42] were they mollified.

Not only did the struggle against ecclesiastical independence in the Second Reich weaken German liberalism by subjecting the churches to civil control, but, paradoxically, it stimulated romantic and *völkisch* interpretations of the Protestant Reformation. Nationalism became "imbued with Lutheran symbols,"[43] and the Christian state appealed to Luther's political doctrines in order to buttress its supreme authority.[44] To the influential court preacher Adolf Stöcker, one of the prophets

of the new nation in the making, Germany became "holy" Germany, the elect people of God and heir of ancient Israel whose "Christian Volk-consciousness" the Jews were constantly attempting to destroy.[45] Not Christians-in-general but German Christians-in-particular were the "modern Gentiles, for they alone had been found worthy to establish a Reich that had renewed the tradition of the Carolingian Empire."[46]

This uncritical transfer of biblical symbolism to the fortunes of a modern power created a crisis of faith for conservative churchmen when the nation suffered a catastrophic defeat in 1918. The God of historic providence had apparently deserted his people! How, wondered the Lutheran theologian Emanuel Hirsch, can Christians regard historic events as meaningful in the wake of Germany's collapse? Surely God, if God truly rules over history, must intend Germany's resurrection. When the so-called hour of spiritual and national rebirth struck in 1933, it was hailed by Hirsch as the "call of the Lord of history" in the "great holy storm of present-day Volk happenings."[47] God had sent a new Moses to a new Israel to lead his people to freedom! In the political miracle of the National Socialist Revolution, faith discerned a transcendent presence, enhanced by the angelic "luminous robes" of its leader that so effectively concealed the devil's "cloven hoof."[48]

41. Cf. Pinson, p. 202.

42. Uriel Tal, *Christians and Jews in Germany*, trans. Noah Jonathan Jacobs (Ithaca: Cornell University Press), 1975, p. 84.

43. Ibid., p. 100.

44. Ibid., p. 122.

45. Richard Gutteridge, *Open Thy Mouth for the Dumb!* (Oxford: Basil Blackwell, 1976), p. 9.

46. Tal, p. 257.

47. Cited in James A. Zabel, *Nazism and the Pastors* (Missoula: Scholars Press, 1976), p. 62.

48. Helmut Thielicke, "Why the Holocaust?" *Christianity Today*, XXII(8): 516 (27 Jan. 1978).

Romanticism

The trauma of 1918 and the ecstasy of 1933 proved too much for the romantic theologians; without hesitation or second thoughts they stepped into the dark and fateful waters of racism. Their misstep was assisted not only by the seductive allure of the Aryan myth, but also by the contemporary Protestant return to Luther's doctrine of society, styled the "orders of creation." These orders, marriage, church, and state, believed by Luther to possess divine foundations, impose a definitive and hallowed structure on the human community that, in Protestant eyes, saves the world from chaos and moral confusion.

There were, however, different possible ways of interpreting the various orders, depending on the concerns and bias of the interpreter. Luther, fearful of social anarchy during an age of serious social unrest, had stressed the authority of the princely rulers as God's appointees, to be disobeyed at one's religious peril. Thus the state was seen as a mighty bulwark against evil and earthly power as the sword of God's left hand. While such a concept had no connection with racism, although it had every connection with authoritarianism, it required only an infusion of romanticism into Lutheran orthodoxy to shift the divine order from the political apparatus of the nation to the nation itself, thereby recasting the shape of Luther's doctrine in a racial mold. Popular feeling, not for the first time in Christian history, swept official theology in its own direction, and its destination soon became clear.

A comparison among the views of four Protestant theologians of our era—Emil Brunner, Friedrich Gogarten, Paul Althaus, and Emanuel Hirsch—reveals the tremendous force of this emotional current. To Brunner, a non-German and non-Lutheran, the family, rather than the state, was the basic order from which the others were derived; he repudiated the notion that the Volk should be considered "the form of life willed by God" because nations are always appearing and disappearing in history and lack genuine integrity.[49] To Gogarten, a German Lutheran with nationalist sympathies, the state rather than the family was the fundamental order, including and transcending the others.[50] To Althaus, a Lutheran theologian associated with the pro-Nazi German Christians, the Fichtean definition of the nation as the "life-unity of men of a similar spiritual type" manifesting itself in language, thought, art, law, politics, and religion, was not only valid but a mark of God's creation.[51] Volk and Volkstum, he declared, are occasions for Christian thankfulness: "We see [God's] creative will in the Volkish [sic] differentiation of humanity."[52] But Althaus, whose ideas were described by Brunner as a "half-way house" between romanticism and the Reformation,[53] shrank from the full implications of this statement, maintaining a distinction between the German Volk and the Hebrew Volk; the latter had received a once-and-for-all revelation from God, and their scriptures, the Old Testament, remain unique.[54]

49. Emil Brunner, *The Divine Imperative,* trans. Olive Wyon (Philadelphia: Westminster Press, 1947), p. 456.
50. Nils Ehrenström, *Christian Faith and the Modern State,* trans. Denzil Patrick and Olive Wyon (London: SCM Press, 1937), p. 115 ff.
51. Cited in Zabel, p. 66.
52. Ibid., pp. 66–67.
53. Brunner, p. 698.
54. Zabel, p. 67.

Hirsch, however, felt somewhat less restraint. With Fichte also as his mentor—the shadow of Fichte fell over Gogarten and Althaus, too—he argued that the state was merely a matrix for the *Volk*, the true order of creation whose unfolding life had sacred and revelatory meaning. History, the sphere of God's lordship, is alive with the divine presence, and the *Volk*, as the "hidden sovereign" of the state,[55] is the medium of this presence. To seek God, therefore, means to turn toward the *Volk* as the concrete expression of the Creator's will, whereas the Christian is called to unconditional discipleship and obedience. "Fidelity to the Lord becomes the sanctification of fidelity to the blood and the people or nation."[56] Hirsch even seems to have regarded war as part of the order of creation.[57]

The invocation of blood in Hirsch's theology was fraught with racial meaning, disclosing a fusion of racism and romanticism at the core of Protestant piety. Blood is an ancient metaphor for the "essence of man, the principle of life," explicitly and intimately linked by the Greeks to the "concept of human generation."[58] As such, it has a spiritual as well as a biological connotation, joining the mystery of man's invisible nature with the mystery of his fleshly origins. This double significance found clear expression in the philosophical musings of the modern racists, who never failed to detect a correspondence between the outer and inner or physical and mental traits of the various races: a beautiful—according to Aryan standards—

body signified a superior mind and a noble soul and vice versa.

The materialistic foundations of this Gobinist belief emerged with special clarity in the writings of H. S. Chamberlain, for whom the laws of race or blood were primary and were the *fons et origo* of man's mental qualities.[59] When Hirsch attached spiritual health to racial determination, he exposed the extent to which the secular and anti-biblical ideas of Gobineau and Chamberlain had seeped into his theology:

All human creating and shaping is limited and bounded by the natural character that we bring into life with us. If the blood is ruined, so also the spirit dies, for the spirit of nations and men arises out of the blood. Only the excessive pride of an intellectual generation that knew no limit to human ability in the mystery of our given creatureliness was able to forget it, causing infinite damage with its forgetfulness. The bloodbond of our nation was in ruin. If another fifty years had unfolded, the bearers of good, old and pure German blood (the leading classes of our nation) would have sunk into a minority. With its belief in creation, the church now has the possibility of keeping sacred the mystery of that power and character given with the blood.[60]

Mysticism

It was not Hirsch's intention to submerge Christianity in a sea of paganism. Rather, while endorsing the National Socialist Revolution, he sought its Christianization in

55. Ehrenström, p. 122.
56. Ibid., cited in, p. 124.
57. Cf. Brunner. p. 697.
58. Jordan, pp. 165–66.

59. H. S. Chamberlain, *The Foundations of the Nineteenth Century*, vol. 1, trans. John Lees (London: John Lane, 1913), pp. 519–21.
60. Emanuel Hirsch, *Das kirchliche Wollen der Deutschen Christen* (Berlin: Verlag Max Grevemeyer, 1933), p. 11 (my translation).

order to prevent a pagan triumph in post-Weimar Germany. But Pandora's box had been opened, and Protestantism was now compromised by racial specters that flew hither and yon in the heads of theologians and churchmen. Their flight was aided by other intellectual winds, notably, a mystical neo-Kantianism that, since the turn of the century, had changed Kant's *Ding an sich* into a "dynamic, eternal essence of things that strives ever upward"[61] that could easily blend with concepts of race and blood. Alfred Rosenberg, for example, spoke of a "mysterious centre which makes fruitful the very cadence of German Being and Becoming whenever Germany draws close to it"[62]—in other words, the *Ding an sich* turned into a pantheistic deity with an Aryan face.

But neither *völkisch* feeling nor neo-Kantian philosophy were necessarily ill-fated. The young Martin Buber, as a *fin de siècle* prophet of Jewish rejuvenation, had conceived of a Jewish *Volk* exemplified by the Hasidim,[63] and the young Paul Tillich had dreamed in neo-Kantian fashion of the rejuvenation of German society through a religious socialism inspired by a rediscovery of the transcendent depths of life.[64] Not romanticism but the loss of its universal dimension led to racism.

EFFECTS OF NEW GERMAN CHRISTIANITY

The moment of truth for German Protestantism arrived when the new regime imposed its Aryan laws almost immediately following its rise to power. Racial dreams could now be animated as political reality, and the "German Christians" lost no time in calling for Aryanization in the church as well as in the state. "It is more important that a theological student should know something about eugenics, heredity, and science than that he should have his head stuffed with the names and dates of Jewish kings."[65]

According to the Erlangen theologians Althaus and Werner Elert, the external organization of the Christian church in Reformation if not in Roman Catholic teaching should correspond to the historical and *völkisch* divisions of the Christian world as well as to the universality of the gospel.[66] This meant, of course, that the universality of the gospel had no bearing whatever on the more vital issue of race, and that Jews, not being Germans, should not be mixed up with Germans in Christian congregations. Baptism was wholly irrelevant—as irrelevant as it had once been to the Spanish authors of the "purity of blood" restrictions which, in strange anticipation of the Aryan paragraph, "old Christians" had introduced into the sixteenth-century Spanish church in order to keep "new Christians," *Conversos* or ex-Jews, from gaining ecclesiastical office.[67]

61. George L. Mosse, *Germans and Jews* (New York: Howard Fertic, 1970), pp. 183–84.

62. Alfred Rosenberg, *Der Mythus des 20. Jahrhunderts*, cited in *Alfred Rosenberg: Selected Writings*, ed. Robert Pois (London: Jonathan Cape, 1970), p. 97.

63. Mosse, p. 85.

64. An old but still reliable account of Tillich's religious socialism is found in Charles West, *Communism and the Theologians* (Philadelphia: Westminster Press, 1958).

65. Cited in Gutteridge, p. 94.

66. Wolfgang Gerlach, "Zwiespältig in der Judenfrage," *Lutherische Monathefte*, p. 463. (8 Aug. 1979).

67. For a good account, *see* Albert A. Sicroff,

During the struggle that ensued, few Protestants, even those most hostile to the German Christian movement, were sufficiently uncontaminated by Germanic nationalism and antisemitism to see clearly the terrible danger in which German Christianity now stood.

Les controverses des statuts de 'pureté de sang' en Espagne du XVe au XVIIe siècle (Paris: Didier, 1960).

A racial virus thus penetrated the religious blood stream of the Reformation churches that Luther, for all his faults, would never have countenanced. The mighty Word of God had become a racist word of blood, *Volk*, and soil, and only the Holocaust still remained as the consummation of its ethic of struggle, violence, and death. The prelude was over. The nation was now prepared for the main event.

Genocide: Was it the Nazis' Original Plan?

By YEHUDA BAUER

ABSTRACT: Since the 1940s scholars have debated the question, Did Hitler and his henchmen plan the Final Solution decades before 1941? Many have answered in the affirmative. However, examination of those developments that led to the Final Solution raises serious questions. Although some have declared that the Nazis with Hitler at the helm did indeed plan the mass execution even before the 1930s, nowhere is there any pronouncement of this before 1939! The plan the Nazis did have was to evict all Jews from Germany. Although several hundred thousand did leave, those left behind as well as the millions conquered as the Nazis swept through Europe provided a dilemma. Hitler wanted them out. No one wanted them. The Schacht-Rublee negotiations and the Nisko/ Madagascar plans, efforts to clear Europe of Jews, had failed dismally before 1939. The last alternative was the Final Solution, which took form in 1941 with the adoption of the *Einsatzgruppen* plan for the mass murder of Jews in Russia, mainly by machine gun, and the Wannsee plan for the mass murder of Jews in Poland in the gas ovens and the crematoria established at six death camps.

Yehuda Bauer earned his Ph.D. from Hebrew University and has been a senior lecturer at the Institute of Contemporary Jewry and head of the Department of Holocaust Studies at Hebrew University since 1968. Currently he is head of the institute. His work in Holocaust studies is the combination of his own experiences as a young man living in Czechoslovakia before 1939 and of his academic preparation. Living with hundreds of thousands of "refugees" pouring into Israel from death camps and hiding places throughout Europe in the 1940s; studying history, philosophy, and English; and attempting to answer the many complex questions relating to the Holocaust caused Yehuda Bauer to become a pioneer in Holocaust studies. In 1975 he was named Jonnah M. Machover Professor of Holocaust Studies. Among his most recent books are The Jewish Emergence From Powerlessness, The Holocaust in Historical Perspective *and* From Diplomacy to Resistance.

THE problem of the origins of the Final Solution has been the subject of much research. One has to make the clear differentiation between the quest for the background of Nazi-type murderous antisemitism and the more immediate problem of the planning for mass murder. The underlying problem of a study of Nazi antisemitism is whether it was the result of a continuity extending from Christian, traditional, or even pre-Christian anti-Judaism to which racial antisemitism added a few new ideas, or whether modern antisemitism, in its late nineteenth-century form is a new departure, qualitatively different from, though influenced by, traditional or Christian antisemitism. My own view is close to that of Franklin H. Littell, Uriel Tal, and Shmuel Ettinger, namely, that while modern antisemitism undoubtedly contains new elements or places new emphases on old ones and leads to consequences that are radically more extreme than those attained by its predecessors, the element of continuity is a predominant factor. Without Christian, or traditional anti-Judaism, modern, nationalistic and racial antisemitism would have been impossible.

THE JEWISH PROBLEM: HITLER'S FIRST SOLUTION

However, the subject of this article is the second problem—the question of the origins of the Final Solution in Nazi theory and practice. Contrary to legend, nowhere in Hitler's writings or pronouncements before 1939 do we find a declaration in favor of the annihilation of the Jewish people. Lucy Dawidowicz, in trying to prove the contrary, argues that as early as 1919 Hitler expressed views that "prefigure the political realities of the German dictatorship . . . when the Jews

were deprived of all rights systematically and 'legally' and then 'removed altogether,' the ambiguity of the word 'removal' is now more apparent than it was in 1919." She bases her views on the first political propaganda letter written by Hitler on 16 September 1919 to Adolf Gemlich. In it Hitler, favoring what he called rational as opposed to emotional antisemitism, stated that "the final objective must unswervingly be the removal [*Entfernung*] of the Jews altogether [*überhaupt*]." Dawidowicz seems to argue from that that the Final Solution in the sense of mass murder was with Hitler from the beginning. That leads her to a deterministic, or teleological, view according to which the ultimate steps unfolded necessarily from a basic Hitlerite concept which already contained mass murder and which remained constant from 1919 to the early forties.[1]

This view is, I think, the popular view. Ask any number of freshmen students, and they will respond with a question, Why did not the Jews flee, or react energetically from the start, if they could have known from Hitler's writings and speeches that he intended to kill them all?

But when one examines the evidence, one finds that Hitler did not say anything like that at all before 1939. Dawidowicz quotes the one and only passage in Hitler's book, *Mein Kampf*, in which a death wish for Jews is uttered: "If at the beginning of the [First World] War twelve or fifteen thousand of these Hebrew corrupters of the people had been held under poison gas, as happened to hundreds of thousands of our very best German workers in the field, the sacrifice of multitudes at the front would not have been in vain."[2] This,

1. Lucy S. Dawidowicz, *The War Against the Jews* (London: 1975), p. 17.
2. Ibid., p. 3.

of course, is antisemitism at its basest, but it is hardly a blueprint for the planned mass killing of all European Jews. Worse things were said by antisemites in and out of power in various countries before Hitler. In fact, it is a solitary sentence in a thick book of turgid German prose.

Was there then a plan? Of course there was, and Hitler stated it plainly on 13 November 1919 in his first public speech, also quoted by Dawidowicz: "We will carry on the struggle until the last Jew is removed from the German Reich." Or, as he said in 1920, he advocated "the removal of the Jews from our nation, not because we would begrudge them their existence—we congratulate the rest of the world on their company—but because the existence of our nation is a thousand times more important to us than that of an alien race."[3]

Until the end of 1938, neither Hitler nor any of the chief propagandists of the regime suggested any other solution for what they called the Jewish problem than eviction from Germany. Why was that their solution? How did they perceive the Jew?

Ideology and practice, 1928–38: The apparent contradiction

In his second book, written but not published in 1928, Hitler made his view of the Jews very clear. He said that they were an antirace, formed out of a hybrid, indeterminate, mongrel core, a nomad people of eternal restlessness, incapable of independent political, territorial existence. He also noted that their religion was a cover for their lust for unlimited power and for absolute rule over all others. Their control of the world was not based on territory, which they never had, and in this they differed from all the other nations; it was based, rather, on financial and other machinations. Hitler wrote that at first the Jew demanded equal rights, and then, finally, superior rights, and that his aim was to rule the world; but, as his character was parasitic and as he was incapable of separate existence, his rule would lead not only to the destruction of the nations oppressed by him, but also to his own demise.

These views can be found, with some variations, in the writings of Alfred Rosenberg, Josef Goebbels, and other close collaborators of Hitler. They contain a number of crucial elements. First among these is the view of the Jew as a demonic presence in the world; the use of the generalizing singular "the Jew" already suggests that. This, of course, is taken from Christian antisemitism, which postulated that only a people possessed by the Devil would have killed the God-Messiah. The Jews, in the Nazi demonology, are out to rule the world, and, in fact, are already well on their way toward doing so. This again is based on Christian foundations, and we can find traces of fear of the Jewish demons controlling the world during the Middle Ages—and even earlier. In modern times, this superstition was reformulated in that famous forgery by the tsarist Soviet police, *The Protocols of the Elders of Zion* (1905), which forms one of the cornerstones of Nazi ideology.

A second basic element in the Nazi view of the Jews is the description of the Jew as a parasite.[4] In Nazi literature Jews are described as vermin, rats, or other

3. Ibid., p. 18.

4. Alex Bein, "The Jewish Parasite," in *Leo Baeck Year Book*, vol. 9 (1964), pp. 3–39.

noxious elements from the insect or animal world, as well as bacilli or viruses. In his previously mentioned second book,[5] Hitler says that in order for the Jews to exist, they use the creative faculties of other nations because they are incapable of establishing a polity of their own. They thus become parasitic, and perforce their aim must be to control as many nations as possible so as to live on their lifeblood. In this way, nazism combined with the two divergent metaphoric pictures it had created for the Jews: that of demons and that of parasites.

For our purpose a third element is most important. Nazism in effect accused the Jew of vices that it was guilty of. The picture of the demonic force out to conquer the world reflects the desires of the Nazis themselves. Years before the wish to murder the Jews became articulate in their own minds, they formulated it in obverse fashion. Thus Hitler stated, in his directives to Goering in 1936[6] regarding the four-year plan, that Germany must be ready for war within four years. The reason for the tight time schedule, according to Hitler, was that "the loss of months may cause damage that will be irreparable in hundreds of years." The reason for that rather surprising statement—in 1936!—was that international Jewry was threatening Germany's existence. The prospective victory of Jewry, said Hitler, "whose most radical expression is Bolshevism . . . will not this time lead to new Versailles treaties, but to the final destruction, that is the extermination of the German peo-

ple." This in turn will cause "the catastrophic destruction of the European nations, such as humanity has not known since the demise of the states of antiquity."

I have chosen a clear statement by Hitler but one can find this idea in many places and at various levels of Nazi officialdom in the thirties: the accusation that the Jews were out to destroy Germany, Europe, and the world and that therefore all Germany could do was to fight a defensive battle against Jewry. Nazi ethics, as I have pointed out in other places,[7] are the ordinary bourgeois ethics reversed, standing very precisely on their head. They could murder because they accused the Jews of wanting to murder them. They extolled murder as a positive ethical command to save the world and white, Germanic supremacy because they accused the Jews of planning that fate for the Germans. Having described the Jews as demons and vermin, that is, as nonhumans, they could murder them, because they were no longer killing human beings, but devils, bacilli, and rats with human faces. In effect, then, they could commit mass murder because they had dehumanized themselves. In other words, they had done that of which they had accused the Jews in a true reversal of values, *Das Umwerten aller Werte*.

It may well appear that the preceding argument ends in a contradiction. On one hand, the claim is advanced that there is no evidence of any Nazi plan to murder the Jews before the end of the thirties, and indeed there is not; on the other hand, great trouble has been taken to explain what it was that enabled the Nazis to murder the Jews as

5. *Hitler's Secret Book* (New York: 1962), pp. 212–13.

6. Wilhelm Treue, *Hitlers Deukschrift zum Vierjahresplan 1936*, vol. 3 (Vierteljahresheftelür Zeitgeschichte: 1955), pp. 184–210.

7. Yehuda Bauer, *The Holocaust in Historical Perspective* (University of Washington Press, 1978).

seen from the point of view of the Nazis' ideological development. But there is really no contradiction. The murder of the Jewish people was inherent in the ideology that the Nazis took from their predecessor in the nineteenth century. It was inherent—as a logical conclusion, not as a practical plan. To become a practical plan, to develop from an unarticulated wish logically embedded in their world view into mass graves and gas chambers, political and military developments had to occur that would make mass murder a practicable proposition.

Antisemitism: central to the Nazi program

Nazi plans for Jews between 1933 and 1938 were to evict them from Germany. But between 1933 and the end of 1937, only 129,000 out of a half million German Jews left the country. In our literature, the accusation is found against German Jews for not having read the signs on the wall and not having left early enough. The description of the Weiss family in the NBC Holocaust film series has made this view even more popular. That does not make it historically correct. There were, of course, large, though diminishing, numbers of German Jews who refused to leave a country where Jews had been living before the Germans had even arrived there; Jews had lived in the Roman towns along the Rhine which were part of the Roman world's frontier defence against the German tribes. After the 1935 Nuremberg Laws, especially, which decreed the Jews to be second-class subjects rather than citizens, the numbers of those wishing to hang on were growing smaller, though no poll exists which could prove this statistically.

The real test lies elsewhere; it is known from historical researches that at no time in the thirties was there any lessening of Jewish emigration pressure on foreign consulates in Germany. There were always considerably more Jews wanting to leave than, in a world stricken by a vast economic crisis, there were places willing to accept them. America did not want them, and they infiltrated there in relatively small numbers. The number of emigrants, both Jews and non-Jews, from Germany was 4,392 in fiscal year 1933/34; 5,201 in 1934/35; and 6,346 in 1935/36. In late 1935, the intervention of some of the so-called German-Jewish aristocracy in America— Felix M. Warburg and Herbert Lehmann—caused President Roosevelt to give more liberal directives to the State Department and the figures show 10,895 immigrants from Germany for 1936/37; 17,199 for 1937/38; and 19,452 for the rest of 1938 (July–December).[8] Of these 63,485 immigrants, probably 85 percent were Jews, or about 55,000. Had Jewish emigration from Germany to the United States and Palestine, which absorbed a similar number, and to other places in which Jews could infiltrate in small numbers continued on this scale, German Jewry would have disappeared by emigration and aging in about 15 to 20 years. But the whole point was that the Nazis saw a demonic, catastrophic threat from an imaginary world Jewry to the Germanic race. War was planned to solve this problem, and if Germany planned to free itself and the world from a demonic force, it could not very well start the process while that demonic force was sitting right in its midst.

8. Yehuda Bauer, *My Brother's Keeper* (Philadelphia: 1974), pp. 168–69.

It is necessary to emphasize here the enormity of what is being said: I am indicating no more and no less than that World War II was unleashed primarily because of the Nazi desire to assert the world dominance of the Germanic peoples of Aryan race in their struggle against world Jewry and its minions, bolshevism in the East, and Western parliamentary democracy, or Anglo-Saxon plutocracy (if one prefers Goebbels' favorite phrase), in the West. Put differently, it is imperative to distill Nazi antisemitism as a major determinant of Nazi aggression culminating in World War II. If one disagrees with this statement, one will have to explain away a whole series of Nazi documents providing circumstantial or direct evidence for these statements: Hitler's instructions for the four-year plan; the Hossbach protocol of November 1937, in which Hitler explains the urgency of war within a short time; the report of the SS (*Lagebericht*) for 1939, in which the Jewish problem is defined as "the problem"[9] of world politics, and many others.

Expulsion

All this meant that the Nazis were bent on radicalizing their anti-Jewish policies in early 1938. Expulsion of Jews was now a central German state interest and had to be achieved quickly. A series of steps in 1938 was indicative of this policy and was aimed at the expulsion of Jews from German economic life: the abolition of the right of Jewish communities to act as legal bodies, registration of Jewish properties, pressure

for so-called Aryanization, various economic restrictions, and from June, 1938, mass arrests of Jews who until then had not populated Nazi concentration camps except insofar as Jews had belonged to the anti-Nazi opposition. Then came the *Kristallnacht* pogrom of November, 1938. Its purpose was to accelerate Jewish exit from Germany. Of the approximately 30 to 35 thousand internees in Nazi concentration camps taken there on *Kristallnacht*, most were set free in 1939 when emigration papers or opportunities were obtained for thĕm from their frantic relatives. Illegal immigration to Palestine was organized by the Jewish Agency representatives and by Zionist Revisionist activists with the Gestapo's encouragement, as was illegal emigration to Latin America. By 1941, 450,000 central European Jews that included four-fifths of Austrian Jewry and close to that percentage of German Jewry, had left Greater Germany, though some of these were caught again later in the German conquest of other European countries.

This second period of Nazi rule, 1938–41, was characterized by an attempt to evict the Jews from the Nazi sphere quickly and radically. According to a circular letter, dated 25 January 1939, of the German Foreign Office to all German representatives abroad, the expulsion of the Jews would cause greater understanding of Germany's stand by foreign powers, because the expelled Jews would cause antisemitic reactions in their new abodes, and this would help Germany!

Ransom: Schacht-Rublee negotiations

What is interesting is that parallel with this radicalization, Nazi Ger-

9. "daas es überhaupt *das* Problem der Weltpolitik im Augenblick ist" II 112: *Das Judentum alz Weltproblem*, quoted in O. D. Kulka, 1:206 (19 Jan. 1939).

many appears to have been willing to sell its Jews. In the so-called Schacht-Rublee negotiations of late 1938 and early 1939, Hitler agreed to release 100,000 young German Jews with part of their property, who would go to establish themselves in a new country with large additional sums to be raised by Jews abroad; their families would then join, and only the old and sick would remain in Germany, to be kept there by the rest of the Jewish capital. The Jews in the United States and elsewhere not only did not have the necessary money at that time, but it was also feared by Jews and non-Jews that this plan would increase German exports and help Nazi Germany economically. The plan was rejected by the American government, though hesitatingly accepted by the American Jewish Joint Distribution Committee (JDC), which represented American Jewish philanthropy toward Jews overseas, as well as the Zionists and the American Jewish Committee.[10] In hindsight, the plan was perfectly logical from a Nazi point of view: if Jews were not really human, one could sell them rather than exorcise them—if there were someone who would buy. The tragedy was that there was no buyer.

Resettlement: Nisko/Madagascar plans

In late 1939 and 1940, two other possibilities emerged, again perfectly in line with what has been outlined: one was to expel the Jews to the Nisko area in the southeastern part of recently occupied Polish territory, with a view of possibly pushing them across the new border

into Soviet Russia. And the second was to ship them to the island of Madagascar off the coast of Africa, then a French possession that would become a German colony at the ultimate peace settlement with defeated France. Both plans were very seriously considered, and in connection with the Madagascar plan, the term "territorial final solution" was used by Heydrich. As late as May, 1940, a memorandum by Himmler[11] rejected the idea of mass murder of peoples and advocated instead enslavement and cultural deprivation.

When did mass murder appear on the scene as a viable alternative in Nazi eyes? We hear the first rumblings in November, 1938, after the *Kristallnacht*, in an article in *Das Schwartze Korps*, the SS journal that on November 24 threatened Jewry with "fire and sword." There followed Hitler's declaration on 30 January 1939, in which he threatened the destruction of the Jewish race in Europe if international Jewry were to unleash another world war. Slightly less explicit threats were uttered in two private meetings with Hitler, one with the South African minister of defence, Otto von Pirow, in November, 1938, and one with the hapless Czech foreign minister, Josef Chvalkovsky, in February, 1939. One may perhaps conclude that Hitler saw mass murder as a possibility then. But he agreed to the Schacht-Rublee plan then (January, 1939) and later supported the Madagascar plan as well. We have every evidence that these plans were meant seriously, and no evidence whatsoever that any mass murder plan exists at that stage! The establishment of ghettos and *Judenraete* (Jewish Councils), as in a fa-

10. The AJC, founded in 1906, represented the upper crust of American Jewry in their endeavor to fight antisemitism and protect the civic rights of Jews everywhere.

11. See *Vierteljahreshefte für Zeitgeschichte*, 2:196–98 (1957).

mous instruction by Reinhard Heydrich, chief of the SS security police, on 21 September 1939, at the time of the conquest of Poland, has often been interpreted as being indicative of a mass-murder plan. Close scrutiny proves the opposite: it was a brutal plan to evict a maximum of Jews, starve them as much as possible, and concentrate them so as to facilitate a later massive expulsion.

With all the suffering and the massive mortality in the ghettos in Eastern Europe between 1939 and 1942, the large mass of Polish Jewry would have survived the war had the decision to mass murder them not been taken. It is therefore crucial to examine when and how this happened.

THE FINAL SOLUTION

It is clear that as late as October, 1940, Hitler himself gave the order to expel the Jews of the Mannheim-Pfalz area in western Germany to France and not to Poland, an act that made sense only if a final expulsion to Madagascar was envisaged. But in May, 1941, special Nazi murder units (*Einsatzgruppen*) were being trained to kill Jews and Communists in the coming campaign in Russia. It has therefore been assumed by most historians that an oral order—there never was a written one—to mass murder the Jews was given by Hitler about mid-March, 1941, together with his other commands and orders relating to the coming Russian war. The fact that such an order was given is seemingly attested to by Himmler in his speech at Poznan in October, 1943, and elsewhere. But nowhere does Himmler or anyone else state exactly when the order was given or what specifically the order said. The date of March, 1941 makes sense. The Nazis expected to find more Jews in Russia—they were thinking of five million—and the idea to send them all to Madagascar was becoming impossible. The Americans had not reacted to the news about ghettos, although American newspapers in 1940 and 1941 had fully reported what was happening to the Jews in Poland and elsewhere up to that point. Therefore, there was nothing to fear from that quarter.

The logical consequence of Nazi ideology could now be drawn, and it was. There followed the mass murders committed by the *Einsatzgruppen* in Russia from June, 1941, when the Germans invaded that country, until late in 1942, when they practically completed the annihilation of that part of Soviet Jewry who had not fled. Rudolf Hoess, the commandant of Auschwitz, said that he received the order to prepare the camp for mass annihilation of Jews in the summer of 1941. On 3 September 1941, the first experimental gassing was done, with Soviet prisoners of war as the first victims. In December, 1941, the Nazis established the first death camp at Chelmno in western Poland, where they killed the Jews from that area, especially from the city of Lodz. In March, 1942, the systematic mass murder of the rest of Polish Jewry commenced.

March, 1941

Most historians agree, then, that the decision to mass murder the Jews was made in March, 1941, and transmitted in an oral order to

Himmler. However, a serious German historian, Uwe Dietrich Adam, in his *Judenpolitik im Dritten Reich* (Düsseldorf, 1972), disagrees and argues that since between June and December, 1941, murder actions took place only in the areas taken from the U.S.S.R., the March decision must have referred to these areas only, whereas a later decision, probably in November, must have referred to the rest of Europe. Another important German historian, Martin Broszat, has since expressed a similar view. The argument appears somewhat problematic, because it presupposes that Hitler regarded Polish Jews differently from Russian Jews, and it stands to reason that the decision to start with Russia was part of a larger decision, implemented a few months later, to carry on with all areas. Even if Adam is right, what difference does it make? We would then have to say that the decision was taken in two stages, but that the principle of murder was accepted in March; the rest followed logically. Besides, the Hoess testimony is ignored. There is no evidence at all for a November decision apart from pure conjecture and the fact that the Chelmno Concentration Camp started operating on December 8. That fact could just as well mean that the decision was taken months earlier and was implemented when the staff and the technical means were ready. What is important is the decision in principle. By December, 1941, well over a million Jews had been killed— the Nazi machine had indeed crossed the Rubicon!

What followed was the Wannsee Conference on 20 January 1942. Top German bureaucrats of the various ministries, of the German occupation authorities in Poland and conquered Russia, and the chief SS henchmen, Heydrich and Eichmann, were present. This conference has been represented as the forum at which the destruction of European Jews was decided. Nothing of the sort occurred. The decision, as we have seen, had been made 10 months before that and had been implemented in the mass executions in Russia. In January, 1942, ways and means were discussed by which the various branches of the German administration would help the SS to implement the decision in areas where their help was required.

The decision of the Wannsee Conference was to murder the Jews from West to East, and to carry on with the Nazi satellites in southeast Europe. These conclusions were not implemented. The main effort of the murderers was in Poland, not in the West, and then intermittently in other parts of Europe. They never managed central Rumania at all, or most of Bulgarian Jewry. They destroyed Saloniki Jewry in 1943, and not in 1942, and so on. Germany under the Nazis was a dictatorship tempered by inefficiency and the squabbles of semi-independent "fiefdoms" belonging to the various top Nazis. The murder of the Jews was done brutally, in factory fashion, in sudden twists and spasms, directed by the SS and aided by practically all the branches of German officialdom.

By the beginning of 1943, as the Nazi empire began to crumble and contract, the old idea of selling the Jewish demons to anyone who would buy them for a desirable equivalent was revived. One might postulate the thesis that Nazi murder of Jews was one of two possible Nazi modes of behavior. The other was barter, or ransom. Between 1942 and 1945 the Nazis, and especially Himmler and some of his collaborators, tried to get rid of the Jews in return for a separate peace agreement with the Western Allies.[12] What seems to be abundantly clear is that the decision to kill the Jews was one logical outcome of Nazi ideology, but not the only one. The trouble with the solution as proposed by Himmler in the latter part of the war was that, as in 1938 and 1939 in the case of the Schacht-Rublee plan, nobody wanted to buy Jews. The Nazis turned to the other alternative. Both resulted from the same premise, namely, that the Jews were not human, and that therefore they could either be killed or sold—in other words, they could be treated as nonhuman elements, as animals or goods.

Definitions

Was the murder of the Jews genocide? We ought perhaps to differentiate very clearly between a planned total annihilation of a national group, on one hand, and what the Nazis did in Poland, Czechoslovakia, or elsewhere on the other hand. The term "genocide," though invented in 1943, did not really cover the Holocaust at all. True, the first sentence of Raphael Lemkin's definition seemingly does so: "The practice of extermination of nations and ethnic groups as carried out by the invaders is called by the author 'genocide.' "[13]

12. I have developed this theme in some recent publications; see fn. no. 7; see also The Jewish Emergence from Powerlessness (Toronto: 1979).

13. Raphael Lemkin, Axis Rule in Occupied Europe (New York: 1943), pp. xi–xii.

But when Lemkin goes on to describe the act he called "genocide," he describes fairly exactly what happened to Poles, for instance, the destruction of the "institutions of self-government . . . disrupting the social cohesion of the nation involved and killing or removing elements such as the intelligentsia . . . destroying cultural institutions . . . introducing a starvation system . . . and mass killings . . . interfering with the Churches," and so forth. If the plan was to kill everyone, then the restrictions in the religious field or the curtailing of cultural activities was hardly a matter of any importance any longer. If genocide meant mass murder, then one did not have to detail the political restrictions: dead people do not have political institutions. What happened to Lemkin in 1943 is typical of what happened then to many Jews and non-Jews: they talked about what they called "extermination" but they did not comprehend it. They talked about the brutal, murderous enslavement of European nations by the Nazis, but what we call "the Holocaust" was beyond them.

The term genocide is appropriate, according to Lemkin's definition, for what the Americans did to the Native American population, for the attempt of the Nazis to destroy Poles and Czechs, for the fate of the Biharis in Bangladesh, perhaps, and so on. The Holocaust, however, was a total act; moreover, it was a sacral act. Hitler said that by destroying the Jew he would be doing the will of God. It was, in Nazi eyes, a fight against Satan, it had cosmic importance, it was a quasi-religious act of the first importance. Therein lies the importance of the Holocaust; *it is unique in the sense that it stands alone.*

Holocaust: logical consequence of ideological antisemitism

Genocide and Holocaust are, therefore, two different concepts. Both are repeatable, and in that lies the universal importance of dealing with the subject. If we then change the name of this article, we can ask, Was Holocaust the Nazis original plan? And our answer will be that the idea of a mass murder of the Jews was the logical consequence of Nazi theories, but that the logical conclusion was not drawn until 1941; that even then mass murder was avoidable because there was a willingness to sell or barter Jews out of the same attitude that produced the readiness to murder them; and that the free world was not prepared to buy the Jews, because its priorities then and now fall short of its declared ethical values. Winning wars was primary; saving human lives was not.

Putative Threat to National Security as a Nuremberg Defense for Genocide

By ROBERT WOLFE

ABSTRACT: Otto Ohlendorf, SS group leader and Lieutenant General of Police, director of the Reich Security Main Office that was responsible for domestic intelligence and public opinion analysis, and lawyer and economist, was the best-known defendant in the subsequent Nuremberg trial of the *Einsatzgruppen* commanders (case 9) for the mass murder of Jews and others in the rear areas of the invading German armies during the first two years of the Russian campaign. Having admitted, as a witness in the precedent trial before the International Military Tribunal (IMT) at Nuremberg, that his *Einsatzgruppe D* operating in the southern Ukraine during one short year under his command executed some 90 thousand Jews and other civilians, Ohlendorf could not deny the charges, particularly because almost daily detailed contemporary *Einsatzgruppen* reports were submitted in evidence. Nor could he claim "superior orders" because the IMT (London) Charter ruled out such a defense, except as mitigation. Ohlendorf and some of his fellow defendants in the same case contended that they were convinced at the time that Soviet Jewry was a mainstay of bolshevism and therefore constituted a direct threat to the security of the Third Reich. Ohlendorf was convicted of crimes against humanity and was executed at Landsberg prison on 7 June 1951.

Robert Wolfe, chief of the Modern Military Branch of the National Archives, has served successively as specialist for captured records and for modern European history and as chief of the Captured Records Branch since transferring in 1961 from the American Historical Association team microfilming captured records at the Worled War II Records Center in Alexandria, Virginia. He received a Ph.B. in history from the University of Vermont in 1942 and a Ph.M. in history from Columbia University in 1955. He taught history at Brooklyn College from 1954 to 1960, was an assistant professorial lecturer for George Washington University from 1961 to 1965, and taught a short course on the Nuremberg trials at Wesleyan University in 1972.

The original version of this paper was read at the Annual Scholars Conference on the Church Struggle and the Holocaust at the Barbizon Plaza Hotel in New York City on 20 March 1974.

THE CRIME of genocide constituted one of the major charges before the International Military Tribunal (IMT) at Nuremberg and of the subsequent twelve trials conducted before United States military tribunals in that city. Along with crimes against the peace, the charge of crimes against humanity was attacked by defense counsel as ex post facto law, as if systematic mass murder were, like the organized slaughter of the battlefield, less culpable than murder in a one-on-one situation. It is this attempt to cloak mass murder with patriotism under the various legal terms of "state of emergency" and of "self defense on behalf of a third party" —in this case the third party being the Third Reich—which in a terminological sea change of time as well as place, will be dealt with here under the blanket heading of "national security."

THE CHARGE

On 15 October 1946, there appeared before United States Military Tribunal II A[1] on trial for his life, charged with mass murder or genocide, Otto Ohlendorf, SS *Gruppenführer* and Lieutenant General of Police; lawyer, economist, analyst of public opinion in a dictatorship as quondam head of the *SD Inland*,[2] the Nazi domestic intelligence service, and under secretary in the Reich Ministry of Economics; father of five children[3]; and confessed mass murderer. How did such a conscientious, sobersided intellectual get into that anomalous position? He was brought to Nuremberg as a witness for the prosecution in the IMT case[4] because during pretrial inter-

---

1. See the *Official Record of the United States Military Tribunals, Nuernberg, Case No. 9, Tribunal II (II-A), U.S. v. Otto Ohlendorf et al.*, 15 Sept. 1947–10 April 1948 (National Archives Collection of World War II War Crimes Records, Record Group 238). A complete microfilm of case 9, consisting of English and German language transcripts of the proceedings, prosecution and defense exhibits and document books, official court files, order and judgment books, clemency petitions, and briefs and pleas are reproduced on National Archives and Records Service Microfilm Publication M895, 37 rolls, as described and indexed in NARS *Special List No. 42* (Washington, 1978). Extensive excerpts from proceedings, documents and court records are printed in English in vol. IV, 3-596, of *Trials of War Crimes before the Nuernberg Military Tribunals under Control Council Law No. 10*, 15 vols. (Washington, DC: Government Printing Of-

fice, 1949–53). Translations (and even transcriptions in the same language) in the mimeographed official court record were hastily prepared for the soonest possible courtroom availability, so direct quotations are to the more polished and more accessible excerpts in *Nuernberg Military Tribunals* (hereafter cited as NMT) vol. IV of the 15-volume series, which were derived by comparison of transcripts and sound recordings. Since these, however, are not always as careful as scholarly quotation should be, citation in such cases is also to the official transcript.

2. *SD* was the abbreviation for the *Sicherheitsdienst der Reichsfuehrer* SS (Security Service of the Reich Leader SS), loosely used in official correspondence as well as on the arm bands of *Einsatzgruppen* personnel, many of whom were never members of the *SD*, although all were SS. For the evolution of the *SD* into a state agency through merger with police agencies after some competitive overlap, and its ultimate incorporation as two offices of the *RSHA, see* pp. 52–53.

3. Ohlendorf's oral testimony on 8, 9, 14, and 15 Oct. 1947 is printed in the *Official Record* of case 9, *Transcripts* (English) vol. 2, pp. 475-756. For biographic data, *see* his SS Personnel File, Nuremberg document NO 3196: Prosecution Exhibit (PEX) 156 (original in Berlin Document Center), his pretrial affidavit of 1 April 1947, document NO 2857: PEX 157, and his oral testimony, case 9, *Transcripts* (English) vol. 2, passim.

4. For Ohlendorf's testimony before the IMT, *see Trial of the Major War Criminals before the International Military Tribunal: Nuremberg, 14 November 1945–1 October 1946*, 42 vols. (Nuremberg, 1947–49), IV, 311–55, 3 Jan. 1946.

rogation[5] he made substantial and specific charges implicating the German army high command and its field commanders as accessories to the genocidal operations of the *Einsatzgruppen*.[6]

Perhaps carried away by his indignation at German military leaders' attempts to whitewash themselves by scapegoating the SS,[7] Ohlendorf under cross-examination estimated on the basis of the top-secret RSHA *Ereignismeldungen UdSSR* (Situation Reports on the Soviet Union)[8]

5. IMT document PS 2620: Exhibit US 919.

6. The *Einsatzgruppen* were SS groups literally set into (in the sense of committed) action in the war areas of the German Army Groups invading Russia. The distinction is between field and garrison troops. The term *Einsatz* has been variously translated as "operational," "action," or "mobile," and *Einsatzgruppe* as "task force." Each group consisted of several *Kommandos*, conglomerates of contingents of SS police, intelligence, security, and combat personnel. Ohlendorf's *Einsatzgruppe D* was so designated because it was eventually to be attached to an abortive Army Group D intended to operate in the Caucasus, but remained subordinate throughout its existence to the Eleventh Army to which it was assigned at the outset of the Russian campaign. (IMT, IV, 316; case 9, transcripts 2:680).

7. For the culpability of the German army leaders as accessories to the Final Solution, *see* IMT document PS 877:RF 273, an army draft of May 1941 entitled "Handling of Enemy Inhabitants," which refers specifically to "bearers of the Jewish-bolshevist world view" and "bearers of the Jewish-bolshevist system." The final version, the "Führer Decree on the Exercise of Courts-Martial" of 13 May 1941 (IMT document C 050: US 554), although granting immunity to commanders and troops meting out swift and severe punishment to the indigenous population, far beyond that allowed by the Hague and Geneva conventions, makes no reference to Jews.

8. *Ereignismeldungen UdSSR*, Nr. 190, 8 April 1942. This entire series of almost daily reports, Nrs. 1–195, 23 June 1941–24 April 1942, as well as its successor series, *Meldungen aus den besetzten Ostgebieten*, Nrs. 1–55, 1 May 1942–21 May 1943, are reproduced in National Archives Microfilm Publication T175, Rolls 233–36.

that 90,000 Jews were killed in southern Russia by commandos of *Einsatzgruppe D* during the 12 months under his command.[9] Chop away though he might at the accuracy of the consolidated reports, complain though he did of the bragging tendency of most *Einsatz* unit commanders to exaggerate their "body counts,"[10] Ohlendorf could not deny the repeated assertions by prosecution counsel in the IMT trial and in his own and other subsequent trials that he had admitted presiding over the murder of many tens of thousands of Jews, perhaps as many as 90,000.[11]

This initial admission, coupled with the overwhelming and damning data in the situation reports and other inadvertently surviving documentary evidence, forced Ohlendorf and some of his fellow defendants to grasp at the last straw defense of "putative national security." Thus he went from star witness for the IMT prosecution to "star turn"[12] as defendant faut de mieux in the absence of Himmler, Heydrich, and Gestapo Mueller; *United States v. Ohlendorf et al.* became the title

9. IMT, IV, 319.

10. Case 9, transcript (tr.) 2:533–41 and 620 ff. Compare IMT, IV, 319, where Ohlendorf uses the word "approximately" and refuses to give a minimum figure; but see also tr. 2:668, where he "stands up for my testimony before the IMT, but not the interrogations in your records," i.e., document PS 2620.

11. *See* Court Opinion and Judgment (tr. vol. 17:6675 and 6786 and tr. vol. 2:620–25 and 651), especially Judge Musmanno's statement that Ohlendorf was "charged with snuffing out the lives of 90,000."

12. This theatrical term is appropriate, not only because of the public attention focused on Ohlendorf during the trial, but because he acquired for many Germans a romantic aura akin to a matinee idol during the three years he and six others known to the press as "the Landsberg Seven" awaited execution in that prison.

for Nuremberg case 9, otherwise known as the "*Einsatzgruppen* case," the genocide case.

But it is not because "Ben Ohlendorf's name led all the rest"[13] and not because he stood in rank, intellectually—and in a peculiar way, morally—above his fellow defendants, that this analysis is focused almost exclusively on Otto Ohlendorf and his defense, but because there was in him a certain warped devotion to principle—at least to conventional bourgeois virtues. He did not lie,[14] he accepted responsibility for his subordinates, and he uncompromisingly, almost compulsively, ventured to differ with his superiors. Although his career suffered, he courageously stood up for his narrow "Prussian"[15] principles in the treacherous bear pit of the most vicious of the Nazi satrapies, the *Reichssicherheitshauptamt* (Reich Main Security Office or RSHA) of the SS.[16]

At one time or another, Ohlendorf was embroiled not only with his SS superiors, Himmler and Heydrich,[17] but with other powerful worthies of the Third Reich who were angered by criticism of performance of their agencies and of themselves in the *SD Inland* reports, although these were circulated only for high-level official use. Drawing on his farm-

bred experience, Ohlendorf early led an *SD Inland* attack on the "hereditary peasant" policies of Walter Darré, minister of agriculture.[18] Criticism of Robert Ley, head of the German Labor Front, "because he interfered with the independent development of social ideas," led to confrontations in 1939–40 and again in 1943.[19] Ohlendorf was involved in an extended quarrel between July 1942 and May 1943 with Gunter d'Alquen concerning articles in the latter's SS publication, *Das Schwarze Korps*, calling for "overcoming of the bourgeois spirit."[20] Ohlendorf also was embittered toward his younger SD colleague Walter Schellenberg, a Heydrich favorite and a careerist and survivor par excellence, who successfully avoided combat service in an *Einsatzgruppe* or anywhere else.[21] Ohlendorf fought a losing battle with Goebbels, who requested, then resented, "defeatist" SD reports about the uniformly unfavorable public reaction to his Berlin Sports Palace speech of 18 February 1943 inaugurating "total war."[22] Accurate SD reports on the corruption of Erich Koch, Reich Commissioner for the Ukraine, were quashed in 1943 by an angry Martin Bormann, who in 1944 forbade distribution of SD reports to Nazi party offices.[23]

Even the stubborn Ohlendorf felt compelled to beat a strategic retreat

13. Apologies to Leigh Hunt, "Abou Ben Adhem."

14. *See* Telford Taylor's assessment of Ohlendorf testimony in the closing statement for the prosecution: "after all the incredible gabbling . . . it is a relief to be given a direct and stark rejoinder" (NMT 14, 3–79; tr. vol. 17: 6591).

15. Actually, Ohlendorf was from Hannover, which until 1866 was more often than not "anti-Prussian."

16. For the evolution of the *RSHA* through organizational merger but functional separation of party intelligence and state police, *see* pp. 52–53.

17. *See* text, pp. 52, 55–57.

18. *See* text, pp. 52 and tr. 2/491 and 565.

19. For Ohlendorf's testimony thereon, *see* tr. 2:499, 505, 565, and 649; for contemporary documentation, see T 175, Roll 239, folder EAP 173-b-05/2A.

20. *See* T 175, Roll 31, Himmler file 307, and Roll 275, *SD Inland* folder EAP 173-b-14-16/17.

21. *See* tr. 2:638-9.

22. *See* tr. 2:505 and 565.

23. For Ohlendorf's testimony, *see* tr. 2:505 and 565, and for a contemporary account *see SD Inland* folder EAP 173-b-14-14/16 reproduced on T 175, Roll 275.

from such formidable opposition;[24] his speech of 31 November 1944 warned his chief assistants that SD reports were not for the purpose of criticizing individuals and agencies, but for presenting an objective picture of domestic conditions and public reactions to these. In 1942, such controversies caused Himmler[25] to enforce secrecy about the network of SD informants operating throughout the Nazi party and caused Hitler to order that derogatory information about subordinates and relatives of Nazi officials must be turned over solely to Bormann.[26]

For such enemies, Ohlendorf deserves at least some grudging respect.

As Eichmann provided Hannah Arendt with a case study for "the banality of evil,"[27] Otto Ohlendorf may provide us with a case study of "conscientious bourgeois morality led astray by ideology." If this premise stands up, his case, unlike Eichmann's, even contains trace elements of classic tragedy.

How did Otto Ohlendorf, SS *Standartenführer* (Colonel) a "desk man" with little military training other than an occasional SS formation or drill, become the commander of one of the four *Einsatzgruppen* charged with securing the rear areas of the German army in the southern Ukraine and the Crimea, involving, among other normal military police activities, the execution of the "Fuehrer Order" to kill all the Jews, Gypsies, and commissars they could round up?

From Ohlendorf's sober bureaucratic memoranda and from his demeanor and testimony on the witness stand, it appears that he had more than his fair share of what the Germans call *"tierische Ernst"* —an officiousness, a lack of proportion and perspective toward his assignments. Himmler called him a "humorless Prussian."[28] For why else would he go to the gallows insisting that the *SD Inland* should and could have performed the function, in the absence of independent information media and informed democratic public opinion, of safeguarding the German people against the mistakes, excesses, and illegalities of officials of the Nazi dictatorship?[29] Did he honestly believe that

24. *See* T 175, Roll 267, folder EAP 173-b-14/2.
25. *See* in folder 22, T 175, Roll 59, EAP 161-b-12/149.
26. *See* Himmler file, folder 22, T 175 Roll 59.
27. *Eichmann in Jerusalem: A Report on the Banality of Evil* (New York: The Viking Press, 1964).

28. Asked by a puzzled Judge Musmanno what specifically were his differences with Himmler, Ohlendorf said these were "differences of temperament and politics . . . I was the unbearable, humorless Prussian, an unsoldierly type, a defeatist, and intelligence monger. . . . I called Himmler a "Bavarian" . . . [who] did not want orderly conditions. . . . The representative of 'Personalism.' . . . [who] tried to imitate Hitler . . . assigning tasks not to organizations but to . . . several individuals . . . this was bound to destroy the whole order of the nation even in peacetime and . . . especially in a serious war" (NMT, IV, 233–4; tr. 2:499–500). For corroborative contemporary documentation of these differences, *see* Himmler's sharp letter of reprimand to Ohlendorf, dated 31 Oct. 1943, threatening his dismissal at his next breach of discipline (Ohlendorf document 33: Defense Exhibit 54).
29. Tr. 2:490: "Since there would be no more public criticism . . . the mission [of the SD would be] to inform the leading organizations of the party and state about . . . mistaken actions and tendencies." Compare his testimony before the IMT, IV, 352–3. For the bulk of the surviving paperwork of *RSHA, Amt* III, i.e., *SD Inland* and its predecessors, *see* T175, Rolls 258–76 and 499–51. Rolls 258–66 contain reproductions of a nearly unbroken run of the consolidated nationwide wartime *SD Inland* reports, *Meldungen aus dem Reich*, Nos. 1–423, 9 Oct. 1939–27 Dec. 1943, plus its unnumbered

through some 33,000 informants in all walks of life, paid and unpaid, he could discover the true attitudes of the German people toward its Nazi masters and, even more incredibly, that Hitler and company would pay attention to these attitudes and would change policies accordingly?[30]

It was, Ohlendorf claimed,[31] for this constant determination to make his *SD Inland* the comptroller and ombudsman of the domestic activities of the Third Reich, that he was punished with the thankless assignment to command an *Einsatzgruppe*. Probably there were also impersonal and weightier general grounds: Himmler's determination that all SS men would undergo the test of com-

bat (*Frontbewährung*) to justify and fortify their elite position in policing a greatly expanded postwar Third Reich and its occupied territories.

THE MAN

How did Otto Ohlendorf, born in February, 1907, son of a Protestant farm owner in Hoheneggelsen near Hannover; brother of a biologist, a farmer, and a businesswoman, respectively; educated in the law and economics at Leipzig and Göttingen, holder of a law degree, an A.B.D. who blamed his failure to cap his studies with a doctorate on his falling victim to an internal party conflict,[32] how did this man seemingly predestined for an academic career become an SS *Standartenführer* and *Amtschef* of *Reichssicherheitshauptamt Amt* III?

Like so many of his German class and generation, too young for World War I, but old enough to grow up in the postwar humiliation and deprivations which Hitler blamed on Versailles and the loss of the war due to the "stab-in-the-back" by Jews, socialists and communists, Ohlendorf became a nationalist and the German equivalent of a *revanchist*. He joined the revived Nazi party in 1925 as a member of his local Brownshirt SA (*Sturmabteilung*) troop, receiving party number 6531, and became one of the early members (number 880) of its still insignificant Blackshirt adjunct, the SS (*Schutzstaffel*), in 1926.[33]

Between 1927 and 1933 he was not very active in the Nazi party, be-

---

successor publication covering Jan.–July 1944, consisting of candid descriptions and analyses of various spheres of life in Germany and annexed territories, including performance of government and party agencies as well as behavior and attitude of the general public.

30. Ohlendorf's postwar claim that his *SD Inland* had tried in vain to make the Nazi regime reponsive to German public opinion, although obviously a defense tactic, was not without justification. But that there were some successes as well as failures, can be seen from a late 1941 *SD Inland* report citing cases of effective application by government, party, and police of information made available in the "law and life" sections of *Meldungen aus dem Reich* from July 1940 to Sept. 1941, reproduced on T175, Roll 271, folder EAP 173–b–14–12/8.

31. See Ohlendorf's account of how his public reprimand at Warsaw in Nov. 1939 by Himmler (tr. 2: 498), and his being dubbed a "defeatist" by the *Reichsführer* during 1940 because of sharp criticism in *SD Inland* reports of Ley's poor leadership of the Labor Front (tr. 2: 499), enabled Heydrich, in a third attempt, to override Ohlendorf's draft exemption as chief of Reich Group Commerce (*see* his draft card dated 20 Nov. 1939, Ohlendorf document 54: DEX 59) to earmark him for wartime duty under the Chief of Security Police and Service, and to assign him to an *Einsatzgruppe* (tr. 2: 513–4). *See also* Ohlendorf's SS Personnel File (document No. 3196: Prosecution Exhibit 156).

32. Tr. 2:489. For family and education, *see* his affidavit NO 2857: Prosecution Exhibit (PEX) 157.

33. SS Personnel File, NO 3196: PEX 156. His courtroom explanation of the attraction national socialism had for him: "Social need was a national problem, and national need a social problem" (tr. 2: 477–8).

cause he was busy completing his studies and beginning his career, first as an apprentice county attorney in Alfeld and Hildesheim, then as a fellow of the Institute for World Economy at Kiel University.[34] But in 1934, he was ousted from his position at Kiel along with his mentor, Professor Jens Jessen, because of his active opposition to what he called "National Bolshevism" in the institute.[35] Presumably, this refers to university radicals sympathetic to Ernst Röhm's Brownshirt street brawlers, the SA.[36] If so, this was a singular case of bad timing for if Ohlendorf had held his tongue until after the Röhm *Putsch* of 30 June 1934, he would have come out on the right side when Hitler, Göring, and Himmler used the SS to liquidate the internal party radical opposition and a few nonparty opponents to boot. Ohlendorf ascribed the thwarting of his academic career to this premature opposition to national bolshevism.[37]

By 1935, he found a position in the Berlin Institute for Applied Economic Sciences, and from there, through Jessen, he was recruited by Professor Hoehn, then head of *SD Inland*, to build up a party economic information service.[38] Once again, because of impolitic criticism of the policies of the Reich Food Estate under Walter Darré and of economic policies of Julius Streicher and other *Gauleiter*, Ohlendorf's mentor was ousted and he was put on the SD shelf.[39] He soon found a nonparty position for himself as business manager of one of the seven Third Reich syndicates, the *Reichsgruppe Handel* (Reich Group Commerce),[40] a position which he continued to hold when Heydrich commandeered him for what Ohlendorf considered the bogus—Americans would say Mickey Mouse—position of chief of *SD Inland*, which became *Amt* (office) III of the newly consolidated *Reichssicherheitshauptamt*.[41] From the beginning of the war until his assignment to Russia, Ohlendorf divided his time between his party and government posts.

Was there anything in this prior career, in his general SS training, and in his specialized SD service that conditioned him for the murderer's role he was assigned in Russia? The Nazi party, seeking exclusive and absolute power, had always put a premium on security and on intelligence and counterintelligence as a means of ensuring it. Before 1933, internal party intelligence and counterintelligence had been the function of the SD. After coming to power, it gradually yielded these functions to state organs, the Gestapo and *Kripo*, the political police and the criminal police, which in turn were subordinated to the Nazi party by the requirement that only SS men could serve in police agencies.

Himmler, *Reichsführer* SS, became Chief of the German Police by 1936, and under his aegis Reinhardt Heydrich between 1936 and 1940 consolidated the Gestapo, *Kripo*, and SD into the RSHA.[42] For our special purposes, we might

34. Tr. 2:487 and 646; affidavit NO 2857: PEX 157.
35. Tr. 2:488-9.
36. Ohlendorf emphatically denied such a prosecution assumption: "These were National Bolshevist and not Roehm circles" (tr. 2: 646-7).
37. *See* Ohlendorf document 35: DEX 56 for his despairing letter of 6 Feb. 1934 to his wife.
38. Tr. 2:489-90.
39. Tr. 2:492 and 565.
40. Tr. 2:493.
41. Tr. 2:491 and 494-7.
42. For contemporary paperwork of this consolidation, *see* T 175, Roll 239, folders

well translate RSHA as "National Security Central Administration." The domestic and foreign intelligence service, *SD Inland* and *SD Ausland*, offices III and VI of the RSHA respectively, were confined to subject matter. The "executive functions" of investigation and surveillance of persons, as well as all counterintelligence, were assigned to the political and criminal police by a Himmler–Heydrich order of early 1940.[43]

These dividing lines, however, were sometimes blurred by the necessity for cooperation, particularly in occupied territories. In the *Einsatzgruppen*, which drew leaders and personnel from the SD and security police, as well as from the uniformed police, from the Totenkopfverbände, made up of concentration camp guards, and from the *Waffen* SS,[44] the dividing line completely disappeared between intelligence and executive functions and between amassing information on the subject matter of "opposition" and "enemies" in contradistinction to dealing with individual opponents and enemies. These combined functions were formidable in Germany as well as in the occupied territories, providing the authority and means for surveillance, interrogation, torture, arrest, imprisonment, hard labor, corporal punishment, or death with or without due process of trial in existing courts or Peoples' Courts, which had at any rate become mere instruments of a police

apparatus executing Nazi party ideology. "Law and order" became "law on order." During his testimony on the IMT witness stand, Ohlendorf summed up the purpose of the RSHA very succinctly: "to prevent the political opposition from becoming a danger to the state."[45]

THE TRIAL

In the trial of *United States v. Ohlendorf et al.*, the prosecution charged the defendants with the crime of genocide under two separate counts, asserting that not only the novel IMT charge of crimes against humanity, but traditional war crimes, were applicable to mass murder of Jews, Gypsies, and others. The Hague and Geneva conventions specifically and international law and custom in general proscribed as war crimes the mistreatment of civilian populations and limited the justification and the scope of reprisals, a particularly critical issue in a war involving ubiquitous guerrilla or partisan warfare. The precedent international rules were written into the London Charter[46] establishing the IMT and into the Allied Control Council law no. 10 under which the subsequent U.S. Nuremberg trials were conducted, as follows:

War Crimes. Atrocities or offenses against persons or property constituting

---

EAP 173-b-05/1A, 2B, 2K, 2L, EAP 173-b-10-16/2, and EAP 173-b-12-05/45, and Roll 432, EAP 173-b-05/2F; *see also* IMT, IV, 326–7 and 352-3, and document L 361.

43. For the separation of functions, see T 175, Roll 232, EAP 173-a-10/20, frames 2720810–14, and Roll 239, EAP 173-b-12-05/45, frames 2728778–81.

44. For composition and strength of the *Einsatzgruppen, see* IMT, IV, 324–7.

45. Ibid., 344.

46. The process by which the victor powers reconciled their considerable differences in legal systems, languages, history, World War II experiences, and postwar aims, in order to achieve the common purpose of the trial and punishment of the major Nazis, can be traced in *Report of Robert H. Jackson, United States Representative to the International Conference Military Trials, London, 1945*, Department of State Publication 3080, February 1949. *See also* Robert Wolfe, "The London Charter, Nuremberg Straitjacket?" presented at the Annual Meeting of the American Historical Association, Chicago, Dec. 1974.

violations of the laws or customs of war, including but not limited to murder, ill-treatment or deportation to slave labor . . . of civilian population from occupied territory. . . .

Crimes against Humanity. Atrocities or offenses, including but not limited to murder, extermination, enslavement, deportation, imprisonment, torture, rape, or other inhumane acts committed against any civilian population, or persecutions on political, racial, or religious grounds whether or not in violation of the domestic laws of the country where perpetrated.[47]

Defense counsel nevertheless attempted to challenge the tribunal's jurisdiction and impartiality but were overruled, not only on the precedent of the international trial, but on the grounds that Control Council law no. 10 was a proper exercise of an occupying power's right and duty to punish war crimes.[48]

The defense also challenged law no. 10 and the charge of crimes against humanity, in particular, as ex post facto law. Citing codified international law, specifically article 46 of the Hague Convention on Land Warfare which provides that invading and occupying armies must respect "family honor and rights, the lives of persons and private property, as well as religious provisions and practice," the court ruled:

. . . But the jurisdiction of this Tribunal over the subject matter before it does not depend alone on this specific pronouncement of international law . . . all nations have held themselves bound to the rules or laws of war which . . . universally condemn the wanton killing of noncombatants. In the main, the defendants in this case are charged with murder. Certainly no one can claim . . . there is any taint of ex post factoism in the law of murder.[49]

47. Tr. volume 1:14–15.
48. Tr. volume 17:6707–8.
49. NMT, IV, 459; compare tr. 17:6711–12.

The criminality of murder goes back, at least, to Cain and Abel.

Finally, the defense argued that the defendants were acting in obedience to superior orders, were conducting a bona fide military assignment to secure the rear areas of an army engaged in life or death combat against "no-holds-barred" partisan attacks, supported by the civilian population of Russia, including and led chiefly by Jews. Furthermore, Dr. Rudolf Aschenauer, Ohlendorf's defense counsel, supported by the expert opinion of Dr. Reinhart Maurach,[50] professor of criminal and East European law, contended that although it was factually untrue, his client was subjectively convinced by his ideological training, which was in turn confirmed by his misinterpretation of objective observations during his year in Russia, that all Jews regardless of age and sex, by their very inborn nature, were a threat to the security of the Third Reich and all of Europe; that Jews had introduced Marxist bolshevism into the Soviet Union as a means for subverting other nations and polluting the bloodlines of Aryan peoples.

THE DEFENSE: SUPERIOR ORDERS

Although the IMT opinion, setting the precedent for the subsequent Nuremberg trials, clearly held that superior orders could not justify commission of war crimes or crimes

50. Aschenauer brought Maurach to the stand as an expert witness (tr. 2:7556–69), but the court soon found much of his testimony irrelevant or long-winded, so the defense settled for his opinion in affidavit form (tr. 3:772–3) Rechtsgutachten erstattet für die Verteidigung im Falle Nr. 9 des amerikanischen Militärgerichtshofes (Prozess gegen Otto Ohlendorf u. Gen.), von Dr. Reinhart Maurach, ord. Professor des Strafrechts und osteuropäischen Rechts (Ohlendorf document 38: DEX 2).

against humanity, Ohlendorf and his codefendants made superior orders a part of their defense, and the court permitted this as being material, at least, to a claim of mitigating circumstances. Ohlendorf contended that the order for extermination of the Jews of Russia was an oral order of the fuehrer to Himmler. On Himmler's and Heydrich's oral instructions, Bruno Streckenbach, then head of the personnel office of the RSHA, transmitted it to the *Einsatzgruppen* leaders, assembled at the Border Police School at Pretzsch on the Elbe River north of Leipzig, in June of 1941, shortly before the attack on the Soviet Union.[51]

The Fuehrer Order[52] was issued within the framework of Hitler's signed Barbarossa directive[53] for planning and conducting that attack. An implementing order delineating areas of military responsibility and authority merely stated: "In the operation area of the army, the *Reichsführer SS* has been assigned . . . special tasks by the *Führer* which derive from the final battle to be waged by two opposing political systems."[54]

But Ohlendorf had been told of the negotiations and had seen the written result of an army-SS agreement by which the army groups and the armies in the field would assign march routes and furnish supplies to the *Einsatzgruppen* and the *Kommandos* attached to them, while the chief of the security police and security service, first Heydrich and later Ernst Kaltenbrunner, would

issue operation orders and general security assignments.[55] Ohlendorf stated that when he and the other *Einsatzgruppen* leaders at Pretzsch had objected vociferously to the extermination order, Streckenbach told them that he had objected just as vociferously when Himmler issued the oral order to him for transmission to the *Einsatzgruppen* commanders.[56]

Neither the order, nor Streckenbach's dislike for it, could have come as a complete surprise to Ohlendorf at Pretzsch in June of 1941, for early in the war, in Warsaw in October, 1939, he and Streckenbach had been harshly rebuffed by Himmler for objecting to large-scale killings of Jews in Poland[57]—Himmler had reproached him for failing to train his SD personnel properly for such tasks—a failure Himmler attributed to Ohlendorf's academic training.[58] When asked by the court how the Polish campaign order differed from

---

51. Tr. 2:515–16 and 634–7.

52. Of all the fuehrer's orders, written and unwritten, signed and unsigned, this one ordering the "final solution of the Jewish question") is known as *the* Fuehrer Order.

53. IMT document PS 46:US 31.

54. "Guidelines for Special Areas to Directive No. 21 (Case Barbarossa)," 13 March 1941 (IMT document PS 447:US 135).

55. For Ohlendorf's recollection of the circumstances and the content of this army–SS agreement, *see* IMT, IV, 313–15 and 340–42. Walter Schellenberg, who kept the minutes of these negotiations, also testified thereon from memory (IMT, IV, 375–7). At that time, Dr. Nelte, counsel for IMT defendant Wilhelm Keitel, questioned Ohlendorf about his statement that he had in his "mind's eye" the letterhead OKW-OKH, which both agreed was unlikely. What Ohlendorf held in visual memory was an OKW "incoming" stamp alongside the OKH letterhead, as became evident when a 26 March 1941 draft of the agreement, "Regulation of the Assignment of Security Police and SD to Units of the Army" (document NOKW 256; PEX 274) was produced late in the case 9 proceedings (tr. 2:687–9).

56. Tr. 2:515–16, 634 and 637.

57. Ibid., 638.

58. Ibid., 498; also 650: Himmler "attacked me in a public place . . . shouting at me across the table that this man was the product of my education . . . he had behaved in an unsoldierly manner, in that instead of acting . . . he had studied the Jewish question in that area [Poland], and the expression 'studied' annoyed [Himmler] so much."

the Russian campaign, Ohlendorf stated that the former involved specific, individual actions, whereas the latter consisted of a general order to kill all Jews.[59]

It seems likely that the genesis of Ohlendorf's selection for an *Einsatzgruppe* command lay in this Warsaw encounter with Himmler, who may have stored in his mind, consciously or unconsciously, the determination to teach his highbrow and contentious underling the lesson needed. Ohlendorf, in turn, would have remembered Himmler's reaction as a threat of dire punishment the next time Ohlendorf questioned orders.[60]

Asked in cross-examination if his negative reactions in Poland and at Pretzsch did not imply that he also questioned the legality of the Fuehrer Order, Ohlendorf replied that he considered the orders legal but "unwise and impossible of execution" because of the "moral and ethical consequences, which would deteriorate the mentality," presumably of anyone who had to execute the order. But he insisted that since the Third Reich found itself in a state of war emergency (*Kriegsnotstand*) and of self defense (*Notwehr*) in a war of national survival against bolshevism, "determining the nature and extent of counter-measures was the sole prerogative of the supreme leadership." Subordinates are not obligated to examine such orders, since "that is legally and practically impossible. . . . Legally, not even a German judge had the right to do so. . . . Practically, it would have been presumptuous, because in our [the defendants'] position we did not

have a basis for judging the conditions prompting the order." Ohlendorf held with the traditional European moral concept "that no subordinate can take it on himself to examine the authority of the supreme commander and chief of state [who in turn is responsible only] to his God and to history."[61]

When Ohlendorf was asked whether article 47 of the German Military Penal Code did not allow a subordinate to interpret a superior order, he replied that while that article was created to prevent excesses by individual officers and men involved in a specific situation, "under no circumstances did it permit questioning a supreme order of the supreme commander—according to the Continental concept, a Chief of State cannot commit a crime."[62]

Neveretheless, Ohlendorf continued to have his misgivings about the wisdom, if not the legality, of the fuehrer's order. In agreement with the Eleventh German Army, Ohlendorf at one point excluded from execution a considerable number of Jewish craftsman useful to the German war effort.[63] Perhaps for that reason, Himmler visited that army's headquarters at Nikolayev on October 4–5 1941, and reproached Ohlendorf for his contravention of orders. Not only did Himmler command that executions should take place as planned, even against the will of the army, but he assembled all the available *Einsatzkommando* leaders of *Einsatzgruppe D* to reiterate the strict order to kill all groups deemed to endanger security. Himmler would carry the sole responsibility as far as accounting to the fuehrer was concerned.

59. Tr. 2:650.

60. For Ohlendorf's account of his relations with Himmler, *see* tr. 2:498 ff. and 646 ff.

61. Ibid., 516 and 518–19; compare 741–3.

62. Ibid., 520.

63. Ibid., 522.

Afterward, alone with the *Reichsführer* SS, Ohlendorf pointed out the inhuman burden on his men; Himmler did not even answer.[64]

Ohlendorf was also asked at Nuremberg, perhaps superfluously since he found the reiterated Fuehrer Order legal if unwise in its consequence, Why did he not try to prevent the liquidations? He answered that there was "only one [possibility] . . . a senseless martyrdom through suicide—senseless because this would not have deterred the execution of the order. . . . If I could imagine a theoretical possibility . . . [it would be] only a refusal [to comply] on the part of those persons . . . in the uppermost hierarchy . . . [with direct access] to the Supreme Commander-in-Chief and Chief of State."[65] Since Ohlendorf asserted that he never met Hitler personally,[66] that left the theoretical responsibility squarely up to Himmler; but the role of a Calvinist ephor, or magistrate, was not fitted to that apostate Catholic, as Walter Schellenberg discovered when he tried for some two years to persuade the *Reichsführer* SS to rebel against Hitler in order to spare Germany the consequences of *Der Führer's* madness.[67] Himmler was just as addicted to superior orders as Ohlendorf.

Judge Musmanno[68] at one point asked Ohlendorf, "Could you not have tried to evade the order by sickness?" The response was: "By simulating illness, I would have evaded the mission, but I would have betrayed my men . . . I would not have been convinced that my successor would care for his men in the same manner. . . . My duty [was] . . . more valuable than the cheap applause I could have won."[69]

In American idiom, he might have said, "But that would be the easy way out."

On another occasion, during cross-examination, it was recalled that at one time the Chief of Staff of the Eleventh Army had threatened that unless Ohlendorf's collaboration with the army improved, his immediate dismissal would be recommended, so that "merely by refusing to be agreeable with other military gentlemen,"[70] as the cross-examiner sarcastically put it, he could have been relieved of his onerous assignment. Ohlendorf responded indigantly, "I do not think you expect that, in order to be relieved, I should have let myself and my men be wrongly accused."[71]

This was no doubt a soldierly response befitting an officer and a gentleman, surprising in a man with so little military training and such avowed disinterest in military position. In explaining why he had used his "indispensable" category position as executive director of Reich Group Commerce twice to avoid Heydrich's attempts to give him an SS military assignment between 1939 and 1941, Ohlendorf stated: "I had not been a soldier and did not

---

64. Ibid., 526.
65. Ibid., 525.
66. Ibid., 506.
67. *The Labyrinth: Memoirs of Walter Schellenberg*, trans. Louis Hagen (New York: Harper & Row, 1956).
68. Presiding Judge Michael A. Musmanno, no shrinking violet, conducted the *Einsatzgruppen* trial as does as a Continental jurist operating without a lay jury, participating in oral examination rather than acting the referee as in Anglo-American adversary proceedings. His reputation for playing to the galleries notwithstanding, his frequent in-

---

terventions elicited a valuable gloss to the records of these unique proceedings.
69. Tr. 2:527.
70. Ibid., 666.
71. Ibid., 667.

have any interest in the military; I was not a policeman, and had no interest in police work, which was against my nature; I had a genuine job in Berlin, most compatible with my abilities, and I knew it would not be filled once I left it."[72]

Nevertheless, once saddled with the *Einsatzgruppe* assignment, Ohlendorf approached it as a soldier, perhaps sensing that only by carrying it out in a strict soldierly fashion might he exonerate himself and his men on the grounds that they were executing a sanctioned military action in pursuit of a proper military security mission. Deeming the never-revoked oral order issued at Pretzsch to be valid throughout the entire Russian campaign as long as the *Einsatzgruppe* existed, he saw no need for him or his subordinate commanders to issue individual orders to individual men to kill people but merely to supervise execution of the standing order.[73] Refusal by anyone of any rank would have brought a court martial in the SS's own courts—the SS had their own "benefit of clergy"—for disloyalty and disobedience were the cardinal sins. *"Meine Ehre heisst Treue"* (my honor is loyalty) read the motto stamped into every SS man's belt buckle.

As Ohlendorf described his procedures, his orders were merely executory, providing coordination and inspection to see that the fuehrer's genocidal order was carried out "as humanely as conditions would permit for the unfortunate victims, and to prevent brutal excesses by any of the [SS] men." Only so many victims were brought to the place of execution as the commandos could handle at one time.

Any individual action by an individual man was forbidden. Executions were conducted by firing squads on command in a military manner: no maltreatment, no undressing, no belated on-the-scene confiscation of personal possessions, and no outsiders present. Any man evincing pleasure in this task was barred from future assignments. No one could volunteer.[74]

THE DEFENSE: NATIONAL SECURITY

Both the procedures he adopted and the way he depicted them on the stand betray Ohlendorf's concern to accentuate that he and his men were soldiers carrying out most difficult and distasteful superior orders in a disciplined military manner. Nevertheless, because the IMT opinion had expressly rejected the claim of superior orders when criminal actions contrary to the Hague and Geneva conventions were involved and because of the quantitative and qualitative enormity of the crimes charged, Ohlendorf's lawyer decided to attempt the back-up defense of "self-defense" and "state of emergency." Standing alone, these defenses also seemed weak; therefore he further decided to buttress them with the concept of a putative or presumed, if mistaken, subjective belief confirmed by objective conditions that the security and survival of the nation was so threatened as to constitute an emergency that justified countermeasures that clearly would be criminal in normal circumstances.

This is reminiscent of the concept of *Überzeugungstäter*—one who commits a "crime of conviction"—by which Imperial hold-

72. Ibid., 630.
73. Ibid., 523; IMT, IV, 330–31.

74. Tr. 2:524; IMT, IV, 320–21 and 331.

overs on the judges' benches of the Weimar Republic justified light or suspended sentences for right-wing political assassins who presumed that murder of Weimar officials, such as Erzberger and Rathenau, or acts like the Hitler *Putsch* of November, 1923, served the welfare and security of the nation. Somehow, left-wing and pacifist, let alone Communist, beliefs were not acceptable excuses to most Weimar judges; concern for international welfare and security was apparently less moral than for national security.

As Dr. Aschenauer, Ohlendorf's chief defense counsel, defined them,[75] the three obviously related defenses were *Notwehr, Nothilfe,* and *Notstand.* Prefixed by "putative" or, to follow the Nuremberg translators, by "presumed," they come out in English as follows:

Putativnotwehr: presumed self-defense against an unlawful or threatened attack.

Putativnothilfe: action for presumed protection of a third party.

Putativnotstand: a presumed state of emergency, that is, an interest protected by law is in presumed imminent danger and can be rescued only by the violation of another interest protected by law.

When the third party is the state, or in this case the Third Reich, then the presumed state of emergency (*Putativstaatsnotstand*) demands *Staatsnothilfe* and *Staatsnotwehr;* a national emergency threatening national security demands that all officials and other citizens give whatever assistance the national

leadership considers necessary and proper in defense of paramount national interests, even if this constrains moral private men to commit official crimes in the process.

Aschenauer also questioned the propriety of applying international law to the defendants, particularly because the Soviet Union, not signatory to the Geneva Convention, did not have to abide by it, and in fact in its partisan warfare openly disregarded it. He argued that either German law should apply since the defendants were being charged for acts committed as officers of a German military occupation or that Soviet law should apply since the crimes were alleged to have been committed on Soviet territory and the victims were chiefly Soviet citizens.

Both Dr. Aschenauer and Dr. Maurach stated a clear preference for the application of Soviet law.[76] Soviet law placed even less restraint on national leadership than Nazi law, which as Hitler and Himmler so often complained was still inhibited by liberal vestiges of the Weimar Constitution. Soviet leadership, it was obvious, was free to do whatever it deemed necessary, not only for the welfare of its domestic proletariat, but for the welfare of the international proletariat anywhere in the .world.

So much for the legal concept of a "putative threat to national security." What was the content, the specific circumstances which defense counsel construed as mitigating or exonerating their clients' guilt for the crimes charged—and admittedly committed? As Dr. Aschenauer put it: the defendants, and in particular Ohlendorf,

---

75. Aschenauer, Opening Statement, (NMT, IV, 59–63 or tr. 1:257–97); compare Maurach (Ohlendorf document 38, DEX 1), pp. 2–12.

76. Aschenauer (NMT, IV, 58); Maurach, pp. 8 and 11–12.

. . . do not claim that the real conditions existed for a case of action in defense of the endangered nation [*Staatsnothilfe*] or participation in the self-defense of the state [*Staatsnotwehr*]. But they do submit that, in view of the special situation in which they found themselves, and in which they were called upon to act, they assumed *subjectively . . . a justification* (*Rechtfertigungsgrund*) existed. . . . *Where precisely* [did] *the defendant Ohlendorf commit the error concerning the permissibility of his action; because the greater the extent to which the objective situation corresponded to the defendant's conception, the weightier is his defense that, by mistake, he considered his action justified or necessary.*[77]

As Dr. Maurach analyzed the conditions prerequisite to the erroneous assumptions of the defendants, the objective or real condition was the total nature of the war against the Soviet Union.

A state of war as such does not in itself justify self-defense or necessity. This presupposes, however, war in the strict sense of international law, that is, armed conflict between two states. If however from the outset the war aims and methods of one of the opponents can be expected to be "total" to such a degree that traditional conceptions and limitations of international law would be disregarded during hostilities, *the opponent of such a state cannot be denied the right to claim self-defense or necessity.*[78]

The implication is, of course, that the Soviet Union, not Nazi Germany, instituted total war. To this end the defense counsel quoted from Joseph Stalin's radio speech of 3 July 1941:

In the areas occupied by the enemy . . . partisan detachments must be formed . . . for kindling partisan warfare every-

where and everyplace. . . . Unbearable conditions must be created for the enemy . . . in the occupied areas; they must be pursued and destroyed at every step. . . . One cannot regard the war against Fascist Germany as an ordinary war. It is not only a war between two armies. It is at the same time the great war of the entire Soviet people against the Fascist German troops.[79]

Defense counsel for one of Ohlendorf's codefendants characterized Stalin's appeal as "an illegal *leveé en masse* on territory effectively occupied by enemy troops," and continued to argue: "Total war has altered the complexion of many rules. At a time when the 'scorched earth' policy in a belligerent's own territory has become widespread practice, general destruction of property ordered as part of broad military strategy cannot properly form the subject matter of a criminal indictment."[80]

This defense, of course, is balderdash since Hitler's Barbarossa order and Fuehrer Order preceded Stalin's order chronologically; the burglar justifies killing the householder, not only because the householder actually resists, but because it is anticipated that he will resist.[81]

The defense also advanced a tu quoque argument of more than passing interest:

In 1941 Hitler may have been convinced that in . . . a war against guerillas draconic measures were necessary to weaken the enemy's will to resist. . . . Henry L. Stimson wrote in his article, *The Decision to Use the Atomic Bomb*: "To extract a genuine surrender from the emperor of Japan and his military advisers, a tremendous

---

77. Tr. 2:63. Aschenauer derived this nearly verbatim from Maurach, p. 13.
78. Maurach, p. 14 or NMT, IV, 345; Aschenauer (NMT, IV, 63–4).

79. Ohlendorf document 39, DEX 2.
80. Counsel Bolko von Stein, closing statement for defendant Martin Sandberger (NMT, IV, 359; tr. 15:6078 and 6080).
81. Compare Telford Taylor's closing statement (NMT, IV, 381–2; tr. 17:6593).

shock must be administered which should carry convincing proof of our power to destroy the Empire. Such an effective shock would save more lives, both American and Japanese, than it would cost." Hitler was similarly convinced that [only] by such harsh measures could he nip the partisan war in the bud or suppress it effectively. The welfare of the whole front was menaced by unrestricted partisan war. Hitler may have expected a shock effect from the [extermination] measure he ordered, which in the end would save the lives of an infinitely greater number of German soldiers.[82]

Dr. Maurach conceded that:

the issuing and executing of orders for mass executions cannot find any justification in international law, even within the scope of a total war of this kind, and in particular cannot allow of any appeal to the objective premises of self-defense and necessity. . . . Here not only the objective circumstances are decisive . . . but the important point is how . . . (the defendants) looked upon and had to, look upon this emergency or danger subjectively. . . . "In truth the defense is not necessity but rather the *assumption* of necessity. . . ." The thing that must be examined now is the compulsion as it developed, and had to develop in the imagination of the defendants. . . . The subjective assumption which brought about the defendant's error about what would constitute the conditions for action in defense of the endangered nation, or in a state of national emergency, was that the *East European Jewish problem was part of the problem of bolshevism*; this led to the defendants' obsession that a solution of the problem "bolshevism versus Europe" could only be brought about by a "solution" of the Jewish problem, and, in their particular sphere, only by unreserved execution of the Fuehrer Order.[83]

One source of this obsession with the solution to the Jewish problem was National Socialist ideology, hammered into the defendants, not only as citizens of the Third Reich and members of the Nazi party, but incessantly inculcated into their very psyches as members of the SS. As Maurach stated:

The following concepts, inspired by the Party, found a wide propagation in pseudoscientific literature and began to influence the imaginations even of *those* strata formerly resistant towards ordinary propaganda: Bolshevism was a Jewish invention; bolshevism was to serve the realization of Jewish plans for world domination; Jewry in its great majority was an active exponent of militant bolshevism; the defense against bolshevist expansion depended on rendering Soviet Jewry harmless. . . .[84]

National Socialist ideology greatly simplified the entire intricate problem. What at the most could be regarded as an accidental communion of interests . . . had become a logically conditioned necessity, a postulate that bolshevism was a mere "Jewish invention" and that the struggle against bolshevism was necessary and in the first place a struggle against Jewry. . . . [Since] following the outbreak of the war in 1941 [Russian Jews] *could only expect a worsening of their situation by the German invasion as a result of the prevailing German policy towards the Jews*, it was obvious that it would support the fight of bolshevism against the German *Wehrmacht* with the greatest intensity. [Thus] the experience and findings made by the advancing German *Wehrmacht* in Russia in regard to the Jewish problem, were at first glance of such a nature as to confirm the correctness of the National Socialist ideology in the eyes of the soldiers fighting in Russia. He who came to Russia in 1941, whether officer or enlisted man . . . found that the percentage of Jews in the Soviet administration was very high . . . and the Jews played a special

82. NMT, IV, 360–61; tr. 15:6080–81.
83. *See* NMT, IV, 346-7 and 345, in that order, or Maurach, pp. 44–5 and 13–14, in that order.

84. NMT, IV, 349; Maurach, pp. 47–8.

role in the resistance movements and particularly in the underground organizations of the partisan movement.

Under these circumstances, among those circles of the German *Wehrmacht* in the East . . . there was a clearly defined resentment against Jews . . . as the spiritual leaders of resistance and sabotage, and this fact in turn created the psychological conditions, the psychological atmosphere, for the liquidation order to be accepted as a "raison de guerre" about which the individual might think as he wanted, but which . . . was to be carried out without discussion.[85]

Argument for the defense has been retailed at some length in the counsels' own words, not so much because court trials are usually decided according to the letter rather than the spirit of the law—at Nuremberg the contrary was usually true—but because it puts the best legal foot forward for the defense theory that the defendants themselves had to buttress on the witness stand.

THE DEFENDANT

But the paramount reason for retailing this approach of defense counsel is to emphasize the dilemma it created for the defendant as a witness. His lawyers conceded that the presumptions of the defendant were erroneous but were sincerely held as a result of his training, which conditioned him to racism and to a friend–foe view of life as well, causing him to misinterpret the salient factors he encountered in Russia.

Under examination on the stand, Ohlendorf, unlike his counsel, therefore found it tactically unwise to

confess that he may finally have come to recognize that the Fuehrer Order, and consequently his own execution thereof, was illegal, unnecessary, and even immoral, lest his "putative" defense go down the drain. At the risk of antagonizing his judges, he reiterated racist and chauvinist beliefs in justification of his actions, earning in the process some grudging respect for his openness[86] but also in June, 1951, eventually earning the gallows at Landsberg prison. It is this which makes so revealing, as well as dramatic, much of the dialogue with his examiners on the witness stand.

During direct examination by Dr. Aschenauer, Ohlendorf asserted that from his own objective observations the Jews of Russia endangered the security of the Reich: "In the Crimea 90% of the administrative and other leading positions of authority were occupied by Jews, and there was evidence that the same was true elsewhere in Russia. For us it was obvious that the Jews in bolshevist Russia played a disproportionately important role."[87]

Three times Ohlendorf observed executions, and each time "the Jews who were executed went to their death singing the 'International' and hailing Stalin." To him it was thus "absolutely certain that these persons would follow without reservation Stalin's call for ruthless partisan warfare by the entire population— peasants and workers, men, women, and children—as found in written

85. NMT, IV, 352–3; Maurach, pp. 53–4.

86. The tribunal's judgment on Ohlendorf concedes: "He will never need to plead guilty of evasiveness on the witness stand . . . a forthrightness which one could well wish were in another field of activity" (NMT, IV, 511; tr. 17: 6787).

87. Tr. 2:522.

proclamations and orders seized by German forces. . . . Our experiences in Russia were definite confirmation that Bolshevist theory and practice was as we had been taught."[88] The following dialogue ensued during cross-examination:

Judge Musmanno: You drew from that a justification for the order, namely, that these individuals had in effect declared their hostility to Germany, and therefore as a matter of security and self-defense or as a war measure in itself, it was justified to dispose of them?

Ohlendorf: I was asked whether I saw any signs that the *Führer* Order really was based on objective facts.[89]

This justification was challenged in cross-examination by the prosecution counsel:

James E. Heath: You don't mean to say that the persons you killed had to endanger security in order to be killed?

Ohlendorf: In the sense of the *Führer* Order, yes.

Heath: [Disregarding the *Führer* Order], did the people you killed in fact endanger security in any conceivable way?

Ohlendorf: There were two different categories to be killed: people who by virtue of the *Führer* Order were deemed to endanger security, and others, namely active Communists or other people whose endangering of security was established by us, and they were only killed if they actually seemed to endanger security.

Heath: But apart from the assumption of the *Führer* Order, from your own objective witnessing of the situation in Russia, did every Jew in Russia that you killed in fact endanger security, in your judgment?

Ohlendorf: I cannot talk about this apart from the *Führer* Order because it was not only aimed at temporary danger but also danger which might arise in the future.

Heath: Did the Jews that you killed, and the Gypsies, endanger the security of the *Wehrmacht*?

Ohlendorf: Many who were killed were members of partisan groups or supported the partisans in some way, sheltering agents, etc.

Heath: Apart from the partisans, and apart from the *Führer* Order, in *your own judgment today* did all of the Jews you killed constitute any conceivable threat to the German *Wehrmacht*?

Ohlendorf: For me, during my time in Russia there is no condition which is not connected with the *Führer* Order.

Heath: Did you kill Gypsies because they were a threat to the security of the *Wehrmacht*?

Ohlendorf: Same as the Jews.

Heath: Blood?

Ohlendorf: From my own knowledge of European history, the Jews during wars regularly carried on espionage service on both sides.

Judge Musmanno: Is it also in European history that Gypsies always participated in political strategy and campaigns?

Ohlendorf: Espionage . . . during campaigns . . . I want to draw your recollection to extensive descriptions of the Thirty Years War by Ricarda Huch and [Friedrich] Schiller.

Judge Musmanno: That is going back pretty far in order to justify the killing of Gypsies in 1941.

Heath: Isn't it a fact that the nationals of any invaded state—Americans, Germans, Russians—are notorious bearers of intelligence?

Ohlendorf: They have permanent homes; unsettled Gypsies are more prepared to change residence and allegiance for economic gain.[90] [Somewhat surprisingly, Ohlendorf passed up this opportunity to mention wandering Jews.]

Seeking to derive from the reluctant Ohlendorf a clear answer

88. Ibid., 522–3.
89. Ibid., 754.

90. Ibid., 654–60.

whether Jews were killed because they endangered German security or because they were the carriers of bad blood, or perhaps both, Mr. Heath on another occasion asked about the distinction in treatment of Krimchaks and Karaites encountered in Ohlendorf's sector of southern Russia. The Krimchaks—or Krimshegs— were Turkish Jews of mixed Jewish and Tartar blood whose Jewish ancestors had come to Russia by way of Italy. Although they had abandoned the Jewish faith, they were killed by the *Einsatzkommandos* on direct instructions from the RSHA in Berlin. The Karaim—or Karaites—who apparently had no Jewish blood, adopted a variant form of the Jewish religion, rejecting the Talmud but accepting the Torah as their sole source of faith. In their case Berlin ruled that they were not to be killed because they had nothing in common with the Jews except their confession. Heath asked Ohlendorf to explain to the court the obvious incompatability of this RSHA determination with his denial that there was any plan to exterminate the Jewish race:[91]

Ohlendorf: Eastern Jews, Jews found in the Eastern Campaign [in Russia] were to be killed according to the order for the reason they were considered carriers of bolshevism and therefore . . . endangering the security of the German Reich . . . it was not known to me that the Jews in all of Europe were killed . . . on the contrary, down to my . . . [departure from Russia], these Jews were not killed, but it was attempted at all costs to get them to emigrate.
Heath: But the Karaims participated in the Jewish confession in Russia.

Ohlendorf: You must understand that Nazi ideology, as you call it . . . [by the criteria of the *Führer* Order] in Russia and in bolshevism the carriers of this blood showed themselves especially suitable representatives of bolshevism . . . not on account of their faith, or their religion, but because of their human makeup and character.[92]

Finally, the proposition was put to Ohlendorf that since he insisted on the legality of the Fuehrer Order, requiring his "obedience until death" although he questioned its wisdom and feasibility, would he care to express an opinion as to its morality?

Ohlendorf: I do not think I am in a position to judge the responsibility of a statesman who rightly saw his people before the question of existence or non-existence, or to judge whether his measures in such a fight . . . were moral or immoral.
Heath: I do not ask for a judgment of Hitler's morals . . . but for an expression of your own moral conception. . . .
Ohlendorf: Your question is circular . . . you are not asking for a moral estimate of an abstraction, but a judgment about a deed of Hitler.
Heath: You surrendered your moral conscience to Hitler?
Ohlendorf: I surrendered my moral conscience to the fact I was a soldier, and therefore a cog in a relatively low position of a great machine. . . .
Heath: You refused to make any moral judgment, then, and you refuse now? . . .
Ohlendorf: Yes.[93]

THE DRESDEN DEFENSE

On the following day, Judge Musmanno tried once again where Heath had failed:

91. Ibid., 626–7. For the contemporary record of this *RSHA* determination, *see* T175, Roll 163, frames 2694761 ff.

92. Tr. 2:627–8.
93. Ibid., 743–5.

Judge Musmanno: You indicated a lack of desire to answer Mr. Heath's question on the moral issue. You indicated that it wasn't for you to decide the moral question at all. But with every order, with every demand, or request, there instinctively goes a moral appraisal—you may agree with it or not —so when this order was given to you to go out and kill, you had to appraise it, instinctively. The soldier who goes into battle knows that he must kill. But he understands that it is a question of a battle with an equally armed enemy. But you were going out to shoot down defenseless people. Now, didn't the question of the morality of that enter your mind? Let us suppose that the order had been—and I don't mean any offense in this question—suppose that the order had been that you should kill your sister. Would you not have instinctively morally appraised that order as to whether it was right or wrong—morally, not politically, or militarily, but as a matter of humanity, conscience, and justice between man and man?

Ohlendorf: I am not in a position . . . to isolate this occurrence from the occurrences of 1943, 1944, and 1945 where with my own hands I took children and women out of the burning asphalt . . . and with my own hands I took big blocks of stone from the stomachs of pregnant women; and with my own eyes I saw 60,000 people die within 24 hours— that I am not prepared, or in a position to give today a moral judgment about that [Führer] order . . . these factors seem to me to be above a moral standard. These years are for me a unit separate. . . . Full of ruthlessness to destroy and to be inhuman. . . .

Judge Musmanno: Those years followed 1941, [the date] when you were confronted with [the Führer Order].[94]

This was not the only time Ohlendorf advanced what one may call the "Dresden defense," although Nuremberg courts uniformly ruled out tu

quoque arguments: "You did it, too" or "Everybody does it." When pressed to justify the extermination of Jewish and Gypsy children, Ohlendorf referred to the Allied bombing of Dresden:

I have seen very many children killed in this war through air attacks, for the security of other nations. . . . I cannot imagine that those planes which systematically covered a city . . . square meter for square meter, with incendiaries and explosive bombs and again with phosphorous bombs . . . from block to block . . . in Dresden including the squares to which the civilian population had fled—that these men could possibly hope not to kill any civilian population, and no children. . . . The pronouncements of the Allied leaders on this [indicate] . . . that these killings were accepted quite knowingly because one believed that only through this terror . . . could the people be demoralized, and under such blows the military power of the Germans would then also break down.[95]

An obvious counterargument to this superficially compelling Dresden defense, is that Warsaw, Rotterdam, London, and Coventry were battered by the Luftwaffe well before Allied blockbusters or firestorms flattened Hamburg, Frankfurt, Berlin, and Dresden, but it is vulnerable to such moral strictures as "Two wrongs do not make a right," or "We are not Nazis!" But the telling refutation came in the prosecution's summation by the chief of counsel, Telford Taylor:

On this whole question we wish to make one final observation. The Einsatz massacres of Jews have been defended here as if it were sincerely believed that the killing of Jews was a military necessity in order to achieve military

94. Ibid., 746–7.

95. Ibid., 662–3.

victory over the Russian Army. But in point of fact this argument is not sincerely made. Whatever anyone may think about atom bombs or ordinary bombs, they have not been dropping here in Germany since the capitulation. But will any defendant dare to suggest to us that the execution of the Jews in Russia would have stopped if Russian military resistance had collapsed? On the contrary, the evidence is compelling that a German victory would have enormously widened the scope of operations of the *Einsatzgruppen* and the holocaust would have been even more staggering. Ohlendorf's own testimony makes this clear beyond a doubt. When questioned as to the necessity for the killing of Jewish children by the *Einsatzgruppen* he replied: "I believe that it is very simple to explain if one starts from the fact that [the *Führer*] order not only tried to achieve security, but *permanent* security, lest the children grow up and inevitably, being the children of parents who had been killed, they would constitute a danger no smaller than that of the parents."[96]

THE SOURCE

So we come, finally, to this barefaced defense, this ultimate aberration of Carl Schmitt's aberrant friend–foe philosophy:[97] You designate your foe, and then justify murdering him and his to prevent his characteristically foelike murder of you and yours. Following Thomas Hobbes's jaundiced view of human nature "seeking power after power

until death,"[98] the only security lies in first-strike extermination of your chosen enemies unto the last generation.

Where did Otto Ohlendorf imbibe this final racist solution which the evidence indicates was foreign to his nature? From his SS training, yes; from the dictates of the fuehrer he had never met, yes;[99] but most directly from the fuehrer's devout apostle of racial hate, Ohlendorf's *Reichsführer* SS and severest critic, Heinrich Himmler. Attempting to avoid the *Einsatzgruppen* command and thus avert his fate, Ohlendorf had twice questioned the wisdom and feasibility of the Fuehrer Order, though wisely not its morality, only to be severely reprimanded by Himmler. Yet when under cross-examination in the dock, his life came down to its bottom line, his instinctive justification was a nearly verbatim replica of passages from Himmler's two 1943 speeches at Posen on October 4 and 6 to the SS *Gruppenführer* and to the Reich and *Gauleiter*, respectively, neither of which Ohlendorf had heard personally:[100] "We know how heavy would be our burden under the bombings, strains, and deprivations of war, if we still had in every city Jews as saboteurs, agitators and instigators. . . . We had the moral right, we had the duty to our people to exterminate this people that wanted to exterminate us."[101]

Addressing the Reich and Gau

---

96. Tr. 17:6593–94.

97. Ohlendorf, however, sternly disapproved of Schmitt's philosophy: "Nothing could contradict the views of National Socialism more than this doctrine, for in a people all members are part of the people, even if they are opponents of a certain point of view . . . they are not enemies to be exterminated but fellow countrymen to be won over" (tr. 2:485 and 640).

98. *Leviathan*, ch. 11.

99. Tr. 2:506.

100. Counsel corrected a misinterpretation of an earlier statement by Ohlendorf from which the court had inferred that he was present among the *Gruppenführer* on 4 Oct. 1943 (tr. 2:621): Ohlendorf "heard about the [Posen] speech here . . . in Nuremberg" (tr. 2:675).

101. IMT document PS 1919.

leaders in the same city two days later, the *Reichsführer* SS had apparently had time to refine his ideas and polish his language, which echoed in Ohlendorf's key testimony:

That which I say to you in this circle, I ask you *really* only to hear it and never to speak of it. The question arose for us: what about women and children? Here, too, I decided to find a perfectly clear solution. I did not consider myself justified to exterminate the men—bluntly speaking, to kill them or to have them killed—and to permit their avengers in the form of their children to grow up for our sons and grandsons to cope with.

For the organization which had to carry out this assignment, it was the most difficult that we have yet had. It has been executed without—as I believe I may assert—our men and our leaders having suffered damage to their spirit or souls.[102]

Whether asserted by Himmler during the full exercise of untrammeled power or by a defenseless Ohlendorf in the dock, this is rationalization of murder and bourgeois morality paired in the same mind, in the same psyche, and in perfect compatibility.

102. T175, Roll 85, frame 169.

Holocaust Business:
Some Reflections on *Arbeit Macht Frei*

By JOHN K. ROTH

ABSTRACT: *Arbeit Macht Frei*, "work makes one free." Those words formed the entry to Nazi death camps. Attention typically focuses on the principal extermination centers— Auschwitz-Birkenau, Belzec, Chelmno, Maidanek, Sobibor, and Treblinka—where countless Jews were dispatched by gas chambers and crematoria. Less well known is the fact that the Nazi program included some 1,600 forced labor operations. During the 12 years of the Nazi regime, millions slaved and perished within them. If survivors were found when Allied forces arrived, it was only because the victims had somehow avoided being worked to death. This article explores the links between industry, slave labor, and the Holocaust. It also examines implications for moral philosophy that spin off from Holocaust business.

John K. Roth is the Russell K. Pitzer Professor of Philosophy at Claremont Men's College, where he has taught since 1966. He received his B.A. from Pomona College and took his M.A. and Ph.D. in philosophy at the Yale University Graduate School. He was a Graves Fellow in the Humanities (1970–71), Fulbright Lecturer in American Studies at the University of Innsbruck, Austria (1973–74), and Fellow of the National Humanities Institute, Yale University (1976–77). His publications include A Consuming Fire: Encounters with Elie Wiesel and the Holocaust (1979).

No one knows who will live in this cage in the future, or whether at the end of this tremendous development entirely new prophets will arise, or there will be a great rebirth of old ideas and ideals, or, if neither, mechanized petrification, embellished with a sort of convulsive self-importance.[1]

SOME writers have uncanny insights about the future. Sigmund Freud, Franz Kafka, and Friedrich Nietzsche are three prominent examples from the past century. Max Weber is another. He saw human rationality constructing its own cage-without-an-exit. His vision is not yet completely true, and it may never be. But we ought not to place sanguine bets on that hope. History itself is the reason why.

Seventy million human beings have been uprooted, enslaved, or killed in the twentieth century alone. Albert Camus made that estimate in *The Rebel* (1951). What the figure should be today, God only knows. It is all too clear, however, that a cage is still in the making. War persists. Scarcity abounds. Misery rages, and business goes on as usual—almost. One difference is that today's work is done after Auschwitz.

Arbeit Macht Frei, "work makes one free." Those words formed the entry sign at Nazi camps of slave labor and death. Attention typically focuses on the principal extermination centers—Auschwitz-Birkenau, Belzec, Chelmno, Maidanek, Sobibor, and Treblinka—where countless Jews were dispatched by gas chambers and crematoria. Less well known is the fact that the Nazi version of Max Weber's cage included some 1,600 forced labor camps. During the

1. Max Weber, *The Protestant Ethic and the Spirit of Capitalism*, trans. Talcott Parsons (New York: Charles Scribner's Sons, 1958), p. 182.

twelve years of the Nazi regime, millions slaved within them. Millions perished, too. If survivors were found more or less alive when Allied forces arrived, it was only because the victims had somehow avoided being worked to death.

Recent concern about the Holocaust has produced much hand wringing about guilt and apostasy. It has renewed moral outrage and indignation. It has even led people to mount campaigns of relief for those who are experiencing a similar plight in Southeast Asia. Sadly, however, such activities, vitally important as they are, may be little more than an attempt to treat symptoms rather than the disease itself. Indeed, the disease could be beyond treatment because it is rampant in a cage where the medicine, if any exists, is beyond the grasp of arms stretched through the bars made by human hands. Such a prospect is grim; it leaves yearnings for a different outcome. Whether there can be one, though, depends on our ability to understand better the cage that is our home. Consider some glimpses of Holocaust business as a step in that direction.

THE "ADVANCE" OF CIVILIZATION

Richard L. Rubenstein's *The Cunning of History* penetrates a process of total domination in which corporate enterprise played a fundamental part. We will see momentarily how that role developed historically, but Rubenstein's framework of interpretation helps to pinpoint crucial questions raised by Holocaust history. A major problem, for example, is the apparently dysfunctional status of moral philosophy and religious ethics. How does it happen that the long and honorable tradition of moral reflection in the West not only seems incapable of providing an effective bulwark against human domination that results in a Holocaust, but even contributes to that process itself? One answer to the former part of the issue is as forthright as it is disturbing. It leads to insights about the second as well. Both dimensions point to *power.*

RIGHT DEPENDENT ON MIGHT

Philosophers and theologians argue whether one can judge what ought to be on the basis of what is. Rubenstein suggests that such considerations are all too often beside the point. As far as history is concerned, right does depend on might. Specifically, those who hold political and economic power also have the authority to define what should and therefore will be. Granted, their claims are often supported by appeals to reason, natural law, inalienable rights, self-evident truth, God's will, destiny, or fate. If those appeals are not without sound arguments behind them, it is also true that such legitimations are never unrelated to desires for power and the privileges that it confers.

Such analysis conjures up visions of the few dominating the many by force. That result is not far off the mark, but it is vitally important to note that the sharing of political and economic power and the diffusion of privileges from it are very often widespread. Indeed, they must be to provide the critical mass of common interests that is required for any regime to work. Hitler's Nazis could not keep such a package together in the long run. They did so long enough, however, to show what is possible. Thus Richard Rubenstein puts a crucial item on the agenda: "Until ethical theorists and theologians are prepared to face without sentimentality the kind of action it is possible freely to perpetrate under conditions of

utter respectability in an advanced, contemporary society, none of their assertions about the existence of moral norms will have much credibility."[2]

The point is simple. Had Nazi power prevailed, authority to determine what ought to be would have found that no natural laws were broken and no crimes against God and humanity were committed in the Holocaust. It would have been a question, though, whether the slave labor operations should continue, expand, or go out of business. Those decisions would have been made on rational grounds.

Right: extermination and slave labor

Although minds are still jarred by the thought that the Holocaust was not a bizarre aberration unleashed by psychopaths, it is more common now to understand that a basic core of rationality formed the Nazi policies of extermination and slave labor. The Nazis perceived a problem—too many people of an undesirable type and a need for labor in a state whose destiny spelled expansion—and they moved to solve it expeditiously. Of course, one can quarrel with their definition of "problem," but the power to define social reality was theirs, and they used it. No doubt the definition process was just that, a process, and it left open varied options for solutions. It is also true that the process took on cagelike qualities as it moved forward. Ultimately, working people to death, coupled with outright extermination, provided the most efficient Final Solution.

2. Richard L. Rubenstein, *The Cunning of History: The Holocaust and the American Future* (New York: Harper Colophon Books, 1978), p. 67.

The dominating power of practical rationality, at least in its Holocaust dimensions, is a most significant consequence of the life of reason. That consequence, however unintended and inconvenient for ethical theory, has a history. One of its chapters involves religion. Religion is often stereotyped as an unthinking phenomenon. That image arises when one considers religion primarily in terms of superstition, dogmatism, and fanaticism. Religious history reveals such qualities, but they are not even half the story. Much more decisive for Western civilization is the fact that religion has been a spur to awaken the human mind. Religion can kill thinking. It also stimulates it, even requires it, which is why the life of religion and the life of philosophy are so closely intertwined.

Life cannot advance without thinking. It is also true that thinking is dangerous business. Thinking is questioning. Questioning, in turn, has no end, except that it can lead one to become self-conscious about power, possibilities, efficiency, and means and ends. Starting from an affirmation of or a search for absolutes, it can lead to skepticism and relativism and then to a will to power. Religion and philosophy were not sufficient to establish Holocaust business. Certainly they were contributing, if not necessary, causes. The issue, Rubenstein suggests, is whether their forms of thought—or any forms of power—have authority enough to forestall the tendencies for destruction that are their own progeny.

"The Holocaust," Rubenstein has written, "bears witness to *the advance of civilization.*"[3] That advance depended on brain power. The power of thought, in turn, gave us the modern political state, high technology, vast networks of transportation and communication, unprecedented military might, and new consciousness that "the decisive means for politics is violence."[4] Such results are not unmitigated evils. Men and women can do amazing things for humanitarian purposes because of those realities. But the same factors also made a cage that took the twentieth century to Auschwitz. Let us look at the situation in terms of labor.

We know that the leaders of German industry under Hitler—men such as Dr. Carl Krauch, chairman of the supervisory board of I. G. Farben; Alfried Krupp von Bohlen, chairman of the Krupp complex of coal, iron, and steel industries; and Friedrich Flick, head of Mitteldeutsche Stahlwerke—were a distinguished group. They had vast scientific knowledge and managerial skill. Nobel prize winners and Rhodes scholars were among them. They were well-educated leaders, their business acumen was high, their loyalty to Germany indisputable, and their innovative ability to solve problems unsurpassed. Before most people could say "multinational conglomerate," these industrialists ran such enterprises.

It was no accident that Hitler had these men on his side, and without them he could never have gotten very far. One of the reasons is that they almost perfected a cost-effective labor policy. Faced with the problem of fueling German industry in wartime, these businessmen, who also condoned Nazi racism at least implicitly, made a more than convenient

3. Ibid., p. 91 (Rubenstein's italics).

4. Max Weber, "Politics as a Vocation," in *From Max Weber: Essays in Sociology*, trans. and ed. H. H. Gerth and C. Wright Mills (New York: Oxford University Press, 1976), p. 121.

marriage with the SS (*Schutzstaffel*). *Arbeit Macht Frei* was the slogan; *Vernichtung durch Arbeit*, "annihilation by work," was the reality. Logistics made the operation difficult to implement. Still, necessity, expediency, and even profitability dictated the course to be rational and, in that sense, good.

Superior Allied might caused the plan to fail partially. In fact, the German industrialists carried out their policies with relative impunity: "It was possible for respectable business executives to participate in and profit from a society of total domination and a venture involving the murder of millions of defenseless human beings without losing their elite status in one of the most advanced modern societies."[5] One moral of this story is that civilization's advance testifies that ethical judgments have authority in history just to the degree that they are backed by political and economic power.

"THE PROBLEM . . . CAN NOW BE REGARDED AS DEFINITELY SOLVED"

In 1935, one of the problems confronting Adolf Hitler was production of a synthetic rubber known as Buna. At the seventh Nazi party congress in Nuremberg on September 11, Hitler boasted that this problem "can now be regarded as definitely solved."[6]

The need: mass production

Hitler's announcement was a propagandistic exaggeration, but not by much. German scientists did know how to produce synthetic rubber, just

as they also knew how to convert coal into synthetic fuels that could power Nazi tanks and planes. The difficulties of mass production, however, were substantial, especially so once World War II was under way. Attempts to cope with them would take I. G. Farben to Auschwitz. Buna was never produced there, but a factory and its supporting operations were well along. The energy that built them was not synthetic. It came from human slaves.

Joseph Borkin's *The Crime and Punishment of I. G. Farben* traces the path that took this world-leading firm into the most grisly depths of the Holocaust, into the dock at Nuremberg for war crimes, and then well beyond. His most noteworthy points for our purposes begin with the observation that Hitler was no fool. German defeat in World War I occurred substantially because the country was deficient in crucial raw materials. British blockades eventually took a heavy toll on German efforts to import required resources for fuel, gunpowder, and rubber. This lesson was not lost on Hitler. Determined that history would not repeat, he successfully wooed I. G. Farben, who wanted governmental support to turn abundant German coal into gasoline by hydrogenation. On 14 December 1933, a bargain was struck. In return for his governmental support, Hitler would not have to worry about oil until Allied bombing raids in May, 1944 razed I. G.'s synthetic oil operations.[7]

The prelude to this mutual interest is intriguing. At the turn of the century, six German companies—BASF, Bayer, Hoechst, Cassella, Agfa, and Kalle—had cornered the world market for synthetic dyestuffs. Still, they battled each other viciously, which

5. Rubenstein, p. 65.

6. *See* Joseph Borkin, *The Crime and Punishment of I. G. Farben* (New York: The Free Press, 1978), p. 62.

7. Ibid., p. 60.

discouraged Carl Duisberg, the general manager of Bayer. Then, on a trip to the United States in 1903, he became aware of the trust movement that was booming in spite of the Sherman Antitrust Act. Duisberg was especially captivated by the example of John D. Rockefeller and Standard Oil. Although war would be required to bring it off, Duisberg would eventually win favor for a similar plan of organization among German chemical plants.

German strategy in World War I called for a short struggle and a swift victory. Care to provide a sound industrial base for a war of attrition was minimal. When it became clear that a long war of attrition was precisely what was in store, the most critical need was to develop German self-sufficiency in the production of gunpowder. Steps in that direction had been taken as early as 1913 when a major breakthrough by Fritz Haber and Carl Bosch made it possible to mass produce synthetic ammonia. Within a year, large quantities of ammonia were available, most of it used in fertilizer. At the same time, however, Bosch was experimentally producing small amounts of saltpeter, the basic raw material for gunpowder, by oxidizing the synthetic ammonia. Little was made of this development until it became apparent in 1915 that Germany would have great difficulty importing the raw materials it needed to produce gunpowder for the war effort.

Now German leadership turned to Bosch, but time was needed to gear up for full production. In the meantime, development of another decisive weapon seemed imperative. As military liaisons discussed the options with German industrialists, it became clear that poisonous chemicals were among the by-products of German dyestuffs. These chemicals could become devastating instruments of war. Thus on the afternoon of April 22, canisters of chlorine gas were opened at Ypres, Belgium. By day's end, Borkin reports, 15,000 soldiers lay on the battlefield, 5,000 of them dead.[8]

Production of the poisonous gas required several steps, which were divided up rationally among the best-suited firms. Meanwhile, Bosch's gunpowder project moved ahead, vastly enriched by government support. All was not well, however. With the Battle of the Somme, July, 1916, Germans found it thinkable that they might lose the war. Taking that eventuality into account, the chemical magnates believed that they would more likely hang separately than together. Thus Duisberg's dream of a more unified dyestuff industry was realized: I. G. Farben—the Interessen Gemeinschaft der Deutschen Teerfarbenindustrie—was born in August.

The solution: I. G. Farben

Although Duisberg's intuitions about the future would prove correct, the immediate future of I. G. Farben was rocky. Not only did the victorious Allies bring sanctions against the companies that had armed German forces, but postwar economic disruptions also made things uncertain. Carl Bosch decided that a more decisive step must be taken. Heretofore I. G. Farben had been an association of cooperating units, but by 9 December 1925, Bosch succeeded in welding them into a single corporation, I. G. Farbenindustrie Aktiengessellschaft, the biggest chemical company in the world.[9]

The company's expansionist ambitions were unslacking. Increasingly,

8. Ibid., p. 18.
9. Ibid., p. 43.

I. G. Farben took control of Germany's munitions industry, and Bosch's dream of German self-sufficiency in oil also kept the hydrogenation project alive. Ever mindful of new sources of capital, Bosch hoped to bring Standard Oil of New Jersey into this operation. In all likelihood, he would have achieved that goal had not the Great Depression and the discovery of vast petroleum reserves in Texas dropped the price of oil so low that Standard Oil lost interest in further development of the process to convert coal.

Meanwhile Hitler and the Nazi party were asserting themselves. Indeed, for a time I. G. Farben was a Nazi target, since Jews were centrally involved with the firm. Bosch defended the Jews in I. G. Farben, and thus his personal relationships with Hitler were never very good, but the two men and their constituents had too many overlapping interests to be seriously at odds for long. Military preparation was Hitler's goal. I. G. Farben could facilitate that aim, and good business required it. Above all, Bosch and his associates knew a rich deal when they saw one.

By 1937, the company had been nazified: all members of the managing board were party members, Jewish leadership had been removed, and Herman Goering had put Carl Krauch in charge of fulfilling all Nazi needs in the chemical field. As Germany invaded Poland on 1 September 1939, I. G. Farben's interests were flourishing. Indeed, Nazi victories in the east were creating attractive possibilities for industrial expansion. Sensing the importance of such options, I. G. Farben successfully courted the Nazi leader most likely to have decisive influence in that area, Heinrich Himmler, head of the SS.

These gains were not without problems; for example, the war might create a labor shortage for German factories. That fact was instrumental in a report filed by Otto Ambros, who was to determine for I. G. Farben the best location for a new plant to produce Buna. The spot Ambros favored had numerous assets: ample coal and water plus ready access to good highway and rail facilities. In addition, a supply of labor would not be in doubt. Ambros argued that the place to build the factory was near the Polish town of Auschwitz.

And I. G. Auschwitz

I. G. Farben, of course, was not the only enterprise planning expansion at Auschwitz in 1941. The SS had similar intentions, only its goal was to manufacture corpses. As events unfolded, these objectives were hardly incompatible. In any case, I. G. Farben was so optimistic about the possibilities in Poland that it was willing to use its own funds to build a new, privately owned firm called I. G. Auschwitz. With a capital investment totaling nearly one billion dollars in today's money, it would be the largest single project in the I. G. Farben system. All that the firm would ask from the government was help in procuring the necessary labor at reasonable rates.

Himmler and his commandant at Auschwitz, Rudolf Hoess, were willing to cooperate. The mutually beneficial agreement was made, and I. G. Farben began to supplement the gas chambers of Birkenau with death by work and starvation. However, if cost-effective efficiency was the goal, the first year at I. G. Auschwitz was a mixed success. Prices for inmate labor were cheap enough, but the workers, already less than energetic because of their meager diet, were further weakened by the long daily trek to the factory site. With valuable time and energy being lost, it was not a rational way to run a business, but the situation could be improved if the laborers were closer at hand. Thus in July, 1942, I. G. Farben decided to build its own concentration camp. It was called Monowitz.

This camp had a rational division of labor: I. G. Farben fed and housed the slave laborers; the SS handled security, discipline, and the supply of workers. If no Buna materialized from this process, its efficiency was remarkable on other counts. One could calculate quite precisely that the vast majority of workers at I. G. Auschwitz would be dead within three or four months after their initial stint. Poor food, inadequate sanitation, brutal guards, periodic selections to weed out the unfit—these realities combined with draining physical labor to make I. G. Auschwitz's most important product: death.

Among the firms dominated by I. G. Farben was the Deutsche Gesellschaft für Schädlingsbekämpfung (the German Corporation for Pest Control) better known as DEGESCH. Among its products was prussic acid, an effective insecticide. Under the trade name Zyklon B, it would work wonders for genocide. As SS purchases of this product increased, DEGESCH did its part by removing from the product a special indicating odor normally used to warn human beings of the deadly presence. "The supply," notes Raul Hilberg, "was kept up to the very end. The SS did not run out of gas."[10]

What should one conclude? Does anything guarantee that it is not good,

rational business to kill?—unless it is a collective will that says, "No!" with force sufficient to command respect?

Arbeit Macht Frei? Those words mock the dead. They also mock the living if we think that Holocaust business is vanquished from the earth. That problem can in no way be regarded as definitely solved.

The camp and its commandant

The most familiar eyewitness accounts of the Holocaust, for example, Alexander Donat's *The Holocaust Kingdom*, Primo Levi's *Survival in Auschwitz*, and Elie Wiesel's *Night*, are by Jewish survivors. The Nazi mind is less inclined to remember things past, but the autobiography of Rudolf Hoess is one telling exception. Among its noteworthy insights is Hoess's confession that he lived only for his work.[11] What was Hoess's work? What relation did it have to *Arbeit Macht Frei?*

One historian calls Hoess "the man from the crowd."[12] Another commentator describes him as "a very ordinary little man."[13] Such observations are true. Hoess was a functionary, a cog in a huge machine, and he was not widely known, except perhaps indirectly by prisoners under his authority, outside of a restricted circle within the SS. And yet to encounter Rudolf Hoess is to meet an unusual individual, for he was the best at what he did, and what he did was no trivial undertaking. In Hoess's case, working one's way to the top

10. Raul Hilberg, *The Destruction of the European Jews* (New York: Franklin Watts, 1973), p. 571.

11. See Rudolf Hoess, *Commandant of Auschwitz*, trans. Constantine Fitzgibbon (London: Pan Books, 1974), p. 122.

12. Joachim C. Fest, *The Face of the Third Reich: Portraits of the Nazi Leadership*, trans. Michael Bullock (New York: Pantheon Books, 1970), p. 276.

13. Lord Russell of Liverpool, "Introduction," in Hoess, p. 23.

meant becoming the commandant of Auschwitz. It could be true that anyone might fill that role, if we mean that the propensity to unleash mass death is something from which no person is immune. On the other hand, to think that just anybody could manage Auschwitz is to underestimate Hoess's ability.

A capsule summary of this man's career highlights the following facts. Born in 1900, Hoess was raised in a devout Catholic home. Obedience to authority was emphasized along with the plan that Rudolf would become a priest. An introverted boy who loved horses and the out-of-doors, Hoess found himself attracted to the army instead. Secretly joining a regiment in 1915, he fought with such distinction on the Turkish front that he not only received the Iron Cross First and Second Class but also at the age of seventeen became the youngest noncommissioned officer in the German army.

At the war's end, his membership in a now-illegal military unit implicated him in a murder, and Hoess received a 10-year prison sentence. He describes himself as a prisoner more obedient than embittered, and he was amnestied in the summer of 1928 after serving about half of his sentence. Encouraged by friends to join the Nazi party, Hoess declined because the party's policies seemed crass. Besides, he had determined while in prison that his life should be that of a farmer and a family man. That dream prevailed until 1934 when Himmler invited Hoess to join the active SS. Acceptance took Hoess to Dachau where he worked his way through the ranks, entering the SS officer corps with promotion to *SS-Untersturmführer* (second lieutenant) on 13 September 1936.

Early in 1940 it was determined that a new concentration camp should be built in Poland. The site was Auschwitz. Assignment as commandant was hardly a plum, and Hoess suggests that he got the post partly because his superior at Sachsenhausen disliked him and was only too glad to let him go. Strict discipline and obedience did not save the SS from personal rivalries. Hoess's narrative complains repeatedly that such conflicts thwarted his conscientious attempts to do the best job possible at Auschwitz.

Still, "every fresh difficulty only increased my zeal," Hoess reported,[14] and despite the obstacles he encountered, Hoess did his work remarkably well. His camp grew; it also diminished. If Hoess rejected a figure of two and a half million dead as "far too high" because "even Auschwitz had limits to its destructive possibilities"[15] that total cannot be far from the mark Hoess achieved before he was through.

Hoess's was not an "ordinary" performance. He worked hard because he believed his tasks were important, meaningful, rational, and even good. Not that he took pleasure, least of all sadistic pleasure, in killing. On the contrary, there simply was a problem to be solved. Part of the problem, of course, was solved before it came to Hoess's obedient hands. Convinced that the Nazi cause was right, and therefore that the orders he received were to be followed without skepticism, Hoess's task was to make the final solution proceed as smoothly as possible. It was also to enable German industry to meet its labor needs. Hoess's ingenuity with Zyklon B went far toward handling the first assignment. Nor did he shirk his duty where the second matter was concerned.

14. Hoess, p. 122.
15. Ibid., p. 219.

Prior to his arrival at Auschwitz, Hoess knew a good deal about forced labor. Prisoners work; that principle had been taught to Hoess firsthand while he was himself an inmate, and it was a cornerstone of his administrative policy, too. In Hoess's early experience, work meant rehabilitation. Working hard and well meant that one was learning a lesson and was paying for wrongdoing in a way that would change consciousness for the better, not to mention breaking the monotony of imprisonment itself. Hoess related that meanings of this kind were behind the sign *Arbeit Macht Frei*, which he first saw at Dachau, and that such a philosophy can apply completely only "where the conditions are normal."[16] If the conditions were less than that when he took over at Auschwitz, neither was Hoess expecting that his new camp would become a full-fledged *Vernichtungslager*. Thus the sign *Arbeit Macht Frei* went up there, too.

According to Hoess, on 1 March 1941, Heinrich Himmler paid him a visit at Auschwitz. Accompanying Himmler were high executives of I. G. Farben. Plans to make Auschwitz an industrial center were well along, and Himmler promised that prisoner labor would be made available as required. Indeed Himmler's proposals reached far into the future. He envisioned a postwar, peacetime operation of some 30,000 inmates, presumably available to work for major branches of the German armaments industry that would be transferred there after the war.

In the summer of 1942, Himmler visited Auschwitz one last time. Meanwhile, he had summoned Hoess to Berlin a year earlier. In effect, the purpose of that meeting was to inform Hoess that Auschwitz would

become "the largest human slaughter house that history had ever known."[17] Hoess was to be in charge. During the subsequent review at Auschwitz, Himmler observed the extermination process without comment, and then went on to inspect the Buna operation. His main concern was to increase worker efficiency. Hoess tried to impress Himmler with the administrative difficulties, but at the end of the inspection tour, Hoess was told that he would have to manage as best he could. Himmler then promoted Hoess to lieutenant colonel and left.

Original plans called for all Jewish arrivals at Auschwitz to be destroyed without exception. However, as the first transports of German Jews arrived, a different order stated that able-bodied men and women would be segregated and formed into labor brigades. Hoess's difficulties compounded. Not only was Auschwitz two camps in one, but there were competing interests among the groups concerned with the labor pool. How many Jews should be selected for work? Which were fit? How would the logistics of security best be handled? In spite of these tough questions, in spite of the smoke and stench from bodies burning in the crematoria under his administration, Hoess claimed that he still hoped to make Auschwitz "a clean and healthy place."[18] Hoess could say that "in Auschwitz everything was possible,"[19] but he was wrong. "Everything" left no room for hopes like those.

A Polish court condemned Hoess to death on 2 April 1947. Two weeks later he was hanged at Auschwitz. The point is not that justice prevails.

16. Ibid., p. 82.

17. Ibid., p. 234.
18. Ibid., p. 231.
19. Ibid., p. 134.

But it may be discovered in a very different place by considering the following question: Was Hoess cynical when he put up his sign, *Arbeit Macht Frei*, at the entrance to Auschwitz and kept it there until the end?

Any reading of Hoess's narrative must allow for his desire to put himself in the best light. Still, at least at the outset of Hoess's tenure at Auschwitz, there is not much reason to suppose that he callously intended *Arbeit Macht Frei* to have the mocking effect that certainly resulted. That adage after all, contained a grain of truth. *If* one got the chance to work, and *if* work did not kill you, then being able to work was the only thing that could keep one alive until rescue from the outside might happen.

I. G. Farben, the SS, and Rudolf Hoess controlled social reality at Auschwitz. They imposed *Arbeit Macht Frei* as a categorical imperative. We claim that their use of power was wrong, and theory after theory tries to back up that judgment. This is good, but not good enough, because when Rudolf Hoess said that he lived only for his work, he was also testifying that the decisive factor in life is who holds power over it.

Normative reflection makes it crucial to ask, Who ought to have power, and what should be the case? Rudolf Hoess made clear that it is equally crucial for normative reflection to ask, Who is and will be in power, and what is going to happen in those cases? Granted, responses to the latter questions alone may not tell us what ought to be done. In that sense the traditional notion that ethics is logically prior to politics still rings true. Such priority, however, guarantees nothing. The human will to power, individual or collective, does not guarantee anything either, but in this world's history nothing goes further to determine what shall be.

At the end of his autobiography, Hoess makes a less-than-impassioned statement that the extermination of the Jews was wrong. Basically, Hoess proclaims that the extermination was wrong because it failed: "It in no way served the cause of anti-Semitism, but on the contrary brought the Jews far closer to their ultimate objective."[20] This unrepentant Hoess is a good soldier to the end, and thus he also admits matter-of-factly: "I am responsible."[21] True, Hoess restricts that admission to those decisions that were in his sphere, reserving to others the responsibility for orders he received. Difficult though it may be, Hoess also wants his readers to try to understand that "he, too, had a heart and that he was not evil."[22] If moral sensitivity finds that plea less than credible, a fundamental point is nonetheless well taken from the commandant of Auschwitz. In this world, theoretical good counts for very little, but what shall in fact count for good matters very much. That determination belongs to people who will take responsibility and hold it.

NO SIGN OF REMORSE

The Universal Declaration of Human Rights adopted by the General Assembly of the United Nations on 10 December 1948, proclaims that "recognition of the inherent dignity and of the equal and inalienable rights of all members of the human family is the foundation of freedom, justice and peace in the world." Such language has a long history, but it is not accidental that the United Nations spoke out in the aftermath of Holocaust business. Flushed into the open by the postwar trials that condemned some Nazi leaders to death,

20. Ibid., p. 201.
21. Ibid., p. 203.
22. Ibid., p. 205.

protest was raised over "crimes against humanity." Moral pronouncements abounded. Who could be against human rights after Auschwitz? Indeed, nowadays we find everyone defending them, at least verbally. And yet how much justice is done remains a question. That question spotlights once again the cage we inhabit.

Benjamin B. Ferencz practices international law in New York City. He also writes about the legal problems of world peace. One of his efforts in that regard is a recent book entitled *Less Than Slaves*. As an American prosecutor at the Nuremberg trials, Ferencz became concerned about restitution for Jewish survivors who had labored in the Nazi camps. His book testifies that too many German industrialists showed "no sign of remorse."[23]

With the outbreak of World War II, the Nazis made labor conscription commonplace. The treatment accorded such workers depended on their classification in a Nazi racial hierarchy that relegated Slavs and Gypsies to subhuman status along with Jews. Germans were affected, too. Political and religious dissidents, criminals, homosexuals—anyone who ran afoul of Nazi law could find themselves imprisoned and enslaved.

Limited restitution

Jews fared worst. If they were allowed to live at all, theirs was the most strenuous and dangerous work. Nevertheless, some of these men and women not only survived but also went on to seek compensation from their captors. Their cases were heard in courts of law as well as in

less legalistic settings aimed at moral persuasion. Ferencz's report is that power—economic and political, but not ethical—determined the verdicts: "Of the hundreds of German firms that used concentration camp inmates, the number that paid anything to camp survivors could be counted on the fingers of one hand. . . . Even the severe hardship cases of those who had survived work for I. G. Farben at Auschwitz got no more than $1,700 each."[24]

One might well ask, Should anything different have been expected? From an ethical perspective, it is not difficult to feel righteous indignation over such trivial individual recompense for wasted lives. But must not we be practical? Ferencz outlines the successful defense mustered by that outlook.

War was the excuse. Germany was fighting for her life. Labor was essential, and nobody could expect favors, least of all Jews whom Nazi propaganda had successfully portrayed as a major cause of global conflict. Indeed, the industrialists' argument went on to say, German industry was under the gun. Disobedience of Nazi commands would have been dealt with summarily. Practically speaking, the German companies had to accept the reality of forced labor. Otherwise their firms were in jeopardy, and with them, Germany as well.

Most ethical perspectives would find such defenses lacking, especially so in the light of SS evidence that called the industrialists to account. Documents and oral testimony by former SS leaders make plain that German businesses could obtain concentration camp labor only if they requisitioned it. True, the other options available were probably scant, but the fact remains that decisions were taken to utilize

23. Benjamin B. Ferencz, *Less Than Slaves: Jewish Forced Labor and the Quest for Compensation* (Cambridge: Harvard University Press, 1979), p. 192.

24. Ibid., p. 188.

slaves. That reality becomes all the more clear when one recalls the treatment received by these workers —starvation diets, virtual absence of health care, and in the case of I. G. Auschwitz, imprisonment in a camp built specifically by and for industry itself.

But could it not be argued that lives were saved by these labor policies? Without them, after all, Jews would have been gassed without further adieu. German industry tried that argument. It is not without validity, but neither will it ring true morally. Had Germany won the war, the fate of those workers would have been sealed. And yet the industrialists' arguments—contrived, rationalized, and ethically unpersuasive as they are—left German industry in very healthy condition, at least from the perspective that seems to matter most: business.

Ferencz argues that there are always exceptions. Some German businessmen took remarkable steps to alleviate the Jewish plight and to save threatened lives. Men such as Hermann Graebe and Oskar Schindler are examples, along with lawyers such as Otto Kuester and Walter Schmidt, who spoke out on behalf of the survivors after the war. It should also be mentioned that some German courts did not hesitate to find in the survivors' favor. These exceptions, however, tended to prove the rule: both during the war and afterwards "too often it was only those who had nothing to be ashamed of who expressed a sense of guilt and culpability."[25] Failure to speak out is understandable, even from a moral point of view, under the duress of wartime in a Nazi state. After the war was over, it became less so, or perhaps it is even more understandable because practical rationality requires that business must get back to normal. Business did so.

Freeing the guilty

Nuremberg, once the site of Nazi rallies, became the scene for postwar trials that put German industrialists in the dock and prison: Alfried Krupp, 12 years; Walter Duerrfeld and Otto Ambros of I. G. Auschwitz, 8 years; and Carl Krauch, 6 years. None of the defendants in the I. G. Farben trial were found guilty for supplying poisonous gas to the concentration camp at Auschwitz.[26]

One other case is particularly noteworthy. In 1947, Friedrich Flick received a prison sentence of seven years for his support of the SS and for the use of slave labor in his vast industrial empire, Mitteldeutsche Stahlwerke, which "controlled over three hundred companies . . . [and] manufactured everything from toilet paper to dynamite."[27] Many of Flick's colleagues were acquitted altogether, but some of them joined their leader in jail. By January 1951, however, the American official in charge of such matters, John J. McCloy, had released them all. Good behavior figured into that decision, but of greater importance was the cold war.

Evidently, German industrial leadership was needed. Quickly it was back at work rebuilding its forces and its bank accounts. When Friedrich Flick died in the summer of 1972, he was the richest man in Germany and among the wealthiest in the world. He had managed well. So much so that he had paid nothing at all to his former Jewish slaves in spite of persistent efforts on their behalf. A fitting epitaph for this man

25. Ibid., p. 192.

26. See Hilberg, p. 696 n.
27. Ferencz, p. 156.

might be the pronouncement he made in self-defense at Nuremberg: "Nothing will convince us that we are war criminals."[28]

Flick's fate and disposition do not make an isolated case, and thus we need to wonder once again: What has happened to justice? What meaning is attached to human rights? If we search for "some credible set of theonomous or autonomous moral norms governing the conduct of men and nations," where are we left?[29]

CONCLUSION: CAN RIGHT MAKE MIGHT?

"The philosophers," asserted Karl Marx, "have only *interpreted* the world, in various ways; the point, however, is to *change* it."[30] Auschwitz did so. I. G. Farben, Friedrich Flick, and Rudolf Hoess contributed to that end as well. And Marx was not completely correct, because even thinking fostered by philosophical and religious minds advanced civilization—however unintentionally—toward the Final Solution. Such factors show how the world works, namely, that without might there seems to be little hope that theoretical right can prevail. In that cage is there any place to stand and say that right makes might?

Holocaust business contains few surprises for anyone who studies history, which G. F. W. Hegel so aptly called a slaughter-bench. At the same time, it cannot be denied that such realities provoke strong feelings that protest and rebel against

what has occurred. Senses of difference between right and wrong live within us, and the Holocaust helps to focus them. Even Heinrich Himmler knew as much. He could never quite be unaware of turmoil created in his men by orders to kill.

Hegel said that "the owl of Minerva spreads its wings only with the falling of the dusk."[31] He thought that philosophy could achieve understanding in retrospect, but that this success arrives too late where "instruction as to what the world ought to be" is concerned.[32] If Hegel is correct, the tools of moral philosophy and religious ethics are more meager than many persons have thought. Still, they have a role to play that nothing else can duplicate.

Moral reflection can clarify and intensify feelings of wrong prompted by Holocaust business. Such thinking can show the importance of those feelings by revealing what happens when they fail to work their way into practice. And yet that understanding alone does very little to change the world. We forget that fact at our peril. For example, if one wants to affirm the United Nations' declaration that "everyone has the right to life, liberty and security of person," it must be emphasized that such claims are as fragile as they are abstract. In truth, rights, liberty, and security of person are real only in specific times and places, only in actual political circumstances, or not at all. At least within history as we know it, apart from such concrete settings those ideals are little more than ideas. Granted, they are ideas that attract. They can lure out the best in people. They can even rally power-

28. Ibid., p. 155.

29. Rubenstein, p. 65.

30. Karl Marx, "Theses on Feuerbach," in *Marx and Engels: Basic Writings on Politics and Philosophy*, ed. Lewis S. Feuer (Garden City: Doubleday Anchor Books, 1959), p. 245 (Marx's italics).

31. G. W. F. Hegel, *Philosophy of Right*, trans. T. M. Knox (New York: Oxford University Press, 1967), p. 13.

32. Ibid., p. 12.

ful forces behind them. Indeed, they may have a transcendent status ordained by God. To assume, however, that they are more than ideas until men and women take responsibility to make them good may well be hope that is illusion.

Can right make might? The answer depends on will. To the degree that a sense of right dwells in feeling and thought, the right has reality, and it takes on greater depth and truth as it is tempered by critical questioning and insightful imagination. In their own way, such developments are advances in civilization, and yet they will change hardly anything unless will intervenes. Where was the spirit of Plato and Kant while six million died? The will to power that might have turned their ideas into actions to thwart Holocaust business arose too late, if at all.

Can right make might? Only a little it seems, and then might must carry on. Might will do so in any case, but how it does so still depends in part on "whether at the end of this tremendous development entirely new prophets will arise, or there will be a great rebirth of old ideas and ideals."[33] Even so, feelings and thoughts that condemn Holocaust business may be so weak as to be functionally insignificant. Our cage, then, appears to warrant an entry sign. Let it read *Arbeit Macht Frei*. Will those words provoke the good work that may set us free? Or will they merely mock us?

33. Weber, *Protestant Ethic*, p. 182.

ANNALS, AAPSS, **450**, July 1980

Children of Hippocrates: Doctors in Nazi Germany

By JACK S. BOOZER

ABSTRACT: One of the more unexplored yet frightening aspects of the Nazi years in Germany, 1933–45, is the conduct of the doctors during those years. Many of them abandoned the traditional guiding norms for the practice of medicine, archaically expressed in the Hippocratic oath, and proposed, carried out, and cooperated with medical experiments without the consent of subjects and with little promise of any contribution to medical science. Many also participated in research and other medical activities, such as euthanasia and mass sterilization, whose purposes had nothing to do with a contribution to medical knowledge that would eventually save or improve life, but were simply for the manipulation and killing of persons. These activities quickly fell under the control of Nazi ideology, with no protest on the basis of the norms of medical practice by societies of medical doctors and psychiatrists, and with little, albeit costly, protest by individuals. A brief survey of what the Medical case and the Auschwitz trial revealed about the conduct of the doctors raises the question of the status and effectiveness of a professional standard like the Hippocratic oath against the power of the state. This, in turn, raises the question about the basis of the rights of man outside of what is enacted and secured by a nation-state. In facing this question, an appeal is made for the nurture of care about human rights, among professional groups with transnational identities as well as among individuals and voluntary nonprofessional associations among the general citizenry. Finally, a claim is made for specific kinds of social-political responsibilities of doctors in modern society.

Jack S. Boozer is professor of religion in the College and Graduate School of Arts and Sciences, Emory University, Atlanta, Georgia. He received the B.Ph. and B.D. degrees from Emory University and the Ph.D. Degree from Boston University. He confronted the Holocaust as an American chaplain in Europe during World War II. His major interest lies between theology and ethics, an interest that is most recently manifest in his editing of a book on the ethics of Rudolf Otto, Rudolf Otto, Aufsätze sur Ethik, *to be published shortly.*

A COLLEAGUE who teaches the history of Germany and of the Nazi period remarked recently that the doctors in Germany had the worst record of all professional groups. Remembering Albert Einstein's claim that the Christian church was stronger than the universities, the newspaper editors, and other groups, and not being particularly proud of the record of the church, I found his comment puzzling. Perhaps the discussion of the Holocaust on other levels has tended to obscure the performance of the doctors, but the issue is an important one and will be discussed in relation to three questions: What did the German doctors do? What strength did professional ethics have with the doctors during this period? What are the social-political responsibilities of doctors in modern society?

WHAT DID THE DOCTORS DO?

It is inconceivable that a group of men trained in medicine and in official positions of power in German government circles could ignore the ethical principles of medicine and the unwritten law that a doctor should be nearer humanity than other men and that all experimental subjects should be volunteers.[1]

The most complete records of the questionable conduct of doctors in Germany, 1933–45, are those of the case of the United States military tribunal against *Karl Brandt et al.* at Nuremberg, 1946–47,[2] and those of

the Auschwitz trial in Frankfurt, 1963–65, the Federal Republic of West Germany against, or proceedings against, Robert Mulka and 21 others, including two dentists and one doctor.[3] The charges in the Nuremberg trial were mainly for war crimes and crimes against humanity, including medical experiments on human beings, sterilization, and euthanasia. The charges in the Auschwitz trial were for "murder and complicity in murder of individuals," and for "mass murder and complicity in mass murder."[4]

THE MEDICAL CASE

The case against *Karl Brandt et al.* included 23 defendants, 20 of whom were doctors. The indictment charged them on four counts: the common design or conspiracy, war crimes, crimes against humanity, and membership in a criminal organization.[5] The

---

1. Andrew C. Ivy, in *Doctors of Infamy*, Alexander Mitscherlich and Fred Mielke (New York: Henry Schuman), 1949, p. ix. Dr. Ivy was vice-president of the University of Illinois, scientific consultant to the prosecution, military tribunal no. 1, Nuremberg, 1946–47, in the case against *Karl Brandt et al.*, generally referred to as the Medical case or the Doctors trial.

2. Military tribunal no. 1, case 1: The United States of America against Karl Brandt, Siegfried Handloser, Paul Rostock, Oskar Schroeder, Karl Genzken, Karl Gebhardt, Kurt Blome, Rudolf Brandt, Joachim Rose, Siegfried Ruff, Hans Wolfgang Romberg, Viktor Brack, Hermann Becker-Freyseng, Georg August Weltz, Konrad Schaefer, Waldemar Hoven, Wilhelm Beiglboeck, Adolf Pokorny, Herta Oberheuser, and Fritz Fischer, *Defendants*.

3. The other defendants were Karl Höcker, Friedrich Wilhelm Boger, Hans Stark, Klaus Hubert Hermann, Dylewski, Pery Broad, Johann Schoberth, Bruno Schlage, Franz Johann Hofmann, Oswald Kaduk, Stefan Baretzki, Heinrich Bischoff, Johann Arthur Breitwieser, Dr. Franz Bernhard Lucas, Dr. Willi Frank, Dr. Willi Ludwig Schatz, Dr. Victor Capesius, Josef Klehr, Herbert Scherpe, Emil Hantl, Gerhard Neubert, and Emil Bednarek. The best source in English to my knowledge on this trial is given in ftn. no. 4. More extensive records may be found at the Central Office of the Land Judicial Authorities in Ludwigsburg, West Germany.

4. Bernd Naumann, *Auschwitz* (London: Pall Mall Press, 1966), p. 8.

5. *Trials of War Criminals* before the Nuernberg Military Tribunals under Control Council Law no. 10, vol. I (Washington, DC: GPO, n.d.), p. 10 ff (hereafter cited as TWC).

wording describing war crimes is typical.

(b) War Crimes. Atrocities or offenses against persons or property constituting violations of the laws or customs of war, including but not limited to, murder, ill treatment or deportation to slave labor or for any other purposes, of civilian population from occupied territory, murder or ill treatment of prisoners of war or persons on the seas, killing of hostages, plunder of public or private property, wanton destruction of cities, towns or villages, or devastation not justified by military necessity.[6]

It is interesting to note that paragraph 4 of that same document claims that the official position of any person in the state "does not free him from responsibility for a crime or entitle him to mitigation of punishment," but that the fact that a person commits a crime pursuant to the order of his government or of a superior, while not freeing him from responsibility for the crime, "may be considered in mitigation."[7] The claim that every person is responsible for a law higher than the state is significant, and is, indeed, contested during the trial. The higher law particularly in point is the Hippocratic oath, a professional standard which, in the terms of article II, would seem to stand above the law of the state, as would universal moral or specific religious law.[8]

The indictment under war crimes involved medical experiments, all using involuntary subjects, as follows: high-altitude, freezing, malaria, lost (mustard) gas, sulfanilamide,

seawater, epidemic jaundice, sterilization, spotted fever, poison, and incendiary bomb experiments; and bone, muscle, and nerve regeneration and bone transplantation experiments.[9] Most of these experiments were requested by the armed forces and were directly related to situations in the military or situations faced by the military. That was not the case, however, in the sterilization experiments. A closer look at that case illustrates the reasoning and actions of the doctors involved.

Mass sterilization

From about April, 1941, until about February, 1945, experiments with mass sterilization were conducted at the Ravensbrueck and Auschwitz concentration camps, mainly on Gypsies and Jewish men and women. These experiments were authorized to find a way of utilizing inmates to the maximum for forced labor while preventing them from procreating. Defendant Brandt described the purpose of the experiments in an affidavit.

Himmler was extremely interested in the development of a cheap and rapid sterilization method which could be used against enemies of Germany, such as the Russians, Poles, and Jews. One hopes thereby not only to defeat the enemy but to exterminate him. The capacity for work of the sterilized persons could be exploited by Germany, while the danger of propagation would be eliminated. As this mass sterilization was part of Himmler's racial theory, particular time and care were devoted to these sterilization experiments. Surgical sterilization was of course known in

6. TWC, Control Council Law no. 10, article II, par. 1, p. xvii.
   7. TWC, Control Council Law no. 10, article II, par. 4, p. xvii.
   8. Cf. June Goodfield, "Reflections on the Hippocratic Oath," *Hastings Center Studies* (Hastings-on-Hudson, NY: Hastings Center), 1(2): 79–92 (1973).

9. TWC, pp. 11–14. Most of the remaining thousand pages of vol. I contain details, documents, and excerpts of testimony about these charges and the strange case of the Skeletons of Jews to complete the collection at the University of Strasbourg.

Germany and applied; this included castration. For mass application, however, this procedure was considered as too slow and too expensive. It was further desired that a procedure be found which would result in sterilization that was not immediately noticeable.[10]

Although the racial policies of the Third Reich were related to some of the other experiments, they affected not the experiments themselves but the "pool" of persons in confinement who might be experimental subjects. In the case of the mass sterilization experiments, race became the central issue. In a letter from Viktor Brack to Himmler (June, 1942), the double intention of getting all the labor benefit from the Jews possible and of destroying them is clear.[11]

Among 10 millions of Jews in Europe there are, I figure, at least 2–3 millions of men and women who are fit enough to work. Considering the extraordinary difficulties the labor problem presents us with, I hold the view that these 2–3 millions should be specially selected and preserved. This can, however, only be done if, at the same time they are rendered incapable to propagate. . . . Sterilization, as normally performed on persons with hereditary diseases, is here out of the question, because it takes too long and is too expensive. Castration by X-ray however is not only relatively cheap, but also can be performed on many thousands in the shortest time. I think, that at this time it is already irrelevant whether people in question become aware of having been castrated after some weeks or months once they feel the effects.[12]

In August, 1942, Himmler indicated to Brack that he would be very much interested in seeing that sterilization by X-rays be tried out at least once in one series of experiments.[13] When the strategy of mass sterilization was adopted, consideration was given to three methods: by medication, by intrauterine irritation, and by X-rays.

The proposal for mass sterilization through the use of caladium sequinum, to be taken by mouth by males and females, was made to Himmler by Dr. Pokorny in a letter of October, 1941. In the proposal he writes, "The thought that the 3 million Bolsheviks, at present German prisoners, could be sterilized so that they could be used as laborers but be prevented from reproduction, opens the most far-reaching perspectives."[14] Although the military tribunal did not possess as much hard evidence as it desired to establish that the experiments with sterilization by medicine actually took place and to determine upon how many persons and with what results, the tribunal was satisfied that experiments had actually been conducted in concentration camps, that there had been difficulty producing sufficient qualities of caladium sequinum, and that the results were not clear. In his affidavit, defendant Brandt admitted that the experiments were conducted.[15]

In May, 1942, Dr. Clauberg proposed an experiment with female inmates of camps entailing "a single injection made from the entrance to the uterus in the course of the

---

10. Document NO-440, Pros. Ex. 141, quoted in translation in TWC, vol. I, pp. 695–96.

11. Cf. Richard Rubenstein's alarming essay, *The Cunning of History* (New York: Harper & Row, 1975), indicating the efficiency of utilizing the labor and then destroying unwanted population.

12. Letter printed in translation, Document NO-205, Pros. Ex. 163, in TWC, vol. I, pp. 721–22.

13. Letter of August 11, 1942, printed in translation, Document NO-206, Pros. Ex. 164, in TWC, Vol. I, pp. 722–723.

14. Pokorny to Himmler, printed in translation, Document NO-035, Pros. Ex. 142, in TWC, vol. I, pp. 713–14.

15. Cited in translation of Prosecution Document NO-440, Pros. Ex. 141, in TWC, vol. I, p. 699.

usual customary gynecological examination known to every physician."[16] Clauberg claims that the method he contrived "to achieve the sterilization of the female organism without operation is as good as perfected" and that with one adequately trained physician with ten assistants in one adequately equipped place, several hundred if not a thousand sterilizations could take place a day. Of course, the experimental subject would not know what was being done to her.

Again Brandt referred to this experiment at Auschwitz in his affidavit. "Dr. Clauberg developed further a method for the sterilization of women. This method was based upon the injection of an irritating solution into the uterus. Clauberg conducted widespread experiments on Jewish women and Gypsies in the Auschwitz concentration camp. Several thousand women were sterilized by Clauberg in Auschwitz."[17]

Defendant Brack proposed to Himmler sterilization of Jews by X-ray as early as the spring of 1941, claiming that with 20 X-ray installations, 3,000 to 4,000 persons could be sterilized a day. The details of the program must be grasped if one is to assess realistically what medical procedures were proposed by some "children of Hippocrates" whose first rule for centuries has been: "Do no harm."

In general, an irradiation period of 2 minutes for men, 3 minutes for women, with the highest voltage, a thin filter and at a short distance, ought to be sufficient. There is, however, a disadvantage that has to be put up with: as it is impossible unnoticeably to cover the rest of the body with lead, the other

tissues of the body will be injured, and radiologic malaise, the so-called "Roentgenkater," will ensue. If the X-ray intensity is too high, those parts of the skin which the rays have reached will exhibit symptoms of burns—varying in intensity in individual cases—in the course of the following days or weeks.

One practical way of proceeding would be, for instance, to let the persons to be treated approach a counter, where they could be asked to answer some questions or to fill in forms, which would take them 2 or 3 minutes. The official sitting behind the counter could operate the installation in such a way as to turn a switch which would activate the two valves simultaneously (since the irradiation has to operate from both sides). With a two-valve installation about 150–200 persons could then be sterilized per day, and therefore, with 20 such installations as many as 3,000–4,000 persons per day. . . . However, it seems to be impossible to do this in such a way that the persons concerned do not sooner or later realize with certainty that they have been sterilized or castrated by X-rays.[18]

In June of 1942, after the invasion of Russia had begun successfully, Brack wrote Himmler again, pressing the case for X-ray sterilization as a way of handling both the labor and the Jewish problems (see the previous excerpt). It is important to note that in the 1941 letter, Brack considered the fact that people would come to know about it a reservation on the X-ray project. In the 1942 letter, a quite different statement is made: "I think, that at this time it is already irrelevant whether the people in question become aware of having been castrated after some weeks or months once they feel the effects." Awareness about the shift to the Final Solution of the Jewish

---

16. Clauberg to Himmler, 7 June 1943, translation, Document NO-212, Pros. Ex. 173, in TWC, vol. I, pp. 730–32.

17. Cited in translation, Document NO-440, Pros. Ex. 141, in TWC, vol. I, p. 701.

18. Brack to Himmler, 28 March 1941, translation of letter and report, Document NO-203, Pros. Ex. 161, in TWC, vol. I, pp. 719–21.

question must have been fairly general among the defendants by June of 1942. In a statement in another document, Viktor Brack is even more explicit: "In 1941 it was an 'open' secret in higher Party circles that those in power proposed to exterminate the entire Jewish population in Germany and in the occupied territories."[19]

Over a hundred subjects—Polish, Russian, and French inmates who were young and healthy—were selected involuntarily for these experiments. Nearly all of the experimental subjects were killed because the severe X-ray burns made it impossible for them to work. In the light of that outcome of the experiment, Viktor Brack's statement in direct examination at the trial is strange if not bizarre: "I never really counted on the realization of these experiments and I never had any intention of submitting a serious proposal to Himmler which would cause the sterilization of millions of Jews. . . . If this suggestion had been serious on my part I would have had to be a fanatical Jew hater, and I think I have already proved that I was not such a person."[20] How different from the letters of 1941 and 1942!

Euthanasia

The other action which the doctors, including the psychiatrists, participated in and which had nothing explicitly to do with the armed forces was euthanasia. Here, as was the case with sterilization, ideology was dominant, and the later application of the technology of euthanasia to the racial doctrine of the party was ominous.

In paragraph 9 of Count Two of the indictment, defendants Karl Brandt, Blome, Brack, and Hoven were accused of being involved in the so-called euthanasia program of the German Reich: "This program involved the systematic and secret execution of the aged, insane, incurably ill, of deformed children, and other persons, by gas, lethal injections, and diverse other means in nursing homes, hospitals, and asylums. . . . German doctors involved in the 'euthanasia' program were also sent to Eastern occupied countries to assist in the mass extermination of Jews."[21]

Hitler himself began this program by a decree signed in late October, 1939, but back-dated to 1 September 1939:[22] "Reichsleiter Bouhler and Dr. Brandt, M.D., are charged with the responsibility of enlarging the authority of certain physicians to be designated by name in such a manner that persons who, according to human judgment, are incurable can, upon a most careful diagnosis of their condition of sickness, be accorded a mercy death."[23]

The program was put into effect quickly and extensively, screened from the public by the names of the three groups that carried it out: the Reich Association, Hospital, and Nursing Establishment, which located patients by the use of questionnaires; the Charitable Foundation for Institutional Care, which handled finances for the project; and the Non-Profit Patient-Transport Corporation, which moved the patients to the euthanasia institutions, the main ones being Hadamar, Hartheim, Grafeneck, Brandenberg-on-

19. Document NO. 426, quoted in translation in Mitscherlich and Mielke, p. 135.
20. Excerpt from testimony, printed in translation in TWC, vol. I, p. 738.

21. TWC, vol. I, p. 15.
22. Mitscherlich and Mielke, p. 92.
23. Hitler to Karl Brandt and Bouhler, translation, document NO-630-PS, Pros. Ex. 330, in TWC, vol. I, p. 848.

Havel, and Sonnenstein. Neither the patients nor the next of kin were consulted in any decisions, and the decision of a physician or psychiatrist must have been made quite superficially because consultants processed over a hundred cases a day. In one instance, Dr. Pfannmueller evaluated 2,109 cases between November 14 and 1 December 1940.[24]

Gradually the program was extended to the insane, the "useless eaters," the deformed children, the "socially unfit," and the concentration camp inmates. "Healthy Jews were exterminated without examination."[25] The program began to operate so mechanically that "standard text" notices were sent to families of euthanasia victims along with urns of ashes. Institutional records were also made routine, as is indicated by the following: "I have the honor to inform you that the female patients transferred from your institution on 8 November 1940 to the institution in Grafeneck, Bemberg, Sonnenstein, and Hartheim all died in November of last year." This memo was dated 6 May 1941.[26] Medical research was tied to some euthanasia programs. For example, Professor Hallervorden requested 600 brains from subjects at euthanasia institutions, with the cooperation of the Non-Profit Patient-Transport Corporation. Dr. Mennecke said that Professor Carl Schneider at Heidelberg also received brains for research.

There are records of protests against the euthanasia program by two churches. Pastor Braune as chairman of the executive committee of the Domestic Welfare Council of the Protestant church wrote a 15-page memorial on behalf of the council in which he strongly protested the program: "It is urgently necessary to halt these measures as quickly as possible, since they strike sharply at the moral foundation of the nation as a whole."[27] He also raised questions about the "socially unfit," calling attention to the vagueness and danger of such a category. The bishop of Limburg, Dr. Hilfrich, wrote a protest on behalf of the Roman Catholic church on 13 August 1941. This protest focuses specifically on the destruction of so-called useless life and on the killing at Hadamar in which families received the same notices saying that their loved ones had died of an infectious disease and had had to be cremated. Bishop Hilfrich emphasized the erosion of authority as a result of these illegal killings and of the deceptiveness practiced to cover the illicit activity: "High authority as a moral concept has suffered a severe shock as a result of these happenings."[28] A protest was also written by the archbishop of Munich-Freising, Cardinal Faulhaber, on 6 October 1940. Records of protest by medical societies or psychiatric societies are apparently not to be found. At least one physician, however, Dr. Schlaich, head of the mental institution at Stettin, did write an inquiry and protest, including the following:

If the government actually wishes to carry out the extermination of these patients, or at least of certain categories of these mental patients, should not a clearly formulated law be proclaimed— one for which responsibility is openly taken before the people, that offers every individual the guarantee that his verdict of death or claim to life is carefully examined, and that entitles the families

---

24. Mitscherlich and Mielke, p. 100.
25. TWC, vol. I, p. 809.
26. TWC, vol. I, p. 852.

27. Cited in translation in Mitscherlich and Mielke, p. 107.
28. Document 615-PS, Pros. Ex. 246, printed in translation in TWC, vol. I, pp. 845–47.

too to voice their opinions, as in the case of the Law for prevention of Progeny With Hereditary Diseases?[29]

As a result of these and other protests, the euthanasia program was temporarily reduced or stopped, only to be put back into action later and then to serve as a model for the mass killing of Jews and others after 1941. It is clear that psychiatrists as well as other physicians played strategic roles in planning and carrying out the euthanasia program, even of the "socially unfit."[30] The number of persons killed in the euthanasia program is variously estimated from 40,000 to more than a million.

THE AUSCHWITZ CASE

The proceedings against Mulka and others have particular interest because of one medical doctor who was a defendant. Dr. Franz Lucas was accused of assisting in the selection of prisoners on the ramp at Birkenau and of having supervised the insertion of Zyklon B gas into the gas chambers. One of the many ironies of the trials was that Dr. Mengele, the well-known killer at Auschwitz, was and remains still at large, and that Dr. Lucas, praised by many witnesses for his gentleness, assistance, and encouragement, was in the block.

Some witnesses were present at the trial and testified against Dr. Lucas. It was established that he was, in fact, at Auschwitz for a few months, and that he participated in the selection process on the ramp. At the same time, it appears that he was suspected of "favoring prisoners"

and was ordered to the ramp under the threat that if he refused to obey the order, he would be arrested on the spot. Mainly, however, there are exceptional, almost unbelievable, testimonies in praise of Dr. Lucas.

Louise Le Porz, a French doctor, praised Dr. Lucas, whom she had known at the Ravensbrueck concentration camp. She said that Dr. Lucas had gotten drugs for sick prisoners and had even given them food from his own ration. Such a thing was unheard of, "an SS man who showed signs of humanity. . . . His attitude was very different from that of the other German military doctors. He did not look on us as unacceptable people; he talked to us. He even examined the patients." She claimed further that he had advised her to remove as many sick people as possible from the hospital. "He said something terrible would happen. Thus he gave me advice which helped me save some fellow prisoners from the gas chambers. I met no other doctor who helped us, only him: Dr. Lucas." To this testimony, Dr. Lucas said only, "I do not remember the witness."[31]

Another witness who spoke for Dr. Lucas was Cäcilie Neideck who had known Dr. Lucas at Ravensbrueck. She, too, told of how he stole from the SS pharmacy, got cod-liver oil and calcium for the prisoners, and bought food with his own money and smuggled it into the camp. "He was ostracized by his comrades; he was a loner. . . . I was imprisoned for more than eight years. I can say with a clear conscience that he was the only doctor who treated us humanely. To us he was a comrade, friend, brother, and father all rolled into one. Had it not been for Dr. Lucas thousands more would have per-

29. Quoted in Mitscherlich and Mielke, pp. 109–10.

30. Cf. Fredric Wertham, *The Sign of Cain* (New York: Macmillan, 1966), especially ch. 9; *see also* Peter Breggin, "The Psychiatric Holocaust," *Penthouse*, Jan. 1979, pp. 81 ff.

31. Naumann, p. 313.

ished." When she had finished her testimony, Dr. Lucas was asked if he wished to say anything. He said only, "I did not know the name of the witness until now."[32]

Most of the accused at this trial made sport of the entire process. "Only one of the defendants, the physician Dr. Lucas, does not show open contempt for the court, does not laugh, insult witnesses, demand that the prosecuting attorneys apologize, and try to have fun with the others. One doesn't quite understand why he is there at all, for he seems the very opposite of an 'intolerable case.'"[33] He was the only defendant who agreed to go with the court to Auschwitz. His closing statement to the court was brief:

Your honor! On the day on which against my will I was assigned to duty in the National Socialist concentration camp began a chapter in my life from which I will never recover. Forced to work on the ramp I naturally sought to save the lives of as many Jewish prisoners as possible. But today as then, I am torn by the question: "And what about the others?" I have fought my way toward the truth. I can only hope that you will arrive at a verdict that will help me to free myself from my bonds and begin a new life.[34]

The court found Dr. Lucas guilty of complicity in joint murder on at least four separate occasions of at least 1,000 persons each, and sentenced him to what was the minimum required penalty according to German law, a total of three years and three months at hard labor. The opinion of the court on Dr. Lucas was striking.

The court believes the defendant—who initially denied having worked on the

ramp and in the gas chambers—did not enjoy his duty on the ramp and in the gas chambers and that he tried to get out of it. But "when his attempts were not successful he chose the way of least resistance" and participated in four selections, in which at least 1,000 persons found their way into the gas chambers.

Lucas' conduct in Auschwitz proved, though, that he did not agree with the extermination plan; he definitely did not perform any "voluntary" jobs. "On the contrary, prisoners have testified that he came to the assistance of the sick." The court believes the statement of the defendant that he was caught in a net and did not have the strength to get out. Also, he had made a confession and shown some understanding. The court believes that the minimum punishment should be meted out.[35]

When Dr. Lucas was first confronted with orders which went against his conscience and his oath as a doctor, he sought counsel from the church and from a high-ranking jurist. The counsel of the bishop was: "Immoral orders must not be obeyed, but that did not mean that one had to risk one's own life." The jurist emphasized the authority of the state and justified the horrors because of the war.[36] The net was strong and tight, and the struggle of conscience and for Hippocrates was, for Dr. Lucas, a lonely one indeed.

What happened to personal and professional ethics in this period?

The first reaction of many people to the discovery of tyranny, brutality, and the kind of designed killing recounted in the two trials is to move with "righteous" indignation to convict and punish the criminals. Indeed, many persons have wanted to be the law themselves and to take out their vengeance on the killers. That must have happened in numbers of instances immediately after

32. Ibid., pp. 322–23.
33. Hannah Arendt, "Introduction," in Naumann, p. xvi.
34. Naumann, p. 408.

35. Ibid., pp. 423–24.
36. Arendt, p. xxvi.

World War II. Simon Wiesenthal, on the other hand, has steadily and deliberately rejected that strategy in favor of turning to the courts, even when it was difficult to procure witnesses and when the people in Germany were not sympathetic to the stretching out of trials against German people for crimes in the Nazi period.

As we have seen, the U.S. government acted shortly after the war to identify, charge, and try the supposed guilty, and to punish them if they were found guilty. The same thing happened within the West German government when accusations began to pile up against persons at Auschwitz. In all these cases, there was a legitimate and important interest in finding the culprits and bringing them to justice. As strained, as tedious, as questionable, as fallible, and as vulnerable as those proceedings were, they represented a constructive effort to affirm the bond of law governing peoples, and they simply had to take place.

But if the crime was beyond "human comprehensibility," so was justice beyond "human jurisprudence." The possibility of justice after the fact was as impossible as was effective protest before the fact. The event recounted about Dr. Mengele by Bruno Bettelheim lays bare the utter illogic of it all. With a pregnant woman at Auschwitz, Dr. Mengele "took all correct medical precautions during childbirth, rigorously observing all aseptic principles, cutting the umbilical cord with greatest care, etc. But only half an hour later he sent mother and infant to be burned in the crematorium."[37]

37. Bruno Bettelheim, *The Informed Heart* (New York: Avon Books, 1973), p. 255. Bettelheim borrows the account from D. Lengyel, *Five Chimneys, The Story of Auschwitz* (Chicago: Ziff Davis), 1947.

Experimentation

Granted the necessity of seeking justice and the impossibility of achieving it in these cases, we must face those events now on quite different levels. A first level of issues lies close to the events. In the Medical case, how many of the experiments resulted in research that advanced medical science? The prosecution admitted that the experiments yielded information valuable for the German armed forces. But at the same time, the prosecution contended that "the true object of these experiments was not how to rescue or to cure, but how to destroy and kill. The sterilization experiments were, it is clear, purely destructive in purpose. The prisoners at Buchenwald who were shot with poisoned bullets were not guinea pigs to test an antidote for the poison; their murderers really wanted to know how quickly the poison would kill."[38]

Almost without exception, the defendants claimed the legitimacy of their experiments in terms of the advancement of science. In the seawater experiment, for example, 44 subjects, most of them Gypsies, were taken from Dachau. The experiment called for them to be fed seawater with Berkatit with the full knowledge that death would inevitably result from 12 days of that diet. Yet in the final statement on behalf of defendant Becker-Freyseng, the following is claimed: "Therefore, in my opinion, it has been proved that Dr. Becker-Freyseng considered these experiments necessary and that he was entitled to consider them necessary. And this question alone can be made the basis of an inquiry into his guilt under criminal law. . . . Inso-

38. TWC, vol. I, p. 37; *see also* vol. II, pp. 61 ff.

far, I consider it proved that the planning of these experiments was in no way objectionable."[39] The subjection of 44 involuntary subjects to probable death to learn whether shipwreck survival kits should contain Berkatit with instructions to take it with seawater was claimed as legitimate research contributing to medical science.

Another question concerns the position of medical societies in Germany. Reports of many of these experiments were made to medical associations and societies with no question raised about informed consent, about consideration of the risk and gain factor, or about the positive contributions to medical knowledge. It would seem that, at least at strategic times, the forthright challenge of a government-sponsored program as a violation of medical standards would have had some effect and would have involved little danger. Cases of recorded protest were by individuals and were at considerable risk. In deciding a crucial moral question in medicine, Dr. Lucas was not only abandoned by his bishop- and his jurist-friend, he was also abandoned by the professional medical associations in Germany. It was a strange fruit of German culture that institutions and professional groups were silent on crucial questions affecting the integrity of the group, while a few heroic individuals, quite alone, put their lives and careers in jeopardy and opposed the power of the state in the name of a higher law.

Response of doctors

A final question of this previously mentioned level concerns the response of the doctors who were accused of crimes during the war. One might have hoped that the public exposure of the record of experimentation and the murder of millions might have caused the accused to respond with some admission of the violation of the standards of medicine. But most of them persisted in living the bizarre picture of things and pleaded their innocence precisely on the basis of those standards of medicine. Dr. Lucas was an example to the contrary. So was Dr. Fritz Klein who was executed after signing a confession of guilt: "I recognize that I am responsible for the slaying of thousands, particularly at Auschwitz, as are all the others, from the top down."[40] With such a response, there is a chance for medicine, for here self-interest, survival, and the will of the state are subordinated to a higher law of humanity and the fundamental tradition of medicine to heal and to promote life.

A second level of question concerns how all of this could have happened to many doctors in Germany. Two Germans, Dr. Alexander Mitscherlich, head of the German Medical Commission to military tribunal no. 1, and Fred Mielke agree with Bruno Bettelheim on the answer to this question. The root of the problem lies in the dominance of objectivity, or facelessness in "an age without mercy." As Mitscherlich and Mielke see it after observing the whole of the medical case:

Only the secret kinship between the practices of science and politics can explain why throughout this trial the names of high-ranking men of science were mentioned—men who perhaps themselves committed no culpable act, but who nevertheless took an objective interest in all the things that were to become the cruel destiny of defenseless men. A profound inhumanity had long

39. TWC, vol. II, pp. 63–64.

40. Naumann, p. 197.

been presaged. This is the alchemy of the modern age, the transmogrification of subject into object, of man into a thing against which the destructive urge may wreak its fury without constraint.[41]

Bruno Bettelheim speaks his distress about the matter in commenting on the autobiographical account of Dr. Nyiszli, a prisoner serving as research physician at Auschwitz.[42] Dr. Nyiszli was proud to be working in "one of the most qualified medical centers in the Third Reich," though it was occupied mainly with proving falsehoods. How could he have done that and survived as a doctor?

The answer was: by taking pride in his professional skills, irrespective of what purpose they were used for. Again and again his pride in his professional skill permeates his story of his own and other prisoners' sufferings. The important issue here is that Dr. Nyiszli, Dr. Mengele, and hundreds of other far more prominent physicians . . . were participants in these human experiments and in the pseudo-scientific investigations that went with them. It is this pride in professional skill and knowledge, irrespective of moral implication, this is so dangerous. As a feature of modern society oriented toward technological competence it is still with us, though the concentration camps and crematoria are no longer here. Auschwitz is gone, but as long as this attitude remains with us we shall not be safe from the indifference to life at its core.[43]

One could not expect the doctors to have practiced and met in associations oblivious to the social and political context in which they and their patients had lived. On the other hand, it also seems reasonable to expect a professional association to nurture and keep alive the central and binding attitudes and commitments of the profession. That does not imply that professionals other than doctors did any better under the circumstances. Nor does it suggest that doctors should have been morally better than other persons. What is claimed is that doctors as a professional group have a norm or ideal as doctors which the state did not create and which the state should not have the power to manipulate or destroy. The two German observers of the Medical trial seem to agree. "We have shown, moreover, the doom awaiting a science that permits itself to be swept along by a political ideology, apparently in the direction of its own goals, only to see itself suddenly engaged in the organization of murder."[44]

Response of Western cultures

The third and more ominous level of question is raised by the Nazi years but applies to the whole of Western culture as well as to Germany. That concerns the heritage of the Enlightenment and the status of the ideals of reason, justice, equality, and tolerance to which we so easily give lip service. The rejection of these by the Nazis who combined *Volk* with racist claims and the "near success" of the effort, forces persons in the West to examine this question with realistic and forthright care. The question is sharply and inescapably posed by Hannah Arendt and Richard Rubenstein.

Arendt discusses the issue in her essay on totalitarianism: "The insane manufacture of corpses is preceded by the historically and politically intelligible preparation of living corpses. . . . This in turn could only happen because the Rights

41. Mitscherlich and Mielke, p. 152.

42. Miklos Nyiszli, *Auschwitz: A Doctor's Eyewitness Account* (New York: Frederick Fell,), 1960.

43. Bettelheim, p. 256.

44. Mitscherlich and Mielke, p. 154.

of Man, which had never been philosophically established but merely formulated, which had never been politically secured but merely proclaimed, have, in their traditional form, lost all validity."[45] Rubenstein goes further in his book on the Holocaust and the American future.

Yet if Auschwitz has taught us the hazards of statelessness, it can also teach us that membership in a political community is no longer a guarantee of the most elemental human rights. . . . The dreadful history of Europe's Jews has demonstrated that *rights do not belong to men by nature.* To the extent that men have rights, they have them only as members of the polis, the political community, and there is no polis or Christian commonwealth of nations. . . . Outside of the polis there are no inborn restraints on the human exercise of destructive power.[46]

It would be a mistake to take these questions lightly. We know too well the failure of noble claims for all persons that was pronounced by the United Nations, the nation-states, and the ethical and religious societies to protect and defend persons under various kinds of assault. To be sure, the process of securing rights is as important as is recognizing them. But it would also be a mistake to limit the meaning of rights to those which are secured by the power of the state. If a right is valid only if it is secured by military, police, economic, or political power, then there is no separate status of rights outside these powers. That would mean that power makes rights, which, in effect, means to deny rights altogether. Rights would only mean

what the power of the state, or of the polis, decides to punish or reward.

The question as put by Arendt and Rubenstein invites two observations. First, while recognizing the necessity of a political process that secures rights, it would be naive to assume that any state could secure rights fully and completely. Not even power in a totalitarian state is isolated from the power of other states. And within a state total control as well as an unchanging policy are not likely. There is inevitable risk on the part of anyone who claims rights on a basis other than the power of the state. One should consider the likelihood, therefore, that the state with all its powers can neither fully secure nor fully deny human rights. Second, the process of securing rights is a complex one entailing persuasion, voluntary associations, and self-understanding and consciousness of persons as well as the instrumentalities of power. For example, the increased recognition of the importance of informed consent in medical procedures moves on the basis of voluntary restraint by physicians and others as well as by enacted law.

The totalitarian years in Germany were tragic and forbid us the naiveté of thinking such brutality to be humanly impossible. The possibility of doing away with "surplus people" in many states is real and frightening. Even so, it would be an unwarranted concession to nazism to conclude, as Rubenstein apparently does, that there are no rights except those created by force.

WHAT ARE THE SOCIAL-POLITICAL RESPONSIBILITIES OF DOCTORS IN MODERN SOCIETY?

It has been assumed in this article that the practice of medicine is both

45. Hannah Arendt, *The Origins of Totalitarianism* (New York: The World Publishing Co., 1958), p. 447.

46. Richard Rubenstein, *The Cunning of History* (New York: Harper & Row, 1975), pp. 87, 89.

an art and a science and that as such it involves a competence based both on skill and on a norm or standard that constantly guides one and to which one is subject. It is on the basis of the expectation of that skill and that normative tradition that society bestows upon a doctor the "privilege" of the practice of medicine. The privilege and the responsibility cohere and are inseparable. With the erosion of the responsibility, an erosion of the privilege is inevitable. Without attempting to be comprehensive, I suggest that the responsibilities fall into two categories, those to the patient and those to society. Responsibility to the patient centers on confidentiality; assisting the life, health, and wholeness of the patient; protecting the patient who, for whatever reason, has limited self-control; and refusing to take advantage of the patient's confidence, weakness, or dependency. The first rule: "Do no harm" is assumed, and "serving life" does not mean simple longevity but is always a combination of longevity and quality of life.

With the increased effect of society and the natural and human environment on individuals, the social responsibilities of doctors become more important. Although this includes keeping costs down and avoiding unnecessary redundancy, the primary social responsibility is to alert society about social pathology that shows up first in the casualties who turn to physicians for treatment. This does not necessarily entail political lobbying, but that is not excluded. If through one's special skill the doctor discovers what threatens health or wholeness, he is obligated to make society aware of those things whether they be pollutants in the air or water, the inhalation of tobacco

smoke, the use of drugs, malnutrition, faults in exercise, intimidation, or physical, psychological, ethical, or religious abuse.

The doctor is not expected to control society, but he is expected from the perspective of his or her privileged position to advise society as to the forces operative in that society which make for life and those which make for death, whether or not that advice is welcomed by the state.

This investigation has led us to recognize that many doctors in Germany between 1933 and 1945 abandoned their professional ideals and traditions and sponsored or cooperated in appallingly brutal experiments and practices desired by Nazi ideology. Without placing extraordinary blame on the doctors, their record, along with those in other professional groups, forced us to question the status of human rights that are not secured by the convictions of the populace and by the power of the state.

I have concluded that rights are not restricted to those persons and things which the state has the power to recognize and reward, yet I have insisted on the importance of political sanction as one way of securing rights. Because rights are also secured by the will of the people, both for all persons and within the traditions and privileges of special groups, I have urged the importance of the nurturing of norms and ideals in professional associations which transcend citizenship in particular states. There is no assurance that any or all of these activities will assure the protection of rights in all circumstances. But there is a possibility that these measures will assure rights in many if not most circumstances. The alternatives seem to be indifference or submission to force which, even in the light of the Nazi years, are unnecessary compromises and restrictions on human possibilities. Danish churchmen proclaimed, "We had rather die with the Jews than to live with Hitler." Our choice may be either to die claiming and working to secure human rights or to live only by the dignity, the vitalities, and the privileges which the state creates and sustains by force.

The Ghetto as a Form of Government

By RAUL HILBERG

ABSTRACT: Isaiah Trunk's classic study of the Jewish Councils in Eastern Europe under the Nazi regime points to four major conclusions. (1) The ghetto was a captive city-state, totally subordinate to German authority while remainng a Jewish entity with traditions and expectations rooted in Jewish experience. The Jewish councils that were placed in charge of the ghettos were facing a dilemma in that they could not follow German instructions without hurting Jews and could not help Jews without obeying the Germans. (2) As a socioeconomic unit, the ghetto was hovering between life and death. The Jewish population could not support itself indefinitely by trading with the outside world; impoverishment spelled out its doom. (3) For the incarcerated Jews, the ghetto was also a mirage. It instilled thoughts of normalcy and continuity in the Jewish community at a time when the Germans were preparing for deportations of the victims to death camps. (4) Finally, the ghetto councils and their police organs were a self-destructive mechanism insofar as they confiscated assets or recruited labor and, in the end, rounded up the people for transport in trains waiting nearby.

Raul Hilberg, who received his Ph.D. from Columbia University, is a John G. McCullough Professor of Political Science at the University of Vermont and a member of the President's Commission on the Holocaust. His work, The Destruction of the European Jews, *is a description of the step-by-step process in the course of which the Jews were defined, expropriated, concentrated, and killed. He is the editor of* Documents of Destruction *and coeditor of* The Warsaw Diary of Adam Czerniakow. *His articles deal with German motivations, ghettos, the German railroads, the* Einsatzgruppen, *and concentration camps.*

IN 1972, MORE than a quarter of a century after the end of the Holocaust, Isaiah Trunk published his pathbreaking *Judenrat*, the first major attempt to portray in systematic terms the institutions and conditions of Jewish life in the ghettos of Nazi Eastern Europe.[1] It is a big volume, some 700 pages long, but it is also, despite its size, an understated work, for Trunk is one of those uncommon authors who promises less than he delivers. His preface deals with limits and limitations: an outline of Nazi administration in the East and a recital of sources at his disposal. The introduction, which was written by Jacob Robinson, is partly philosophical, partly polemic, and in no event foreshadows the dimensions of the contents. The substantive account is presented by Trunk in ordinary matter-of-fact language without intensification or climax. As he traverses his terrain, from schools to synagogues, or from labor to deportations, his tone remains constant. In this evenness, Trunk has managed to submerge everything: his range, depth, and findings.

The title of the book is *Judenrat*, "the Jewish Council," or, rather, hundreds of them in various Eastern European ghettos. Trunk wanted to "achieve an objective history of the councils," and thereby "find the key to internal Jewish history under Nazi rule,"[2] but his book is not merely a depiction of that key; it deals with the whole house, for it is a full-scale political, economic, and social history of the ghetto as such. The various headings of chapters and subchapters indicate the scope of the

discussion which comprises a gamut of topics including organizational developments in the ghetto bureaucracy, commissions, and police; the problem areas of finances, taxes, production, and purchases; and programs involving bathhouses, kitchens, welfare, or medical aid.

There is a similar richness of documentation. Although Trunk calls special attention in the preface to a survey which netted replies from 927 respondents concerning 740 former council members and 112 ghetto police, this questionnaire material constitutes only about 5 percent of the 2,000 citations in the notes, which are filled with references to orders issued by German supervisory agencies, reports of councils to the Germans, minutes of council meetings, newspapers, diaries, memoirs, and memorial books. Text and sources reveal the extent of Trunk's effort, and intricate facts on every page reflect the author's long preoccupation with numerous aspects of ghetto life.[3]

Trunk cautions against overgeneralization. At the outset he stresses the importance of local conditions and the individuality of leaders in the Jewish communities.[4] Yet he does not present the Warsaw ghetto in one chapter, Lodz in another, and additional ghettos down the line. The fragmentary nature of the source material would not in any case have allowed for an approach of that kind. Instead, he addresses himself to the

---

1. Isaiah Trunk, *Judenrat—The Jewish Councils in Eastern Europe under Nazi Occupation* (New York: Macmillan, 1972).

2. Ibid., p. xviii.

3. Trunk does concentrate his attention on ghettos that were located within the prewar boundaries of Poland and Lithuania. There are a few details about Riga in Latvia and Minsk in White Russia, but the ghettos farther east as well as the Jewish communities under Rumanian administration between the Dniester and the Bug are almost entirely, if understandably, omitted.

4. Trunk, pp. xvii, xviii.

essence of the ghettos, that is, the mode of their operations in regard to such all-pervasive problems as crowding, hunger, or the demands of the Germans; and he does so implicitly by using almost any item of information about a particular ghetto as illustrative of the situation in all of them. In this manner, he builds a mosaic which is generalization par excellence.

More than that, his whole book is a demonstration rather than a mere assertion that, notwithstanding the different internal structures of the Jewish communities or the diversity of personalities in the councils, the stories of all of these ghettos must be read as one history. This impression is underscored when we consider that Jewish perceptions and reactions were remarkably similar across the occupied territories, despite the relative isolation of the communities and their councils from each other. In the final analysis, the variation among ghettos is not as crucial as their commonality, nor is it primarily the classification of ghettos in terms of demographic or economic factors that counts, but the singularity of meaning in the phrase "Jewish ghetto" compared with everything else that has transpired in recent times throughout the world.

If Trunk had done no more than organize a compendium of facts in subject-matter categories, he would have furnished us with significant additions to our knowledge, but beyond any compilation, he also set forth a series of propositions about the nature of the ghettos and of the councils that governed them. Of course, it would be useless to look for these thoughts in some final chapter—Trunk eschews discoveries, and there is no recapitulation at the end. His summation is confined to five pages and there he considers

solely an issue raised by Jacob Robinson in the introduction: the question of the councils' "collaboration" with the Germans. Thus an entire set of observations and conclusions is left buried in the text, some in lengthy passages, others in single sentences, still others in recurring themes and characterizations. For a review of *Judenrat*, nothing is more important than a consolidation of these points in analytic form. Here they are, under four headings, partly condensed from his account, partly developed from it, but mainly rooted in his evidence.[5]

THE GHETTO AS A POLITICAL ENTITY

The principal characteristic of the ghetto was the segregation of its inhabitants from the surrounding population. The Jewish ghetto was a closed-off society, its gates permanently shut to free traffic, so much so that Trunk labels as relatively "open" those of the ghetto communities in smaller cities that dispatched labor columns daily to projects outside the ghetto limits.[6] That is not to imply the total absence of contacts with Germans or Poles. There were telephone, electrical, gas, and water connections; removals of human waste; exports of manufactured goods; imports of coal, food, or raw materials; mail and parcel shipments through ghetto post offices; loans from banks, payments of rents, and so forth. In examining these links one must, however, always differentiate between institutional transactions that had to be maintained if the ghetto was to function and

5. To allow for deeper treatment of some of the problems, illustrations in this discussion will be drawn mainly from the Warsaw ghetto.

6. Trunk, p. 104.

private bonds, across the boundaries, that could no longer be tolerated because they were incompatible with the function of the ghetto.

Even the official correspondence of Jewish ghetto authorities with neighboring German or Polish agencies or firms was largely severed, and the flow of orders and reports was confined as much as possible, though never completely, to a channel running from the German supervisors to the Jewish council. The horizontal relationships which are built into so much of modern life were consequently replaced by an almost all-embracive vertical regime, sometimes complex, as in the case of Warsaw and Lodz, often simple, as in outlying localities, but always standardized in a dictatorial manner.[7]

The hierarchical system of German supervision was designed for the purpose of absolutism. German orders were unqualified and council members were required to carry them out promptly and in full. Trunk underscores the fact that the members of the councils were not Nazi sympathizers, that, although some were ambitious and many deluded, they were not, and could not be regarded as, a German institution.[8] They were, in short, Jews, and they could not fail to perceive the fate of Jewry as their fate as well.[9] All the

more bitter then was their task of receiving and implementing German decrees. Yet the directives of the Germans were only half of their problem. Less stark but equally burdensome was the necessity of asking for authorization to carry out every function of government, including duties expected of them. The councils had to obtain clearance for a variety of revenue measures; they had to "borrow" Jewish funds previously sequestered or confiscated under occupation ordinances; they even had to request permission to post German orders.

If the councils were thus rendered totally subordinate and dependent in their relations with the Germans, a corresponding status was fashioned for the Jewish population subjected to council rule. The German sentiment in this matter was expressed unambiguously by one official when he asserted, "It lies in the interest of the difficult administration of the Jewish district that the authority of the Jewish council be upheld and strengthened under all circumstances."[10]

Jewish executives, like the Germans in charge, could make use of coercion and take advantage of helplessness. Compliance and acquiescence were ensured by the Jewish

---

7. Trunk discusses at some length intra-German rivalries for control of the ghettos, ibid., pp. 264–76. The police in particular wanted power over the Jews. *See* letter by the SS and Police Leader in Warsaw (*Wigand*), 11 November 1941, claiming jurisdiction of his Protective Police (*Schupo*) over the Warsaw Ghetto "Order Service." YAD VASHEM microfilm JM 1112 (YIVO microfilm MKY 76).

8. Trunk, pp. 572–74.

9. In statistical terms, membership in councils was in fact hazardous. Trunk reports on the basis of his questionnaires that the incidence of violent death among councilmen

in the period before the deportations was somewhat high; in his group of 720, about one in four was killed in the ghetto, most were deported, and one in nine survived, ibid., pp. 326–28. However, the 99 councils covered in his survey must cumulatively have contained several times as many members as the number of recollected names. If the forgotten members died in the gas chambers, the ratios would be less striking.

10. Mohns, deputy chief of the Resettlement Division in the office of the governor of the Warsaw District, to Leist, plenipotentiary of the governor for the City of Warsaw, 11 Jan. 1941, YAD VASHEM microfilm JM 1113 (YIVO microfilm MKY 77).

police, which had the power to make arrests and guard prisoners.[11] Relief could be dispensed in that the councils controlled food and space: the German shipments of flour, sugar, or coal were doled out under conditions of constantly increasing privation.[12]

Throughout the system, power was exercised in levels of dominance, and each level was fortified in every way. An illustration of such reinforcement was the principle of limiting correspondence and conversations to immediate superiors and inferiors. In conformity with this arrangement, the council could make appeals only to the German supervisory authorities in its locality —it could conceivably urge the city commander or ghetto commissioner to submit a plea to higher officials[13] —but it could not carry messages directly to regional governors or their staffs. The ghetto inhabitants in turn might stand in line to see the Elder of the council, but they had no ordinary access to German agencies. In fact, there is reason to suppose that the councils acquired a stake in establishing themselves as the sole representatives of the Jewish population vis-à-vis German officialdom. They certainly felt themselves empowered to govern the Jews, and, in some ghettos, announced that persons who had failed to pay taxes or report for labor would be handed over to a German organ because of their recalcitrance.[14] For Jewish bu-

reaucrats, no less than German, there was no substitute for authority.

The physical and administrative constrictions of Jewry reduced its space and narrowed its horizon but, at the same time, intensified its organizational activity. While the Germans outside became invisible,[15] the Jewish community machinery within evolved into the government of a captive city-state. Trunk explains the transformation as clearly stemming from two causes: one was the necessity of rendering those regular municipal and economic services from which the community was now cut off and without which it could not have survived; the other was the burden thrust upon the council by the Germans who used it as a tool to fulfill German needs.[16] The multiplication of tasks inherent in this dual evolution, coupled with continuing unemployment and periodic fears of disaster, led also to swollen ghetto bureaucracies that were filled with minor functionaries and clerks, both paid and unpaid. In ghettos featuring public enterprise (particularly Lodz and Vilna), the council payrolls at the beginning of 1942 encompassed as much as a fifth of the employable population.[17]

Although ghetto office personnel were often doing very little, some of the officials wielded power—at times almost undisturbed power— in specialized spheres of jurisdiction. One area in particular lent itself to what Trunk calls, albeit between quotation marks, ghetto self-government. This island of Jewish freedom

11. Trunk, pp. 82–83.
12. Ibid., p. 99.
13. For an example of such a request, *see* the diary of Czerniakow, 7 Jan. 1942, in *The Warsaw Diary of Adam Czerniakow*, eds. Raul Hilberg, Stanislaw Staron, and Josef Kermisz (New York: Stein and Day, 1979), pp. 312–13 (hereafter cited as *Diary of Czerniakow*).
14. *See* Trunk on Lublin, Bedzin, Zamosc, Vilna, p. 484.

15. *See* Trunk, pp. 528–29, on the psychological implications of this shift.
16. Trunk, p. 44.
17. Ibid., pp. 50–51; *see also* Trunk, "The Organizational Structure of the Jewish Councils in Eastern Europe," *YAD VASHEM Studies* 7:147–64 (1968).

was located in the courts, where disputes between Jewish litigants were settled by Jewish judges without German interference.[18]

Consequently, the ghettos were political entities with governmental attributes much larger and fuller than the social, cultural, or religious functions carried out by the prewar communities. Soon, however, councils everywhere came face-to-face with the basic paradox in their role as preservers of Jewish life in a framework of German destruction. They could not indefinitely serve the Jews while simultaneously obeying the Germans. A good deal of what Trunk calls the strategy and tactics of the councils[19] was in fact their futile attempt to resolve this contradiction. The Jewish leadership was completely nonprovocative: It did not fight the Germans—it seldom fought the orders—but in its distress it made numerous offerings. From time to time the councils offered words, money, labor, and finally lives.

Appeals were probably the most frequently used device. They were often generated by upheaval, especially at the beginning of the German occupation, during ghetto formation, and at the onset of deportations, but anything could be the content of a plea. The councils asked for permission to turn on the lights after 8 P.M. (Lublin), for reductions of confiscations (Bialystok), or for the return of hostages (Warsaw). "Seldom did Jewish petitions have any success," states Trunk, yet one has the feeling from such documents as the Czerniakow diary that an occasional or partial German concession, even

if only for the mitigation or postponement of some harsh measure, fueled the pleadings time and again. They remained, throughout, the strategy of first resort.

Trunk devotes considerable space to bribes, which he believes to have been widespread, but which obviously could have been used only under special conditions. They must have been more successful than intercessions, but the objects attained by bribery are likely to have been limited and the effects short-lived. Typical were payments to effect the transfer of a particularly troublesome official or policeman, the ransom of young girls from forced prostitution (a practice which under German "race-pollution" law was in any case prohibited), or the tender of money to avert "resettlement."

Most extensive is Trunk's discussion of the "rescue-through-work" strategy[20] that reflected the consideration that the Germans actually needed the products of Jewish manufacture, not only war material, but also simple things, such as brushes that in labor-hungry Axis Europe could not be turned out in quantity with ease. In Lodz, Vilna, and Czestochowa, this policy led to the construction by the councils of fairly large-scale industries. The factories bought time for tens of thousands, but the Jews were playing a predetermined game in which the outcome was always under German control.[21]

18. Trunk, *Judenrat*, pp. 180–81, 185; other areas of autonomy were Saturday as a day of rest and the use of Hebrew or Yiddish in schools, etc., pp. 189, 196–215.

19. Ibid., pp. 390–95.

20. Ibid., pp. 400–420.

21. Trunk indulges in the thought that if, in August, 1944, the Red Army had not stopped about 75 miles outside Lodz, some 70,000 Jews in the ghetto might have been saved, ibid., p. 413. The same speculation is offered by Robinson in the introduction (ibid., p. xxix) and was reiterated on another occasion by Yehuda Bauer (Holocaust Conference at the Hebrew College, Boston, 1973). The

The mass deportations forced the Jews to the extreme ends in the spectrum of alternatives. There was no longer any middle ground between open opposition and total compliance: the Jewish communities were bound to choose the one or the other. Trunk gives some examples of councils with a "positive attitude" toward resistance. However, most of the manifestations of that inclination turn out to have been actions of individual council members in aiding escapes or in establishing contacts with partisans.[22] The predominant pattern was the active implementation of German directives.

The councils themselves organized confiscations and forced labor. In most ghettos, they themselves delivered the victims for the death transports. Of course, the Germans would frequently ask for only a certain number of deportees. It is this request that ignited an internal Jewish argument to the effect that if 1,000 Jews were given up, 10,000 would be saved, that if none were sacrificed, all would be lost. In delivering a part of the community, the councils could also choose the less worthy.[23] Trunk quotes Zalman Shazar, a president of Israel, as pointing out in 1964 that the negative selections in the ghettos had been preceded by similar behavior in czarist times when

the Jewish community leaders were forced to designate youngsters for 25 years of service in the imperial army. Then, too, the councils chose the simpletons.[24]

Because of the compliance strategy, the *Judenrat* could be a dangerous organization precisely when it functioned most smoothly. Impersonality, as in the recruitment of the strong and the weak or the healthy and the sick for heavy labor, could become brutality. Order, as shown in Lodz where smuggling was curbed, could intensify deprivation. Efficiency, in the collection of taxes or furs, could bring about more suffering. Thus many of the virtues of Jewish ghetto government became vices; responsibility was turned into unresponsiveness and salvage into loss.

THE GHETTO AS A SOCIOECONOMIC ORGANIZATION

The Jewish ghettos mark an interim phase between prewar freedom and wartime annihilation. These last moments of organized existence in the Jewish community were endured in a vise of progressively diminished space and gradually increasing hunger. If social and economic policies in normal societies may have long-range effects on large groups of people seeking comforts, security, or some pleasure in life, the internal measures and practices of ghetto councils were bound to have an immediate, massive impact on a population hovering between survival and death.

We may safely assume that many times the meager resources at the disposal of the councils were strained for the benefit of the community. There were occupational training

---

question is counterfactual. Red Army offensives, though broad, were conducted for limited territorial gain to allow for resupply and regroupment. The halting of the Russian drive so many miles from Lodz was in no sense "accident." The chance event would have been its opposite—a rapid German collapse.

22. In the Minsk ghetto, the entire council appears to have favored a liaison with partisans, ibid., p. 466. Also of interest are the councils in Bialystok and Vilna that had "ambiguous" attitudes, ibid., pp. 467–71.

23. *See* Trunk on the Lodz resettlement commission, p. 52.

24. Trunk, pp. 435–36.

programs, workshops, rationing systems, housing authorities, hospitals, ambulances, and other services in a large number of ghettos. Their very existence demonstrated what Jewish bureaucrats and technocrats could accomplish even under these conditions. At the same time, Trunk leaves little doubt that the ghettos as a whole were no triumphs of social equality and economic justice. The ghetto was the scene of all forms of corruption, including bribery, favoritism, and nepotism. Moreover, in the critical areas of labor, food, and taxes, the prevailing regulations were particularly harsh for the most destitute families.

Instances of dishonesty are difficult to document, but Trunk cites relevant testimony of survivors from several ghettos. Council members accepted personal bribes for exemptions from labor duty (Zamosc) or deportation (Horodenka and other ghettos).[25] Bribes were said to have been taken for appointments to the ghetto police (Warsaw).[26] Patronage in awarding jobs to inexperienced applicants, sometimes resulting in the employment of entire families, was apparently rampant in Warsaw, Lodz, Bialystok, Lublin, and elsewhere.[27] Friendships were also important in the soup kitchens of Lodz, and the Lodz ghetto chairman, Rumkowski, is reported to have issued supplementary food ration stamps "at whim," favoring particularly Orthodox groups and rabbis.[28]

While abuses for private ends may be regarded as transgressions of individuals, a regime of exploitation through official routines can only be described as systemic. The dif-

ference is important, for the concealed bribes and favors were intrinsically unjustifiable, whereas the open decrees and decisions, which so often took advantage of the most helpless portion of the population, were defended by councils as being the best they could do under the circumstances. Nowhere is this posture more clearly expressed than in the pronouncements, correspondence, and diary of Adam Czerniakow, chairman of the Jewish Council in the laissez-faire ghetto of Warsaw.

During the early days, Czerniakow excused the well-to-do from forced labor for a fee, in order to finance the compensation of poor families whose men were digging ditches for the Germans.[29] Later, as he struggled with the council's unbalanced budget, he proposed as his principal revenue source a monthly tax on bread.[30] Still later, when the council was threatened with declining German food shipments, cash reserves were created as a precautionary measure by increasing the surcharges on the bread and sugar rations.[31]

One of the effects of ghetto class structure was the emergence of what

25. Ibid., pp. 385–87.
26. Ibid.
27. Ibid., p. 354.
28. Ibid., p. 385.

29. Czerniakow to plenipotentiary of the Warsaw District for the City of Warsaw, 21 May 1940, YAD VASHEM microfilm JM 1113 (YIVO Institute microfilm MKY 77). The Warsaw district chief was Gouverneur Fischer, his City Plenipotentiary Leist. For examples of similar labor recruitment in other ghettos, see Trunk, pp. 379–80.

30. Czerniakow to Warsaw District Chief/ Resettlement Division/Exchange, 8 Jan. 1941. JM 1113. (Schön was in charge of the Resettlement Division.) Krakow also instituted a head tax, see Trunk, p. 381. Levies on earnings were considered problematical, because in ghettos like Warsaw smuggling accounted for considerable income.

31. *Diary of Czerniakow*, proclamation of the Warsaw Ghetto Provisioning Authority, signed by Czerniakow, 31 August 1941, pp. 273–74; on 2 Feb. 1942, he noted that the reserve had made possible free distributions of bread and sugar, pp. 321–22.

Trunk calls a "food pyramid." Quite simply, the social ladder became more and more conspicuous by the number of calories consumed. Thus a survey in the Warsaw ghetto during December, 1941 revealed that council employees were receiving 1,665 calories; artisans, 1,407; shopworkers, 1,225; and the general population, 1,125.[32] A similar picture of relative starvation may be observed in the Lodz ghetto. There, differential rationing, by type of employment, was official policy.[33] This is how status became instrumental in the prolongation of sheer survival. Czerniakow himself made the point obliquely at the end of 1941 when he observed that the intelligentsia were dying now.[34]

In retrospect, the tiers of privilege in ghetto society should not surprise us. Ghetto life rewarded special talents such as smuggling or wheeling and dealing. It accommodated the more usual skills of the doctors, artisans, or people who could speak German. The ghetto protected its rabbis as well, for the Jews clung to the past and approached even their most extraordinary problems with all traditional means. Finally, the Jewish bureaucrat who ran the ghetto during its formation and who presided at its dissolution was granted his reprieve. In the vast majority of instances, however, the last occurrence of even the most shielded existence was a violent death.

THE GHETTO AS MIRAGE

Adam Czerniakow was the sort of man who did not want to draw a salary as long as there was not enough money to pay his staff.[35] In the midst of starvation, he shunned elaborate meals, eating soup for lunch in his office.[36] During a contraction of the ghetto boundaries, he refused a German offer that would have allowed him to keep his apartment on a street from which the Jews were being expelled.[37] In July, 1942, when he realized that the Jews were going to be deported en masse, he took his own life. Yet in February, 1942, just about six months before that fateful day, Czerniakow had decided to have stained glass windows installed in the council chambers.[38] Czerniakow, as well as most of the other Jewish leaders, acted on the premise that there was a future. From the outset, the councilmen at their desks and the crowds in the streets bore their crushing burdens as temporary inflictions to be suffered until liberation. To the end, Jewish hospitals were trying to heal the sick, schools were continuing to train the young, and kitchens went on feeding the starved. To the ghetto inmates, there was no alternative.

Many ghetto activities, especially in education and culture, bordered on illusionary behavior; the Vilna ghetto, for example, established a music school in the summer of 1942.[39] Readers in the Warsaw ghetto fantasized in the pages of Tolstoy's *War and Peace* that a German collapse was imminent.[40] In the upper eche-

32. Trunk, pp. 356, 382. For a detailed discussion of the medical aspects of food deprivation in the Warsaw ghetto, *see* Leonard Tushnet, *The Uses of Adversity* (New York: Thomas Yoseloff, 1966). *See also* Trunk, pp. 146–48.

33. Trunk, p. 383. In several ghettos (Kutno, Kolomea, Chelm, etc.) the social pyramid was particularly visible in housing, pp. 374–77.

34. *Diary of Czerniakow*, 4 Dec. 1941, p. 305.

35. Ibid., 24 May 1941, pp. 241–42.
36. Ibid., 23 June 1941, p. 251.
37. Ibid., 6 Oct. 1941, pp. 285–86.
38. Ibid., 4, 10 Feb. 1942, pp. 322, 324.
39. Trunk, p. 227.
40. Emmanuel Ringelblum, *Notes from the Warsaw Ghetto* (New York: McGraw-Hill, 1958), p. 300.

lons of ghetto leadership, a kind of unreality surfaced in power struggles in and around the council headquarters.

Jurisdictional questions were a major preoccupation of the ghetto managers. One of these contests was waged between the councils and a centralized Jewish Welfare Service (JSS), which reported to the German Population and Welfare Division of the *Generalgouvernement* in Krakow and which maintained local committees in the ghettos.[41] A complex federal structure with built-in frictions evolved in the Warsaw ghetto in which more than a thousand "house committees" began to perform all sorts of voluntary and assigned functions, including the provision of shelter for refugees, the staging of one-act plays, emergency assistance, reports of illnesses, and collections of taxes.[42] In the same ghetto, the council was challenged by an organization known as the Control Office for Combatting the Black Market and Profiteering in the Jewish District under Abraham Gancwajch. Czerniakow won that battle when the Gancwajch apparatus was dissolved, with provision for the incorporation of its members into the regular Jewish Order Service (police).[43]

The following story, told by Czerniakow in his diary, illustrates the manner and extent to which administrators in the Warsaw ghetto were absorbed with problems of entitlement. A Provisioning Authority had been formed as a quasi-independent agency in the summer of 1941 to deal with the approaching food crisis. In the council's own labor department, an official wanted the local German labor office to approve applicants for positions in the authority. Incensed, Czerniakow wrote on 15 February 1942: "This clearly amounts to undermining the authority of the council and diminishing its prerogatives. According to the [council's] legal department, there is no basis for this position in law."[44]

Ghetto government at times became a distorted facsimile of a viable political system. The politics in the administrative processes of the ghetto may strike us as a caricature, because so many of the functionaries in this bureaucracy had come to think of life in a German enclosure as a stabilized condition of existence; they claimed not only some of the food, space, or medical services for themselves and their families, but they also fought for a share of power in this "weird, crippled structure." Yes, even in this rundown machine, which could no longer cope with its narrowest tasks, they wanted a piece of the action.

Trunk speaks at some length of "The German Policy of Fraud and Deceit."[45] He says that the Germans kept the Jews in the dark about their intentions. Indeed, the German perpetrators did not install a warning system in the ghetto. They did not practice chivalry toward their victims. On the other hand, the Jewish leaders did not attempt to acquire information about the Germans systematically, and they did not come to grips with disturbing news in time.

At the start, the Polish Jews viewed ghettoization as the culmination of German plans. They failed to think

41. Trunk, pp. 332–42.
42. Ibid., pp. 343–45; *Diary of Czerniakow*, 27 June 1941, pp. 252–53, 3 Dec. 1941, pp. 304–5. Trunk mentions house committees also in Bialystok, Trunk, pp. 515–16.
43. Trunk, pp. 505, 644. The text of the agreement between the council and the "Control Office," dated 5 August 1941, appears in the *Diary of Czerniakow*, pp. 265–67.

44. *Diary of Czerniakow*, pp. 325–26.
45. Trunk, pp. 413–36.

in terms of a further, more drastic stage in the destruction process. The diary of Adam Czerniakow, leader of the largest ghetto in Europe, is the most detailed record of that characteristic train of thought in the face of the imperilment.

Anyone with a deep interest in the Warsaw ghetto might well approach the diary with the direct question, What were Czerniakow's predictions? What were his plans? What did he think the Germans would do eventually, and what did he see as his alternatives? Nothing, almost nothing of this kind will be found in these notes.

Czerniakow does not make forecasts. He does not draw up options. He does not refer to the Germans as a foe. From October, 1941, to the spring of 1942 he expresses himself only in subdued tones, very briefly in passing, about ominous reports. As early as 4 October 1941, he quotes an ambiguous and enigmatic statement of a German official: "Bischof disclosed yesterday that Warsaw is merely a temporary haven for the Jews."[46] The entry for October 27 states: "Alarming rumors about the fate of the Jews in Warsaw next spring." On January 17, he asks whether Lithuanian guards were coming. There are more rumors on February 16. Disturbing news reached him on March 18 from Lvov (30,000 resettled) and from Mielec and Lublin. As of April 1, he hears that 90 percent of the Jews of Lublin were to leave their ghetto within the next few days. All this was written in entries of a sentence or two, in the middle of paragraphs which contained other sentences on other subjects.

Czerniakow viewed himself as having taken over an impossible task to be pursued from morning to night against increasingly unfavorable odds. He lived through daily nightmares of blocked funds, labor columns, apartment allocations, bricks for the wall, furs for the Germans, and soup for the poor. There was hardly anything that could be put off—everything was urgent. This is why, when the Germans accepted his revenue statute imposing a tax on bread, he felt that he had accomplished something and that he could face the next day. That is also why a modest collection of money for children was entered as a notable success. And this is the reason why in February, 1942, when most of the ghetto had not yet starved to death, he could feel a sense of vindication.

Czerniakow, and hundreds more on Jewish councils all over Eastern Europe, had fallen into a cadence which did not allow for prolonged reflection about the real meaning of the ghetto in the Nazi scheme of things. In fact, any German laxity or inefficiency only served to reinforce the pace and to intensify the activities of the Jewish offices, which worked in tandem with their German supervisors, reporting to them, seeking clarifications, and requesting authorizations. Thus an administrative and economic dependence was increasingly becoming psychological as well. This was the trap into which the Jewish leadership had slipped and from which it could not extricate itself.

On 20 July 1942, the deportations in Warsaw were imminent. Trunk cites an excerpt from the diary which describes that day.[47] It was a moment of panic in the ghetto, and Czerniakow went from Gestapo man to Gestapo man in desperation to ask whether the rumors of a "resettlement" were

46. The remark is cited in another connection by Trunk, p. 292.

47. Ibid., p. 414.

true. The Germans assured him that they did not know anything and that the reports were all nonsense (*Quatsch and Unsinn*). The passage is a fairly good example of how crude the Germans could be in their policy of "fraud and deceit." One has the feeling that their simple denials were almost lame. Not so simple are Czerniakow's frantic requests for reassurances. He was not a naive man. At the beginning of the paragraph, he himself states that he left the office of the Gestapo mán Mende "unconvinced," and that later in the day he asked for permission to transmit the German denials to the Jewish population. The Germans could see no harm in that, and, by evening, in *Kommissar* Auerswald's office, they promised an "investigation" of the rumors. Three days after that meeting, all the camouflage was gone, and Czerniakow killed himself with poison. We do not know how long he had kept that pill in his drawer.

The Jewish communities were lulled by the continuation of sheer routines, including the endless rebuilding of walls and fences, the periodic exactions, confiscations, and arrests, and even the desultory firing by German guards into the ghetto. Yet they did not lack indexes of danger. The whole economic system of the ghettos was not geared to longterm survival. There was large-scale, chronic unemployment, and, as Trunk points out in one of his important findings, a finite supply of personal belongings was mobilized to supplement the insufficiency of production in an effort to pay for legally and illegally imported food.[48] The clock was running down, and soon there were signs of massive German violence. As German armies crossed the

Bug and San rivers in June, 1941 to assault the U.S.S.R., mobile units of the SS and Police began to kill Jews by the hundreds of thousands in eastern Poland, the Baltic states, White Russia, and the Ukraine. By the spring of 1942, deportations to death camps commenced in the heart of Poland. The deported Jews were not heard from again.

In the remnant ghettos of 1943, the issue of life and death could no longer be avoided. The alternatives were brought forth and discussed: one could plan escapes, prepare resistance, or redouble an effort to produce goods for the Germans. Even in this drastic situation, there was a tendency to veer away from methodical dispersal or organized battle because of the belief that, while it was not feasible for the entire population to participate in acts of defiance, it was possible for everyone to suffer the consequences.[49]

This is how the doctrine of "rescue through work" became paramount from Upper Silesia to Vilna. It was, in more ways than one, the strategy of least resistance. It was founded also on the presumption that if only the Germans were rational, they would not obliterate the work force which was engaged in so much war production for them. The thought was, of course, a misconception. Once, the Jews had placed their trust in rules and regulations for protection against the ravages of totalitarianism; now they clung to contracts and deliveries for safety from destruction. Thus the Jews in Czestochowa were bewildered by the report that in the Warsaw ghetto workers had been dragged from their shops.[50] Still, the rationale of work salvation was not dispelled. If the

48. Ibid., pp. 101–2.

49. Ibid., *see* pp. 451–74.
50. Ibid., p. 404.

unskilled were lost, it was hoped that the skilled would remain, and when some of those were removed, it was reasoned that the raids would occur only once in a while. In this manner, Jewry sacrificed more and more for less and less until it was annihilated.

THE GHETTO AS SELF-DESTRUCTIVE MACHINERY

We have seen now that the Jewish ghetto was a provider of administrative services, a social and economic laboratory, and a state of mind. It was also a form of organized self-destruction.

Once more, it should be emphasized that the councils were not the willful accomplices of the Germans. Within the German superstructure, however, they were its indispensable operatives. Even when their activities were benign, as in the case of housing refugees or promoting sanitary conditions, they could contribute to the overall purposes and ultimate goals of their German supervisors. The very institution of an orderly ghetto was, after all, an essential link in the chain of destructive steps. In building this order and preserving it, the councils could not help serving their enemy.

We know, of course, that the Germans expected much more than general government of their Jewish deputies. It was German policy to transfer to Jewish middlemen a large part of the physical and psychological burdens of destroying millions of men, women, and children. One aspect of that assignment was financial, another entailed selections, and the third called for enforcement.

The destruction of Jewry generated administrative costs, and, throughout Europe, German agencies attempted to obtain some of the necessary resources from the Jews themselves. As far as possible, the destruction process was to be self-financing. In Poland, too, an effort was made to balance the books without drawings from the budget of the German Reich. Trunk cites the fact that the German administration of the Lodz ghetto (the *Gettoverwaltung*) covered expenses by taxing deliveries to the ghetto.[51] In Warsaw, there was wall building. The Jewish engineer Marek Lichtenbojm and a large crew of Jewish laborers were engaged at the site, and financial responsibility for the wall was passed on to the Jewish community.[52]

Indirectly, the Warsaw Jews may have subsidized Treblinka. From a letter written to the Warsaw Ghetto Commissioner Auerswald by the first Treblinka commander, Dr. Eberl, it appears that the commissioner was to supply various materials to the camp where shortly afterward the ghetto inhabitants were to be gassed.[53] This is not to say that the Jewish leadership was able to decipher the nature of Treblinka while it was under construction.[54] There may also

51. Ibid., pp. 282–83; *see also* requisitions of furnishings, etc., pp. 66–67, 296; *Diary of Czerniakow*, 22 July 1941, p. 260, 28 Nov. 1941, p. 302.

52. Documents in YAD VASHEM microfilm JM 1112 (YIVO film MKY 76); Czerniakow letter of 8 Jan. 1941, JM 1113 in *Diary of Czerniakow*, 5 July 1941, pp. 254–55, 30 Dec. 1941, pp. 310–11. In Warsaw, Lodz, and Kaunas, the councils had to build bridges to connect ghetto sections divided by Aryan streets, Trunk, p. 110.

53. Eberl to Auerswald, 26 June 1942. Facsimile in Jüdisches Historisches Institut Warschau, *Faschismus-Getto-Massenmord*, ed. 2 (Berlin: Rütten & Loening, 1961), p. 304.

54. While Czerniakow became aware of "resettlement" and was told about Treblinka, he did not connect the two. On 17 Jan. 1942, he asked whether Lithuanian guards were coming and was assured that the rumor was false, *Diary of Czerniakow*, pp. 316–17. That

have been remote funding of death transports from Jewish sources. We know, for example, that the German railways in Lodz billed the Gestapo in the city for the one-way fares. The Gestapo passed the bill to the Lodz *Gettoverwaltung* for payment.[55] We can only surmise how this debt was ultimately discharged.

First the Jewish councils handed over money; then they delivered human beings. Let us remember, though, that the process of selecting victims began with the social structuring of the ghetto population. We have seen that from the moment of their incarceration, the Jews were discernably divided according to their advantages and privileges in life. To be sure, few individuals had any inkling then that these stratifications would acquire a special meaning during the Final Solution. However, growing suspicions and forebodings had the effect of accentuating the differentiations. Everyone was now concerned with his position all

of the time, and soon the passes and identification cards made out by the councils became more varied and colorful.[56] The papers spelled out a rank order of protection and, by the same token, vulnerability. At last, separation was bound to be a selection per se, since in the course of a roundup quotas were often filled with readily available old people, hospitalized patients, or children.[57] In the final analysis, the councils only had to save some to doom all the others.

Jewry became at least passively a participant in its own undoing, underwriting German operations through financial mechanisms and involvements and arraying its own people on an axis that defined degrees of safety or danger. Jews were engaged also in a more active and virulent mode of self-destruction when the Jewish police was employed for German designs. Trunk devotes an entire chapter to the order service.[58] Much attention has always been riveted on the Jewish police because of the role that these semiuniformed auxiliaries of annihilation performed in the pivotal occurrences of 1941 and 1942.

The order service exercised all the expected functions of a regular police department, such as traffic control and the pursuit of petty thieves. Furthermore, it carried out tasks that were normal only in an abnormal society, from the collection of ghetto taxes, to the enforcement of compulsory labor, and to the seizure of families for deportation, including the penetration of their hiding places. In some of the large ghettos the organization of the Jewish police revealed distinctly German features,

---

same day, he talked to Auerswald who informed him of a conversation with Generalgouverneur Frank as a result of which Jewish prisoners held in Warsaw's Pawiak prison would, if fit for labor, be sent to Treblinka to work. Two days thereafter, Czerniakow noted that Auerswald was going to Berlin. In this entry, Czerniakow also expressed fear of mass resettlement. (In fact, a conference of bureaucrats on the Final Solution was held in Berlin on 20 Jan. 1942. Trunk comments on Auerswald's deception on pp. 295–96.) On 19 Feb. 1942, Czerniakow complains that German prosecutors had failed to produce the appropriate papers for the "release" of prisoners to Treblinka, ibid., pp. 323–24. A day later, the prisoners left. On March 10, he records the departure of five Jewish clerks to the camp, and on April 7 some 160 young German Jews, recently arrived from the Reich, were sent there, ibid., pp. 333, 341.

55. Facsimile, *Getto-Faschismus-Massenmord*, p. 214; both items of correspondence, dated 19, 27 May 1942, on a single sheet of paper.

56. Trunk, pp. 175–77. The crass illustration is Vilna.

57. Ibid., pp. 507–8, 514.

58. Ibid., pp. 475–527; *see also* passages in other chapters.

particularly, a division into ordinary and security police components, but even more visible was the adoption of German methods, such as the arrest of parents whose sons did not report for labor duty[59] or the sealing of houses in which individual tenants had not paid taxes.[60] The Jewish police arrested people in the middle of the night and beat up smugglers or the reluctant volunteers for death transports. They ate well and frequently filled their pockets with the bribes and ransom payments of frightened fellow Jews. So many were the instances of sheer brutality and corruption that Trunk patiently recites case after case of exceptions.

Yet the very personnel composition of the order service deepens the paradox of Jew acting against Jew. Whereas some of the recruits may well have been drawn from the underworld, and Ringelblum complains that also a hundred baptized Jews were serving in ranking positions of the Warsaw ghetto force,[61] some were included for their prior military experience, a large number was fairly well educated, and many were idealistic.[62] Here there was a concentration of healthy young men, uniquely capable of conducting intelligence operations or psychological warfare against the Germans, or of aiding in escapes, or even engaging in physical resistance. On isolated occasions, Jewish police may have done just that, but most of the time they were the most conspicuous Jewish instrument in the German destructive machine.

Ringelblum wrote in his notes on 19 February 1941 that the Jewish population had an understanding of the difficulties of being a Jewish policeman. It was hard for Jews to take a Jewish policeman seriously, and often, in those days, the order service would refrain from ordering people around and would "discuss" things with them instead. At one point it was therefore said, "You would have minded a Polish policeman, so why don't you mind a Jewish one!"[63] However, this very trust in the Jewish police was to result in one of the greatest moral disappointments of the Holocaust—an experience from which Jewry has not recovered to this day. Irving Louis Horowitz, in reviewing Trunk's *Judenrat*, concludes, "Jewish policemen of Lodz, Vilna, and Warsaw were, after all, still policemen."[64]

The Jewish ghetto has just been opened, and we see it now with all of its institutions and processes. This is Trunk's lasting achievement. On the other hand, the moral questions raised over so many years have not been closed; they have only become more complicated. We know that already the ghetto leaders themselves were fully aware of their dilemma and that for some it was always on their minds. A small, sensitive book by Leonard Tushnet recently illuminated the lives of just three of these figures: Rumkowski of Lodz, Czerniakow of Warsaw, and Gens of Vilna.[65] They were different men by background as well as in their ideas, but in the end all three declined to save themselves after they had not succeeded in saving their people.

59. Bedzin, Sosnowiec, Zawiercie, Bialystok, ibid., p. 584. In Warsaw, members of house committees were taken hostage, if a tenant did not present himself for labor. Ringelblum, p. 176.

60. Czestochowa, Radom, etc. Trunk, p. 483.

61. Ringelblum, p. 138.

62. Trunk, pp. 489–998. Interesting is the finding that Jewish militants (Betar, etc.) were well represented in the police.

63. Ringelblum, pp. 125–26.

64. Horowitz, *Israeli Ecstasies/Jewish Agonies* (New York: Oxford University Press, 1974), p. 197.

65. Tushnet, *The Pavement of Hell* (New York: St. Martin's Press, 1972).

Failure to Rescue European Jewry: Wartime Britain and America

By HENRY L. FEINGOLD

ABSTRACT: During the years of the Holocaust, British leadership was unable to perceive that the smoke of the chimneys of the death camps meant that their own world was also aflame. Bernard Wasserstein, in a superbly documented book, relates the disheartening story of the consequence of that failure of imagination and will. Britain's rescue policy frequently tended to serve as an adjunct to Berlin's murderous plans for the Jews of Europe. It was a reflection of the low estate of British power and of an altered perception of Jewish influence in the world. Far more than Washington, London decision makers felt threatened by the Nazi ability to "dump" thousands, perhaps millions of Jews. That accounts for the 1939 White Paper and for the consistent failure to act on rescue opportunities. But Wasserstein is able to document how the reluctance of British decision makers to save Jewish lives often went beyond the question of wartime priorities and strategic needs. They rejected plans to send food packages to certain camps even while they fed occupied Greece throughout the war; they blocked the forming of a Jewish army, and the bombing of the death chambers was thwarted despite the approval of Churchill and Eden. Clearly the failure to seriously attempt the rescue of millions of Jewish lives went beyond the exigencies of war.

Henry L. Feingold is currently professor of history at the Graduate Center of the City University and at Baruch College. He is also chairman of the editorial board and editor of the American Jewish History, *is on the editorial board of* Shoah *and* Reconstructionist, *and is chairman of the Faculty Seminar on the Holocaust of the National Jewish Resource Center. He was awarded the Leon Jolson award for the best book on the Holocaust in 1974. Among his books are* Politics of Rescue: The Roosevelt Administration and the Holocaust, 1938–1945 *and* Zion in America: The Jewish Experience from Colonial Times to the Present.

OF THE several sources of national vitality and power, quality of leadership is perhaps the most difficult to concretize. Isolating leadership from factors such as national morale or the extent of the development of industry and technology is problematic because it is much more illusive. There is one factor, however, which good leadership must demonstrate. It is the ability to perceive in the flow of events, even when they seem remote from the national interest, a possible impact on the future national welfare. During the war, British leadership failed, for the most part, to perceive that the final solution of the Jewish problem imposed by Nazi racial policy somehow impinged on their own future national well-being. They thought that the smoke of the chimneys of the death camps pertained only to the Jews and other unfortunate victims of Nazi barbarity. They never fathomed that after Auschwitz their own world could never be the same. Bernard Wasserstein, in a superbly documented and written book[1] which serves as a sequel to A. J. Sherman's prior *Island Refuge*, tells the disheartening story of the failure of British leadership to understand what was happening in the death camps of Europe and of how their policy tended to serve as an adjunct to Berlin's murderous plans for European Jewry. It is a story of the failure of imagination, power, and will. In the final analysis, Britain's unwillingness to play a more active rescue role can be attributed to its leadership, which in itself was symptomatic of the island kingdom's declining vitality.

One need not, of course, turn to Britain's relation to the destruction of the Jews of Europe for evidence of decline. That failure was already in evidence in the policy of appeasement and, undoubtedly, well before that. If London would not respond to the threat to Czechoslovakia, why should there be an expectation that there would be a response to a threat to European Jewry, which was not represented by a nation-state? Indeed expectations for succor might well be lower since Britain, fighting a bitter war of survival, could hardly be expected to give the rescue of the Jews a higher priority when there was a sense that doing something for Jews, such as allowing them to enter Palestine, would weaken Britain's strategic position. Beset by a sense of weakness, British leaders saw the Jews as a liability to their survival.

There seemed to be two secret weapons in the Nazi arsenal that the British feared most, the V-bombs, which Goebbels touted endlessly even before they rained on London, and the "dumping" of Europe's Jews. Had Hitler not been so fixated on liquidating the Jews, he might have realized that from the British perspective these Jews represented an even more lethal weapon in the minds of leading officials in the Foreign and Colonial Office.

THE PALESTINE PROBLEM

It is that sense of danger which partly accounts for the series of horrendous words and deeds of the British authorities during the period of the Holocaust. Britain was closer than the United States to the Final Solution, which, in a perverse way, relieved it of what it felt was a potentially terrible burden. What one senses after reading Wasserstein's troubling account is that British leadership succumbed to a policy based on the notion that it was better to have these "surplus people" erad-

1. Bernard Wasserstein, *Britain and the Refugees from the Third Reich, 1933–1939* (London: Clarendon Press, 1979).

icated by the Nazi killing process than to have them become a burden to the British war effort. British authorities took the lead in barring possible escape routes at the war's outset. The first shots fired by British combatants on the second day of the war were not aimed at German soldiers but at Jewish refugees trying to enter Palestine. Like the United States, Britain found itself in the midst of a popular security psychosis at the outset of the war. It manifested itself in the arbitrary arrest and internment of enemy aliens.

Even after it became clear that Berlin was not using the refugee stream to infiltrate its agents, British officialdom nevertheless clung to that notion and acted accordingly. When rumors of a Nazi plan to create a special reserve for Jews in the Nisko-Lublin area were heard shortly after Poland was overrun, an official in the Foreign Office expressed relief to his superiors. The proposed Jewish state, he thought, "would apparently offer an alternative refuge for Jews from Russia and occupied Poland and would make it unnecessary for us to consider the request for their immigration to Palestine" (31 October 1939). That was a primary consideration.

When the *Salvador*, formerly an unseaworthy ship the S.S. *Tzar Krum*, sailed from the Black Sea port of Varna en route to Palestine and foundered in the Sea of Marmora on 12 December 1940, with the loss of over 200 Jewish lives, including 70 children, the head of the Foreign Office refugee section observed: "There could have been no more opportune disaster from the point of view of stopping this traffic."[2] The fate of the ship was widely publicized to deter other refugees des-

parately seeking a haven in Palestine. But the mounting death toll, which included the *Patria* and several other disasters, hardly softened the heart of British officialdom which was able to observe firsthand that refugees who would brave such dangers really had little choice but to become illegals.

A 1943 offer from the Rumanians to release 70,000 Jews caused consternation in London which, nevertheless, felt compelled, considering the known circumstances of Rumanian Jewry, to encourage the Bucharest authorities. But by the year's end, when the plan actually showed signs of coming to fruition, the ardor of the British authorities cooled noticeably, and all means were sought to prevent the implementation of the plan. A similar reluctance to find a place for Jews could be noted in July, 1944, when it appeared that the Hungarian Regent Horthy would make good on an offer to release thousands of Jews. Even the 75,000 who might have received the cherished Palestine certificates in 1944 never reached that haven.

British authorities could muster little love for seeming American generosity on the refugee front. They saw it as putting pressure on London. The establishment of the War Refugee Board in January, 1944 was not well received and neither was the establishment of a temporary refugee haven in Oswego, New York. Such breakthroughs were viewed in London as additional evidence of the growing effectiveness of American Jewish pressure. They had already learned from diplomatic dispatches of the growing strength of American Zionism.

One might easily conclude from such incidents that London's record in relation to the rescue of the Jews is worse than that of Washington. Certainly because of its proximity

2. Ibid., p. 77.

and strategic interest, Britain was more directly involved in the Final Solution. While Washington authorities were able to employ what I call a "politics of gestures," the British experienced considerable difficulty in concealing their real interest in preventing large numbers of Jews from leaving Europe. A submarine-infested ocean separated America from Europe, and, if that was insufficient to dissipate the notion of bringing large numbers of European Jews to American shores, State Department officials could always point to the lack of shipping or the difficulty of screening out potential agents that Nazi intelligence had surely planted in the refugee stream. Separated only by a narrow channel from occupied Europe and with its mandate in Palestine accessible via the Black Sea and Turkey, Britain could make no such claim. If Britain seemed more direct in its opposition to rescue, it was because its interest was more directly involved.

INSUFFICIENT HELP FROM WASHINGTON

Nevertheless, researchers interested in the comparative role played by the two Allies in relation to the destruction of European Jewry will find their appetites whetted by this study. Throughout the war there were subterranean tensions between a Britain declining in power and a United States still in its ascendency that were concealed behind a veneer of unity in the face of a common enemy. But conflicts had a way of coming to the surface on issues such as the Jewish refugees. Both governments shared a common distaste for the Jewish burden Berlin was compelling them to bear. But they sometimes differed markedly in approach.

Some of the conflicts regarding Jewish refugees and rescue of Jews were in fact a spillover from larger issues that were best left unspoken during the war. Britain harbored some resentment against America even while she was grateful for aid extended. It nettled that Britain saw herself bleeding to death fighting a "common enemy" of the North Atlantic community while the United States between September, 1939, and December, 1941, played the role of a "reluctant belligerent." Impatient with American dallying, more than one British decision maker must have felt that the "garden hose" Roosevelt mentioned in his Lend-Lease address was not enough and that Washington was playing a waiting game to pick up the pieces of the British empire.

Men like Ambassador Joseph Kennedy had made no secret that the proper policy of America was not to place all the American eggs in the British basket. That resentment was reinforced at the Argentia Conference in August, 1941. There Churchill succeeded in making the United States a silent partner in the war but the issue of the disposition of the British empire after the war created some rancor. It compelled Churchill to explain to Roosevelt that he had not come to that conference to dispose of that empire. It was difficult for the British, watching their substance draining away, to observe the ideal position of an upstart America, naive in the ways of world power. American isolationists, on the other hand, endlessly suspected the British leadership of expecting Washington to pull its chestnuts out of the fire as America had done during World War I. On the vexing Jewish question, America had a much easier time of it. Geographic distance and size gave it a better ability to absorb

Jewish refugees. Why could not Washington be more generous?

The domestic situation in both nations was unfavorable for the absorption of Jewish refugees since both were in the throes of a rising tide of antisemitism. Wasserstein, perhaps too kindly, classifies the British situation as compounded by "habitual island xenophobia," but the net effect was the same. There was another commonality: a similar gap in both governments between policymakers and the actual implementation of decisions. In Washington, the oppositionists could be found in the middle and upper echelons of the State Department and of the defense establishment. In London, oppositionists were in the Foreign Office and the Colonial Office. In the case of bombing, for example, Wasserstein finds "striking testimony to the ability of the British civil service to overturn ministerial decisions."[3] There existed in Washington a similar disparity between the professions of good intentions emanating from Roosevelt's Oval Office and the blocking actions taken at the administrative level. Unanswered is the question of why supreme leaders like Churchill and Roosevelt did nothing to close the gap, even though they were undoubtedly aware of it. One can hardly avoid the conclusion that they, too, were not overly enthusiastic about making the war into a war to save the Jews.

The parallels of inaction are striking. The security scare at the outset of the war was as manifest in America as it was in Britain, though there was much less excuse for allowing it to run rampant in a nation that was still neutral. It was used by officials in both nations to halt the flow of

Jewish refugees. The reaction of confirmed news of the actual implementation of the Final Solution was also similar in both countries. There was no attempt, as there was in Washington, on the part of British officials to halt the flow of news at its source but there was similar reluctance to accept the Riegner cable, and there was a postponement of the announcement of its contents until "further confirmation." High officials in the State Department and the Foreign Office were convinced that "wailing Jews" were guilty of atrocity mongering or at least of special interest pleading. In America they would be more careful about accepting such stories at face value. Revisionist historians had, after all, confirmed that America had needlessly been sucked into World War I by skillful British atrocity mongering.

Both the Jewish community of Britain and of the United States encountered inordinate difficulty in getting the fact of the Final Solution believed. Neither ever learned the method of convincing the public of the unbelievable fact; they never solved the problem of gaining credibility. The role of government officials did not help.[4] The reluctance of both allies in making public statements of retribution specifically for crimes committed against Jews compounded the problem of gaining credibility and, incidentally, must have gone far in convincing Nazi leaders like Goebbels that the Allies approved of their getting rid of the Jewish riffraff.

The two governments often dif-

3. Ibid., p. 316.

4. In that connection, the role of the Augudath representative in Switzerland in embroidering the horrible facts with the erroneous notion that the Nazis were using soap made from the fat of the Jewish victims did not help. It simply made the story sound more incredible.

fered on specific steps. In some cases London was more generous than the United States. That was true, according to A. J. Sherman, in the admission of Jewish refugees before hostilities began. The United States did not make a distinction between refugees in dire need and normal immigrants. But in the case of breaking the blockade so that food packages might be shipped to some camps, London leaders, more cognizant of the role played by the British blockade in bringing Germany to her knees during World War I, proved far more reluctant than Washington to make exceptions. Yet what is one to believe when one is reminded by Wasserstein that throughout the war, occupied Greece was fed by Britain despite the rigid blockade? British blockade stringency was limited to Jews.

ADOPTION OF THE RESCUE-THROUGH-VICTORY PLAN

Like the Roosevelt administration was, British authorities were reluctant to play "the air for the Jew string," that is, to focus propaganda on the Final Solution so that the world, and especially the occupied people, might become aware of what was happening to the deported Jews. It was argued that Jews were not the only group being victimized by the Germans and that should Jewish wishes be acceded to, others would soon insist on their fate being made public. The result would be not only undue attention to the fate of the Jews at the expense of other groups, but an emphasis on "greuel" propaganda which would surely "debase the currency" and create a kind of Gresham's law in which bad propaganda would chase out good. The Germans, it felt, could outdo the Allies in atrocity mongering since

they had so much firsthand experience. It was a strange and bitter irony for rescue advocates. They were being told that the truth was so unbelievable that to publicize it would make for counterproductive propaganda.

Yet the real problem was that the British simply insisted that what was happening to Jews be grouped with the other victims of nazism: that universalization of the Final Solution was a reflection of the low priority given to the rescue of Jews and was, at the same time, a rationale for keeping the priority low. It permitted officials in both nations to wash their hands of the rescue question and argue that the only sure means of saving Jewish lives was to win the war quickly. "The blunt truth is," read a Foreign Office dispatch to the British embassy in Washington on 26 February 1943, "that the whole complex of human problems raised by the German domination of Europe, of which the Jewish question is an important but by no means the only aspect, can only be dealt with completely by an Allied victory, and any steps calculated to prejudice this is not in the interest of Jews in Europe."[5] One wonders if the policymakers who conceived of the rescue-through-victory strategy were fully aware that it entailed a death sentence for European Jewry.

Behind such thinking in London and Washington was the failure, or perhaps the unwillingness, to recognize that something *sui generis* was occurring in the death camps of occupied Europe. A system had been put in place by means of which Europe, especially the people in its Eastern portion, could literally have been consumed in the gas chambers.

5. Wasserstein, p. 215.

The Jews were merely the first of many targets. There were reasons why the rescue of Jews was given a low priority. The war itself threatened the survival of the would-be rescuing nations until well into 1943 and, naturally, they were more concerned about that. They viewed the destruction of the Jews as one of many barbarities in a particularly cruel war. The Holocaust did not have a special significance; it was universalized and lost its uniqueness, a phenomenon which continues to this very day. Then as now few could fathom that what was happening in the death camps was a *novum*. The production process which had enabled Europe to dominate the world was beginning to consume itself. It was starting with the very group that had played a pivotal role in creating that system, especially the modern mental set and the ethos that went with it.

INABILITY TO RECOGNIZE PLIGHT OF VICTIMS

The inability to recognize the true nature of the event made the Final Solution merely another atrocity in a war full of atrocities and made the Jews merely another group of victims in a war that counted its victims in the many millions. The result was that the priority given to rescue in the Allied camp never remotely matched the priority given by the Nazi leadership to liquidating the Jews. In concrete administrative terms, that meant Berlin found cattle cars and ships to deport the Jews to the death camps from the remotest corners of Europe and that they did so even when it meant denying needed war material to their scattered fronts. They continued to hold fast to these priorities even when it was clear that the war was lost for them.

Britain and America, on the other hand, never found the needed transportation for those that might have been saved nor found a haven where they might be sheltered. Yet thousands of Axis prisoners of war were transported across the Atlantic to camps in the interior. That was also true of the internment of Axis sympathizers from Latin America. Hundreds of ships were returning empty to the American arsenal but they carried no Jews. That continued to be the case even after the Allies had good reason to believe that victory would ultimately be theirs. The unwillingness to rescue Jews was thus at once a reflection of a low priority and of a transcendence of these priorities as well.

Retributive bombing rejected

Wasserstein is most instructive in discussing the failure to bomb the camps and to consider retributive bombing. Considering that such bombing required no major alteration of strategic priorities and contained the promise of saving many thousands of lives at relatively little risk, the failure to do so is especially tragic. It also provides additional evidence that the failure to rescue Jews went beyond the question of wartime priorities.

The full story of the failure to bomb has been told elsewhere so that only certain salient points need be reiterated here. In the United States, the relatively late request to bomb the death camps and the rail lines leading to them (August, 1944) was rejected by John J. McCloy because such raids were considered to be of "doubtful efficacy," meaning that they would not help bring victory faster. There was also the additional fear that the raids would provoke "more vindictive" action by the Nazi leadership. But in London, where Churchill and Eden eventually approved the idea of bombing the camps, the plan was sabotaged at the administrative level by the use of dilatory tactics including the convenient misplacement of topographical data, including photo intelligence of Auschwitz, Birkenau, and Treblinka. By mid-1944 it was argued that the deportations from Hungary had in any case been halted. In actual fact, the gas chambers continued to operate until October consuming among others the Jews of the Lodz ghetto. Surely bombing might have saved a portion of these unfortunates.

Even if one accepts the dubious notion that bombing the camps entailed a diversion of resources and planning away from the primary task of winning the war—although it did not, since nearby targets were in fact being bombed—that could not be said of retributive bombing, which required no change whatsoever in priorities. How effective such tactics might have been was demonstrated in the case of Hungary. Raids on Budapest were among the several factors which triggered Horthy's decision to halt the deportations. In July, 1944, Moshe Shertok explained to Eden what bombing might achieve: "It would mean that the Allies waged direct war on extermination of the victims of Nazi oppression . . . it would mean the lie to the oft repeated assertion of Nazi spokesmen that the Allies are not really so displeased with the work of the Nazis in ridding Europe of Jews . . . it would go far towards dissipating the incredulity which still persists in Allied quarters with regard to the report of mass extermination perpetrated by the Nazis."[6] The announcement of retri-

bution was never made and the Nazi hierarchy and the German people, over a half million of whom lost their lives in such raids, never learned that the practice of genocide entailed a price. It was probably a price which many Germans would not have thought worth paying. As it was, the processed murder of a people occurred amidst an eerie silence that convinced Nazi leaders that the Allies secretly approved of the Final Solution and allowed many Germans to close their eyes to what was happening in the death camps.

The idea of retributive bombing was raised by General Sikorsky, head of the Polish Government in Exile as early as June, 1942. He requested "bombing on a large scale of non-military objectives . . . in retaliation for German savagery."[7] At one point the efficacy of mounting an "operation retribution" was under consideration, but little came of it. After the United Nations War Crimes Declaration of 17 December 1942, the Poles again requested such raids (January, 1943). The Polish case was strengthened when Churchill suggested that a raid be made on Berlin accompanied by leaflets announcing that it was in reprisal for atrocities committed against Poles and Jews in the East. But again nothing came of the suggestion. Not even the lethal V-1 and V-2 raids on London could convince British authorities that such an announcement might be effective.

Behind their reluctance was a notion that seems appallingly unreal today. They feared that by abandoning the idea that saturation bombing of German cities was aimed at fulfilling a purely military objective and was therefore "lawful and justifiable," they would lay themselves open to Nazi charges of

6. Ibid., p. 310.

7. Ibid., p. 306.

terror and atrocities against civilians. What a bitter irony. The Allied high command allowed itself to be hand-cuffed by notions of legality while involved in a war with a criminal regime, which they knew was involved in genocide, and thereby lost an opportunity to save thousands, perhaps millions, of lives while simultaneously winning a psychological victory by making the world and the German people aware of the true nature of the Nazi regime. Even more paradoxical is the posture of Jewish rescue advocates who did not fully take up the cudgels for retributive bombing. It was probably something they could have achieved, but the question was not raised in the highly publicized rescue program emanating from the giant Madison Square Garden rally held in March, 1943.

FAILURE

By the time he reaches the end of his research, Wassestein is left wondering why the rescue effort was so meager. He locates at least one of the reasons in the changed image of the Jews. During World War I an exaggerated notion of Jewish power was prevalent in both London and Berlin. It was one of the factors that led to the issuance of the Balfour Declaration and to the matching strenuous efforts by German authorities to win the favor of the Jews.

The interwar period saw a significant alteration in the image of the Jews. Even while they spoke incessantly of Jewish power and acted as though they were at war with a concrete Jewish national entity, Nazi leadership was actually demonstrating that the reverse was true. Jewish unity and international leverage was illusory; its power, nonexistent; they were in fact a weak and vulnerable people without even a national sovereignty that might come to its protection.

British leaders no longer thought of Jews as a distinct nation. They became not cobelligerents in the common struggle against the Nazi threat but merely troublesome victims who insisted on special treatment. It was never extended to them because, with some few noteworthy exceptions, British leadership was unable and unwilling to recognize that what was transpiring in the death camps was unprecedented in history and so special that it required a response. They experienced, according to Wasserstein, "an imaginative failure to grasp the full meaning of the consequences of decisions, when the consequences were distant, unseen, and bore no direct relation to the actor."[8] It may well be that the low estate of British power, particularly as it was reflected in the quality of its second-rung leadership, makes assigning it a responsibility for the rescue of Jews an exercise in futility. They simply could not perceive it.

8. Ibid., p. 356.

Jewish Organizations and the Creation of the U.S. War Refugee Board

By MONTY N. PENKOWER

ABSTRACT: Confronted by the Holocaust, the Anglo-American Alliance moved slowly to meet this unique tragedy during World War II. Refusing the initial appeal of Jewish organizations in the free world that food and medical packages be dispatched to the ghettos of Europe, London and Washington argued that supplies would be diverted for the Germans' personal use or would be granted the Jews just to free the Third Reich from its "responsibility" to feed them. A license granted in December, 1942, for such shipments had minimal effect. The World Jewish Congress' subsequent plan to rescue Jews through the use of blocked accounts in Switzerland received the U.S. Treasury Department's approval in mid-1943, but the State Department and the British Foreign Office procrastinated further. Jewish groups failed at times to measure up to the catastrophe but the fundamental obligation lay with the Allied councils of war, which discriminated in their unwillingness to save a powerless European Jewry. The persistence of Treasury Secretary Henry Morgenthau, Jr., and his staff in bypassing State and ultimately confronting Franklin D. Roosevelt in January, 1944, along with increasing calls from Congress and the public for a presidential rescue commission, resulted in the executive creation of the U.S. War Refugee Board. The lateness of the hour and Hitler's ruthless determination to complete the murder of all the Jews of Europe made the odds for the new board's success more than questionable.

Monty N. Penkower is a professor and chairman, Department of History, Touro College, New York City. A graduate of Yeshiva, B.A., 1963, and Columbia, M.A., 1964; Ph.D., 1970, Universities, he previously taught at City and Bard Colleges. The author of The Federal Writers' Project: A Study in Government Patronage of the Arts *(1977), his writing has appeared in the* Herzl Yearbook, Jewish Social Studies, Moment, American Jewish History, Journal of American History, *and* Martyrdom and Resistance. *A member of the Oral History Advisory Committee of the Holocaust Survivors' Memorial Foundation, he is currently completing a volume of studies in diplomacy during the Holocaust.*

This article, first presented to the Association for Jewish Studies' convention in Boston on 18 December 1979, forms part of a broader study on diplomacy during the Holocaust, to be published by the University of Illinois Press.

O NE WEEK before Warsaw surrendered to the Nazi blitzkrieg and the curtain fell on the first act of World War II, German Security Police Chief Reinhardt Heydrich took the initial step to extend the Final Solution beyond the borders of the Third Reich. Empowered by Hermann Goering the previous January to "solve the Jewish question," Heydrich ordered the mass resettlement and later concentration into ghettos of the two million Jews in German-occupied Poland as measures "leading to the fulfillment of the ultimate goal." Until eventual destinations would be approved, the Nazis turned these closed urban centers into death traps. Spotted typhus, tuberculosis, dysentery, and starvation ravaged the inhabitants. By September, 1942, 80,000 had died in the Warsaw ghetto alone. The Lodz Jewish community of originally 160,000 had a death–birth ratio of about 29:1 between 1940–42; its Warsaw counterpart, originally 470,000, registered 45:1. Raul Hilberg has estimated that in the end, one-fifth of Polish Jewry under the swastika died behind such sealed walls.[1]

WORK OF THE JOINT DISTRIBUTION COMMITTEE (JDC)

The American Jewish Joint Distribution Committee (JDC) kept warm a spark of life in this Jewish heartland. The JDC had spent some $2.6 million in Poland alone during 1933–38; in 1939 its expenditures reached $1.2 million. In 1940 and 1941, $859,400 and $972,000 reached the beleaguered Polish ghettos, respectively. By 1942, one in every nine Jews obtained meals at the JDC soup kitchens in Warsaw; the ratio stood at 1:3 in Lublin and 1:4 in the Radom and Warsaw districts. Medical aid helped 34 hospitals, and 30,000 children received daily care.[2]

Not one dollar of these funds entered Nazi-occupied Poland. Soon after the advent of Adolf Hitler to power, the JDC had decided not to extend aid that might benefit the German economy. All campaign monies raised were placed in U.S. banks while zlotys arrived in Poland through the extension of a financial clearance agreement which the JDC employed with its affiliated groups in the Reich: Berlin, Vienna, Prague, and Bratislava. This insistence on a relief policy "conforming in the closest degree" with U.S. State Department regulations had its drawbacks. For example, the JDC refused to transmit funds from Geneva to Poland at the higher black-market rate or to send foodstuffs there from Bratislava against *valuta* or Swiss

1. Raul Hilberg, *The Destruction of the European Jews* (New York: Franklin Watts, 1973), pp. 128, 140, 144, 168–69, 173–74.

2. Memo, 8 Feb. 1940, Poland genl., American Jewish Joint Distribution Committee Archives, New York (hereafter cited as JDCA); Kahn report for 1941–44, Poland genl., 1942–43, JDCA.

franc payments since this would aid the German economy.[3]

Other organizations

Other Jewish organizations in the United States felt less constrained in the face of the unparalleled crisis facing their people in Europe. The World Jewish Congress (WJC), through its Geneva RELICO office directed by Abraham Silberschein with the aid of Gerhart Riegner, dispatched food parcels, visas, medicines, and clothing to the General Government. The Jewish Labor Committee and the Bund used contacts in London to forward sums to comrades in Warsaw; Agudas Israel employed ties to the Polish consulate in New York through which messages, monies, and parcels safely arrived in the ghettos.[4]

THE BOYCOTT: REACTIONS

Few in the free world grasped in the first years of the war that Germany had consciously made starvation a weapon of annihilation, whereas public opinion felt that the blockade was the deadliest weapon in the British arsenal. "No form of relief can be devised," categorically asserted Prime Minister Winston Churchill on 20 August 1940, in the House of Commons, "which would not directly or indirectly assist the enemy's war effort." The British embassy in Washington reaffirmed this position on 9 March 1941, and in a letter to the Foreign Relations

Committee a half a year later, Secretary of State Cordell Hull opposed plans to feed occupied Europe on the assumption that "the responsibility and manifest duty to supply relief rests with the occupying authorities."[5]

The issue divided the Jewish organizations in the United States and ultimately halted all sending of food packages from there to the Polish ghettos in the summer of 1941. The Joint Boycott Council, formed during the 1930s by the American Jewish Congress and the Jewish Labor Committee to boycott all trade with Germany, opened a drive in July, 1941, to "end the food package racket" and prevent "the feeding of Hitler's war machine." The WJC and the Federation of Polish Jews in America stopped their activities in this regard as a result, while the council boycotted the offices of Agudas Israel of America for disregarding British official requests to halt package service to Poland.

Ultimately, the Agudas Israel Executive in London, under the direction of Harry Goodman, announced at the end of August that it would be "guided entirely by the wishes of the British authorities in Washington" henceforth. RELICO's Dr. Silberschein, aided by Isaac Weissman in Lisbon, continued quietly to send food at the rate of 1,500 food parcels per week, but this could hardly meet a situation where one-third of the Warsaw ghetto could not even afford to pay the two-zloty tax on ration cards imposed by the *Judenrat*, and living corpses collapsed and died every day in ghetto streets.

The inability of Jewry in the free world to ease the Allied blockade

3. Ibid; Bienenstock report, Jan. 1942, 212/20, World Jewish Congress Archives, New York (hereafter cited as WJCA); Lisbon to JDC, 20 Dec. 1940, Poland genl., 1940, JDCA.

4. Gerhart Riegner interview with Monty N. Penkower, 1 Nov. 1977; K. Iranek-Osmecki, *He Who Saves One Life* (New York: Crown Publishers, 1971), pp. 228–29; Isaac Lewin interview with Penkower, 5 Oct. 1979.

5. A. Leon Kubowitzki, "Survey of the Rescue Activities of the WJC, 1940–1944," mimeographed (1944), 153, WJCA.

was especially frustrating when the Anglo-American Alliance allowed food to reach Nazi-held Greece in early 1942. Fifteen thousand tons of wheat and three thousand tons of other materials could be sent to hold off starvation in Greece with the help of the Allies and the International Committee of the Red Cross (ICRC), one ship even leaving Haifa Bay, but Jewry's singular agony went unheeded.[6]

ALLIED AND RED CROSS AID TO GREECE

At this juncture, the General Jewish Council in New York decided to consider sending a delegation to intercede with the State Department regarding relief supplies for Jews in Poland. On 17 April 1942, the Jewish Labor Committee, B'nai B'rith, and the American Jewish Committee, in conjunction with the American Jewish Congress, drew up a draft memorandum. At the suggestion of the JDC's vice-chairman, Joseph Hyman, the group invited Christian and nonsectarian organizations to the deliberations. The issue, not confined to Jews, presented international, military, and diplomatic questions which had to be viewed "in relationship to the necessities of our country in prosecuting the war," Hyman argued. Delay thereby ensued; on November 13 the memo was ready.[7]

A promising breakthrough occurred simultaneously in London.

Following a suggestion in mid-February from Agudas' Harry Goodman, the Board of Deputies of British Jews requested its government to permit food shipments to Poland's ghettos along the lines of the Greek relief example. On June 23 the British Ministry of Economic Warfare (MEW) agreed to the board's sending one-pound packages from neutral Portugal to specific individuals, with the Polish government-in-exile transferring funds for these shipments, up to a maximum of $12,000, to its representatives in Lisbon. Whitehall insisted on secrecy as the British authorities were not prepared to sanction the project on any large scale or to encourage the sending of foreign exchange to Portugal. The *Jewish Telegraphic Agency (JTA)* broke the story, however, on September 10, leading Hyman to insist that the JDC had to be "governed entirely" by American policy, which had not been ascertained.[8]

The WJC in the meantime had independently raised the question in Washington of relief to Jews in Poland. On July 23, the WJC's Aryeh Tartakower and the president of the Central Representatives of Polish Jewry suggested to the U.S. Board of Economic Warfare that two tons of tea be sent to Poland for valuable barter purposes via the Red Cross in Lisbon. James Waterman Wise, son of WJC president Stephen Wise, submitted a memorandum and legal brief to the Washington representative of the ICRC asking that the ICRC ship medicaments and condensed milk to the ghettos and that the Jews there be accorded the treatment demanded by international law under the 1929 Geneva Convention for all war prisoners.

6. Ibid., p. 9; *Jewish Telegraphic Agency (JTA)*. 1 April, 10 July, 5 Sept., and 27 Sept. 1941; *Unity in Dispersion, A History of the World Jewish Congress* (New York: Institute of Jewish Affairs, 1948), p. 175; *Inter Arma Caritas* (Geneva: n.p., 1947), pp. 79–80.

7. Hyman to Baerwald et al., 1 April 1942; Minkoff to Hyman, 17 April 1942; Hyman to Buchman, 1 May 1942; Leavitt to Lehman, 13 Nov. 1942; all in Poland genl., 1942–43, JDCA.

8. *JTA*, 8 Feb. 1942; Rosenheim to JDC, 10 Sept. 1942, and Hyman to Waldman, 14 Sept. 1942, Poland genl., 1942–43, JDCA.

The Wises, father and son, together with WJC administrative committee head, Nahum Goldmann, urged the Greek precedent on Assistant Secretary of State Dean Acheson. On October 5 they heard from Secretary of the Treasury Henry Morgenthau, Jr., that the State and Treasury departments had agreed "in principle" to follow the British example and to grant licenses of $12,000 monthly for the Belgian, Dutch, and Polish governments, two other organizations, and the WJC. Elated, the WJC began reporting to its affiliated bodies that antityphus vaccine could be sent to the Warsaw ghetto, and it asked the JDC for financial support.[9]

Hearing this, the JDC promptly notified the other groups of the Central Jewish Council, which quickly sent off a delegation to Washington. Council spokesmen assured Treasury Foreign Funds Control director John Pehle that the JDC, as the oldest and most substantial relief organization in the country, should be granted the license. In the meantime, the WJC and the JDC hurled verbal brickbats at each other with no hope for a mutual settlement. The JDC received the Treasury license on 11 December 1942, just as the Allies first acknowledged that 2 million Jews had already fallen victim to the Nazis' Final Solution.[10]

But the twelfth hour had already struck for Polish Jewry. The license was not even changed to allow packages to individuals; Portugal also made export of commodities very difficult. Of 12,000 packages of figs dispatched through the Board of Jewish Deputies between February and April, 1943, 7,000 remained unaccounted for; in September, the JDC's Lisbon representative reported that addresses for Warsaw and Crakow, along with Upper Silesia and the entire General Government except for Galicia, had to be eliminated on German orders. "For the time being," the ICRC's Washington delegate concluded in a letter to Agudas Israel two months later, the sending of supplies to Poland was "impossible."[11] Indeed, for the large core of Polish Jewry had long since met death in the ghetto and labor camps or had gone up in smoke in Treblinka, Chelmno, Belzec, Maidanek, and Auschwitz.

The WJC refused to forsake sending packages to Jewry in Poland. It first urged the ICRC to extend the use of its food parcel service from Geneva to Jews in Europe. In February and March, 1943, the WJC pressed the Board of Economic Warfare to extend a new board regulation of the previous November, allowing gift parcels to specified war prisoners and civilian internees, to Jews deported from Allied countries to Eastern Europe and to those in the ghettos. While the board, the State Department's Office of Foreign Relief Operations, and the ICRC delayed their replies, they all cautioned that American authorities would not approve of such schemes without firm guarantees that the Nazis would recognize the Jews as

9. Tartakower to Wise et al., 24 July 1942, 267/46, WJCA; J. Wise memo to Peter, n.d., 212/20, WJCA; J. Wise memo to Peter, 6 and 14 Oct. 1942, 264, WJCA; Susman to Hyman, 9 Nov. 1942, Poland genl., JDCA.

10. Hyman memo, 17 Nov. 1942; Minkoff to Pehle, 17 Nov. 1942; Baerwald to Wise, 27 Nov. 1942; Baerwald to Wise (not sent), 1 Dec. 1942; Hyman to Minkoff, 15 Dec. 1942; all in Poland genl., 1942–43, JDCA.

11. Schwartz to Leavitt, 6 Jan. 1943; Katzki to Brotman, 2 July 1943; Katzki to New York, 19 and 21 Aug. 1943; Peter to Rosenheim, 11 Nov. 1943; all in Poland genl. 1942–43, JDCA.

civilian internees and would not confiscate the parcels. The full burden had again been shifted to the enemy's shoulders.[12]

Obstruction of aid by the State Department

But unknown to the WJC, at that very moment the State Department's career officers moved to withhold further information about the Holocaust from the Jewish community and even from certain authorities in the govenment. State officials had spent three months the previous year before confirming Gerhart Riegner's first report in August, 1942, about a rumored Nazi plan to kill all of European Jewry. On 21 January 1943, Minister Leland Harrison in Geneva forwarded cable number 482 for Wise to Under Secretary of State Sumner Welles in which Riegner reported that 6,000 Jews were being killed daily in one Polish town, that Berlin Jews were facing their end, and that of 136,000 Jews deported to Rumanian-controlled Transnistria in the Ukraine, 60,000 had died. Welles passed this on to Wise, and the WJC prepared for a mass Madison Square Garden rally to "Stop Hitler Now!" Yet on February 10, cable number 354 arrived on Harrison's desk, referring to "YOUR CABLE 482, JANUARY 21," and suggesting that he *not* accept reports destined for "private persons" in the United States unless under "extraordinary circumstances." Welles ap-

parently signed this routine-sounding dispatch without realizing its connection to cable number 482, for he sent off a wire on April 10, following Wise's request of March 31, that Harrison contact Riegner for "important information" about the fate of European Jewry that the WJC delegate wished to send to Wise.[13]

Welles's new order bewildered Harrison and especially mystified Riegner, who suddenly found his channel to Wise through Welles open once again. Harrison paraphrased Riegner's detailed two-page message of April 14, and mailed it to State four days later, along with his personal plea that the "helpful information" which Riegner's messages "may frequently contain" *not* be subjected to the restriction imposed by cable number 354.[14]

Riegner's report, dated April 20 from the American legation at Berne, proposed a revolutionary change to WJC headquarters: funds from the United States could bring about the rescue—not just relief—of a substantial number of Jews within Nazi Europe. His report stated that German authorities had approved ICRC collective shipments to the Theresienstadt ghetto and might do likewise for Jewish labor camps in Upper Silesia. Much more significantly, "considerable amounts" of currency could bring about "wide rescue action" in Rumania, especially Transnistria, and France. An urgent appeal from Rumanian Jews for 100 million lei ($600,000), 60 million immediately to clothe and feed Transnistrian children and orphans who should be transferred

12. Tartakower to Kubowitzki, 9 Feb. 1943, 265, WJCA; Tartakower to Wise et al., 19 Feb. 1943, U-134, WJCA; Tartakower to Peter, 4 March 1943, 265, WJCA; for more on ICRC intransigence, *see* Penkower, "The World Jewish Congress Confronts the International Red Cross During the Holocaust," in *Jewish Social Studies*, 41: 229–56 (summer–fall 1979).

13. Arthur Morse, *While 6 Million Died, A Chronicle of American Apathy* (New York: Random House, 1967), ch. 1, and pp. 42–43, 64–65.

14. Ibid., p. 65; Riegner interview with Penkower, 22 April 1977.

to Palestine, could be met by guaranteeing that the funds would be deposited to Switzerland or the United States and paid *after* the war. Large sums, not to be transferred to French territory, would also aid in maintaining Jewish children underground in France and in transferring young people and certain "political friends" from that country to Spain and North Africa.[15]

The WJC central office in New York, seizing this new ray of hope, pressed the State Department to approve the financial arrangements hinted at in Riegner's telegram. Wise wrote Welles to support a Treasury license for food packages to the ghettos. A week later he and Goldmann asked the under secretary in an interview if he would recommend to Treasury that a license be issued to the WJC to deposit a substantial amount of money with the American legation in Geneva for rescue work, as Riegner had outlined. Welles replied that "he saw the point," and asked for a memo on the subject.[16]

Welles then handed the matter over to State's economic advisor, Herbert Feis, who turned to Bernard Meltzer, acting chief of its Foreign Funds Control Division, for advice. Feis and Meltzer, after meeting with Nahum Goldmann on May 12, worded a cable to Harrison which sought information, rather than envisaged "immediate action," about Riegner's scheme. These two Jews in Foggy Bottom, aware of their superior's negative attitude to the relief and rescue of Jewry—as

formulated by Assistant Secretary Breckenridge Long—since the beginning of the war through the recently concluded Bermuda Conference, thereby kept the matter afloat.[17]

Three weeks later, Riegner confirmed through Rumanian sources that wealthy Rumanian Jews could provide the necessary funds to support the 70,000 remaining Jews in Transnistria and would be reimbursed at black-market rates in American dollars or Swiss francs after the war through the American Jewish Congress' blocked account. Wilhelm Filderman, former president of the Jewish communities in Rumania, would disperse the WJC-backed funds via an underground relief agency manned by WJC members in that country; the WJC would try to evacuate immediately as many of these Jews as possible. As for France, at least 15 to 20 thousand francs a month would be necessary. People in Switzerland having francs in France would release these to the underground through intermediaries trusted by the WJC in return for American dollars converted into Swiss francs within Switzerland at the prevailing black-market rate. Harrison, for his part, warned that these sums could not be controlled and that the transfer of enemy funds would be involved. At the same time, he con-

15. Morse, p. 65.

16. Wise to Welles, 14 April 1943, Emergency Joint Committee on European Jews, 1942–43, American Jewish Committee Archives, New York (hereafter cited as AJCA); Wise to Welles, 23 April 1943, 264, WJC; Wise-Goldmann-Welles talk, 20 April 1943, State Dept. files, Zionist Archives, New York.

17. Meltzer-Goldmann talk, 12 May 1943, 840.48 Refugees/3827, State Department files, RG 59, National Archives, (Washington, DC (hereafter cited as SD); DuBois memo, 9 Dec. 1943, in Morgenthau Diaries, vol. 688-I, Franklin D. Roosevelt Library, Hyde Park, New York (hereafter cited as MD, FDRL); State to Harrison, 25 May 1943 862.4016/2269, SD; for Long and the Bermuda Conference, see Henry Feingold, *The Politics of Rescue, The Roosevelt Administration and the Holocaust, 1938–1945* (New Brunswick, NJ: Rutgers University Press, 1970).

veyed that the Rumanian government had taken a "helpful attitude toward the amicable settlement of Jews."[18]

Riegner's response of June 14 only strengthened the division in State. While Feis and Meltzer favored action to implement the Riegner proposal, Long, his executive assistant, George Brandt, and his specialist on refugee matters, Robert Reams, particularly opposed the step. The trio emphasized that foreign exchange would thus be made available to the enemy, although Meltzer noted that the "economic warfare" aspects of the matter were questions for Treasury's decision. They finally made a slight concession: Meltzer could present the Treasury Department with the economic warfare aspects at stake. Accordingly, John Pehle received a copy of Riegner's cable on June 25.[19] With this step, Treasury had been brought for the first time officially into direct contact with the Final Solution.

Aid from the Treasury Department

The State Department's decision that the Treasury Department had to be consulted on the WJC rescue proposal for Rumania and France delighted WJC headquarters. When first approached by the WJC to permit a license for food packages to the Polish ghettos, Treasury had unhesitatingly consented. In addition, in the WJC's view, bribery could achieve results: it had just received information that deportations from Slovakia had temporarily

ceased in this manner, and now Riegner's letter suggested further possibilities. The American Jewish relief organizations, which alone had the large sums needed for significant rescue, hesitated to accept the WJC's repeated urgings to take action. The WJC could probably raise the ransom funds necessary to permit the evacuation, but the millions suggested for relief and larger rescue projects would be the responsibility of others. And they refused to apply to the American government for permission to transfer money to Europe for rescue in Nazi-held territory, claiming that such deals, contravening the Trading With the Enemy Act, were deemed unpatriotic. At the end of May, for example, the JDC emphasized to State its interest in offering financial aid for "every possible measure of rescue and relief that will not conflict with military considerations" which the U.S. government "may devise and undertake." Its representative in Geneva, Saly Mayer, hesitated in relaying the $2 million requested by the Slovakian Jewish "Working Group" partly on the assumption that the Allies would not permit him to make this transfer in the necessary Swiss francs. Consequently, the WJC had no alternative but to challenge the financial blockade on its own. Treasury seemed a far better address than State for this purpose.[20]

Indeed, these views proved to be well founded. James Wise and Gold-

18. Harrison to State, 14 June 1943 862.4016/2275, SD.

19. DuBois memo, 9 Dec. 1943, in MD, vol. 688–I, FDRL; Harrison to State, 14 June 1943, 862.4016/2274, SD (with notation about Pehle's receipt of same).

20. Tartakower to Wise et al., 12 April 1943, 266, WJCA; "Relief and Rescue" memo, mimeographed (1944), 153, WJCA, pp. 27–28; Nahum Goldmann interview with Penkower, 14 March 1974; Baerwald to Welles, 28 May 1943, Paul Baerwald MSS., Herbert Lehman Papers, Columbia University, New York; Livia Rothkirchen, *Churban YaHadut Slovakia, Taiur Histori BeTeudot* (Jerusalem: Yad Vashem, 1961), pp. xxxv–xxxvi.

mann met with Pehle and an associate in Treasury on July 1, and they in turn reported to Secretary Morgenthau. Riegner and Harrison in the meantime prodded State for a reply, pointing out that a Red Cross representative could expedite the rescue project. But at a meeting with Treasury on July 15, State officials dragged their feet; Feis and Meltzer could do no more than send a memorandum to Hull against the economic warfare arguments of Long and company.

Wise's intervention with President Franklin D. Roosevelt, on July 22, appeared to break the bottleneck, for the chief executive and then Morgenthau approved the proposal in principle.[21] Morgenthau, having learned the previous September of the Final Solution through Wise, subsequently intervened with the Papal Nuncio in Washington to have the Vatican intercede for Jewry's sake and had just sent a personal message to a special "Emergency Conference to Save the Jewish People of Europe" calling for "every possible step" to "stop this needless slaughter." As State preferred to make "no comments" on the Riegner proposal, however, Harrison only received Treasury's approval on August 6. At the end of September, the minister finally received word that he could definitely issue Riegner the license, and Treasury quickly gave its approval to additional matters raised by Riegner and Harrison "in view of the broad humanitarian considerations involved." By this time, Treasury officials

had had some indications of State's attitude toward assisting European Jewry: its objections to the immediate release of 1500 Jewish refugees from camps in Algiers, its firm support for a joint Anglo-American statement aimed at quieting public discussion of Palestine during the war, and its stalling in the grant of JDC food packages to Theresienstadt. Foreign Funds Control director Pehle wished now to make sure that State would do nothing further to hold up the Riegner plan.[22]

Hull and Morgenthau

Suddenly, Minister Harrison mentioned two difficulties concerning Treasury's green light for the proposal: he required specific instructions from State and the British Commercial Secretary in Geneva also opposed the scheme so long as MEW had not given its approval. Pehle, who only heard of this cable through an undercover source in State, informed Long immediately on October 26 that U.S. funds had been transmitted in the past to other foreigners in need abroad whereas British clearance was never necessary after Treasury had exercised its licensing authority in a specific case. Long finally gave a qualified approval, but Harrison, realizing State's dissociation from Treasury's enthusiastic approval, checked with the British commerical secretary. The latter official received word from his superiors—three weeks later

21. Pehle and O'Connell memo to Morgenthau, 1 July 1943, in MD, vol. 646, FDRL; Morse, p. 67; Paul memo to Morgenthau, 12 Aug. 1943, in MD, vol. 688-I, FDRL; Stephen Wise, *Challenging Years, The Autobiography of Stephen Wise* (New York: G. P. Putnam's Sons, 1949), pp. 277–78.

22. Henrietta Klotz interview with Penkower, 14 March 1977; *The Answer*, Aug. 1943, p. 4; DuBois memo, 9 Dec. 1943, in MD, vol. 688-I, FDRL; Paul to Morgenthau, 17 Dec. 1943, in MD, vol. 688-II, FDRL; Monty N. Penkower, "The 1943 Joint Anglo-American Statement on Palestine," *Herzl Yearbook*, 8:212–41 (New York: 1978); Pehle to Leavitt, 14 Sept. 1943, Genl. and Emerg., Czech., Terezin, JDCA.

—that the proper Washington authorities would have to be consulted before MEW would finally agree.[23]

Morgenthau's circle in Treasury, stunned at State's dilatory tactics, urged Hull to support MEW withdrawal of its objections. On December 6, however, Secretary Hull replied to Morgenthau's letter in the matter by shifting responsibility to Treasury for the delay! Hull countered that the Treasury Department had never formulated a workable proposal for financing the program, and it had never obtained British agreement.[24] The ball was back in Morgenthau's court.

Again, Morgenthau's "boys" provided a strong response. General Counsel Josiah DuBois, Jr., shared with the staff Meltzer's confidences about the division within State during the previous summer, and a 10-page memorandum by Randolph Paul, refuting Hull's contentions, arrived in Morgenthau's hands on December 17. A cable just received from U.S. ambassador in London, John Winant, added fuel to the fire by hinting darkly that, according to MEW, "the Foreign Office are concerned with the difficulties of disposing of any considerable number of Jews should they be rescued from enemy-occupied territory." Recovering from this message, which shocked the normally silent Morgenthau, the Treasury Department prepared a two-page brief for Hull and Roosevelt asking for immediate action on the Riegner proposal. Pehle, DuBois, and the others,

however, with the strong support of the Foreign Economic Administration's Oscar Cox, urged that the time had definitely come for the president to establish an agency which would deal sympathetically with all rescue possibilities. The secretary agreed, but insisted that he confront Hull with the facts personally before turning to Roosevelt in the last resort. Paul's revised memorandum concluded that the time had come for the State and Treasury departments to "cut the Gordian knot *now* by advising the British that we are going to take immediate action to facilitate the escape of Jews from Hitler and *then* discuss what can be done in the way of finding them a more permanent refuge. . . . Even if we took these people and treated them as prisoners of war it would be better than letting them die."[25]

An even more jolting revelation moved Morgenthau to face head-on what Pehle called the "real issue." In early December, DuBois asked a friend at State if he could provide a copy of the mysterious cable number 354 referred to in Harrison's dispatch of April 20 which Pehle had received in mid-July. DuBois obtained cable number 354 and the telegram to which it referred, 482, thus giving Tresury the sudden realization that State wished to suppress vital information about the Holocaust.

At the meeting with Hull on December 20, Morgenthau read therefore with "astonishment" Hull's sharp cable to the British, refusing to accept the Foreign Office's view about the disposal of many Jews.

---

23. Harrison to State, 6 Oct. 1943; Paul to Morgenthau, 2 Nov. 1943; both in MD, vol. 688-I, FDRL; Pehle-Long talk and memos of 26 Oct. 1943 862.4016/2292, SD.

24. "Jewish evacuation" meeting, 23 Nov. 1943; Morgenthau to Hull, 24 Nov. 1943; Hull to Morgenthau, 6 Dec. 1943; all in MD, vol. 688-I, FDRL.

25. DuBois memo, 9 Dec. 1943; Paul memo, 17 Dec. 1943; Winant to State, 15 Dec. 1943; "Jewish evacuation" meeting, 17 and 20 Dec. 1943; all in MD, vol. 688-II, FDRL.

Long chimed in, self-defensively, that he had even ordered Harrison two days earlier to issue the license to Riegner. Still, Morgenthau and Paul jointly agreed then and there to show Treasury's memorandum to Hull. After a hasty reading of the document, the genuinely furious secretary of state conceded that the "people down the line" got "hold of these things and didn't understand them. . . . You just sort of have to rip things out if you want to get them done."[26]

President Roosevelt

Despite this victory, the Treasury staffers decided to bring their righteous indignation to the White House. Morgenthau had taken a great risk in pushing State: Hull might not have wished to be bothered with the issue or anti-Roosevelt congressmen might still get a copy of the memorandum. Yet Cox reported that Welles's newly appointed successor, Edward Stettinius, Jr., had privately expressed sympathy for the Jewish refugee question, while Long sent over cable number 354 to Morgenthau after the State–Treasury confrontation *without* the reference to cable number 482.

Long's continued obstruction for the past eight months over the Riegner proposal, together with his attempt to defend State's miserable record before a closed session of the House Foreign Affairs Committee at the end of November—a statement attacked by the public as soon as his testimony was released—convinced Morgenthau and others on his staff that Long would have to go. A scheduled appointment with Roosevelt was set for 16 January 1944.

Morgenthau's gambit was to be an explanation of the delay between Wise's July meeting with Roosevelt over the Riegner proposal and the issuance of the license on Christmas Eve.[27]

While Paul and his associates revised the memorandum, they heard of additional information about State's willful obstruction to prevent rescue ever since Riegner's first cable arrived in Washington. WJC executives informed Pehle and DuBois about the "run-around" they had received from State and about the way in which State had torpedoed the Bermuda Conference even before it convened. Pehle also discovered that Treasury's approval four months earlier for a JDC license to rescue Jewish children in France had been stymied by the State Department, and he issued the license forthwith on his own.[28]

Meeting with Morgenthau on January 12, Hull agreed with his Cabinet colleague that the U.S. government's record in rescuing the doomed Jews was "most shocking," yet he showed no knowledge of British Foreign Secretary Anthony Eden's view, cabled by Winant five days earlier, that possible "transportation and accomodation problems" which might be "embarrassing" to both governments could well ensue from adoption of Riegner's scheme. Long sought unsuccessfully to hold back the official record of his suggestion to the British minister in Washington that His Majesty's Government make havens available for Jewish refugees in the former Italian colonies of North Africa and so divert mounting

26. Morse, p. 75; "Jewish evacuation" meetings, 20 Dec. 1943, in MD, vol. 688–II, FDRL.

27. Ibid.; Feingold, pp. 230–37.
28. "Jewish evacuation" meeting, 31 Dec. 1943, MD, vol. 688-II, FDRL; Paul memo, 3 Jan. 1944, in MD, vol. 690, FDRL.

public pressure away from the most logical refuge, the Jewish National Home in Palestine. Only days earlier, the British had also turned down the JDC's request to set aside sufficient Palestine immigration certificates under the limited quota of the 1939 White Paper, to assure the evacuation from Switzerland of 5000 French Jewish children after the war.[29]

The final brief for the president, authored by DuBois, Pehle, and Paul —three Protestants—flayed the State Department's failure to use the available governmental machinery to rescue Jews from Hitler and its clandestine attempt to use this machinery to prevent the rescue of European Jewry. Included was a most recent revelation about the WJC's inability to obtain Anglo-American funds for aiding European Jewry through ICRC auspices. Goldmann had suggested to Long in September that the two governments contribute $8 million to the ICRC for medicines and concentrated foods to Jews in central Europe. Long replied then that State had no money, the president possessed limited special funds, and the WJC would have to obtain a congressional appropriation. He agreed, however, to recommend the measure if approved by the Intergovernmental Committee in London, a move which effectively stifled Goldmann's proposal from the start. The JDC, informed by Goldmann of Long's interest, had immediately offered State to make an initial grant of $100,000 to the ICRC while a decision on the larger proposal

would be pending. While the Intergovernmental Committee had no quick response, the Treasury staff reported to Morgenthau on January 14 that the President's Fund had some $70 million allocated, and that State officials could get whatever funds they wished "with a snap of their fingers."[30] Long had apparently not made the crucial gesture.

CREATION OF THE WAR REFUGEE BOARD

Morgenthau, Pehle, and Paul confronted Roosevelt in the White House on 16 January 1944, as he quickly read the secretary's *Personal Report to the President*. The secretary had condensed the original draft and had altered its initial title, *Report . . . on the Acquiescence of This Government in the Murder of The Jews*, but he had left the original sting intact. The indictment focused on the delays regarding Riegner's evacuation proposal and the fate of his cables about the Holocaust at the hands of men "who are indifferent, callous and perhaps even hostile." The overwhelming weight of the argument and Morgenthau's rocklike stance, along with increasing calls for a presidential commission from Congress and the public after their reading Long's testimony, combined to produce the desired effect.

The president responded with enthusiasm to the group's prepared Executive Order and urged a greatly relieved secretary of the Treasury

29. "Jewish evacuation" meeting and Pehle memo of 12 Jan. 1944; "Jewish evacuation" meeting, 7 Jan. 1944; Eden to Winant, 7 Jan. 1944; and Leavitt to Hayter, 7 Jan. 1944; all in MD, vol. 693, FDRL.

30. "Report to the Secretary on the Acquiescence of This Government in the Murder of the Jews," 13 Jan. 1944, in MD, vol. 693, FDRL; Long-Goldmann talk, 16 Sept. 1943, Box 202, Breckenridge Long MSS., Library of Congress, Washington, DC (hereafter cited as LC); Hyman to Long, 6 Oct. 1943, 840.48 Refugees/4556, SD; "Jewish evacuation" meeting, 15 Jan. 1944, in MD, vol. 694, FDRL.

to discuss the proposal with Under Secretary Stettinius. Six days later, Roosevelt announced the formation of the War Refugee Board with John Pehle to be its acting director. Roosevelt assigned the new agency $1 million from the emergency funds but private rescue agencies would have to cover all expenses thereafter.[31]

With Stettinius's strong support, "the whole government policy," as Pehle put it, began to change in the field of rescue. The under secretary assigned Long, who convinced Hull to keep the "hot potato" entirely out of State, to drop all refugee questions and to shift to congressional relations. Treasury's draft of an unequivocal cable from State on January 25 to all its diplomatic missions abroad—at a record cost of $10,000—to facilitate by all possible means the War Refugee Board's future work for the rescue and relief of "the victims of enemy oppression" also went forward under Stettinius's guiding hand.[32] This telegram directly reversed cable number 354, as well as State's previous stance regarding the food package program and Riegner's evacuation proposal.

A promising beginning had finally been made. But the lateness of the hour and Adolf Hitler's ruthless determination to complete the murder of all the Jews of Europe made the odds of success more than questionable.[33]

RESULTS

Four years had elapsed between the Nazi conquest of Poland and Roosevelt's removing the jurisdiction over refugee activity from the State Department to the War Refugee Board. State's inaction and "gross procrastination"—Morgenthau's characterization[33]—regarding the killing of European Jewry had been clearly reflected in the case of food relief to the ghettos, cable number 354, and Riegner's rescue proposal. Especially striking was State's opposition to the WJC evacuation plan, given Roosevelt's initial encouragement and the support of the State Department's own economic specialists and the Treasury Department's Foreign Funds Control Division. Only Treasury's increasing pressure finally brought about the State Department's retreat in these matters.

The Foreign Office's record suffered even more by comparison. While it approved a limited license for food to Poland and Theresienstadt before State did, Whitehall expressed reluctance on political grounds even to accept its *own* Ministry of Economic Warfare's approval of the preliminary financial arrangements for Riegner's scheme. Morgenthau appropriately termed its views "a Satanic combination of British chill and diplomatic doubletalk; cold and correct, and adding up to a sentence of death."

The persistent worry of "disposing" of any "considerable number of Jews" from Nazi-occupied Europe also explains the vexation

31. "Personal Report to the President," in MD, vol. 694, FDRL, pp. 111–18; Morse, pp. 78–81. The effort of Jewish pressure groups, especially the Emergency Committee to Save the Jewish People of Europe, regarding the War Refugee Board's creation lies beyond the scope of this article.

32. "Jewish evacuation" meeting, 26 Jan. 1944, Box 202, Long MSS., LC; Fred Israel, *The War Diary of Breckenridge Long* (Lincoln, NE: University of Nebraska Press, 1966), p. 337; "Jewish evacuation" meeting, 25 Jan. 1944, in MD, vol. 696, FDRL.

33. "Personal Report to the President," 13 Jan. 1944, in MD, vol. 694, FDRL.

of a prominent Foreign Office official on suddenly hearing of the War Refugee Board's creation: "It is fundamentally all part of a Zionist drive and is liable to make much trouble for us in Palestine and with our relations with America over Palestine."[34] The British never set up a parallel refugee agency to the board during the remainder of the war.

Both British and American governments appeared ill at ease with the possibility of truly aiding the Jewish people in their blackest hour. According to the Allied rationale, supplies to the ghettos would "almost certainly" be diverted for the Germans' personal use or granted the Jews just to free the Third Reich from its "responsibility" to feed them. Either way, the argument could not lose and the Jews died. Actual rescue, on the other hand, raised "technical difficulties" which might be "embarrassing" to both governments. Anthony Eden's choice of words in January, 1944, simply echoed his earlier fear, expressed to Hull and Roosevelt in March, 1943, that acceptance of Bulgaria's 60 to 70 thousand Jews might cause Hitler to make similar offers in Poland and Germany just when shipping and accommodation could not "handle" the Jews. State's European Division had turned down a related offer for Rumanian Jewry in November, 1941, on similar grounds. Both governments jointly took this position at the abortive Bermuda Conference on Refugees, Robert Reams of Long's staff later informing Stettinius that "in the event of our admission of inability to take care of

these people, the onus for their continued persecution would have been largely transformed from the German Government to the United Nations."[35]

Morgenthau and the Treasury circle reacted differently, understanding the moral issue involved and the possibility of helping Jews without sacrificing the major war effort. Realizing, with Cox and Stettinius, that the annihilation of the Jews by the Nazis challenged the basic principles of humanity and civilization for the which the Allies had taken up arms, they argued that bringing the Jews relief and rescue would have the effect of thwarting the Axis and of furthering a fundamental objective of the United Nations in view of Germany's announced policy to annihilate the Jews. A proud American, Morgenthau deeply believed in the concept of the United States as a refuge for people persecuted the world over; as a Jew, the Holocaust shocked him profoundly. Guided by a concerned staff, he displayed courage and statesmanship in first approving Riegner's evacuation project, then challenging State, and finally confronting Roosevelt himself.[36]

Had the definite possibilities of relief and rescue which existed been taken up without delay by the Anglo-American Alliance, as Treasury alone championed, countless thousands of Jews would have survived the German Götterdämmerung. Food and medical supplies could have pro-

---

34. Henry Morgenthau, Jr., "The Refugee Run-Around," *Collier's* 1 Nov. 1947; Hankey minute, 4 Feb. 1944, Foreign Office 371/42727, Public Record Office, Kew, England.

35. *Foreign Relations of the United States, 1943*, 3:38, (hereafter cited as FRUS); *FRUS, 1941*, 2:875–76; Reams to Stettinius, 8 Oct. 1943, Box 202, Long MSS., LC.

36. Paul memo to Morgenthau, 26 Aug. 1943, in MD, vol. 688-I, FDRL; "Jewish evacuation" meeting, 2 Dec. 1943, in MD, vol. 688-II, FDRL; Henrietta Klotz interview with Penkower, 14 March 1977.

vided immediate sustenance through-out Europe, while dollars and Swiss francs would have been used for false documents, South American passports, bribes, and large ransom efforts. Some in the Nazi hierarchy did allow wealthy Jews to buy their way to safety. Taking note of this fact when defending State's "reluctance" to allow blocked accounts in Switzerland, which "apparently could not be used by the Nazi leaders" during the war, Cordell Hull unwittingly admitted in his memoirs the probability of rescue: "The State Department did not have the large sums of money and the personnel needed to carry out a plan of reaching and bribing the German officials in charge of the extermination program."[37] Treasury revealed, however, that the attitude of State and the Foreign Office militated against attempting such plans in the first place.

Some Jewish efforts had shown what successes even limited funds could achieve in underground activities. JDC funds enabled a French interfaith relief organization to shelter thousands of children in Christian homes throughout 1942, until the U.S. government cut diplomatic relations with Vichy and the Trading With the Enemy Act closed off funds in November. The three Palestinian Jewish emissaries in Istanbul, assigned to work exclusively for relief and rescue in Europe, reported to American Jewish organizations in May and July, 1943, how "with money one can save lives." They wrote that bribery had postponed the expulsion of the entire surviving Slovakian Jewish community three times and that Jews could be smuggled out of Poland, Slovakia, and

Hungary. But by the time the War Refugee Board managed to take its first concrete steps to alter the financial blockade, the German armies occupied Hungary and speedily carried out the last act of the Final Solution with a ruthlessness unsurpassed heretofore. And even then, the board favored drawn-out negotiations over Gestapo offers at the end of 1944, rather than allow the payment of ransom for the swift release of Jews in Nazi hands.[38]

Errors in judgment

Organized Jewry in the United States failed at times to measure up to the unparalled catastrophe. The inability to grasp that the Third Reich employed starvation as a weapon to destroy European Jewry, coupled with sincere but misguided doubts about challenging the Allied blockade against Germany, ended organized Jewry's food parcel projects in August, 1941. As for the more established JDC, it insisted on complying with all American regulations and refused throughout the war to contemplate some *modus vivendi* with the WJC while Jews abroad underwent mass annhilation. Patriotic considerations not to confront the financial blockade, coupled with fears of dual loyalty charges, overrode the desperate need to raise and transmit through all means substantial funds for ransom and similar activities. A traditional philosophy of relief in accordance with governmental law, rather than obligatory,

37. Cordell Hull, *Memoirs* (New York: Macmillan, 1948), 2:1539.

38. Morse, pp. 60–62; Pomeraniec to Mereminski et al., 30 May 1943, 266, WJCA; Pomeraniec and Shind to Mereminski, 25 July 1943, Z6/17/9, Central Zionist Archives, Jerusalem; Yehuda Bauer, "The Negotiations Between Saly Mayer and the Representatives of the S.S. in 1944–45," in *Rescue Attempts During the Holocaust*, eds. Y. Gutman and E. Zuroff (Jerusalem: Yad Vashem, 1977), pp. 5–45.

large-scale rescue measures, could not cope fundamentally with the unprecedented tragedy.

Even those organizations which challenged the economic warfare argument did not always comprehend the dimensions of Nazi policy. One major Agudas Israel leader, for example, continued to focus as late as March, 1943, on sending the already doomed ghettos food to save the Jews and thereby "disrupt" the Nazi propaganda line in occupied countries: "One Jew less—one bread more!" In mid-July he still pressed the Joint Emergency Committee for European Jewish Affairs, which covered all the major Jewish organizations, to dispatch food by boat for the "still several million Jews in Poland." WJC headquarters in New York, although maintaining constant pressure on various circles in Washington and elsewhere to save Jewry, also erred occasionally in evaluating the crisis. Thus in a memorandum to the Bermuda Conference, the WJC expressed a conviction that starvation represented the major cause of Jewish death at German hands. It declared that the second factor was the high death rate Jews suffered while being transported from Poland to labor camps on the Nazi-Soviet front.[39]

In the final analysis, however, the JDC correctly concluded that the ultimate solution to helping European Jewry lay "in the hands of governments from which permission must be secured." Rather than grapple with the "technical difficulties" involved in relief and rescue, the State Department and Foreign Office, the Board and Ministry of Economic Warfare, the ICRC, and the Intergovernmental Committee on Refugees all passed their responsibilities onto the enemy. Roosevelt did nothing either until pressed in July, 1943, by Wise and, far more importantly, by Morgenthau and political considerations in January, 1944, even though he received an eyewitness report on 28 July 1943, from a Polish underground messenger about the gassing of Jews at Treblinka and Belzec.

"I don't know how we can blame the Germans for killing them when we are doing this," observed Randolph Paul in December, 1943. "The law calls them *para-dilecto*, of equal guilt." At a time when the two closest Allies received accurate information on the full scope of the Jewish tragedy, the *New York Post*'s Samuel Grafton raised the issue most succinctly in a column which found its way into Morgenthau's personal diaries: "Either we consider the Jews part of Europe, and therefore we retaliate against their murderers as against the murderers of Europeans, or we must consider them a special case, and therefore devise a special means of rescue. There are no other alternatives, in logic or in honor; only these two."[40] The powers of the free West refused to pick up the challenge.

---

39. WJC Relief Committee meeting, 24 March 1943, 216A/33, WJCA; Joint Emergency Committee minutes, 15 July 1943, Emergency Joint Committee on European Jews, 1942–43, AJCA; S. B. Beit-Tsvi, *HaTsiyonut HaPost Ugandit BeMashber HaShoa* (Tel Aviv: Bronfman, 1977), pp. 324–26; Wise to Frankfurter, 16 Sept. 1942, Box 109, Stephen Wise MSS., American Jewish Historical Society, Waltham, MA.

40. Hyman to Rosenberg-Silver, 6 Oct. 1943, Vaad HaHatsala MSS., Yeshiva University, New York; Jan Ciechanowski, *Defeat in Victory* (Garden City, NY: Doubleday & Co., 1947), pp. 182 ff.; Paul comment, in "Jewish evacuation" meeting, 17 Dec. 1943, in MD, vol. 688-II, FDRL; Samuel Grafton, *New York Post*, 22 July 1943, in MD, vol. 688-I, FDRL, p. 61.

Confronted by the Holocaust, the American and British governments discriminated in their unwillingness to save European Jewry. State Department wires regularly sent reports from Switzerland to private American and British firms giving the status of their property holdings in Europe, but cable number 354 argued that further cables from Riegner about the Final Solution should be suppressed because such "private messages" might endanger official secret communications. The telegram permitted this service in "extraordinary circumstances," but State did not regard the mass murder of millions of Jews as such. A massive food relief program to Greece could be carried out but not to the ghettos of Poland and only slight quantities to Theresienstadt and elsewhere. (The Jewish organizations, particularly the JDC, immediately covered the substantial cost of these relief services when tardy government approval provided an opportunity to do so.)

Whitehall quickly transferred three thousand pounds sterling to Guernsey to feed English children in the Channel Islands occupied by the Germans without even asking for U.S. approval, but Whitehall turned a deaf ear to similar relief for Jewish children in Rumania, France, and all over Axis Europe who faced certain death. British political considerations kept the people most in need from their national homeland in Palestine, tantalizingly close to the charnel house of Europe. State did finally challenge these considerations over the Riegner proposal, but it acceded to the more basic White Paper at the Bermuda Conference and zealously guarded entry into the United States.[41]

Hidden behind the unique classification "stateless refugees," the Jews could not hope to exercise any meaningful leverage in the international arena. Assistant Secretary Acheson attempted to explain the fundamental differences between the Greek and Jewish ghetto situations in terms of a German perspective, but actually, as Goldmann observed at the end of 1944, the Jews could not duplicate the Greek "bargaining point" with the Allies of ships, a geographic base, and other factors.[42]

Riegner mused after the event that the most expensive cable he ever sent in his life, 700 francs for the April, 1943, telegram about evacuation possibilities, was really his cheapest since it eventually made possible the breaking of the financial blockade and the subsequent sending of large funds abroad by the American Jewish organizations for relief and rescue.[43] But had State and the Foreign Office felt compelled, as they did for other groups of civilian refugees and prisoners of war, to lift such restrictions once they comprehended German designs, the annihilation of the Jews could have been considerably checked before Riegner's first rescue proposal crossed their desks.

By the mutual consignment of the two Western Allies, the unique tragedy of the Jewish people was either lost among "suffering civilian populations" of different nationalities or dismissed as a separate circumstance which could only achieve redress after victory in a new "free society." Other peoples already possessing the benefits of statehood

41. Josiah DuBois, The Devil's Chemists (Boston: Beacon Press, 1952), p. 188; Paul memo, 2 Nov. 1943, in MD, vol. 688-I, FDRL.

42. J. Wise memo, 14 Oct. 1942, 264, WJCA; Goldmann remarks, 29 Nov. 1944, War Emergency Conference, 81/1, WJCA.

43. Riegner interview with Penkower, 22 April 1977.

fared far better than the Jews, although operating as governments-in-exile. Even the title of the War Refugee Board, like the camouflaged vocabulary Germans specifically employed for their attempt to kill all the Jews, followed the example of the Evian Conference and the Bermuda Conference and the Intergovernmental Committee on Refugees to disguise its real objective. The WJC, under such circumstances, could do no more in the war years than besiege Washington regularly and hope that some understanding would result in action.

"Only a fervent will to accomplish, backed by persistent and untiring effort, can succeed where time is so precious," read Morgenthau's January, 1944, memorandum to Roosevelt. That fervent will and compassion were missing in the Allied councils of war. The Jews could not wait for the Allied victory. Adolf Hitler would not let them wait. His grim executioners, working day and night, reaped a bloody harvest.

The Ecumenical Community
and the Holocaust

By ARMIN F. C. BOYENS

ABSTRACT: The ecumenical fellowship of the churches became manifest in a special way in the work of the World Council of Churches (WCC) and its members, not only for the Christian non-Aryans, but for all persecuted Jews in Europe. In almost all of the churches there were small minorities who took up the fight for the rights of the persecuted and who tried to help the refugees. In some instances whole churches protested publicly, and thereby resisted Hitler's policy of extermination by their word and deed. In the work for the persecuted Jews, cooperation between Protestant member churches of the WCC and the Roman Catholic church began to be developed on the regional level. This work for the rescue of the Jews also led to Christian-Jewish cooperation on the national and the international level. To rescue Jewish people, Christians had to act illegally. The cooperation of the churches and the WCC with the resistance movements in the occupied countries of Europe and with national liberation movements was not born out of the theory of an abstract theology of revolution but out of the daily practicing of Christian love of one's fellowman. Finally, the persecution of the Jews stimulated among Christians a new and deeper understanding and a theological re-examination of the role of the people of Israel, of God's revelation, and of the nature of the Church itself.

Armin F. C. Boyens received his Ph.D. from the faculty of Protestant theology of the University of Geneva, Switzerland, (Dr. theol. avec mention sciences oecuméniques) and is a pastor of the Lutheran Church in Hamburg, West Germany. From 1961 to 1967, he worked as executive secretary on the staff of the World Council of Churches in Geneva. After his return to West Germany, he lectured at the faculty of Protestant theology at the University of Mainz. He presently is a military dean in the Evangelisches Kirchenamt für die Bundeswehr in Bonn. He is the author of several books and articles on subjects of contemporary church history.

IN JULY, 1940, the general secretary of the World Council of Churches in process of formation (WCC), W. A. Visser'tHooft, a minister of the Dutch Reformed church, wrote to the member churches in a report on the activities of the WCC:

Non-Aryan Refugees: Sometimes it has been said that the Ecumenical Movement expresses itself in words only but very little in deeds. The work for non-Aryan refugees, however, proves that this is not true. . . . If there was ever a task which requires ecumenical solidarity, it is this one. And if there was no Ecumenical Movement one would have to create such a movement in order to practice Christian cooperation in this type of assistance work.[1]

THE ECUMENICAL REFUGEE SERVICE

When Visser'tHooft wrote these lines, the WCC found itself in a very difficult situation. After Hitler's victory over France, the headquarters of the WCC in Geneva, Switzerland, was in danger of being cut off from its member churches in the United States and Great Britain. Therefore the Federal Council of the Churches of Christ in the United States had urged Visser'tHooft to leave Europe and transfer the headquarters of the WCC to New York. But Visser'tHooft refused to desert his post because he felt it to be his duty to stay with the churches in Europe and to continue their common work. As he wrote to a friend in the United States: "It might be that the reality and vitality of the Ecumenical Movement will depend on the spiritual resistance against the evil forces which it can manifest in those many

countries which are being submerged."[2]

In the critical months of summer, 1940, the small staff of the WCC in Geneva helped to manifest the reality of the ecumenical movement in two ways: the five executive staff members continued the work for the prisoners of war and the ecumenical refugee service.

The ecumenical refugee service was devoted particularly to the assistance of non-Aryan refugees. It had been founded by the Provisional Committee of the WCC in January, 1939. Adolf Freudenberg, a German pastor of the Confessing church had been appointed secretary for ecumenical assistance to refugees. Being a refugee himself, Freudenberg was especially qualified for this task. Married to a non-Aryan, this former diplomat, who had served in the German Foreign Office, until 1935, had then began to study theology. He joined the Confessing church and became a member of Martin Niemöller's congregation in Berlin-Dahlem. When he was called by the WCC to set up a secretariat for the assistance to refugees, the diplomat-pastor Freudenberg gladly accepted this call.

In his first report to the member churches of the WCC, Freudenberg wrote that his "main concern was to enable further emigration out of Germany." With this goal in mind the policy of the ecumenical refugee service was defined by Freudenberg and his friends as follows:

1. To coordinate the work of the Christian refugee committees in the various countries,
2. to look for possibilities for emigration,
3. to mobilise Christian forces for active and adequate support of the refugees,

1. Visser'tHooft, "Report on the Activities of the Provisional Committee," (Jan. 1940–July 1941), p. 10, AWCC, Box Gen. Sec. 1.

2. Visser'tHooft to H. S. Leiper, 14 June 1940, AWCC, Gen. Sec.

4. to raise funds for the assistance to refugees,
5. to care for the spiritual needs of the refugees.[3]

Raised funds

Raising funds was the task to which Freudenberg had to devote most of his time and energy after he took office with the WCC's refugee service. By the summer, 1940, this was to prove the most urgent task to perform for several reasons.

First, the budget for the staff of the WCC in 1940 was limited to the annual amount of 132,000 SwF. The actual financial reserves available to the WCC at that time (when Visser't-Hooft decided to stay in Europe) were only sufficient to carry on the activities of the staff for two months.

Second, Freudenberg had to finance the passage of almost 200 refugees from Germany who wanted to emigrate to the United States. The names of these refugees had been passed on to Freudenberg by the Büro Grüber in Berlin, the refugee service of the Confessing church in Germany. By the outbreak of the war, through his refugee service, Heinrich Grüber had helped 1,138 refugees emigrate from Germany. His assistance consisted in providing the necessary exit permits from Germany and the entry visas to foreign countries and in raising the necessary travel expenses in German marks. After the outbreak of World War II (1939), foreign travel agencies no longer accepted German money but insisted on being paid in U.S. dollars. This applied to the Western shipping lines as well as to the Russian Trans Siberian railway which, until 1941, was open for refugees who tried to reach Shanghai.

Heinrich Grüber estimated that there were about 500 refugees with valid exit permits and entry visas who could not emigrate because they did not have the necessary U.S. dollars. He urged Freudenberg to help him find the required foreign currency. Freudenberg immediately sent out a fund-raising appeal to the member churches of the WCC. He estimated that $100,000 would be necessary.

This appeal was first directed to the member churches of the WCC in the United States. Their response was rather disappointing. Until the end of 1941, the ecumenical refugee service had only received $13,000 from America instead of the $100,000 it had asked for.[4] When, in February, 1940, the terrible news about the deportation of 1,200 Jews from Stettin to Poland found its way into the U.S. press, Visser'tHooft renewed the appeal for American financial support for the refugees. He asked the Federal Council for $4,400 a month. In March, 1940, Henry Smith Leiper, who was in charge of the office of the WCC in New York, received a cable, signed by Visser'tHooft, Freudenberg, Grüber, and Adolf Keller which read: "In view new threats transfer Non-Aryans Lublin urge most serious consideration appeal made in letter 'tHooft February 24." H. S. Leiper's answer was the following cable: "Deeply regret funds dependent on receipts impossible estimate large amounts improbable stop can you use two steamship tickets Geneva-New York Leiper."[5]

---

3. A. Freudenberg, "Die Kirchen und die nichtarischen Christen," AWCC Interchurch Aid B 2.

4. See A. Boyens, Kirchenkampf und Ökumene 1939–45 (München: 1973), p. 44 f.

5. Leiper to Visser'tHooft, 27 March 1940, AWCC, Gen. Sec.

Members of the National Study Conference organized in 1940 by the Federal Council of the Churches of Christ in America passed a resolution in which they said: "We are ashamed to confess that the amount of money which our Protestant Churches and church members have contributed to the support of the suffering people is comparatively small and terribly inadequate."[6]

Looking back at the work of the ecumenical refugee service during the years 1939 and 1940 in which the $10,800 available helped to finance the emigration of 71 persons from Germany, A. Freudenberg wrote in 1969 in his book *Rettet sie doch!*: "Wenig genug im Vergleich zu den Hunderttausenden Todeskandidaten; und dennoch: alles für 71 Menschenbrüder!"[7] ("Very little compared with the several hundred thousand people doomed to death; but nevertheless all we had available was for 71 fellowmen!").

Cooperated with the resistance movement

On 15 August 1941, Berlin stopped issuing exit permits to non-Aryan refugees. Legal emigration was no longer possible. Together with the halting of emigration, large-scale deportations of Jews began. Already in October, 1939, Jewish citizens of Austria had been deported to the district of Lublin in Poland, and in October, 1940, 6,500 Jewish people from Baden and the Saar had been sent to internment camps in the unoccupied zone of southern France. But October, 1941, signaled a new

6. Retranslated from A. Freudenberg, *Bericht des Ökumenischen Ausschusses für Flüchtlingshilfe* (Jan. 1942), AWCC.
7. A. Freudenberg, *Rettet sie doch!* (Zürich: 1969), p. 23.

intensification of Hitler's antisemitic policy. The stages of the Nazi policy against the Jews in occupied Europe are well known: first, the introduction of special legislation for the Jewish population, which included a definition of the term "Jew"; second, the branding of the Jews by the yellow star; third, the confiscation of Jewish property; and finally, the concentration of the Jews in special areas (ghettoization).

The fact that the Jews in all of Nazi-occupied Europe were placed under special legislation meant that any form of assistance to Jews had become illegal. In this new atmosphere of illegality, the ecumenical refugee service had to look for new ways and means to continue its work.

Under these circumstances it was quite natural that contacts developed between the ecumenical refugee service and the resistance movements in the various countries. France is a good example, the Netherlands another one.

Aided refugees in southern France

Young French Christians, members of the CIMADE (*Comité Inter-Mouvement auprès des évacués*), took the lead in helping the Jewish internees in southern France. They managed to get into the camp of Gurs and set up a center of both spiritual and material aid for the deportees. Later, similar posts were set up by the CIMADE in the camps of Rivesaltes, Brens, le Récébédou, and Nexon. The ecumenical refugee service provided for their financial support. In June, 1941, Visser'tHooft wrote: "Some 500,000,-Fr.frs. have been distributed during the last six months amongst the most needy of the 6000 refugees with whom we are in touch. The bulk of the money has come from the Swiss Churches."[8] The leader of the CIMADE was a young woman, Madeleine Barot. Being also a member of the French *résistance*, she played an important role when in summer, 1942, the CIMADE organized the clandestine passage of Jews from France to Switzerland.

Helped churches in the Netherlands resist

The resistance of the Protestant churches in the Netherlands against the occupation authorities began with a protest against the introduction of special legislation for Jewish civil servants. On 27 October 1940, the eight member churches of the Protestant Church Council sent a letter to the German *Reichskommissar* Seyss-Inquart in which they said: "In our view the spirit of these regulations . . . is contradictory to Christian mercy."[9] The content of the letter was made public throughout Holland. Visser'tHooft reported this event in a letter to his British colleague William Paton in London: "This is probably the first time in recent history when a church under an aggressively anti-semitic government protests publicly against the persecution of the Jews."[10]

Served as spokesman for the persecuted

In Proverbs 31, verse 8, we read: "Open your mouth for the dumb, for the rights of all who are left desolate." The ecumenical refuge

service of the WCC tried to do its best to live up to this biblical precept. Again and again the WCC tried to be the mouthpiece of the persecuted Jewish people in Europe. One example may suffice. On 29 October 1941, the general secretary of the WCC wrote an official letter to Professor Max Huber, president of the International Red Cross and to Professor Carl Burckhardt, president of the Commission Mixte de Secours des Sociétées de la Croix Rouge, in which he asked them "to pay special attention to the situation in the Warthegau and the General-gouvernement."[11] A "Memorandum on the situation in Poland" was added to the letter. It described the situation in several Polish cities and ghettos and provided detailed information about the most recent deportations. Visser'tHooft gave the following reasons for the WCC's acting in behalf of the Jews:

It is because of Christian responsibility that the WCC in process of formation cannot pass over in silence the need of the refugees living in Poland. . . . On the whole Jewish organizations are no longer able to act effectively on behalf of their people. The Jewish question is related to the heart of the Christian message; if the Church failed to raise its voice in order to protect and to warn and if it failed to do its best to help, it would not be obedient to its Lord. It is, therefore, the duty of the Christian Churches and especially of their ecumenical representative; the WCC in process of formation, to act as the spokesman of the persecuted.[12]

At the end of his official letter, Visser'tHooft suggested that "the Red Cross should make preparations for the setting up of a special mission to Poland, which would include a

8. Report from the Geneva Office of the Provisional Committee for the period Jan. 1–July 1, 1941, AWCC.

9. A. Boyens, p. 100.

10. Visser'tHooft, "Notes on the state of the church in Europe," (Jan. 1941), p. 4, AWCC.

11. A. Boyens, p. 116.

12. Ibid., p. 116.

medical doctor."[13] What was the reaction of the leaders of the International Red Cross? A. Freudenberg writes:

The Committee's basic concern was limited to their care for prisoners of war. It could do very little for civilians. The members of the Committee were convinced—and we could not prove that they were wrong—that actions on behalf of the Jews whom Hitler hated, would endanger the indispensable work of the Red Cross for millions of allied prisoners of war.[14]

RESPONSE TO THE FINAL SOLUTION

Historians like G. Reitlinger,[15] R. Hilberg,[16] H. Krausnick,[17] and many others[18] have done basic research about the problem of the origins of the Final Solution and about the execution of Hitler's terrible policy of extermination. I do not need to repeat here what they have discovered. The question that concerns us is, When did the WCC receive the first information about the Final Solution and how did its staff in Geneva and its member churches react?

The first definite reports that deportation meant extermination seem to have reached the WCC during August and September, 1942. On 25 September 1942, A. Freudenberg reported to a meeting of some members of the Provisional Committee of

the WCC: "According to different trustworthy reports deportation means in many cases extermination."[19] The source of these reports was Gerhart Riegner, director of the office of the World Jewish Congress (WJC) in Geneva. According to Visser'tHooft, the two Germans, Freudenberg of the WCC and Riegner of the WJC, had established good working relationships, and since 1939 had exchanged information as often as possible.

On 1 August 1942, Riegner had received terrible news from a German industrialist with close connections to the *Führer Hauptquartier*. The informant presented Riegner with a detailed account of the plans for the Final Solution and told of thousands of victims murdered by means of prussic acid, a prime ingredient in Zyklon B gas. On August 8, Riegner transmitted this information to Samuel Silvermann, representative of the WJC in London, who forwarded it to Rabbi Stephen Wise in the United States. Riegner also seems to have informed Freudenberg, who immediately began to take action, particularly on behalf of Jewish refugees fleeing to Switzerland.

Helped "non-refoulables"

During the period from 1 September 1939 to July, 1942, Switzerland had accepted only 1,200 refugees. With the onset of the deportations, not only from Germany but also from the occupied countries, the number attempting to reach this haven vastly increased. Under pressure the Swiss authorities in September, 1942, admitted 3,800. However, from August to December, 1942, the same au-

13. Ibid., p. 116.

14. A. Freudenberg, *Rettet sie doch!*, 25 f.

15. G. Reitlinger, *Die Endlösung*, 4. Aufl. (Berlin; 1961).

16. R. Hilberg, *The Destruction of the European Jews* (Chicago: 1961).

17. H. Krausnick, "Judenverfolgung," in *Anatomie des SS-Staates*, Bd. 2 (München: 1967).

18. Henry L. Feingold, *The Politics of Rescue* (New Jersey: 1970). Karl A. Schleunes, *The Twisted Road to Auschwitz* (London: 1972).

19. Minutes of a Meeting of a group of members of the Provisional Committee at Geneva, (Sept. 1942), p. 8, AWCC.

thorities officially denied entry into Switzerland to 1,056 refugees.[20] The official term was *refouler*. Freudenberg now asked A. Koechlin, president of the Swiss Church Federation, to see the Swiss police authorities and to demand the application of a still more generous policy in admitting Jewish refugees. This move turned out to be successful. Together with his French colleague Marc Boegner, president of the Eglise reformé de France, who came to visit the WCC headquarters in Geneva, Koechlin negotiated with the Swiss government. Koechlin and Boegner managed to reach an understanding with the Swiss authorities about which persons the CIMADE in France would be responsible for admitting to Switzerland. From this time onward the World Council's Refugee Secretariat was able to give very active support to these courageous French Christians who organized the clandestine passage of Jews from France to Switzerland.

Urged more aid from American churches

A special visitor to beleaguered Geneva in September, 1942, was Samuel McCrea Cavert, general secretary of the Federal Council of the Churches of Christ in America.[21] There he heard for the first time from Freudenberg that the Nazi policy of deportation of the Jews involved deliberate extermination measures. This was a point which Rabbi Stephen Wise had specifically asked him to find out in Geneva: Did deportation really mean extermination?

After his return to the States, Cavert was still unsure. In a speech on November 5 about the deportations, he stated: "The destination, though unannounced, was presumably the Jewish reservation in German-occupied Poland, where it is assumed the deportees will undergo forced labor in camps and mines. Their future existence will be virtually a process of slow death from exhaustion and semi-starvation after they are no longer useful for forced labor."[22] Why did he not use the term "extermination"? In March, 1965, looking back at the events of 1942, Cavert wrote: "It seems clear that on that date I had no knowledge (at least not of the kind that would be regarded as reliable enough to use in a public address) about extermination."[23] But a month later, presumably on the basis of more information, he did use the term "deliberate extermination"[24] when he addressed the biennial assembly of the Federal Council in Cleveland, Ohio, on 11 December 1942. In his speeches and reports, Sam Cavert tried to reactivate the American Protestant churches' financial support for the WCC and its refugee service. This was not without success, because as Freudenberg could report to his committee, American churches' contribution rose from 43,600 SwF in 1942 to 202,300 SwF in 1943.

Cooperated with Jewish organizations

The contacts established through the refugee work with Jewish organizations led to different types of collaboration. The cooperation be-

20. A. A. Häsler, *Das Boot ist voll, Die Schweiz und die Flüchtlinge 1933–1945* (Zürich: 1967), p. 334–38.

21. For more details, *see* A. Boyens, 122 ff and 233 f.

22. Speech given at a meeting in the Town Hall Club, New York, held under the auspices of the American Christian Committee for Refugees and the American Friends Service Committee, Federal Council Bulletin (Dec. 1942).

23. A. Boyens, p. 123.

24. A. Boyens, p. 123.

tween the CIMADE and Jewish organizations in France has already been mentioned. The refugee secretariat of the WCC was also able to act as intermediary for the large-scale help to Jewish families and children in hiding in Belgium and Holland.[25] An especially close co-operation existed with the WJC in Geneva. Gerhart Riegner has stated that during certain periods he and Freudenberg were "in nearly daily contact,"[26] 1943 and 1944 being such periods. Riegner later described their cooperation in these years: "I know that at a certain number of other occasions we have used the same device, and some of the very forceful speeches by Dr. Bell and other dignitaries of the Anglican Church in the House of Lords were based on reports which we have communicated to them."[27] One of these occasions was the time shortly before the Bermuda Conference on the refugee issue.

On 19 and 22 March 1943, Visser't-Hooft and Gerhart Riegner sent a common memorandum of the WCC and WJC to the British and the U.S. ambassadors in Berne to be communicated to the governments in London and Washington. Copies of the memo were also sent to Allen W. Dulles, director of the U.S. Office of Strategic Services in Berne, to the Papal Nuncio in Berne, to the League of Nations' high commissioner for refugees, and to the president of the Provisional Committee of the WCC, William Temple, then archbishop of Canterbury. The authors declared: "The Secretariats of the World Council of Churches and of the World Jewish Congress have in their pos-session most reliable reports indicating that the campaign of deliberate extermination of the Jews organised by the Nazi officials in nearly all countries of Europe under their control, is now at its climax."[28] Therefore they urged the Allied governments to organize

without delay a rescue action for the persecuted Jewish communities on the following lines:

1. Measures of immediate rescue should have priority over the study of post-war arrangements.
2. The rescue action should enable the neutral states to grant temporary asylum to the Jews who would reach their frontiers.

For this purpose a definite guarantee by the Governments of the United States of America and Great Britain . . . should be given to the neutral States, that all refugees entering their territory would be enabled to be repatriated or to reemigrate as soon as possible after the end of the war.[29]

Riegner and Visser'tHooft emphasized that only such "explicit and comprehensive guarantees of re-emigration of the refugees" would "lead the neutral countries to adopt a more liberal and understanding attitude towards the Jewish refugees."[30] They added to this request that "these guarantees should provide for the granting of facilities concerning the supply of food and funds for the maintenance of refugees during their stay in the neutral countries."[31] Their third suggested measure was the most radical one: "A scheme for the exchange of Jews in Germany and the territories under German control for German civilians in North

---

25. A. Boyens, p. 137.
26. G. Riegner to Visser'tHooft, 14 April 1965, AWCC, D274.3.2. Box 1.
27. Ibid.

28. WCC action at time of the extermination of the Jews, March 19 and 22, 1943, AWCC, D 274.3.2. Box 1.
29. Ibid., p. 2.
30. Ibid.
31. Ibid.

and South America, Palestine, and other Allied countries, should be pressed forward by all possible means."[32]

Their explanation given for this previous suggestion was:

We should like to stress the fact that the number of nationals of Axis countries living in Allied countries—particularly in North and South America—exceeds by far the number of nationals of Allied countries living in Axis countries. We feel that in spite of the great difficulties which we do not underestimate, a workable scheme of exchanging Jews for Germans would constitute an important method of rescuing a considerable number of persecuted people from the countries under Nazi control.[33]

The wartime files of the British Foreign Office prove that this memo arrived in London on 29 March 1943. Anthony Eden read it. On April 15 he forwarded it to the archbishop of Canterbury and wrote him a letter saying that this problem was not the business of His Majesty's government alone but of the Bermuda Conference.[34]

Visser'tHooft's British fellow general secretary in the WCC, William Paton, discussed the memo with Sir Hubert Emerson, the League of Nations high commissioner of refugees. His conclusion was that he could agree with the first two suggestions but not with the third. He wrote:

It means, in effect, that we should offer to take any number of Jews simply because they are Jews from German-controlled countries and exchange for them German civilians of all kinds. The popular opinion of this country would demand that, in exchange for the sending back of German civilians to Germany who might

conceivably be of value to the war effort of Germany at least British wounded should be exchanged, and it would increase anti-Semitism if the exchange were to be made of German civilians for Jews in German-occupied countries without any relief to British prisoners.[35]

Paton and Emerson were not anti-semitic. But were they free from prejudice? Emerson himself criticized the memo when he said, "the Jews made a great mistake in emphasizing only the plight for the Jews, and giving the impression that there are no other refugees in the world."[36]

Paton was critical. The memorandum, he assumed, "is the work of 'tHooft and his colleagues and I should a little judge from the contents that they had been in touch with the Zionist group and had to some extent swallowed their stuff."[37] And in a letter to the archbishop of Canterbury dated May, 1943, Paton said, "I must say that I a little regret that 'tHooft should have gone in so definitely with the World Jewish Congress, which is, of course, Zionist."[38]

Although Visser'tHooft and Riegner did not succeed in convincing the Allied governments or even their friends that some quick and extraordinary measures ought to be taken in order to rescue millions of people who were threatened by extermination, they continued their cooperation in trying to mobilize world public opinion, the Allied governments, the international humanitarian organizations, such as the Red Cross, the neutral governments,

32. Ibid., p. 3.
33. Ibid.
34. Eden to Canterbury, 15 April 1943, AFO 371/36657.
35. W. Paton, note of conversation with Sir Hubert Emerson, 20 April 1943, AWCC, D274.3.2 Box 1.
36. Ibid.
37. W. Paton to H. Carter, 16 April 1943, AWCC, D274.3.2 Box 1.
38. W. Paton to Canterbury, 14 May 1943, AWCC, D274.3.2 Box 1.

and the member churches of the WCC. There is ample proof for such common actions in the files of the WCC and the WJC in Geneva, as, for example, in the Hungarian crisis of 1944.[39]

ACTIVITIES OF SOME WCC MEMBERS

The reaction of the churches of the WCC in Europe was one of protest, in varying degrees.

Great Britain

On 29 October 1942, William Temple protested publicly against the "deliberate policy of extermination which the Nazis have declared against the Jews whereever [sic] they are to be found."[40] His actions were supported by the archbishop of York and Bishop Bell of Chichester. In public meetings and in speeches in the House of Lords, Temple and Bell repeated their protests on 10 November 1942, at the beginning of December, on 27 January 1943, February 24, March 23, and 28 July 1943. They also kept writing letters on this subject to the *London Times*.[41] Because of this attitude, the British church leaders were criticized by the British press as well as by their government. Bell complained in May 1943: "The attitude of the Government is peculiarly lukewarm and unhelpful . . . and I am dreadfully depressed about it."[42]

Norway

At the end of October, 1942, the Nazi prime minister of Norway,

Vidkun Quisling, started his campaign against the 1,700 Jews in Norway. On 11 November 1942, the bishops of the Lutheran state church in Norway, together with the leaders of the Baptist's, Methodist's, Salvation Army's, and the Foreign Mission's societies, wrote a letter to Quisling in which they raised a solemn protest against the government's violation of the constitution, the human rights and the Lutheran Confession that is "according to the constitution the religion of the State."[43] They said, "If we were to keep quiet with regard to this legalised injustice against the Jews, we too would become responsible and guilty of this injustice."[44]

Their letter to the government was read to all congregations in the country on 22 November 1942. In their pastoral letter on the First Sunday in Advent, 1942, the Swedish Lutheran bishops referred to the protest of their fellow bishops in Norway and asked their countrymen to help and receive the persecuted Norwegian Jews in Sweden.[45] In fact, 930 Jewish refugees from Norway were brought to safety in Sweden.

Denmark

The Lutheran church in Denmark had learned from the experience of their sister churches in other countries. In October, 1943, preparations for the arrest of the 7,700 Jews living in Denmark began. The Danish resistance movement had received warnings from members of the German opposition, like George Fr. Duckwitz and Helmut James Graf von Moltke.[46] And it thus became

39. *See* A. Boyens, 139 ff.
40. J. M. Snoek, *The Grey Book* (Assen: 1969), p. 238 f.
41. Ibid., 239 ff.
42. Bell to Paton, 21 May 1943, AWCC, D274.3.2 Box 1.

43. *Norwegische Kirchendokumente*, ed. 2 (Zürich: 1946).
44. Ibid., 69.
45. A. Boyens, 132 f.
46. Ibid, 133.

possible to mobilize the whole Danish nation to support the rescue operation of the Jews.[47]

The Lutheran church was an integral part of this protest movement of the Danish people. Its official protest was handed over to the German occupation forces even before the arrest of the Jews started. On Sunday, 3 October 1943, this protest was read from all the pulpits in the country. The bishops declared: "We shall therefore struggle to ensure the continued guarantee to our Jewish brothers and sisters of the same freedom, which we ourselves treasure more than life. . . ."[48] Out of 7,700 Jews living in Denmark, 7,220 persons were rescued by fleeing to Sweden. Hannah Arendt calls this action "the only example of *open* resistance of a people known to us."[49]

The Netherlands

There is something special about the reaction of the Dutch churches in their protests against the deportation of the Jews. On 5 January 1942, all Christian churches in the Netherlands, the Roman Catholic church and the Protestant churches, together signed a letter of protest against the deportations which they sent to the German *Reichskommissar*. For the first time in the history of the Christian church in Holland—and maybe even in the world—Catholic and Protestant church leaders joined in a common action.[50] This truly ecumenical action was continued by Catholics and Protestants in Holland throughout the German occupation. If today

we speak of a Dutch ecumenism there can be no doubt that the experience of the war and the common fight against injustice and persecution contributed to the growth of an ecumenical conscience among the Christians in the Netherlands.

The Confessing church in Germany

A presentation of the attitude of the European churches when confronted with Hitler's policy of extermination of the Jews would be incomplete without a brief look at the reaction of the German Protestant church when it learned that deportation meant extermination.

On 9 December 1941, Bishop Wurm of Württemberg, the speaker of the Confessing church in Germany, came to Berlin and handed a letter of protest to an official in the *Reichskanzlei* in Berlin addressed to Hitler as the "Führer of the German people." In this memorandum Bishop Wurm pointed out the fatal consequences which the attacks of the Nazi party and other officials on Christian organizations, particularly the measures against the non-Aryans, were likely to have in the life of the nation.[51]

On the same day, Bishop Wienken handed a letter of protest from the German Catholic bishops to the *Reichskanzlei*, which was also addressed to Hitler. In Germany, too, Catholics and Protestants acted together. However, this was not the only representation made by Bishop Wurm. Besides his sermons, in which he condemned the persecution of the Jews without fear, he addressed three letters to Joseph Goebbels in 1941 and 1942. He wrote again to Hitler on 2 March 1942 and sent

47. H. Flender, *Rescue in Denmark*, (New York: 1963).

48. AAPol. Arch. Inland I-D, 1/18-20, 19/4.

49. H. Arendt, *Eichmann in Jerusalem* (München: 1964), p. 215.

50. *See* W. A. Visser'tHooft, ed. *Holländische Kirchendokumente* (Zürich: 1944), p. 53 ff.

51. G. Schäfer, ed., *Landesbischof D. Wurm und der nationalsozialistische Staat 1940–1945, Eine Dokumentation*, (Stuttgart: 1968), p. 277.

several letters of protest to Reichsminister Lammers in the *Reichskanzlei*.[52] When the Nazi authorities did not answer these protests, Wurm wrote again in a more urgent tone to Hitler on 16 July 1943:

> In the Name of God . . . we urgently request the responsible leaders of the State to put an end to the persecution of thousands of men and women under German rule without legal reasons. All Non-Aryans within the German sphere of influence having been practically eliminated, there is every reason to fear as various incidents prove, that the socalled [sic] "privileged Non-Aryans" who have so far been spared, are again in danger of being treated in the same manner. We emphatically protest against all measures that threaten marriage life in law-abiding families. . . . Such aims, together with the destructive measures against other Non-Aryans, are entirely contrary to all Divine law and undermine the fundamental principles on which life and civilization are built upon—the God given right of human life and dignity."[53]

Nazi documents prove that Hitler read the protests of Bishop Wurm. There exists a special file in the Archive of the German Foreign Office entitled "*Landesbischof Wurm, Stuttgart.*"[54] From a memo included in this file we learn that Hitler, Goebbels, and other Nazi dignitaries had a conference in 1942 in the *Reichskanzlei* to discuss possible measures to be taken against the bishop.

Heydrich, chief of the *Reichssicherheitshauptamt*, had accused Bishop Wurm of high treason and of a "stab-in-the-back policy."[55] He asked for "security police measures" against the bishop. But in a top-

secret letter (*Geheime Reichssache*) of 19 March 1943, written by Hitler's right-hand man, Martin Bormann, to the minister of justice, we read that Hitler himself decided that "at present for political reasons Landesbischof Wurm ought not to be accused officially."[56] The only answer which Bishop Wurm received to his letters came on 3 March 1944. On behalf of the Reich government, Reichs-minister Lammers wrote to warn Bishop Wurm that if he were to persist in his attitude toward the government and were to continue sending in protests, which had become known to the enemy, he would no longer be treated with leniency. If he were to go on speaking of "Divine judgment" in his sermons and other public speeches, such a course would be looked on as defeatism for which reason he would be arrested and treated with the utmost severity.[57]

The protests of Bishop Wurm, the official spokesman of the Confessing church in Germany, prove that this church did not keep silent on Hitler's policy of extermination of the Jews. There are also examples of a very small number of Protestants in Germany, some of them members of the Confessing church, who dared to help the persecuted Jews by hiding some of them and by providing those in hiding with food and falsified passports.[58]

STATEMENT, 1948: ANTISEMITISM IS A SIN AGAINST GOD AND MEN

The member churches of the WCC and the staff of the WCC raised their voices in protest against the persecution of the Jewish people. In almost all of the churches there were small minorities, brave men and

---

52. Ibid., 273, 289, 296, 291, 295.
53. Ibid., 305 f.
54. Pol. Arch. AA. Inland I-D, Deutschland Kirche 2/3.
55. Heydrich to Ribbentrop, 12 April 1942, Pol. Arch. AA, Inland I-D, Deutschland Kirche 2/3.
56. BA, R 22/4008.
57. G. Schäfer, 313 ff.
58. For more details, *see* A. Boyens, 111 ff.

women, who took up the fight for the rights of the persecuted and who tried to help the refugees. In some instances whole churches protested publicly and thereby resisted Hitler's policy of extermination by their word and deed. Nevertheless it is true what Visser'tHooft has said in his memoirs, "I know now that I ought to have done much more."[59] Having this in mind, I would like to sum up this article in the following theses:

1. The ecumenical fellowship of the churches became manifest in a special way in the work of the WCC and its member churches not only for the Christian non-Aryans, but for all persecuted Jews in Europe.

2. In the work for the persecuted Jews, a pattern of cooperation between Protestant member churches of the WCC and the Catholic church began to be developed on the regional level, especially in Holland, France, and also in Germany.

3. The work of the churches of the WCC for the rescue of the Jews also led to Christian-Jewish cooperation on the national as well as on the international level.

4. In order to rescue Jewish people Christians had to act illegally, that is, to falsify passports, hide people, smuggle them across frontiers; in brief, they had to resist. The cooperation of the churches and the WCC with the resistance movements in the occupied countries of Europe and with national liberation movements, was not born out of the theory of an abstract theology of revolution but out of the daily practicing of a spirit of Christian love of one's fellowman.

5. The persecution of the Jews stimulated a new and deeper understanding and a theological reexamination of the role of the people of Israel, of God's revelation, and, finally, of the nature of the Church itself. In a paper, "The Protestant Churches in Europe—Their Presence and Their Future," Karl Barth wrote in September, 1942: "Der Jude sorgt ohne sein Zutun dafür, daß diese (alt- und neutestamentliche) Offenbarung wohl verkannt, aber nicht ganz übersehen, nicht ganz vergessen werden kann."[60] ("By their very existence the Jews witness to the fact that this revelation from both the old and the new testament may be disguised but cannot be completely overlooked, still less forgotten.")

Barth pointed out that the people of Israel reminded the churches of the WCC of their proper task, that is, to testify to this revelation. This task of theirs was bound to lead them into opposition, into the resistance against national socialism. Therefore he declared: "Wo die Offenbarung, deren faktischer Zeuge der Jude ist, erkannt und verstanden wird, da hört der Gegensatz und Kampf gegen den Nationalsozialismus auf, zufällig und äußerlich zu sein, da wird er grundsätzlich und notwendig."[61]

This new understanding of the people of Israel born out of the experience of the churches of the Ecumenical movement during the time of the Second World War was reaffirmed by the first Assembly of the WCC in Amsterdam in 1948. In their resolution against antisemitism the delegates of 164 member churches stated: We call upon all our churches to reject antisemitism . . . as absolutely incompatible with Christian religion and life. Antisemitism is a sin against God and men.[62]

60. Karl Barth, *Eine Schweizer Stimme* 1938–1945 (Zürich: 1945), p. 251 ff.
61. Ibid.
62. "Das christliche Verhalten gegenüber den Juden," in *Die erste Vollversammlung des* Ökumenischen Rates der Kirchen, ed. W. A. Visser'tHooft (Zurich: 1948), p. 213 f.

59. W. A. Visser'tHooft, *Die Welt war meine Gemeinde* (München: 1972), p. 208.

ANNALS, AAPSS, **450**, July 1980

The Holocaust and the Historians

By John S. Conway

ABSTRACT: The impact of the Holocaust has been interpreted by historians largely according to the present needs of their audiences. Jewish historians, both in Israel and outside, see these events as the culminating tragedy of their people before the rebirth in statehood. German historians are more concerned with the attempt to overcome their knowledge of guilt and therefore concentrate, not so much on Jewish sufferings, as on Nazi rule. Christian historians and theologians have sought to eradicate the long tradition of Christian prejudice against Jews, which some of them see as culminating in the Holocaust. Historians of nazism are divided into rival schools and have yet to reach any firm conclusions on such topics as the genesis of the Final Solution. Was the persecution of the Jews something unique or just the prelude to other genocidal measures against unwanted groups of society? The impact of ideology in governmental policies and the weakness of the traditional barriers to the corruptions of absolute power are subjects which need to be reexamined in the light of the Holocaust experience.

John S. Conway is professor of history at the University of British Columbia, Vancouver, Canada. After emigrating to Canada in 1955, he began research on the position of the churches in Nazi Germany, which led to his book The Nazi Persecution of the Churches 1933–1945. Since then, he has written many articles on the Holocaust on the role of the Protestant churches and on the prudent but unheroic position of the Vatican. He also introduced the first courses on the Holocaust to be taught in western Canada and is currently engaged on a study of the impact of the Holocaust on church policy in Western Europe and North America since 1945.

THIRTY years have now elapsed since the world first learned of the tragic and terrible experiences of Jews at the hands of Nazi Germany. A whole generation has grown to manhood for whom the names of Auschwitz, Treblinka, Maidanek, Dachau, or Belsen are only memorials, not memories. The intervening years have seen striking changes both in the position of the Jewish community in the world, particularly with the establishment of the state of Israel, and in the attitudes adopted by non-Jews, particularly Germans, to this dark, atrocious period of the recent past. It has also been a period of intense activity by historians whose concern to record and evaluate the Holocaust has provided an enormous body of literature in an attempt to place this terrifying example of genocide in a framework of German and world history, to explain the circumstances of anti-semitism, and, of course, to draw the lessons from it.

HISTORIANS' VIEWS

If at first historians, especially German historians, were reluctant to examine the "unassimilated past" of the systematic, bureaucratically administered extermination of millions of human beings by the Nazis, more recently a truly international and multisided debate has been engendered to come to terms not only with the facts of the Holocaust but also with their significance. It is perhaps now time to share the findings of these historians briefly from the point of view of their impact on the four different groups of people most affected by the Holocaust: the Jews, the Germans, the gentile world, and finally the historians.

The Jews

The connection between the Holocaust and the determination to create an independent state of Israel is, of course, obvious. The Zionist cause, which before 1939, had been only a minority movement among Jews, was validated by the persecutions and its premises vindicated. The need for a secure homeland in which Jews would no longer be at the mercy of a hostile world has been the most constant theme in Israeli thought, supported by the personal memories and strivings of the survivors who emigrated to Israel in the subsequent years. Virtually everyone in that country has lost members of his immediate family; even if he has not, the frequent ceremonies and memorials, such as Yad Vashem, provide one of the poignant forms of national ideology for the new nation.

The result has led to extensive writings to record and preserve the tragic history of the Nazi persecution in all its horrifying detail. The earliest accounts, such as Gerhard Reitlinger's *The Final Solution*[1] and Leon Poliakov's *Harvest of Hate*,[2] sought to give the broad contours of the mass murders and were the first to tackle the still unresolved question of the total Jewish losses in these terrible years.[3]

A more comprehensive and reliable guide is Raul Hilberg's *The Destruction of the European Jews*,[4] first published in 1961, shortly before the trial of Adolf Eichmann, which was analyzed in the polemical and controversial work by Hannah

1. Gerald Reitlinger, *The Final Solution: the Attempt to Exterminate the Jews of Europe, 1939–1945* (London: 1952).
2. Leon Poliakov, *Harvest of Hate* (Syracuse, NY: 1954).
3. Reitlinger's figures have recently been subject to a close scrutiny by D. Luck, "Use and Abuse of Holocaust Documents: Reitlinger and 'How Many?'" in *Jewish Social Studies*, XLI:(2):95 (spring 1979).
4. Raul Hilberg, *The Destruction of the European Jews* (Chicago: 1961).

Arendt, *Eichmann in Jerusalem*.[5] Arendt not only raises significant questions about the Nazis' motivations, which she attributes to the banality of evil, but also about the extent of Jewish resistance or lack of it, an issue which has been hotly debated ever since, especially among Israelis.

Five more recent books have now taken up the latter theme. Norah Levin's *The Holocaust*[6] is particularly useful concerning the part played by non-Germans and the failure, as she sees it, of other bystanders to oppose the German plans. Reuben Ainsztein's *Jewish resistance in Nazi-Occupied Eastern Europe*[7] is a detailed account of the various uncoordinated and ineffectual attempts of Jews to fight back, though one-sided in its repeated claim that the charge of Jewish passiveness was and always has been groundless. Isaiah Trunk is more cautious in his treatment of the unique institution imposed by the Nazis on the Jewish communities. In *Judenrat*,[8] he outlines the dilemmas faced by the leaders as they sought to bargain and compromise with their oppressors. This evidence is drawn largely from Poland and Bohemia, and in this he is followed by Lucy Dawidowicz in *The War Against the Jews: 1933-1945*.[9] Most recently of all, Helen Fein has attempted a more statistical and sociological study. *Accounting for Genocide*,[10] in which she rightly remarks that

the fatal deterrent to previous research on *Judenräte* was not only the lack of evidence but the unconscious expectation that if we did not find all victims to be heroes or martyrs, we would be debasing their image. . . . Many earlier Holocaust researchers have had an unacknowledged bias either to evaluate their victims' behaviour by singular normative standards, not related to how people in general behave under given stresses, or to deny any evidence of human corruptibility by selective aggregation of cases, idealizing the noble and rationalizing the ignoble. Both biases are pernicious for analysis, judgment, or evaluating the implications of given tactical policies for the future.[11]

Fein also takes up another hotly disputed issue—the uniqueness of the Holocaust. She seeks to show that the sociological preconditions that enabled the Nazis to discriminate against, segregate, and finally exterminate the Jews were not markedly different from those pertaining to the Armenian massacres in 1915-16 or, she might have added, from the Cambodian decimations from 1975-79. All were murdered in order to fulfill the state's design for a new order by eliminating groups conceived as enemies and as responsible for previous national defeats in conditions of war which effectively removed both internal and external sanctions against genocide.

At a deeper level, these works have sought to tackle the obtrusive question, What did the Holocaust mean? Was there any historic significance behind all the unprecedented suffering? Without going into the theological field, one can say that most of the literature, especially that generated by the trial of Adolf

5. Hannah Arendt, *Eichmann in Jerusalem: A Report on the Banality of Evil* (New York: 1964).

6. Nora Levin, *The Holocaust: the Destruction of European Jewry, 1933-1945* (New York: 1968).

7. Reuben Ainsztein, *Jewish Resistance in Nazi-Occupied Eastern Europe* (New York: 1974).

8. Isaiah Trunk, *Judenrat: the Jewish Councils in Eastern Europe under Nazi Occupation* (London: 1972).

9. Lucy Dawidowicz, *The War Against the Jews: 1933-1945* (New York: 1975).

10. Helen Fein, *Accounting for Genocide* (New York: 1979).

11. Ibid., p. 142.

Eichmann, sought to show that the Holocaust must not be forgotten, not merely for the sake of the martyred, but for all time as an example without comparison of the fatefulness of racial prejudice and national idolatry. The Holocaust has immeasurably increased the self-awareness of all peoples, not only of the Jewish people, and has led to a determination that this record of man's inhumanity to man shall never be allowed to become merely an episode of past history.

The Germans

The early attempts made by many Germans after the war to deny any knowledge or complicity in the Holocaust's tragic developments have now given way to a virtually universal acceptance of responsibility—not guilt—for these crimes.

Historians have been careful, after the unfortunate experiences following World War I, to avoid pronouncing a verdict of war guilt on all Germans. We have recognized that there were different levels of acceptance of Nazi ideas, different degrees of complicity, and different responses to the personal sufferings and tragedies involved. Similarly, German historians have been active in exposing the fallacies of the racial and national theories which provided the seedbed for antisemitism.

There is, however, a striking difference in tone between the historians of West and of East Germany. East Germans have sought to recast all German history in a Marxist mold, as Marxism is understood within the Soviet bloc. The Jewish Holocaust is largely attributed to the fantasies of the collapsing capitalism of which Hitler was the culminating disaster. They claim that racial prejudice,

and in particular antisemitism, has now been eradicated because of the structural changes brought about by the establishment of the People's Democracy in East Germany. This does not, however, prevent them from adopting a highly critical policy toward the state of Israel. They have refused to accept any liability toward the survivors and have refused all payments of reparations.

West Germans have been more sensitive. Not only has the West German government accepted during the last 20 years the responsibility for physical and financial reparations, but their historians have diligently sought to channel the feelings of shame and responsibility into more constructive paths. This has been helped by an increasing awareness of the nature of the Nazi regime. There is no longer the attempt made to claim that the German people as a whole were ignorant of or antipathetic to the Nazi rule, including the antisemitism that is now seen as its most vital characteristic. Recent studies of Nazi leaders, such as the excellent biography of Hitler by Joachim Fest,[12] have sought to show that the chief motivating force of his career was not the love of power or even the desire to restore Germany as a world power but, rather, his apocalyptic hatred of Jews as a race.

Certainly, the effect on West German opinion in general has been profound. The Holocaust, beyond any other event, disillusioned Germans concerning their infatuation with racialist theories. The growth of a moderate liberal democracy in that part of the country can undoubtedly be attributed to the often painful process of coming to terms with the awful shadows of the past.

12. Joachim Fest, *Hitler* (New York: 1975).

The gentile world

Undoubtedly the most active debate over the Holocaust outside Germany or Israel has taken place in the ranks of the Christian community. The responsibility of Christian antisemitism for the fate of the Jews is now widely acknowledged. The task of revising Christian attitudes toward the Jewish people has engrossed theologians and scholars, both of the Protestant and the Catholic communities and both in Europe and North America, though to a far lesser extent among the Eastern Orthodox churches of Russia and not at all in other areas, such as the Arab countries.

One very active Protestant group in North America has accepted in full the view that the contempt for the Jewish people and the vilification of the Jewish religion by Christians culminated in the radical antisemitism of the Nazis and thus contributed to the Holocaust. Rosemary Ruether's book *Faith and Fratricide*[13] is the most scholarly presentation of this thesis. She traces Christian antisemitism back to the rejection of the Jews in the New Testament and through the many centuries of persecution by the Church to the final apotheosis at the hands of the SS. She naturally calls for an abandonment of such lingering attitudes within the Protestant ranks. The Catholic church has been led similarly to alter its traditional views, though not as far or as fast as some would like to see.[14]

This debate has, of course, gone further. It has led some Christians, out of a justified feeling of guilt, to take up a unilateral position on behalf of the state of Israel and a total opposition to its opponents, particularly the Palestine Liberation Organization. These writers insist that the Holocaust was an event in Christian, not merely Jewish, history. They accuse those who do not accept this view of still harboring antisemitic or racial sympathies. To them, the recent resolution about Zionism and racism at the United Nations is "obscene." As one of the most notable advocates of these opinions, Franklin Littell, professor of religion at Temple University, Philadelphia, in his recent work *The Crucifixion of the Jews* forcibly reminded his audience:

The cornerstone of Christian Antisemitism is the superseding or displacement myth, which already rings with the genocidal note. This is the myth that the mission of the Jewish people was finished with the coming of Jesus Christ, that "the old Israel" was written off with the appearance of "the new Israel." To teach that a people's mission in God's providence is finished, that they have been relegated to the limbo of history, has murderous implications which murderers will in time spell out. . . . The existence of a restored Israel, proof positive that the Jewish people is

---

13. Rosemary Ruether, *Faith and Fratricide: The Theological Route of Anti-Semitism* (New York: 1974); *see also* A. R. Eckardt, *Elder and Younger Brothers: The Encounter of Jews and Christians* (New York: 1967).

14. On 28 October 1965, the Second Vatican Council issued the declaration *Nostra Aetate* "on the relationship of the Church to non-Christian religions" which marked an important breach with previous statements of the Roman Catholic church on the subject of Judaism. Nine years later a newly created Vatican Commission for Religious Relations with the Jews issued *Guidelines and Suggestions* for the implementation of the 1965 declaration. *See also* Eva Fleischner, ed., *Auschwitz: Beginning of a New Era* (New York: 1977) and Clemens Thoma, ed., *Auf den Trümmern des Tempels* (Vienna: 1968). On the other hand, the Vatican has still not extended diplomatic recognition to the state of Israel.

not annihilated, assimilated, or otherwise withering away, is substantial refutation of the traditional Christian myth about their end in the historic process. . . . It is not the Jewish people that has become incredible. In the meantime our problem is the incredibility of Christianity.[15]

Other writers take a different view. In their opinion, to lay the blame for Auschwitz upon all Christians and their understanding of the New Testament is as grotesque and untenable as the equally farfetched, if durable, belief that the Jews deserved their fate because of their alleged complicity in the crucifixion of Jesus. To suggest as Littell and Reuther do that the Nazis' Final Solution was a logical extension of the thought of those church fathers and councils who declared God was finished with the Jewish people is to take impermissible shortcuts through history. The "culmination" theory, which sees Hitler as the heir to Innocent III or even as the "best Catholic of the lot," ignores the fact that a seismic change occurred with the rapid growth of racialist doctrines in the late nineteenth century.

Admittedly, not enough has yet been learned about those rabid German writers who translated Darwin's biological insights into a political ideology of racism, though Uriel Tal in *Christians and Jews in Germany*[16] shows how their extreme polemic against both Judaism and Christianity was nevertheless laced with a religious vocabulary. By the 1930s the influence of Christianity in Germany—or indeed elsewhere —was far less prominent than the advocates of the "culmination" theory suggest. It would be unhistorical to exaggerate the part religious sentiment may have played in fomenting Nazi extremism. These doubts about the part played by Christian antisemitism, as opposed to other more radical currents, have been strengthened by the most recent studies of the Nazi persecutions of the Jews from the point of view of the Nazis themselves.

The Nazis

As is well known, the overthrow of Nazi Germany and the total rejection of its ideological foundations has meant that no one has sought, in the last 30 years, to defend its policies or even to write its history from the inside. Albert Speer's apologia is probably the best-known attempt but its evasiveness and falsification of major issues hardly lends it credibility.[17] As a result, historians from outside have had to undertake the unrewarding task of seeking to explain Nazi policy on its own terms, with a certain commendable degree of success.

Perhaps the most successful study is by U. D. Adam, *Judenpolitik im Dritten Reich*.[18] In English, the most notable contribution is by Karl Schleunes, *The Twisted Road to*

15. Franklin Littell, *The Crucifixion of the Jews: the Failure of Christians to Understand the Jewish Experience* (New York: 1975), pp. 2–3; *see also* F. Littell and H. G. Locke, eds., *The German Church Struggle and the Holocaust* (Detroit: 1974) and J. E. Wood, Jr., ed., *Jewish Christian Relations in Today's World* (Waco, TX: 1971).

16. Uriel Tal, *Christians and Jews in Germany: Religion, Politics and Ideology in the Second Reich 1870–1914* (Ithaca, NY: 1975); *see also* U. Tal, *Political Faith of Nazism Prior to the Holocaust* (Tel Aviv:

1978) and Richard Gutteridge, *Open Thy Mouth for the Dumb: the German Evangelical Church and the Jews, 1879–1950* (Oxford: 1976).

17. Albert Speer, *Inside the Third Reich* (New York: 1970).

18. U. D. Adam, *Judenpolitik im Dritten Reich* (Dusseldorf: 1972).

Auschwitz,[19] who, however, takes the story only up to 1939. He makes several important points. He joins those who have disputed the view that Nazi Germany was a monolithic police state in which the individual citizen was helplessly trapped, unable to take any preventive measures to oppose Nazi policies or practices. Rather, he points out that the totalitarianism of the Nazi state was inefficient, particularly at first, in its practical measures to offset the Jewish "menace." He shows that despite the unanimity within the Nazi party hierarchy about the evil and dangerous impact of the Jews on German life, there were for the first seven years, 1933–40, serious divisions of opinion about how to deal with it.

Various factions within the party proposed their individual remedies, which proved self-contradictory in their results and led to bitter infighting, not only between the party officials and the civil service ministries, but within the party itself. In 1933, no one, not even Hitler, had any clear idea of the practical measures which could be implemented, despite the centrality of this issue in all Nazi propaganda.

There were four main policies proposed. Goebbels, Streicher, and the leaders of the SA favored a root-and-branch attack on the Jewish community, which led to individual acts of brutality and thuggery and culminated in the savagery of the notorious Crystal Night of November, 1938: 177 Jewish synagogues were destroyed, countless Jewish shops and businesses were looted and burned, and some 40,000 Jews were taken off to concentration camps and not released until they had promised to emigrate. But the damage done to the German image abroad by these acts of violence was immense.

Others, such as Göring, favored an economic squeeze through the Germanization or nationalization of Jewish business and property and were strongly opposed to the reckless destruction of valuable property. But these measures only increased the economic difficulties Germany faced at a time when its economy was being put on a war footing.

A third group advocated legal and bureaucratic measures, such as the Nuremberg Laws of 1935, which turned German Jews into second-class citizens. But these in turn did nothing to alter the ideological nature of the problem. A further group, led by Himmler and the SS, at first favored speedy emigration.[20]

It is paradoxical that until 1940, the SS encouraged the Zionists in their attempts to persuade Jews to leave their homeland. But the refusal of the economic ministries to allow German Jews to take their property with them was matched by the refusal of most other countries, such as Canada, to accept them without it. Although almost half the German Jews, nearly 300,000 in all, had fled the country by 1939, with or without property, the problem, from the Nazi point of view, remained. Following the conquest of Poland, the sudden accession of several million Jews, none of whom had any prospect of emigration, forced the SS to adopt a far more radical policy which led to the erection of the Polish ghettos

19. Karl Schleunes, *The Twisted Road to Auschwitz: Nazi Policy Towards German Jews* (Urbana, IL: 1970).

20. *See* Rolf Vogel, *Ein Stempel hat gefehlt, Dokumentation zur Emigration deutscher Juden* (Munich: 1977).

and hence to the extermination camps.

Karl Schleunes' account has now been taken further by the short but excellent study by Christopher Browning, *The Final Solution and the German Foreign Office, 1940–1943*,[21] which describes the role of the Foreign Office in the Madagascar Plan, the Wannsee Conference, and the ensuing waves of deportations of Jews from Nazi-dominated Europe. In his view the Jewish "experts" under Ribbentrop were guided by careerism rather than racial ideology, but their capacity for meticulous efficiency and surrendering their consciences to whomever was in power proved to be just as murderous to the victims in the long run.

The emphasis placed by Adam, Schleunes, and Browning on the polycratic form of the Nazi system, with their close attention to the internecine disputes among the bureaucrats about Jewish policy, stresses the internal chaos and rivalries in the allegedly monolithic Nazi state and runs parallel to similar findings about other aspects of Nazi policy.[22]

But another school of historians argues vehemently against this interpretation. Andreas Hillgruber, Hans-Adolf Jacobsen, and Eberhard Jäckel are among the best-known German scholars who argue that ideology, not bureaucratic politics, was the key factor in nazism, especially in Hitler's mind.[23] Hitler's violent hatred

of the Jews dominated his whole career from beginning to end and conditioned all his policies, supplanting even his desire to restore Germany's great power status in the world and motivating his dynamic rise to political supremacy. So argues Hillgruber in his most recent contribution,[24] supporting the view already advanced most cogently in English by Lucy Davidowicz in her previously mentioned book. These writers stress both the continuity of ideological motives and the priority of antisemitism in contrast to earlier historians, such as Alan Bullock or A. J. P. Taylor, who saw Hitler as just another German politician, eager to advance his country's territorial interests or to gratify his personal megalomania.

To Taylor and to the more sensational writer David Irving,[25] the Holocaust was merely incidental or a by-product of the wartime circumstances, even if they do not share the extreme views of the so-called revisionists, such as the Frenchman Rassinier or the American professor of electrical engineering A. R. Butz[26] who deny that it took place at all. Needless to say, such opinions are anathema both to the Hillgruber school and to the supporters of the

21. Christopher Browning, *The Final Solution and the German Foreign Office: A Study of Referat D III of abteilung Deutschland, 1940–1943* (New York: 1978).

22. *See* Reinhard Bollmus, *Das Amt Rosenberg und seine Gegner: Studien zur Machtkampf in nationalsozialistische Herrschaftssystem* (Stuttgart: 1970) or Edward Peterson, *The Limits of Hitler's Power* (Princeton, NJ: 1969).

23. *See* Andreas Hillgruber, "Die 'Endlosung' und das deutsche Ostimperium als

Kernstück des rassen ideologischen Programmes des Nationalsozialismus" in *Vierteljahrshefte für Zeitgeschichte*, 20(1):148 ff. (1972); Hans-Adolf Jacobsen, *Nationalsozialistische Aussenpolitik, 1933–1938* (Frankfurt/Main: 1968); and Eberhard Jäckel, *Hitler's Weltanschauung, A Blueprint for Power* (Middletown, CT: 1972).

24. Andreas Hillgruber, "Die ideologischdogmatische Grundlage der nationalsozialistischen Politik der Ausrottung der Juden in der besetzten Gebieten der Sowjetunion und ihre Durchführung 1941–1944," in *German Studies Review*, II(3):263 ff. (1979).

25. David Irving, *Hitler's War* (London: 1977).

26. A. R. Butz, *The Hoax of the Twentieth Century* (Torrance, CA: 1977).

pluralistic or bureaucratic image of Nazi Germany.

At the moment, fierce debate continues among all these historians about one crucial issue—the decision to implement the Final Solution.

Martin Broszat, director of the prestigious Institut für Zeitgeschichte in Munich, has cogently argued that in the summer of 1941 there was still indecision about the future fate of the Jews.[27] Various quotations from Hitler's conversations with foreign politicians, from Goebbels' diaries, or from Himmler's correspondence at that time seem to indicate that the expulsion of the Jews "to the east," which was to begin with mass deportations from Berlin, Vienna, and Prague, did not yet mean a commitment to extermination in gas chambers. Broszat claims that the latter process was developed "spontaneously" by the Nazi officials in Poland, who could not cope with the vastly increased numbers of deportees.

On the one hand, the already constructed ghettos, such as Litzmannstadt (Lodz), were hopelessly overfilled. On the other hand, the more-or-less open mass executions, such as those which had taken place in Riga in October and November, 1941, had led to unwelcome publicity and repercussions. Such local measures were inadequate to the task created by the ideological pressures for a *Judenrein* Europe. The military failures on the eastern front had caused both a lack of rail transportation and of more reception areas in newly conquered Russia. Therefore Broszat concluded that the extermination program grew out

of these individual actions and was gradually institutionalized by the spring of 1942, when the death camps in Poland were erected or developed for this explicit purpose.[28]

This preceding view has been hotly disputed. Broszat's critics, while admitting that no explicit order or directive signed by Hitler ordering the mass extermination of Jews in the tightly sealed concentration camps in Poland exists or survives, nevertheless claim that such instructions must certainly have been given at the highest level. It is indeed inconceivable that these measures could have been taken without Hitler's knowledge and approval. It is equally inconceivable that such a policy and its implementation, which was extensively discussed at the notorious Wannsee Conference of January, 1942, would have been launched without a large segment of the ruling elite being aware of it—Albert Speer's apologia notwithstanding.

Hillgruber has rightly pointed out that the blanket extermination of Jews by the *Einsatzgruppen* in Russia paved the way for a similar treatment of the rest of Europe's Jews. Poland was chosen because the rail connections made transportation more feasible and because the absence of any non-Nazi controls ensured secrecy. Surviving evidence shows that the first major extermination camps at Belzec, Chelmo, Maidanek and Auschwitz-Birkenau were all equipped with gas chambers and crematoria in the winter months of 1941–42. But just when or whether an explicit *Vernichtungsbefehl* was ever issued remains an open question.

The priority given to the Holocaust proves its centrality in Nazi thinking.

27. Martin Broszat, "David Irving, Hitler und der 'Befehl' zur Judenvernichtung" in *Vierteljahrshefte für Zeitgeschichte*, 25(4): 739 ff. (1977).

28. Ibid., p. 753, fn. 26.

Not only are there Hitler's innumerable public and private utterances on this point but the implacable efficiency with which his intentions were carried out, even when defeat was obvious, disprove David Irving's view that the extermination of the Jews was merely an "escape from an unfortunate dilemma."[29]

We know, for example, that as late as 1944, when military supplies were desperately needed on the eastern front, vital trains were being diverted to Budapest to round up Hungarian Jews for deportation to Auschwitz, instead of carrying munitions to the battlefront. Historians are still disputing whether the implementation of the Final Solution was an indication of Hitler's confidence in his military victory, or whether it was his determination to rid the world of the enemy he increasingly regarded as responsible for his defeat. In either case, the evidence is clear, not only that Hitler's fanatical policies were both remorseless and unrelenting, but that they met with approval from the majority of his followers.

Jews at the time, and most Jewish writers since, were not aware of the countervailing variations in Nazi policy. To the victims, the repeated blows rained down upon them were all attributed to a masterminded campaign of hatred and violence. They were unable to know that the Nazi policies were directed by different factions all fighting among themselves. The natural tendency has been to depict the Nazi persecution in terms of a black-and-white saga of innocent victims and brutal oppressors. This overlooks the nuances and divagations along the twisted road to Auschwitz just as it avoids the awkward question

of whether the Jews could have done more to defend themselves—as Hannah Arendt unfeelingly pointed out. Historians are usually adept at pointing out that the record is not always black and white but often a murky shade of grey.

One of the most crucial questions which has still to be researched centers on the problem of what role the Holocaust played in the evolution of Nazi political goals. Although, as has been stressed, Hitler's ideology was grounded in his conviction that he was the secular messiah called to lead his people in a life-and-death struggle against the forces of darkness, represented by the Jews, the question nevertheless remains what he would have done had he been successful. In this view the Nazi goal was not limited by the Jewish factor. Rather, the eradication of the Jewish menace has to be seen as only one part of the whole Nazi attempt to recast German and hence European social and political institutions on an entirely new radical basis.

The Nazi aim was to reconstitute society, no longer on the foundations of law, tradition, and morality but solely on the basis of race, under the control of the dynamic leadership of the fuehrer, whose will was to constitute the final and absolute authority. Every institution in society was to be transformed or *gleichgeschaltet* as part of the totalitarian nature of Nazi rule.

Even more ominously, the purposes and moral foundations of social life were to be reorientated into new racial channels. This left no room for alternative life-styles or scales of values. The Jews were to be eradicated because for so long they had resisted exactly that process of forcible assimilation which the Nazis intended to carry through. But equally, one should note that all

29. Ibid., p. xiv.

other groups in society were to be subject to the same processes. The churches, the universities, the schools, and the law courts were all to be nazified in this fashion.

Roland Freisler, the notorious president of the People's Court which conducted the trial of the 20 July 1944 Resistance leaders, expressed exactly the Nazi concept of law in this regard. Freisler proclaimed that the judge should be based on his faith in the fuehrer and nation and on "the sound sense of the people." Punishment should not be meted out according to a law prescribed for a specific deed. It should be based on the will of the fuehrer. The Holocaust, then, was not a punishment for Jewish crimes. It was justified solely by the will of the fuehrer. Only the timely military defeat of nazism prevented this doctrine from being applied to all other areas of German life. Who can doubt that if the genocide of the Jews could be justified by the will of the fuehrer that equally radical measures would have been taken to reshape all German institutions in the name of the Nazi ideology?

Others

One final area of discussion must also be briefly mentioned, namely, the debate about the response of other countries to the Jewish suffering. In 1963, Rolf Hochhuth launched a vigorous attack on the Papacy for the supposed failure of Pius XII to prevent the persecution of the Jews.[30] Historians have since exhaustively studied the facts of the

case and have come to a more balanced conclusion. The pope was undoubtedly a cautious and prudent man, but not the heartless monster of inhumanity portrayed by Hochhuth. It is true that more could have been done by the Catholic church; it is not true to say that nothing was done.

An equally scathing condemnation of American policy is provided by Henry Feingold in his book *The Politics of Rescue*[31] which examines the failures of Roosevelt's administration to take timely measures on behalf of the Jews both before and after the outbreak of war.

A similar study of British policy by Bernard Wasserstein, *Britain and the Jews of Europe*,[32] shows how the British government's response was overshadowed by the fear that increased assistance to Jewish refugees would lead to insoluble difficulties in the British mandate of Palestine. Helen Fein, in her writing on these countries, is severely critical of the local Jewish communities, which she claims failed to mobilize support for a more appropriate and energetic policy.[33] It is encouraging to note that other studies of a similar kind are now being undertaken, such as a study of Canadian policy toward the Jewish refugees.[34]

30. Rolf Hochhuth, *The Deputy* (New York: 1963); E. Bentley, ed., *The Storm over the Deputy* (New York: 1964); *see also* J. S. Conway, "The Silence of Pope Pius XII" in *Review of Politics*, 27:105–31 (1965) and Anthony Rhodes, *The Vatican in the Age of the Dictators* (London: 1973).

31. Henry Feingold, *The Politics of Rescue* (New York: 1970); David Wyman, *Paper Walls: America and the Refugee Crisis, 1938–1941* (Amherst, MA: 1968); and Saul Friedman, *No Haven for the Oppressed: United States Policy Towards Jewish Refugees, 1932–1945* (Detroit: 1973).

32. Bernard Wasserstein, *Britain and the Jews of Europe, 1939–1945* (Oxford: 1979).

33. Ibid., ch. 7.

34. Irving Abella and Harold Troper, "The Line Must be Drawn Somewhere: Canada and Jewish Refugees, 1933–1939," in *Canadian Historical Review*, LX(2):182 ff. (1979).

Conclusion

For years the traumatic experience of the Holocaust was, for the survivors, a subject for tears, stammering, and screams of anguish. Thirty years after these events, we have only begun to digest the lessons taught by this unparalleled atrocity. We know too much now to be persuaded that the tragic events of 1933–45 were merely an accident, or even an aberration by a few malevolent individuals. We have been forced to take a more profound look at antisemitism, at racism of all kinds, as a force in ideological conditioning of peoples. We have been obliged to consider the role of ideologies of this power in the manipulation of populations through propaganda in the modern state. We have to reflect more deeply upon the values which should control the actions of governments and upon the means to be employed to ensure that they are not perverted in the name of the modern heresies of class, nation, or race.

The Holocaust of the Jewish people stands as the most terrifying example of inhumanity in our recent past. Here, if anywhere, we should heed the wise words of the historian who said, "People who refuse to learn the lessons of the past are condemned to relive them in the future."

ANNALS, AAPSS, **450**, July 1980

The Holocaust and the Enigma of Uniqueness: A Philosophical Effort at Practical Clarification

By ALICE L. ECKARDT and A. ROY ECKARDT

ABSTRACT: This philosophical analysis seeks to foster understanding between representatives of diverse disciplines in the study of the Holocaust. The article inquires whether there are ways to avoid the mystification of the Holocaust without losing its singularity. Three concepts of uniqueness are utilized: ordinary uniqueness, unique uniqueness, and transcending uniqueness. Eight propositions are submitted that concern: the salience of facticity, the challenge of the Holocaust to conventional tools of study, the relation of historic antisemitism and the Holocaust, the relevance of eschatological images, the bearing of the Holocaust upon soteriological expression, ideology as a weapon against the Holocaust's concreteness, the theft of the Holocaust for antisemitic and anti-Israeli purposes, and the jointure of nomothetic and idiographic interpretation as a possible aid to understanding. In conclusion, the category of transcending uniqueness is applied to the moral dimension of the encounter with the Holocaust in a way that links a social ethic and the sociology of knowledge.

Alice L. Eckardt and A. Roy Eckardt are members of the Department of Religion Studies faculty, Lehigh University, Bethlehem, Pennsylvania. Contributors of numerous articles to scholarly journals in the United States and Europe, they have co-authored two books, Encounter With Israel *(1970) and* Long Night's Journey Into Day *(forthcoming). They spent 1975–76 in Germany at the University of Tübingen and in Israel at the Hebrew University engaged in research on the aftermath of the Holocaust under a Rockefeller Foundation grant. In 1979, the Eckardts served as special consultants to President Carter's Commission on the Holocaust.*

The authors thank Carey B. Joynt and Park McGinty, two colleagues at Lehigh University, for fruitful conversations aiding the preparation of this article.

IN A recent book, Yehuda Bauer of the Hebrew University in Jerusalem, a leading historian of the Holocaust, argues against the mystification of the Holocaust, an event to be identified as the murder of some 5.8 million European Jews by the German Nazis. To Bauer, today's widespread tendency to mystification is open to the charge of obscurantism: "If what happened to the Jews was unique, then it took place outside of history, and it becomes a mysterious event, an upside-down miracle, so to speak, an event of religious significance in the sense that it is not man-made as that term is normally understood." On the other hand, Bauer is quite sensitive to the historical and moral failure, or refusal, to face up to the Holocaust as it actually occurred. He asks, If that event is not at all unique, where then are its parallels or precedents?[1] To turn one's back upon the singularity of the Holocaust is to violate the event's integrity and to assault implicitly the dignity of its victims. But to identify the Holocaust as absolutely inexplicable and incredible may have, paradoxically, these very same consequences.

This article seeks to cope with the enigma of the Holocaust's uniqueness through coming to terms with several different understandings of "uniqueness."

KINDS OF UNIQUENESS

It was Wilhelm Windelband who first applied the terms "nomothetic" and "idiographic" to two modes of epistemological activity within the human mind. In nomothesis, attention is directed to the generality of things and to what they have in common. Upon that foundation the abstractive and symbolist asseverations of certain dominant forms of science are put forth today. In idiography, stress falls, by contrast, upon the distinctiveness of the individual happening and the individual case. Quantitative considerations are supplemented and sometimes replaced by qualitative ones.[2]

The practical question before us is associated with the idiographic extremities of the continuum, nomothesis-idiography.[3] Three discrete meanings of uniqueness are suggested, the sequence of which drives us further and further into particularity and incomparability.

Ordinary uniqueness

As against our memorable high-school indoctrination with the idea that "history repeats itself," it is apparent that all historical events are unique, by which is meant simply that they are qualitatively different from each other. The philosophic grounding for this practical observation derives empirically from the shifting conditions of the spatio-temporal flux and is, accordingly, twofold: succeeding events must perforce occupy physical locales that are alternative to those that earlier events have occupied; and succeed-

---

1. Yehuda Bauer, *The Holocaust in Historical Perspective* (Seattle: University of Washington Press, 1978), pp. 30–31.

2. See A. Roy Eckardt, "The Contribution of *Nomothesis* in the Science of Man," *American Scientist* 49:76–87 (1961); see also A. Roy Eckardt, ed., *The Theologian at Work: A Common Search for Understanding* (New York: Harper & Row, 1968), pp. xix–xxx.

3. In elucidating the dialectic of generality-particularity we intend a kind of continuum. This implies that there are no absolute breaks as we move along the continuum. However, the absence of such breaks does not imply that salient types cannot be distinguished.

ing events take place within temporal frames of reference that are alternative to those that previous events involved.

From within this initial and mundane point of view, the unqualified proposition that the Holocaust is a unique event is judged to be at best a truism and at worst an excrescence. A like judgment applies to the proposition that the Holocaust could occur another time—as long as that proposition is left similarly unqualified.

Unique uniqueness

Since all happenings within space-time bear unique marks, the concept of uniqueness has to be elaborated and qualified if we are to grasp the fabric of uniqueness in its manifoldness.[4] As the mind reviews the dramas of human history and seeks after the meaning of that history, it quickly resorts to the continuum of insignificance-significance. The mind freely concludes that while many happenings appear to be more or less trivial, others are possessed of singular importance and may be characterized as, in truth, "epoch-making": they make the epoch in which they transpire. We find ourselves captivated and even dominated by the great watersheds of history. Some of these epochal events are constructive while others are catastrophic, but all are regarded as decisive within the story of the human race.

That the Holocaust of the Jews is a uniquely unique event scarcely requires argument. It is noteworthy that for all his polemic "against mystification," Bauer insists upon the need to distinguish "Holocaust" and "genocide":

Clearly, what was happening to quite a number of peoples in Nazi Europe was genocide: their institutions of learning closed, their political leadership decimated, their language and national culture discarded, their churches eliminated from a free exercise of their functions, their wealth despoiled, and subjected to killings of groups and individuals as the Nazis pleased. . . . The difference between that and the Holocaust lies in the difference between forcible, even murderous, denationalization, and wholesale, total murder of every one of the members of a community. Contrary to legend, there never was a Nazi policy to apply the measures used against the Jews to other national communities. . . . [There] may be no difference between Holocaust and genocide for the victim of either. But there are gradations of evil, unfortunately. Holocaust was the policy of the total, sacral Nazi act of mass murder of all Jews they could lay hands on. Genocide was horrible enough, but it did not entail *total* murder if only because the subject peoples were needed as slaves. They were, indeed, "subhumans" in Nazi terminology. The Jews were not human at all.[5]

The Holocaust was an unprecedented event. "[For] the first time in history a sentence of death had been pronounced on anyone guilty of having been born, and born of certain parents. . . . This Nazi decision was based on an ideology in which the Jew was defined as the anti-race, . . . as that mixture of characteristics that could be described, in Nazi terms, as an absolute evil."[6] The fact that all Jewish babies and children were to be murdered along with all adults discloses at once, and for all time, the unique uniqueness of the Holocaust: not a single Jew was to remain upon earth. Such an eschatological decision and

4. Cf. Carey B. Joynt and Nicholas Rescher, "The Problem of Uniqueness in History," *History and Theory* I:150–62 (1961).

5. Bauer, pp. 35, 36.
6. Ibid. p. 32.

hope contrasts sharply with Nazi policy toward the Gypsies, as it does with the earlier Turkish slaughter of the Armenians.[7]

Significantly, Yehuda Bauer emphasizes that the failure to recognize that the Jewish situation was unique is itself an instance of the mystifying of history—equally as mystifying as the assertion that the Holocaust is inexplicable or that it bears no parallels at all to other murderous events.[8] Deborah E. Lipstadt criticizes the increasingly common attempt to subsume the Holocaust under man's inhumanity to man, whereby the event is made into a case study in human pathology to be assigned a "universal" frame of reference, along with Hiroshima, Wounded Knee, and Mai Lai. Such revisionism is "unfaithful to historical reality. . . . 'Jew' by definition meant 'enemy or vermin to be exterminated.' This all-encompassing definition of 'victim' alone renders the Holocaust unique."[9]

Transcending uniqueness

Nomothetic science may not desire to concern itself with uniquely unique events, or it may wish, for the sake of its own operations and purposes, to abstract from the realm of the uniquely unique those elements or characteristics that are ostensibly shared by more than single events. But there is nothing within nomothetic science to rule out a priori the actuality of uniquely unique events or data. The scientist and the historian are able to live under a common roof without going at one another's throats. However, with our third eventuality, conflict appears unavoidable within the community of disciplined thought.

The concept of transcending uniqueness refers to events that are held to be essentially different from not only ordinary uniqueness but even unique uniqueness. With transcending uniqueness the quality of difference raises itself to the level of absoluteness. One way to situate the qualitative shift to transcending uniqueness is to speak of a radical leap from objectness to subjectness,[10] a total existential crisis and involvement for the party who makes one or another affirmation of transcending uniqueness. This extraordinary about-face is accompanied by a marked transformation in modes of language.

Now, in place of relatively calm, descriptive references to the merely unprecedented character of the Holocaust or to its singularly catastrophic nature, the witness to transcending uniqueness is heard to testify that this event is simply unbelievable or inexplicable. The witness asks, How could there ever be such an event

7. The Nazis seem to have been highly ambivalent toward the Gypsies. Some Gypsy tribes were murdered but others were protected. As for the Armenians, during World War I about half the Armenian population of Anatolia was murdered by Enver Pasha's troops. But in Istanbul, the very heart of the Ottoman Empire, Armenian residents were not killed (Bauer, p. 36).

8. Bauer, p. 36.

9. Deborah E. Lipstadt, "We Are Not Job's Children," in *Shoah: A Review of Holocaust Studies and Commemorations* 1: 14, 15 (1979); *See also* A Roy Eckardt, "Is the Holocaust Unique?," *Worldview* 17: 31–35 (1974).

10. We resort to the terms "objectness" and "subjectness" instead of the more customary "objectivity" and "subjectivity" as a means of offsetting somewhat the usual connotations of "arbitrariness" or "illusoriness" or "taste" within the popular usage of "subjectivity." The proponent of transcending uniqueness will simply deny that he has sold objective (real) truth for the pottage of mere whim or personal preference. At this juncture we are simply endeavoring to *describe* a point of view.

at this one? Often this person will plead that the only really sensible response to the Holocaust is a kind of holy, or unholy, awe and even a consuming silence. Many times it is the survivors of the Holocaust who have reacted in this way (cf. the works of Elie Wiesel).

But sometimes nonsurvivors are caught up in the same spirit, taking into themselves the very abyss of the Holocaust. Thus Dalton Trumbo, the well-known writer of screenplays, tried for no less than 16 years to create a novel on the Holocaust and died with the work still unfinished. A non-Jew, Trumbo was conscience-stricken and overwhelmed by the ultimate horror and incomprehensibility of the Holocaust.[11]

The response that finds in the Holocaust a transcendent, crushing mystery incarnates the dimension of the numinous, as described by Rudolf Otto in *Das Heilige*. The mental state called the numinous by Otto presents itself as *ganz andere*, wholly other, a condition absolutely *sui generis* and incomparable whereby the human being finds himself utterly abashed. There is a feeling of terror before an awe-inspiring mystery, but a mystery that also fascinates infinitely.[12]

EIGHT PROPOSALS

A clear and decisive difficulty with attestations to transcending uniqueness arises in connection with the

11. Dalton Trumbo, *Night of the Aurochs*, ed. Robert Kirsch (New York: Viking Press, 1979); see review of this book by Irving Abrahamson, *Chicago Tribune*, 18 Nov. 1979.
12. The English version of Otto's work bears the misleadingly intellectualistic title, *The Idea of the Holy*, trans. John W. Harvey (New York: Oxford University Press, 1958); *see also* Mircea Eliade, *The Sacred and the Profane* (New York: Harper & Row, 1961), pp. 8–10.

fundamental presuppositions and methodologies of history and science, including the social sciences. Does not transcending uniqueness defy the canons of empirical and rational comparison and discourse? Accordingly, is it not devoid of practical historical and scientific meaning? A problem in the sociology of knowledge is at issue here: no matter how the historian or scientist may feel as an individual, the norms of the professional and scholarly community to which he or she belongs appear to rule out, as a matter of principle, the legitimacy of transcending uniqueness. These norms center in the ideal of treatability. Any datum or claim that cannot be treated by means of accepted procedures lacks, in effect, any positive historical or scientific worth or relevance.

It does not follow from this state of affairs that dialogue between adherents of different understandings of uniqueness is wholly out of the question. True, there are formidable intellectual, spiritual, and moral conflicts over the interpretation of the Holocaust. While the considerations in the following pages will not resolve those conflicts, they may be of some aid in the attempt to address the question of the singularity of the Holocaust.

Salience of facticity

The advocacy of transcending uniqueness is preveniently guilty of improper mystification if it fails to honor the facticity of the original events in the context of their original background. Yehuda Bauer provides one selected listing of the kinds of data that cannot be avoided:

[What] were the bases of Nazi Jew-hatred? What in Christian theology, in popular antisemitism, prepared the ground? Who were the murderers? What social strata did they come from? What did they think? When was the mass murder planned and how? How did the bureaucracy work that was able to sit behind their desks and direct the murder? Who built the gas chambers? What was the reaction of the victims? Sheep to the slaughter? Glorious resistance? Was there a way to rescue? What were the relations between Jew and non-Jew in the European countries occupied by the Nazis? What were the demographic, cultural, psychological consequences of the Holocaust? How did the State of Israel, into which two-thirds of the survivors immigrated, emerge just three years after the end of the mass murder? What are the effects of the Holocaust on the Jewish people, in Israel and in the Diaspora? What is the responsibility of the free world towards this event?

. . . Without a return to the very hard and arduous task of actually knowing something about the Holocaust, the symbolic descriptions that occupy, quite legitimately, the center of the stage in Holocaust literature, become just another escape route for the superficial.[13]

Any theory of transcending uniqueness that is incompatible with the specific and real data that we can all learn and share has fled into arbitrary speculation and is not to be taken seriously.

Threat of the Holocaust

On the other hand, Lipstadt refers to the threat posed by the Holocaust itself to the usefulness and applicability of the historian's conventional tools. The very fact that the Final Solution could be so exhaustively documented has contributed, ironically, to the difficulty of comprehending it. "If something can be broken down into its component parts, if each step can be isolated

and analyzed, and if the most minute elements can be substantiated, should the event . . . not be understood and therefore understandable? . . . [Yet in] this case the contrary supposition seemed more correct: the more known, the less comprehended."[14] After we have assembled all our data and marshaled all the "causes" of and "reasons" for the Holocaust, we are not spared yet the haunting question, How could all this have taken place?

The logic of the first two considerations taken together is that while the disposition to transcending uniqueness cannot ignore facticity, factual and analytic knowledge does not possess, in and of itself, the right to subvert the higher reaches of uniqueness. A principled exclusion of metahistorical and metascientific issues cannot be permitted to place these issues objectively and finally out of bounds—not without begging the entire question.

Historic antisemitism

The linkage between the Holocaust and the long history of antisemitism—a linkage that appears self-authenticating—suggests that nomothesis and idiography may be construed dialectically, each side presupposing and driving toward the other. In the nomothetic method, particular realities or events gain understanding through being assigned to a more comprehensive category. In the present instance "Holocaust" may be placed all too obviously within the larger category "antisemitism." But this very act impels us in the direction of the extremities of idiography because antisemitism, as it has manifested

13. Bauer, pp. 46, 47.

14. Lipstadt, pp. 13–14.

itself within the entire history of the West, is itself a markedly unique phenomenon. This phenomenon is radically discontinuous with ordinary forms of "prejudice," such as in race and religion, forms that have their occasions and their locales and then atrophy or are superseded. Antisemitism is the one perennial malady of its kind within the history of the Western world, and it is spread universally within the entire geography of the West. Distinctively, it is pervasive in time as in space.

Thus is the peculiar generality of antisemitism wedded indissolubly to the peculiar particularity of the Holocaust.

Eschatological images

In the Holocaust and its ideology, certain eschatological images of salvation and death act to draw into history the transcendent realities of heaven and hell. Lucy S. Dawidowicz writes:

"Final" [in the term "Final Solution"] means definitive, completed, perfected, ultimate. "Final" reverberates with apocalyptic promise, bespeaking the Last Judgment, the End of Days, the last destruction before Armageddon. "The Final Solution of the Jewish Question" in the National Socialist conception was not just another anti-Semitic undertaking, but a metahistorical program devised with an eschatological perspective. It was part of a salvational ideology that envisaged the attainment of Heaven by bringing Hell on earth.[15]

The psychiatrist Robert Jay Lifton comments:

One of Hitler's greatest rhetorical talents was to evoke in the German

people a sense of perpetual life-or-death crisis. Always at stake was the spirit, essence, vitality, and purity—that is, the life-power—of the German people. And the threatening force was the Jew, by his very existence. . . . The project, through murdering the Jews, was to "murder death"—which is always, psychologically speaking, the project behind mass killing.[16]

Accordingly, nothing could be allowed to interfere with the transcendent duty to exterminate the Jews, not even the vital and compelling needs of the German war effort.

The Christian vision and hope of the "conversion of the Jews" is the other side of the Nazi "annihilation of the Jews." It is *eine geistliche Endlösung*, a spiritual Final Solution. In both cases there are to be no more Jews. Thus would be realized, as Lifton puts it, a Christian utopia in which such menaces as doubt and meaninglessness are at last overcome.[17]

From the Nazi eschatological viewpoint, those who remain today are confronted by a choice: to reaffirm the Aryan anti-Antichrist to the ends of purity, life, and heaven—neonazism is at present a growing international movement—or to stand with the Jewish Antichrist for the sake of corruption, death, and hell. But for those who represent the anti-Nazi persuasion, it is Aryan "purity" that constitutes the real Antichrist and hell while Jewish reality means, accordingly, life and the anti-Antichrist.

Yet we are painfully aware—the television series *Holocaust* did much to bring this home—that the life for

15. Lucy S. Dawidowicz, *The War Against the Jews 1933–1945* (New York: Holt, Rinehart and Winston, 1975), p. xiv.

16. Robert Jay Lifton, *The Broken Connection: On Death and the Continuity of Life* (New York: Simon and Schuster, 1979), pp. 317, 332–33.

17. Ibid., p. 316.

which we may choose to stand has been identified once and for all with total petrifaction and death.[18] This state of affairs induces in us a condition of death-anxiety. For many who simply try to live out their lives in ordinary or harmless ways, the Holocaust yet persists as a terrifying sign of obliteration as such.

As mentioned earlier, not only every "eligible" adult but every child and baby were marked for annihilation. Could not the same policy come to enshroud us, our loved ones, our friends, our people? Within the Holocaust a singular death-threat is carried: herein is found that event's existential uniqueness.[19] In the contemporary confrontation with the Holocaust, the end of our personal time coalesces with the awful end of the entire human reality.

In sum, through the Holocaust the power of the end insinuates itself into the historical process in a twofold and paradoxical sense: in the utopian promise of ultimate meaning and salvation and in the terrible threat of ultimate meaninglessness and destruction.

Soteriological expression

Some theologians and philosophers today are raising the question of the transcending uniqueness of the Holocaust. As pointed out previously, the historian and social scientist are

18. In a paper and a journal of this kind any plea in behalf of a certain eschatological position would be improper. However, we believe that the destructive power of Nazi eschatology was granted meaning, and was able to realize itself in human history, only by virtue of the absolutely opposed eschatology of Judaism.

19. What functions as this type of sign for the people of one epoch will, of course, vary for the people of another epoch. Thus the Black Death doubtless signified a dread end-possibility for the people of the fourteenth century.

hard put, in principle, to assimilate this form of uniqueness in their own methodologies. They may be prepared, however, to give attention to such a claim, if only as phenomenological material for critical response. More positively, the claim may be treated as a datum within the dialogue between secular and nonsecular thinking. Some will argue that we cannot ignore completely this claim with its potentially world-shattering consequences for human life and thought.

The category of the numinous has been mentioned. One potential outcome of that kind of experience is metanoia, an entire about-face at the point of conviction and behavior. The distance from such experience to *heilsgeschictliche* claims, that is, claims that are held to encompass sacred history—the very history of salvation—is short. A few examples may be sketched.

From the Jewish side, Richard L. Rubenstein has declared that after Auschwitz, he could not possibly believe in a God whose will it was to enable Adolf Hitler to slaughter six million Jews nor could he any longer believe in Israel as God's chosen people.[20] Rubenstein's existential *via negativa* does not, it is evident, conflict with some secular presumptions.

In contrast, Irving Greenberg has identified the Holocaust as positively revelational in an unqualifiedly revolutionary way. The transcendent lesson of the Holocaust is that God's covenant with Israel, while by no means annulled, no longer enshrines a deontological structure. Its yoke may nonetheless be borne by Jews upon a wholly decisional,

20. Richard L. Rubenstein, *After Auschwitz: Radical Theology and Contemporary Judaism* (Indianapolis: Bobbs-Merrill, 1966), p. 46.

voluntary, and, incredibly joyful basis.[21]

From the Christian side, it has been asserted with a revelational presupposition comparable to that of Greenberg, that the Crucifixion and the Resurrection are all-decisively transfigured at the hands of the Holocaust. The Crucifixion is transfigured because the absolute God-forsakenness of Jewish children renders the ostensible absoluteness of the cross of Jesus nonabsolute, and the Resurrection is transfigured because in the Holocaust the intrinsically triumphalist nature of the dogma of the Resurrection of Jesus is finally revealed as an absolute seal of hostility and guarantor of the destruction of Jews.[22]

It is sometimes protested that attributing transcending uniqueness to the Holocaust will, if successful and as a presumed species of "mystification," make futile those human efforts to learn from the Holocaust and to work to prevent other such occurrences in the future. The overall danger here is a genuine one. But the danger need not be inherent in the affirmation of transcending uniqueness. This is made apparent in the three illustrations just given.

Paradoxically, attestations of transcending uniqueness do not have to be so "absolutist" or "wholly other" that they are emptied of immediate, historical application. On the contrary, the consequences of transcend-ing uniqueness may be of a morally helpful and even a soteriologically positive kind. "Religious faith involves a movement in which the believer goes beyond the categories of present experience and posits a met-aempirical ground for hope."[23]

Ideological attack

It is essential to be alert to the current utilization of ideology within the disposition of the Holocaust. Ideology is being widely resorted to in the service of denials of the distinctiveness of the Holocaust.

Such denials were made vivid to members of President Carter's Commission on the Holocaust during its study mission in the summer of 1979 to Poland and the Soviet Union, among other places.[24] Within those countries the commission was exposed to the full force of Marxist "universalism." The practical application of universalism, negating as it does Jewish particularity— the Jews of 1933–45 are regularly reduced to "victims of Fascism"— was the subjecting of the commission to long lectures by Communist political functionaries concentrating upon the "equal" suffering of "all" the Poles or the "much greater" suffering of a total of 20 millions of Soviet citizens. As pointed out previously, Nazi ideology and practice respecting Jews was in fact radically different from its disposition of non-Jews.

An additional and highly relevant aspect of the Holocaust's singularity is the concerted effort to destroy the

21. Irving Greenberg, consultation with one of the authors, Southampton, England, 21 July 1977.

22. A Roy Eckardt, "Christian Responses to the Endlösung," Religion in Life 47: 40 (1978); A. Roy Eckardt, "Christians and Jews: Along a Theological Frontier," Encounter 40:107–8 (1979); for a more general analysis of theological and philosophical responses to the Holocaust, consult Alice L. Eckardt, "The Holocaust: Christian and Jewish Responses," J. Am. Acad. Religion 42:453–69 (1974).

23. Sam Keen, "Hope in a Posthuman Era," The Theologian at Work, ed. A. Roy Eckardt (New York: Harper & Row, 1968), p. 220.

24. We accompanied the study mission as special consultants. A fuller chronicle is "Travail of a Presidential Commission," in Encounter (in press). Several passages are here taken from that narrative.

evidence that the event ever happened. The German Nazis worked hard at this point. Their attempt finds its parallels today. At Babi Yar, just outside Kiev, the stone inscription in Ukrainian pretends that not Jewish bodies but instead "more than 100,000 citizens of Kiev" lie beneath that ravine. The Jews who were cut down there did not die as citizens of Kiev, though they were that. They died solely because they were Jews. This truth applies to the Holocaust in its entirety. The Germans never reviled or killed Jews because they were Poles or Czechs or Latvians. The opposite was the case: Polish, Czech, and Latvian Jews were destroyed only because they were Jews. The Marxism of the Presidential Commission's hosts kept them from the acknowledgment of such historical truths.

The ideological aspect of the preceding conditioning is further revealed via the truth that Poles, Russians, Ukrainians, Lithuanians, and others were not only victims of the Nazis but also very often willing and enthusiastic collaborators with Germans in the annihilation of the Jews of Europe. In significant respects Hitler and his cohorts were heirs of a special East European antisemitic tradition that had reigned for centuries, as well as being heirs of the Christian anti-Jewish tradition as a whole.[25] Few countries in the world can be expected to excel the historic antisemitism of Poland; not without significance is that every killing center was placed within that land.[26] And there is little need to recite here the parallels to Nazi policies in the treatment of three million Soviet Jews today.

25. See John Toland, Adolf Hitler (Garden City: Doubleday & Co., 1976), pp. 102 ff.
26. See Celia Heller, On the Edge of Destruction (New York: Columbia University Press, 1977).

The world-Communist reiteration of non-Jewish, universal suffering at Nazi hands is much more than a sympathy-arousing tribute to historical fact. It is equally a subterfuge whereby the particularities of one's own antisemitisms are covered over. The protestation, drearily repeated, that "we all suffered together from a common foe" is a distortion. Every effort is made to hide guilt and to obscure responsibility for the hatred and oppression of Jews that the people of Communist countries bear equally with the peoples of the West, the Christian world—a hatred that continues to afflict the inhabitants of Eastern Europe and the Soviet Union. All in all, were the Communist and neo-Nazi program of suppression of the truth ever to prevail, within 50 to 100 years the world would have no way to know that there had ever been a Holocaust.

Antisemitic and anti-Israeli campaign

We make brief reference to a consideration allied to the previously mentioned point of ideology as a denial of the distinctiveness of the Holocaust: the present and increasingly widespread effort to steal the Holocaust from its specific victims by giving it to someone else and transforming the Jewish people into the victimizers. The campaign today to particularize the concept "Holocaust" in behalf of non-Jews and to reverse actual historical roles is the other side of the coin from false universalization, a more patently antisemitic side.

Edward Alexander documents this campaign in a recent piece. He concentrates on the effort to transubstantiate the Jewish survivors of the death camps into Nazi militarists and the Palestinian Arab refugees into "Jewish" victims. This has been a prominent technique within Arab and Soviet propaganda.

A triumphant climax in the campaign to steal the Holocaust from the Jews was the United Nations' resolution equating Zionism with racism. In Europe for almost a century, the concept "racism" was virtually equivalent to "antisemitism." To turn the country of Israel into the inheritor of nazism is, as Alexander puts it, to transmute "public memory of the Holocaust into a potent instrument of destruction." He concludes:

To make of the murdered Jews metaphors for all humanity is not to exalt but to degrade them, and to render easier the dirty work of those who would make them the representatives, not of humanity in general, but of their polar opposites: the enemies of the Jews in particular. Those who deprive the dead Jews of that for which they died are of necessity in collusion with those who wish to deprive the living Jews of that for which they live.[27]

Jointure of enomothetic and idiographic interpretation

A final item takes us back to the specific philosophic frame of reference with which we began.

The physical image behind such a continuum as generality-particularity is one of a single line that extends in diametrically opposed directions. Further reflection may suggest a profounder state of affairs. First, as already suggested, the relation between our two modes of knowledge can be treated as a dialectical one: on the one hand, the most abstract

27. Edward Alexander, "Stealing the Holocaust in the name of 'humanity,'" the *Seattle Times*, 4 Nov. 1979; *see also* Rael Jean Isaac, "From Friendly Persuasion to PLO Support," *Midstream* 25:23–29 (1979); Marvin Maurer, "Quakers in Politics: Israel, PLO, and Social Revolution," *Midstream* 23:36–44 (1977).

symbol-system conceivable could at the last be adjudged unique in and of its own Gestalt. On the other hand, ways may be sought to prevent a radically peculiar datum from being excluded from a highly generalizing model.[28]

Second, a much more venturesome eventuality presents itself. Is it not possible that the ostensibly rigid, single line of generality-particularity may be grasped at points near its two extremities by, so to speak, the left and right hands of the human spirit and then curved upward and finally inward until at the last it is granted the form of a circle? The theoretical end-terms of our continuum are "absolute abstractness," or common Being as such, and "absolute peculiarity." Are we prepared to realize and endure an encounter between these two absolutes? Or will such a meeting shatter our minds and our lives?

The theologian has dared to behave in this very way. Thus he makes bold to bring forward both the most generalizing concept of all, Being

28. Within the behavioral sciences, an exclusive concentration upon nomothesis is subject to serious dispute. Thus, in personality theory a consequence of such exclusivism could well be the disintegration of the very subject that was to be analyzed: the wholeness of personality. Individual personality affords manifold evidence of defying subjection to precise quantitative treatment. Idiography seems required, as reflected in the very phrasing "case history." The individualizing thrust within clinical psychology points to a link between the disciplines of psychology and history. The need for idiography within psychology hardly establishes that need within the political and social sciences. It does serve to remind us, however, that a certain school of thought constituent to the human sciences insists that nomothesis places limitations upon human understanding. Our own purpose is to inquire whether the limitations upon understanding within nomothesis may also be found within idiography. The "case history" of the Holocaust has here been singled out.

as such, and the most peculiar concept of all, *this* Individual. And then, presumption of presumptions, he acts to merge them into the single concept, God. A potentially appropriate observation within the bounds of the present analysis is that this God is reputed to utilize the world-determining events of history for certain purposes.

There is a more modest, non-theological way of putting the matter that will perhaps be less offensive to many persons. May it be that our frontier conceptualization, according to which absolute abstractness and absolute peculiarity are assigned convergence, could function heuristically to foster a metahistorical structure of reasoning for grappling with such an overwhelming event as the Holocaust of the Jewish people? The hope that this might transpire is prompted by the extraordinary and almost unbearable consideration that something within this incredible happening seems to have the power to drive us infinitely in the direction of singularity and yet, at the very same moment, to impel us infinitely in the direction of generalizing interpretation. It almost appears that all the race were somehow imploded here.

We restrict ourselves, in sum, to a two-sided question: idiographically expressed, is there some way in which the Holocaust is to be identified as a mutual impingement of alpha and omega? Nomothetically expressed, is there the possibility of a happening that, while radically unique, could also be received as a boundary-event, as somehow revelatory of the meaning and tragedy of human life and death itself, and hence as embodying the most generalizing insight that could be garnered? Here, perhaps, an eventuality is given form that we may come to

share with the scientist and the historian—not on the ground of something integral to scientific and historical methodology but instead upon the soil of our common humanity. Human intellectuality in its natural philosophical heights and depths may upon occasion contribute to a shared universe of meaning and thence to mutual decision making.

It is interesting in this connection to reflect upon the work of Albert Einstein within the context of Nazi Germany, from which he was a refugee, and within the general frame of reference of the relation between truth and morality. The Einsteinian equation $E = MC^2$ falls very far along the extremity of nomothesis. From the standpoint of Nazi ideology, this equation had to be total nonsense and a positive threat to the only particularity that is possessed of absolute or genuine value, Aryan man. The equation was devised by an *Unmensch*, someone who did not belong within the category of humanity but was a deadly bacillus seeking to destroy truth and goodness. Thus from within Nazi ideology, nomothesis and idiography had to stand in conflict. Need this be the case once the human mind is free?

THE MARRIAGE OF SOCIAL ETHICS AND THE SOCIOLOGY OF KNOWLEDGE

We may remind ourselves, in conclusion, that moral obligation can fill the role of arousing convictions of absoluteness respecting a given event even if it appears that the event itself will not manage after all to gain philosophic categorization as something transcendently unique.

Reference may be made to Gertrude Stein's famous sentence, "Rose is a rose is a rose is a rose." We are given three choices. One is to subject all roses to an abstract fate, in good nomothetic fashion. Second, we may select out one rose from all other roses and concentrate upon its unique uniqueness within time and space. But, third, we may establish a moral-existential relation with *this* rose, perhaps determining to do what we can to fight against the unhappy transitoriness of so fragile and beautiful a thing. Thus if fortunate enough to be blessed with requisite talent, we may resolve to convey to others the being of this rose artistically so that it may, in a sense, not have to die. The tie between moral obligation and the philosophic quest appears at this third level of choice: this rose differs transcendently from all other roses because of our human relationship to it. We do not want it to become a victim.

The singularity of the Holocaust is measured by the specific identity of its victims. It is from within the context of historic and abiding Jewish victimization that the moral peculiarity and challenge of the Holocaust may be said to emerge. This state of affairs itself exemplifies the dialectical character of nomothesis-idiography: "Holocaust" is here assimilated to the more general concept "Jewish victimization." Moral claims do not take form apart from specific historical conditions and milieux. The Jew has been the traditional enemy and scapegoat of Christendom and, subsequently, of the secularizing West.[29] Even the international readiness after World War II to sanction a land of refuge for the miserable remnant of the

Jews of Europe cannot be comprehended apart from the social psychology of victimization: the widespread and concerted opposition to Israel over some years, not excepting the identical parties that supported the U. N. partition of part of Palestine, bespeaks an ongoing refusal to tolerate Jews and to have compassion for them in a role other than that of victim or underdog.

As Edward Alexander writes, after 1967 "Israel discovered that the price she would have to pay for winning a war that, if lost, would have meant her obliteration, was the universal loss of the sympathy that Jews [had amassed through the Holocaust]."[30] The victor will sometimes go to the aid of the victim. But once the victim loses or overcomes his victim's status, the victor will tend to turn upon him. In adaptation of conclusions from both Jean-Paul Sartre and Robert Jay Lifton, victimization is the cowardly *sine qua non* of one's own immortality.[31]

The challenge of the Holocaust is addressed concretely to the Christian and Western worlds, although, as has been implied, this is hardly to exclude from culpability the non-Western world. The singular relation that Christians and other Gentiles have to Jews, a psycho-moral relation of victor to victim, takes us beyond many forms of unique uniqueness, including its most epochal forms. Those who continue to identify themselves with the Christian community are confronted by certain transcendent questions, questions of absolute moral import: "Am I my brother's keeper? I can, to be sure, renounce my place in and my allegiance to the Christian community. But if I choose to remain

29. *See* Bauer, pp. 28–29; for the history of antisemitism *see* Leon Poliakov, *The History of Antisemitism*, vols. 1 & 2: (New York: Schocken Books, 1974); and vol. 3 (New York: Vanguard Press, 1979).

30. Alexander.
31. Lifton, p. 330.

within that community, do I not thereby take upon myself, in tacit yet positive and ineluctable ways, the burden of the church's guilt for the antisemitism that helped make the Holocaust inevitable? And am I not then faced with the obligation to engage in such thinking and behavior as will help to purge away that guilt?"

The historic relationship that the Christian church bears to the Jewish community, epitomized in the phrase "the teaching of contempt" from the French historian Jules Isaac,[32] demands a revolution within those religious doctrines that are still prom-

ulgated today, most especially a critical transformation in teachings that are traceable directly to the many anti-Jewish elements in the church's prevailing authority for faith, the New Testament.

Improper mystification is indeed a pitfall whenever we seek to characterize the Holocaust as transcendingly unique in any objective, impersonal sense. The transcending uniqueness of the Holocaust is made manifest in an existential way by virtue of the special relation that many human beings have to that event. It is at this juncture that a social ethic for the post-Holocaust era comes together with a sociology of knowledge applied to the Holocaust. Herein lies the Holocaust's uniqueness, in an absolute sense, for our time.

32. Jules Isaac, *The Teaching of Contempt: Christian Roots of Anti-Semitism*, trans. Helen Weaver (New York: Holt, Rinehart and Winston, 1964).

ANNALS, AAPSS, **450**, July 1980

The Christian Response to the Holocaust

By ROBERT F. DRINAN

ABSTRACT: The reaction of the Christian community to the Holocaust can generally be described as mild, vague, and belated. While there are notable exceptions to the general ineffectiveness of the Church to affect its concern over rising antisemitism, it failed in any significant way to provide political or moral leadership to combat the antisemitic designs of Hitler's Germany. The reappraisal of past teaching coupled with acknowledgement of past complicity with antisemitism has contributed to a heightened sense of ecumenical responsibility. Since World War II, the Christian community's statements condemning the Holocaust have increased Christian sensitivity to the horrors of the past and to the potential dangers of the future.

Robert F. Drinan, LL.B. Georgetown University Law Center and Doctor of Theology, Gregorian University, Rome, is currently serving as United States Congressman, 4th District, Massachusetts. An ordained priest, his chairmanship of the Subcommittee on Criminal Justice as well as of numerous other governmental committees reveals Father Drinan's concern with man's relation to man and the many problems of aging, retirement, income and employment manpower, housing, and individual rights. His publications include Religion, the Courts and Public Policy, Democracy, Dissent and Disorder, Vietnam and Armageddon, *and* Honor the Promise: America's Commitment to Israel. *He has also served as corresponding editor of* America, the National Catholic Weekly, *and on the editorial board of* A Journal of Church and State.

179

THE CHRISTIAN response to the Holocaust may be said to have begun as early as the second half of 1943 when, according to the *Encyclopedia Judaica*, "knowledge of mass murder was widespread" and "the truth, even if not the whole truth" of the systematic killing of the Jews "gradually spread all over Germany."[1] The reaction of the German churches is characterized by the *Encyclopedia Judaica* as "mild, vague, and belated." The response of Christian leaders and churches generally during the years of anti-Jewish persecution by the Nazis which led up to the Holocaust has been judged by some in similar terms.[2]

It may not be possible to arrive at any historic judgment which does full justice to the complex factors involved: the degree to which reliable information of what was happening had become available; the subtle interplay among worthy and unworthy motives—prudence, credibility, fear, and cowardice; and the dreadful ambivalence posed by the dilemma of whether "to speak or to save." All these must be considered in the larger context of people confused by propaganda, enflamed by wartime passions, and terrorized by totalitarian rule.

"The darkness of the holocaust was so great," writes Johan Snoek, "that one can hardly comprehend it." Hence his measured judgment on the reactions of the churches: "The picture is neither completely black, nor purely white."[3] The grey halftones of history—darkened as much

1. *Encyclopedia Judaica*, vol. 8 (New York: Macmillan, 1971), p. 874.
2. *See* Alan T. Davies, *Anti-Semitism and the Christian Mind* (New York: Herder and Herder, 1969), pp. 23–67.
3. Johan M. Snoek, *The Grey Book* (Assen, Netherlands: Von Gorcum and Co., 1969), p. 289.

by indifference as by deliberate brutality, yet lightened by the faith and courage of the few—reflect the ambiguities inherent in the actual responses of Christendom to an event such as the Holocaust.

It has been the troubled conscience of the Christian community that, since the end of World War II, has sought to come to terms with the meaning of the Holocaust both by self-examination, critically scrutinizing whatever in the Christian tradition may have fostered antisemitic attitudes, and by ecumenical dialogue with Judaism and the Jewish people, opening new areas of understanding and respect. In this sense, the actions of the Second Vatican Council, repudiating the ancient charge of deicide and condemning all forms of anti-Jewish prejudice, are a vital part of the continuing Christian response to the impact of the Holocaust.

ANTISEMITISM AND THE CHRISTIAN TRADITION

The special character of the Jews in Christian teaching as God's Chosen People under the Old Dispensation helps explain the underlying ambivalence of the Christian community toward the Jewish community in the past. The Church at once protected and restricted the Jews. Its protective measures—crucial to Jewish survival in medieval Christendom—were inspired by the hope of conversion. Its restrictive measures were designed to prevent Christians from apostasy to Judaism. Thus Jews, though abused, persecuted, and feared, were regarded and treated in a different light than were Christian heretics.

While racism was no part of what was essentially a theological tension in the Middle Ages, the popular image of the Jews was a factor in the rise of modern antisemitism, incorporating, as it did, racist and economic elements. The term "antisemitism" was first employed in 1897 by the German racist Wilhelm Marr.[4]

While modern antisemitism was born from the racist and nationalistic theories of the last century,[5] it cannot be wholly divorced from the context of Christian-Jewish relations in European history, particularly in what Jules Isaac has called "the teaching of contempt" in Christian circles and the popular emphasis on Jewish culpability for the death of Christ.[6] The reception given Professor Isaac in 1960 by Pope John XXIII, who forwarded Isaac's proposals for purifying Catholic teaching from anti-Jewish prejudice to Cardinal Augustin Bea, then director of the Vatican Secretariat preparing for Vatican Council II, was a landmark in the movement among Chistians since the Holocaust to alter "centuries old antipathy and misconceptions" regarding the Jews.[7] It should be noted that Isaac's first meeting with a pope was in 1949 when Pope Pius XII bestowed his blessing upon him.[8]

Similarly, the major non-Roman Catholic churches and ecumenical bodies throughout the world have spoken out against antisemitism with increasing vigor since the end of World War II, most dramatically in the "Resolution on Anti-Semitism" adopted in 1961 by the Third Assembly of the World Council of Churches, meeting at New Delhi. In 1964, the General Board of the National Council of Churches of Christ in the United States reaffirmed the World Council's position. These and other statements emanating from the Christian community have reflected—and strengthened—Christian self-examination. The reappraisal of past teaching, coupled with acknowledgement of past complicity in antisemitism, has led to a renewed sense of ecumenical responsibility in dialogue with the Jewish community.[9]

THE GERMAN CHURCHES

The situation of the German churches, Catholic and Protestant, under Hitler has received treatment at the hands of scholars. Protestant unity was weakened by the rise of the "German Christian" movement, which was both racist and ethnic in character. Opposition to collaboration with the Nazi state found expression in the confessing church. Among Catholics, memories of Bismarck's *Kulturkampf* against the church fostered an ultranationalism which gave uneasy support to the regime. Hence, in the words of Richard Grunberger, "the Confessional Church of Prussia was the only Christian body in the twelve-year history of the Third Reich to protest publicly against the unspeakable outrages inflicted upon the Jews." The protest, read from pulpits in 1943, dramatizes the "overwhelming silence" of the

4. For the religious background of modern antisemitism in Germany, see Fritz Stern, "The Hostage of the New Anti-Semitism," in *Gold and Iron* (New York: Vintage Books, 1979).

5. See Koppel Pinson, *Essays on Anti-Semitism* (New York: Conference on Jewish Relations, 1946).

6. Jules Isaac, *The Teaching of Contempt* (New York: Holt, Rinehart and Winston, 1964).

7. Pinchas Lapide, *Three Popes and the Jews* (New York: Hawthorn Books, 1967), p. 26.

8. Katherine T. Hargrove, *The Star and the Cross* (Milwaukee: Bruce Publishing, 1966), p. 131.

9. Interfaith dialogue guidelines are discussed by Arthur Gilbert, *The Vatican Council and the Jews* (Cleveland, OH: World Publishing, 1968), ch. 14, pp. 219–42.

rest of the German churches throughout the Holocaust.[10]

The reasons for this silence were many. Prudence, fear of the consequences, which were invariably swift and brutal, and reluctance to alienate public opinion by undermining what were perceived to be national interest and national unity—these were among the factors which, after the war, moved the German churches to repentance and to adoption of a series of statements acknowledging their guilt in "crimes committed by people of our nation toward the Jews."[11]

Guenter Lewy, in his study of the German Catholic church during the Nazi Era, has noted "the passivity of the German episcopate in the face of the Jewish tragedy . . . in marked contrast to the conduct of the French, Belgian, and Dutch bishops."[12] The same judgment applies to the general attitude of the Protestant churches in Germany. There were remarkable exceptions—Provost Lichtenberg and Dr. Gertrud Luckner, to name but two among the most forthright—but indifference, abetted by fear, was more common. Thus in 1950, a group of Protestant and Catholic theologians could state that "among the Christians, a few courageously helped the persecuted, but the majority failed disgracefully in face of this unheard of provocation."[13] The effect of this failure is emphasized by Grunberger, who writes that "basically the holocaust was not a real event to most Germans, not because it occurred in wartime and under conditions of secrecy, but because

Jews were astronomically remote and not real people." The sense of national interest had become "so total that imagination and conscience alike were anaesthetized."[14]

German Christian response since the war has addressed itself to these issues—notably, in the 1961 Report of the German Evangelical *Kirchentag*.[15] Similarly, the Synod of the German Evangelical Church spoke in 1964 of the guilt shared by "ordinary" Christians:

Even the citizen who had no direct share in the crimes, nay, even he who did not know of them, has shared in the guilt because he was indifferent towards the perversions of all moral standards and all notions of right and wrong among our people. Nor can we exempt ourselves and our congregations from the guilt. For where all Christians were called upon to uphold the Gospel entrusted to us, to make public affirmation of the everlasting dominion of God in all spheres of our lives, and, thus armed, to protect the victims of the regime, especially the Jews living amongst us, only few had the insight and the courage to resist.[16]

The Holy See

The pontificate of Pope Pius XII poses a special problem, one fraught with controversy, stimulated at the popular level by Rolf Hochhuth's 1963 play, *Der Stellvertreter (The Deputy)*, which raised serious questions of motive and character regarding the larger issue of alleged papal silence in the face of the Nazis' Final Solution to the Jewish problem.

Writers such as Guenter Lewy have argued that the "silence" of Pius XII represented a failure in moral leadership. "Influenced by a long condition of moderate anti-Semitism,"

10. Richard Grunberger, *The 12-Year Reich* (New York: Holt, Rinehart and Winston, 1971), p. 453.

11. Snoek, p. 292.

12. Hargrove, p. 168.

13. *See* Freiburger Rundbrief, II (1949–1950), No. 8/9, cited by Guenter Lewy in Hargrove, p. 170.

14. Grunberger, p. 466.

15. Snoek, p. 294.

16. Ibid., p. 294–95.

Lewy writes, the pope "did not view the plight of the Jews with a real sense of urgency and moral outrage."[17] Defenders of Pope Pius have emphasized his role in saving many thousands of Jews from death. Others have stressed his inability to act more openly without endangering the lives of Jews and Catholics alike. It is asserted that papal caution and circumspection resulted in the saving of more lives than a more outspoken, forceful stand would have accomplished. Joseph Licten has maintained, for example, that the pope's course of action was "dictated by his long experience as a Vatican statesman and his great desire to save lives."[18]

In his *Pius XII and the Third Reich*, Saul Friedlander presents an overview of pertinent documents, mostly from the German diplomatic archives, matched with public documents from the Holy See and other collections. In 1943, in a letter to the archbishop of Berlin and in a secret address to the College of Cardinals, the pope alluded directly to the extermination of the Jews—some three million had already been murdered by June of that year. "Every address to the competent authority, and all our public utterances, have to be carefully weighed and measured by us in the interests of the victims themselves, lest, contrary to our intentions, we make their situation worse and harder to bear."[19]

A clear judgment may never be possible. The continuing debate on

the pope's stand reflects the depth of concern which the Holocaust has stimulated in the Christian conscience. Thus scholars will continue to differ over specific events, variously interpreting the pope's actions—for example, in the deportation of Italian and Roman Jews in late 1943.

Friedlander conveys an impression of the pope's attitude in this instance quite different from that given by Anthony Rhodes in his *The Vatican in the Age of the Dictators*. Friedlander relies upon reports by Baron von Weizsacker, the German ambassador to the Holy See, who praises the pope for "making [no] demonstrative pronouncement."[20] Rhodes quotes the report of the British ambassador, Sir F. D'Arcy Osborne, regarding the protest made to Berlin by Cardinal Maglione, papal secretary of state, which resulted in release of "a large number" of Jews. Osborne added that "any publication of [this] information would probably lead to renewed persecution."[21]

Finally, no evaluation of the pope's public silence can ignore the possibility that Christian response to antisemitic measures by the Nazis was determined less by the policy of the Holy See or other religious authorities than by national feeling and popular attitudes in each country. In Poland and Rumania, for example, antisemitic feeling ran deep and found open, vigorous support. In Bulgaria, Denmark, and the like, antisemitism received little or no backing from people or churches. Germany was a special case, influenced by Vatican anxieties at the possibility of German Catholic sep-

17. Guenter Lewy, "Pius XII, the Jews, and the German Catholic Church," *Commentary*, 27:22–25 (2 Feb. 1964).
18. Cited in Edward H. Flannery, *The Anguish of the Jews* (New York: Macmillan, 1965), p. 314.
19. Both texts are given in full in Saul Friedlander, *Pius XII and the Third Reich* (London: Chatto & Windus, 1966), pp. 135–45.

20. Ibid, p. 207.
21. Anthony Rhodes, *The Vatican in the Age of the Dictators (1922–1945)*. (New York: Holt, Rinehart and Winston, 1973), p. 351.

aratism and by that intense fear of communism which the Holy See shared with German Catholic leadership.[22]

The terrible lessons provided by the Dutch Catholics and by the situation in Poland must also be considered in examining the policy of the Holy See. In 1942, the Catholic and Reformed churches in the Netherlands protested in secret against the deportation of Dutch Jews. The Nazi authorities yielded only to the extent of sparing baptized Jews. In response, the archbishop of Utrecht publicly condemned the Nazi persecution of Jews, whereupon all baptized Catholic Jews were also arrested and deported, the philosopher Edith Stein among them. In Poland, Nazi reaction to the pope's 1939 Encyclical *Summi Pontificatus* was particularly severe. These and similar experiences served to alarm the pope and to induce great caution in his public statements.[23]

OTHER COUNTRIES

The reaction to the Holocaust in countries other than Germany is divided by *The Grey Book* into categories: occupied countries (Norway, Netherlands, France, Yugoslavia, Greece, and Denmark); satellite countries (Slovakia, Rumania, Bulgaria, and Hungary); neutral countries (Switzerland and Sweden); and countries at war with Germany (Britain and the United States). A special category, "Territories in which Churches Kept Silent," includes Austria, Belgium, Poland, Finland, Italy, Russia, and the Protectorate of Bohemia and Moravia, formed out of Czechoslovakia.[24]

In general, in countries under German occupation, "efforts made by the Churches had hardly any direct practical result."[25] However, while public protests were helpful in counteracting the Nazi propaganda, "in many cases individuals acted quietly and behind the scenes" with courage and decency largely unnoted in history. The rescue of Danish Jewry remains a heroic feat, achieved by the church and the people together, after a remarkable public protest, which stated that "every man is precious in the eyes of God."[26] In the satellite nations, the churches were sometimes able to mitigate the suffering of the Jews, most dramatically in Bulgaria where the churches, led by the Metropolitan Stephan, intervened to prevent deportation of Bulgarian Jews. "Do not persecute" Stephan wrote King Boris, "so that you may not be persecuted. With what measure ye mete it shall be measured to you again."[27]

In the neutral countries, the churches did give help to Jewish refugees. In the nations at war with Germany, Christian churches helped combat antisemitism and break "the wall of secrecy [which] concealed the terrible tragedy"[28] but effective rescue activities were largely frustrated. For the most part, protests by the churches "came too late," except in Denmark and the Netherlands, where resistance to persecution of the Jews was manifest from the beginning.[29]

In Norway, the church spoke out

25. Ibid, p. 21 et passim.
26. Ibid, p. 169. The legend that King Christian defied the Germans by publicly wearing the Jewish "yellow star" is wholly without foundation and is most likely the product of wartime British propaganda. *See* Richard Petrow, *The Bitter Years* (New York: Morrow Quill Paperbacks, 1979), pp. 227–29.
27. Snoek, p. 192.
28. Ibid, p. 23.
29. Ibid.

22. *See* Helen Fein, *Accounting for Genocide* (New York: The Free Press, 1979), pp. 93–120.
23. Ibid, pp. 286–91, 321–22, 344–45.
24. Snoek, pp. 19–24.

publicly in 1942, though it was not able to prevent the deportations. Public protest was made in the Netherlands with some effect, though mercy rather than justice was usually stressed. Significantly, after the war, the Dutch Reform church was moved to public confession "[T]hat in this struggle we have not been sufficiently faithful."[30]

The situation in France was complicated by the existence of the unoccupied and occupied zones until late 1942. Protests against antisemitic measures were directed to Marshall Petain by Protestants and Catholics but they were largely ignored. Heroic assistance was rendered by the Cimade, a Protestant youth group. The story of Andre Trocme, pastor at Le Chambon, whose people aided Jewish refugees to safety has received wide attention in recent years.[31] The Catholic bishops in both zones protested the deportations. Archbishop Saliege of Toulouse vigorously denounced the arrest of Jews in a letter read from the pulpits of his diocese:

That men, women and children can be rounded up like a herd of cattle, that members of the same family can be separated from one another and transported to unknown destinations—to live through this horror, is that what is reserved for us today? In the concentration camps of None and Recebedon disgraceful scenes have taken place. Jews are men too! Jewesses are women too! They too belong to the human race, they are our brothers and sisters. Let no Christian ever forget this!

These protests were supported by the Vatican, and, although Jews continued to be hunted down and taken away, the breach thus effected between church and state in Vichy France was permanent.[32]

In Greece, Archbishop Damaskinos of Athens, the primate of the Greek church, was able to save countless thousands of Jews. Friedman asserts that the Orthodox church in Greece "used its considerable influence" to oppose Nazi antisemitism.[33] However, it is doubtful whether any Church in any country had a 'considerable influence' with the German occupying forces."[34] Most Greek Jews were eventually killed.

Repeated protests by Christian authorities in Hungary in 1944 succeeded in stopping deportations until the Nazis intervened in force to overthrow the Horthy regime. In Rumania, Orthodox leaders intervened personally and in private to rescue the Jews, thereby saving the majority. The direct appeal of Chief Rabbi, Dr. Safran to the metropolitan of Bucharest, Archbishop Balan —known as antisemitic—was successful. A similar personal appeal won over the Patriarch Nicodemus, previously indifferent.[35]

In Belgium, as in France, Catholic authorities, at first moderately cooperative with the Occupation, moved gradually toward opposition. The churches in Poland, where the whole population was subject to the most severe oppression, were preoccupied with national survival and were compelled to do what little could be done in strict secrecy. Indeed, almost everywhere the majority of people was preoccupied with the problems of war or of military occupation. "The persecution of the Jews was not the only challenge confronting the Churches in those days, though we only now can perceive better that it was the most important one."[36]

30. Ibid, p. 136.
31. *See* Philip Hallie, *Lest Innocent Blood Be Shed* (New York: Harper & Row, 1979).
32. Rhodes, p. 315–18.
33. Philip Friedman, *Their Brothers' Keepers.* (New York: Crown, 1957), p. 109.
34. Snoek, p. 153.
35. Ibid., p. 175.
36. Ibid, p. 11.

In Britain, leadership in this issue was provided by the archbishop of Canterbury, William Temple, in a 1942 broadcast, following reports of the mass murder of Jews in Poland. Public protests by all the churches continued throughout the war.[37] In 1943, the archbishops of Canterbury, York, and Wales called for "sanctuary for the victims" and retribution after the war. The government, reluctant to admit refugees on a mass scale, yielded in 1943 to public pressures by the Council of Christians and Jews, concerned at "reports of mass extermination of Jews and others." (Archbishop Temple had received full details from the World Jewish Congress and other sources.) The Bermuda Conference, held that year in response to the appeal by the churches, accomplished nothing tangible. Bishop Bell of Chichester criticized the conference in the House of Lords, noting that "the Jews were not even mentioned."

Archbishop Temple's words in 1943 spoke for the Christian conscience in Britain and generally. "It is one of the most terrible consequences of war that the sensitiveness of people tends to become hardened," he said. "We could hardly live these days if we felt the volume of suffering of others in the world as acutely as we felt in peacetime." He added, "There is a great moral danger in the paralysis of feeling that is liable to be brought about. It is most important for our own moral health and vigor that we express horror at the persecution of the Jews." The public stand taken by the churches in Britain is eloquently represented by the statement of the General Assembly of the Church of Scotland in 1943:

The General Assembly protest anew against the atrocious persecution of the Jews in Nazi-occupied countries, and in the name of Christ condemns the inhumanity and sacrilege of anti-Semitic policy.

They warmly approve of the steps taken by the Government to assist refugees, and respectfully urge it to continue and extend its efforts as far as possible.

They assure the Jewish people of their deep sympathy in their grievous distress, and earnestly commend them to the prayerful concern and compassion of the Church.[38]

UNITED STATES

The Federal Council of Churches of Christ and other groups in the United States strongly denounced antisemitism during the period of American neutrality. In 1942, the Federal Council spoke out in response to reports of the Holocaust which were reaching America:

It is impossible to avoid a conclusion that something like a policy of deliberate extermination of the Jews in Europe is being carried out. The violence and inhumanity which Nazi leaders have publicly avowed toward all Jews are apparently now coming to a climax in a virtual massacre. We are resolved to do our full part in establishing conditions in which such treatment of the Jews shall end.

The feelings of the Jewish community throughout the world have recently been expressed in a period of mourning, fasting and prayer. We associate ourselves with our Jewish fellow-citizens in their hour of tragic sorrow, and unite our prayers with theirs.[39]

Mass meetings of Christians and Jews in 1943 supported the holding of the Bermuda Conference, which, as we have seen, failed to address itself to the urgency of the crisis.

37. Ibid, pp. 235–56.

38. Ibid, p. 251.
39. Ibid, p. 261.

Numerous public statements were issued by Protestant, Catholic, and Jewish authorities, sometimes acting together. As news of the full dimension of the Holocaust reached America, Christian feeling was profoundly shocked, and statements warning against antisemitism in American life were increasingly common.

At the same time, "published studies indicate that close to one half of the American people were expressing different shades of anti-semitism right up to 1942 and 1943."[40] Isolationist feeling still ran strong. These factors—and President Roosevelt's concern not to move too far ahead of public opinion[41]—shaped American policy at Bermuda. Similar concerns influenced the British government,[42] despite pressure from the clergy, Catholic and Protestant, members of Parliament, and the press. Fear of being inundated by refugees was endemic generally in the West.

It seems clear, however, that the basic problem was not so much who knew what or how credible such information might be. Rather, as Bauer has argued, "the thing was unbelievable, and indeed was not believed."[43] He adds:

In the end this boils down to an epistemological question: when does information become internalized knowledge, and when does this knowledge become a guide to action? The information regarding the Holocaust was there in the late spring of 1942, about one year after the Nazis had begun their mass murder

of European Jewry. . . . The point was that it took time before it became knowledge. As far as the western powers were concerned, it became the guide to action partly, very late, or not at all.[44]

With noteworthy exceptions and some qualifications, a not dissimilar judgment can be made regarding the response of the churches. This was the background to the failure of the Bermuda Conference and of the Evian Conference in 1938 to provide practical help for refugees. Saul Friedman has noted that even refugee children were regarded with fear as a potential Fifth Column menace.[45] While groups such as the American Friends Service Committee and the Unitarian Service Committee—and such religious leaders as Dr. John Haynes Holmes of New York's Community Church—labored valiantly to save Jews and other refugees fleeing Nazi terror, sustained public pressure by the Christian community in America as in Europe was largely inadequate and ineffective. Rhetoric did not translate into tangible proposals for immediate rescue of those who might have been saved.

CONCLUSION

In the perspective of history, the Christian response to the Holocaust has acquired new and continuing dimensions—a deepened awareness of what Simone Weil described as "the Hitler in ourselves";[46] a greater sensitivity to the human rights of all

40. See Yehuda Bauer, *The Holocaust in Historical Perspective* (Seattle, WA: University of Washington Press, 1978), p. 79.

41. See Henry Feingold, *The Politics of Rescue* (New Brunswick, NJ: Rutgers University Press, 1970).

42. Barnard Wasserstein, *Britain and the Jews of Europe, 1939–1945* (London: Institute of Jewish Affairs, 1979).

43. Bauer, p. 81.

44. Ibid.

45. Saul Friedman, *No Haven for the Oppressed* (Detroit: Wayne State University, 1973), p. 113.

46. Her essay "Some Reflections on the Origins of Hitlerism," is discussed in Simone Petrement, *Simone Weil* (New York: Pantheon Books, 1979), pp. 356–61.

persons, Christian and non-Christian; and a common concern to avoid similar tragedies in the future.

Many groups have sprung up throughout the Christian world, committed in word and deed to reparation for the crimes of the Holocaust. One such group, representative of many, is the Aktion Suhnzeichen (Action for Atonement), organized by Pastor Lothar Kreysig in Germany as a "penance corps." In this way German youth from all faiths have given their labor and talent to projects for rehabilitation and renewal in Israel, Britain, the Netherlands, and France. Similar reparative ministry is carried on by the German Lutheran sisterhood organized by Mother Basileia Schlink. At the Dachau Concentration Camp there is a community of Carmelite nuns engaged in prayer and intercession. The visit of Pope John Paul II to Auschwitz in 1979, and the Memorial Mass celebrated there by him, and his eloquent homily honoring those who perished in the death camp, with explicit reference to the Jews, gave expression to the Christian conscience today.

While reparation—moral and material—is seen by some as an appropriate response from Christian individuals and communities alike, collective guilt would be an unhelpful basis for Christian-Jewish understanding. "Unless the lessons drawn from the Holocaust are kept in perspective—one aimed to benefit all peoples (Jew and non-Jew alike)— they could," writes Richard Harley, "foster some of the intolerances they are intended to counteract."[47] He distinguishes four "broad streams of interest" which relate to Holocaust history and the future of Holocaust studies, interests which bring Christian and Jew together:

1. Mutual concern for human rights. In the words of Rabbi Marc Tannenbaum, "In a world with increasing violence and torture . . . there appears to be a growing callousness to human suffering. The Holocaust issue helps us ask, 'Where am I in all this?' and 'What should be my responsibility?' "

2. Mutual concern for the ethical character of modern education in days to come. "[The Holocaust was] carried out in a highly civilized society with fine educational systems, and in the heart of European Christendom," according to Franklin Littell. "Both institutions were largely indifferent to what happened to the Jews."

3. Mutual concern at overt antisemitism.

4. Mutual concern for Holocaust history and for the lessons it may teach in the present.

The educational context of Holocaust studies is emphasized by Henry Friedlander as a means of imparting "civic virtue" by showing "how the only defense against persecution and extermination is citizens prepared to oppose the power of the state and face the hostility of their neighbors to aid the intended victim."[48] For Professor Friedlander, "the Holocaust is not sacred history. [It] is a public event" whose focus must be expanded to shed light on the human condition.

For Christians, however, the Holocaust continues to have a special significance, over and above civic responsibility: it touches theology, social ethics, and ecumenical concerns at their deepest levels. Thus in 1974, an International Symposium

---

47. Richard Harley, "Holocaust Lessons Not Just For TV," *Christian Science Monitor*, 31 (8 May, 1978).

48. Quoted in Fred Hechinger, "Educators Seek to Teach Context of the Holocaust," *New York Times*, 15 May, 1979, p. C5.

on the Holocaust met at the Cathedral of St. John the Divine in New York City. Its papers, published that year under the title *Auschwitz: Beginning of a New Era? Reflections on the Holocaust*, deal with various aspects of the Holocaust in relation to Christian and Jewish theology, history, education, culture, and politics. The symposium itself was a landmark in Christian-Jewish dialogue, "a joint effort . . . to speak of the unspeakable."[49] The symposium includes a balanced appraisal of Christian history in its impact upon the Jews by Professor Yosef Hayim Yerushalmi, who notes the twofold Christian tradition of "reprobation" and "preservation" concerning the Jews.[50]

An outgrowth of the symposium, urged by Father John Pawlikowski, was renewed interest in liturgical commemoration by Christians and in ecumenical gatherings of Holocaust Day, observed in Israel on the twenty-seventh day of the Hebrew month of Nissan. Already in 1972, at a Chicago conference on "the Holocaust and the Contemporary Religious Condition," it was proposed that the Sunday closest to Holocaust Day be so designated. In 1979, following passage of a joint congressional resolution, signed into law by the U.S. president, April 28–29 were kept as Days of Remembrance for the victims of the Holocaust. By choosing a Saturday and a Sunday, both Jews and Christians could honor the dead in their respective communities and with their own or ecumenical rites.

On April 24 of 1979, a moving service of remembrance was held in the rotunda of the United States Capitol, attended by President Carter, members of Congress, and others, at which Elie Wiesel, Holocaust survivor, author, and chairman of the President's Commission on the Holocaust, spoke of the "forgotten [of whom] the world knew—and kept silent." Appropriately, the massacred Armenians of World War I, traditionally remembered on April 24, were included in the prayers and ceremonies.[51]

Observance of Holocaust Remembrance Sunday may spread among Christians of every denomination. Educational programs sponsored by Christian and Jewish groups jointly, stimulated by the President's Commission on the Holocaust as well as by the ecumenical impulse of recent decades, are increasingly underway across the nation.[52]

These activities can serve an instructive and useful purpose of remembering the atrocities of the past and of understanding the failure of the Christian community to respond in a meaningful, effective manner. It is unfortunately necessary to realize the potential for another holocaust in our time. The Christian community, based on the perspective of history, should stand ready to participate actively and virulently to prevent a holocaust from threatening humanity again.

49. Edited by Eva Fleischner, the *Auschwitz* Symposium is published by the Cathedral of St. John the Divine in cooperation with the Anti-Defamation League of B'nai B'rith and the KTAV Publishing House, New York.

50. *See also* Alan. T. Davies, *Anti-Semitism and the Christian Mind* (New York: Herder and Herder, 1969).

51. Michael Kernan, "The World Knew— and Kept Silent," *Washington Post*, 25 April 1979, p. C1.

52. An example of "ongoing Jewish-Christian dialogue" is the 1971 Symposium on Jewish-Christian Relations and Education, held at Baylor University and sponsored by the Anti-Defamation League of B'nai B'rith and J. M. Dawson Studies in Church and State at Baylor. *See* James Wood, ed., *Jewish-Christian Relations in Today's World* (Waco, TX: Baylor University Press, 1971).

The First German Church Faces the Challenge of the Holocaust: A Report

By HEINZ KREMERS

ABSTRACT: After 20 years of discussion about the relationship of Christians and Jews, caused by the reflection of the Holocaust, the Evangelische Kirche im Rheinland, regional church of the Evangelische Kirche in Deutschland, has passed a resolution. It states the responsibility of Christianity for the Holocaust, the everlasting election of Israel as the people of God, and the common vocation of Jews and Christians to be witnesses of God to the world and to each other; it refutes the opinion that the Jewish people have been rejected by God and accordingly have been substituted by the church; and it stresses the impossibility of *Judenmission*. Furthermore, the synod demands better information on Judaism and wishes to build up a new partnership between Jews and Christians. First impulses in this direction came from the Reformed churches of the Netherlands and from the Deutsche evangelische Kirchentag in Berlin, 1961. Since then, many Jewish teachers have helped the Evangelische Kirche im Rheinland to reach a new understanding of Judaism and of the Christian guilt for the Holocaust. The American Holocaust research has vastly affected German theologians, one of whom, Eberhard Bethge, has composed thesis I for the committee "Christians and Jews" of the Landessynode, thereby preparing the resolution aforementioned.

Heinz Kremers was born in 1926 in Mönchengladbach, West Germany. He was a soldier and a prisoner of war in 1944–45, was educated at Wuppertal Theological Seminary and the Universities of Tuebingen and Goettingen in 1946–51, and received his Dr. theol. in Old Testament in 1951. From 1951 to 1958 he was clergyman in the Protestant church of the Rhineland and, since 1972, has been professor of Bible and religious education at the University of Duisburg. Since 1974, he has been first speaker of the Institute for Research of the History and Religion of the Jewish People at the University of Duisburg (cooperating with the National Institute on the Holocaust in Philadelphia, Pennsylvania).

English translation of this article by Ruth Olemesdahl.

AFTER 20 years of learning and redirection of thought, the Evangelische Kirche im Rheinland was the first German Protestant church to face the challenge of the Holocaust. On 11 January 1980, the synod (the Church-Parliament), which meets once a year, passed a resolution[1] (out of 251 members only 3 voted against it and 6 abstained).

STEPS LEADING TO THE RESOLUTION OF 11 JANUARY 1980

The resolution of the Synod of the Evangelische Kirche im Rheinland in January, 1980, is the result of 20 years of learning and redirection of thought in this church. There are two events which mark the beginning of this process in 1961. From 1945 until this year, the Church in the Rhineland was so preoccupied with the reconstruction of its own institutions that it had no time for the questions concerning the Holocaust and its relationship with the Jewish people. This is proved by the reports of the synods of this church from 1945 to 1960.

Recognition of a need

A first impulse for the Church in the Rhineland to face the Holocaust and to renew the relationship with the Jewish people came from the Netherlands. Representatives of the three Reformed churches of the Netherlands asked the Protestant churches of Germany in 1961 to take part in an act of reconciliation and renewal of relations between the churches and the Jewish people. They wanted the German churches to take part in the building up of a Christian settlement in Israel, Nes Ammim, which should be *nes*, that is, a sign for the confession of the

churches of their guilt concerning the Holocaust, a sign for the end of *Judenmission* (mission among the Jews), and the sign of a new beginning in the relations of the churches with the Jewish people. It was to be an offer of cooperation in brotherly solidarity and in an open ecumenical dialogue.[2]

Formulation of a meeting

The *sozial-ethische Ausschuß* (committee for ethics in social life) of the Protestant church in the Rhineland, whose chairman was Professor Karrenberg, arranged a meeting between the representatives of the Dutch and German churches and institutions, for example Lutherischer Zentralverein für Mission unter Israel, represented by Professor D. K. H. Rengstorf. The Dutch representatives reported that they had rediscovered the Jews as their "elder brethren in faith" by the common sufferings and resistance during the time of the occupation of their country by German troops. They were therefore unable to continue their missionary activities toward their "brethren in faith." Now all European churches had to acknowledge their guilt toward the Jewish people during their long history, which reached its climax in the Holocaust, and they had to repent and return into the community of the people of God, consisting of Jews and Christians. The settlement of Nes Ammim was intended as a sign; therefore they asked the German churches to cooperate.

But there were only three German representatives who were in-

1. Resolution of the Synod, 11 Jan. 1980.

2. S. Simon Schoon and Heinz Kremers, *Nes Ammim. Ein christliches Experiment in Israel* (Neukirchen-Vluyn: Neukirchener Verlag, 1978), especially the documents on pp. 171–97.

duced by the Dutch to cooperate with them. They were three young representatives of the Rheinische Kirche, the oldest being 34 years of age: Landeskirchenrat Nikolaus Becker, today Oberkirchenrat und juristischer Dirigent der Evangelischen Kirche im Rheinland; Horst Dahlhaus, today Direktor der Bundeszentrale für politische Bildung bei der Bundesregierung in Bonn; and myself. We founded the German Nes-Ammim-Verein and started to take part in the building up of the settlement in Israel and to ask for a renewed relationship with the Jewish people by lectures and publications in the Church of the Rhineland.

A second impulse to face the Holocaust and bring about a readjustment with the Jewish people started from the Evangelischer Kirchentag in Berlin in 1961, where a committee "Jews and Christians" came into existence and addressed the public for the first time.[3] The continued work of this group during the *Kirchentage* from Berlin, 1961, to Nuremberg, 1979, and the publications edited by it[4] have finally affected the process of learning in the Evangelische Kirche im Rheinland.

Development of a Christian-Jewish dialogue

Numerous excellent Jewish teachers have pushed on this process. Even earlier than 1961, they have informed us about Judaism and together with us have looked for a new way in the relationship between Jews and Christians. Above all, we

think of Robert Rafael Geis. He was a gift of heaven to our church. Geis, the former rabbi of Baden-Württemberg, lived in the Rhineland as a very active pensioner. He was the first to enter into a dialogue with Professor H. J. Iwand, H. J. Kraus, and myself, and this dialogue reached broadening circles of our church.

Eva Fleischner describes the outcome of this cooperation with R. R. Geis in her book *Judaism and German Christian Theology Since 1945:*[5] "The last position to be examined is that taken by certain authors, such as myself and Hans Joachim Kraus, who believe that only a total renouncing of Judenmission can open the way to true dialogue. I see such a renouncing of mission as resulting not simply from historical considerations and the awareness of the Church's guilt, but from the full recognition that Israel is still Israel.[6] Judenmission is a denial of God's covenant with Israel. "The Church must renounce all Judenmission. . . . By Judenmission we understand all attempts by the Church to draw Jews away from their people, which is still today more than a people, that is to say, the Covenant-community Israel, in order to make them members of the Church of the gentiles."[7]

Dialogue must indeed replace mission, and great care be taken

3. S. report in "Der ungekündigte Bund," ed. D. Goldschmidt and H. J. Kraus, (Kreuzverlag Stuttgart: 1962).

4. For example, "Das gespaltene Gottesvolk," ed. H. Gollwitzer and E. Sterling (Kreuzverlag Stuttgart: 1966).

5. Eva Fleischner, *Judaism and German Christian Theology Since 1945, Christianity and Israel Considered in Terms of Mission*, Atla monograph ser. no. 8 (Metuchen, NJ: The Scarecrow Press, 1975), pp. 115ff. My own position of 1965 has been further developed in "Judenmission heute? Von der Judenmission zur brüderlichen Solidarität und zum ökumenischen Dialog" (Neukirchen-Vluyn: Neukirchener Verlag, 1979).

6. Das Verhältnis der Kirche zu Israel, Düsseldorf, Presseverband der Evangelischen Kirche im Rheinland, (1965), p. 25.

7. Ibid., p. 25.

that it not become a new and covert form of Judenmission. "The Jews must be subject as well as object in this dialogue, that is, genuine partners."[8] On the basis of the Old Testament, which Christians and Jews have in common, both should interpret for each other their respective traditions: the Christians, the New Testament; the Jews, the Talmud. Through such open, honest discussion among equals there will come about mutual understanding and greater knowledge, and each will be challenged to a new depth of understanding and living his own faith.[9] What this may mean for the Christian is hinted at by Martin Stöhr, who asks whether Israel's way of constantly questioning, of doing without dogmatic systematization, may not be more worthy of God's revelation than the Christian systematization of dogma.

It is here that this position goes beyond any examined so far. Genuine dialogue involves the willingness to confront ultimate questions about one's own faith. This is emphasized also by Kraus, who sees such a questioning "as the one essential condition for encounter and dialogue"[10] without which the other will not be understood in his existential reality. "Judaism today confronts Christianity with question upon question. . . . Nothing is more important than a greater willingness to listen on the part of Christians, nothing more urgent than letting themselves be questioned by the other."[11]

There is not a doubt that in the first years, R. R. Geis was the most important teacher of the Rheinische

8. Ibid., p. 27.
9. Ibid., pp. 26 ff.
10. H. J. Kraus, *Begegnung mit dem Jedentum*, p. 108.
11. Ibid., p. 124.

Kirche, in the last years being professor at the University of Duisburg until 1972, when he left because of serious illness. Rabbi Yehuda Ashkenasy, who has survived Auschwitz and Buchenwald, became his successor as a teacher, professor, and team-member of the center of research for "Geschichte und Religion des Judentums" at the University of Duisburg, after having worked together with R. R. Geis in the beginning. With myself, he founded the "Christlich-jüdisches Lehrhaus" in Duisburg in 1969, where he regularly teaches to this day.

Other important teachers of our church (acknowledgedly, the number may not be complete) were Professors David Flusser and Shmuel Safrai of Jerusalem University, who have regularly come to the Rhineland since 1964 to teach in seminaries and congresses. Other professors of Jerusalem University, who have not come quite as often, were Shlomo Pines, Shmarjahu Talmon, and Ernst Simon, and in 1980, Zwi Verblowsky. We must not forget the Duisburg visiting professors from Israel, Aharon Oppenheimer and Jehoshua Amir, as well as Dr. Pinchas Lapide, who has often visited us. One must also mention Rabbi Dr. Moshe König from Amsterdam, deceased a short time ago, and Professor Henry van Praag of Utrecht University, who holds regular weekend seminary lectures for teachers of various schools. Then there is the great pioneer of Jewish-Christian dialogue Schalom Ben Chorin, who worked through numerous lectures and books for the continuing of the learning process in our church.

Finally there are a few speakers of European Jewry who have become our teachers: Dr. Ernst-Ludwig Ehrlich, *Landesrabbiner* N. Peter Levinson and his wife Pnina Navé-

Levinson, as well as Edna Brocke, who has come into the Rhineland together with her husband, Dr. Michael Brocke, who has been assistant professor for Judaism at the University of Duisburg since 1978.

ADOPTION OF A RESOLUTION

A significant step for the Rheinische Kirche has been the Landessynode in 1965. The synod passed the following important resolution:

The Federal Republic of Germany is faced by difficult decisions concerning the relationship with Israel and with the Arabic world. In this situation the Synod reminds us that for moral and human reasons, it is our duty to use every possible way for reconciliation and for giving assistance to Israel for a life in peace. Considering the responsibility connected with this resolution and its possible disadvantage, we most urgently ask the Bundesregierung to overcome opposing difficulties and to offer normal diplomatic relations. The Synod authorizes the "Praeses" [that is, the head of the Synod] to inform the Bundesregierung of the resolution.

I stood up for the acceptance of the resolution, but I strove for more. Therefore I put forward the following motion: "The Landessynode der Evangelischen Kirche in Rheinland asks the Evangelische Kirche in Deutschland to set up a committee like that concerning the questions arising with the Lord's Supper. This committee is to clear the theological relationship between the Church and the Jews and to prepare an adequate pastoral word."

There were enough of my friends from the Nes-Ammim-Verein among the members of the synod to sign my motion, so that it had to be dealt with by the theological committee. This committee weakened my motion to such an extent that I had to fight hard for the restitution of the original motion. The then-Praeses Professor Dr. Beckmann asked "not to burden the Evangelische Kirche in Deutschland with binding resolutions, as it cannot take decisions concerning the doctrine of the Church" (protocol of the synod). My motion was accepted by the synod without a member voting against and with two members abstaining.

Not until 1967 did the Rat der Evangelischen Kirche in Deutschland set up the committee asked for by the Rheinische Kirche. My colleague Wolfgang Wirth and I were asked to serve on the committee as representatives of the Rheinische Kirche. After years of hard struggle, the committee presented in 1974 the study "Christen und Juden" and proposed that it be accepted by the Rat der Evangelischen Kirche in Deutschland. After some of the members of the Rat and several professors of the school of Bultmann had called for corrections, the study was accepted and published by the Rat in 1975, slightly altered and weakened.

The study was appreciated by Jewish critics as an important step toward reconciliation between Jews and Christians. The passages criticized by them were those that have been changed lately. Many a member of the committee was glad that the Rat authorized us to write an *Arbeitsbuch Christen und Juden zur Studie des Rates der Evangelischen Kirche in Deutschland* that needed no correction by the Rat. We made up our mind to cut out the weak passages of the study in our commentary, in which we—thank God—succeeded.[12]

12. R. Rendtorff, ed., *Arbeitsbuch Christen und Juden, Zur Studie des Rates der Evangelischen Kirche in Deutschland* Gütersloher Verlagshaus Gerd Mohn Gütersloh, 1979.

The publication of the study gave cause to my assistant H. J. Barkenings in the research group "History and Religion of Judaism" to push forward the development during the Rheinische Landessynode in 1976. We were not satisfied by a mere study; we aimed at a "binding theological declaration," respectively, a confession. An initiative of Barkenings[13] was accepted nearly unanimously in the following form:

The Landessynode authorizes the Kirchenleitung to set up a committee on the theme "Christians and Jews" and ask Jews for their participation in the committee. The purpose of the committee will be to formulate a comment on the study of the Rat der Evangelischen Kirche in Deutschland "Jews and Christians" as to the practical consequences. This comment will be discussed at the next Landessynode.

With this resolution the Rheinische Kirche entered a final stage of learning. It was the first time in the history of the Church that Jews were asked to take part in a committee of the synod. In one of the first meetings, the Jewish members of the committee declared that their cooperation depended on the renunciation of the Judenmission by all other members of the committee. They declared that they were willing to work with us only if looked upon as true partners, not as objects of our missionary aspirations. Now it was the turn of the Christian members of the committee to begin a continued and often difficult process of learning.

During several meetings we formulated a statement on Judenmission, which was incorporated into the proposal under point 4(6) and was "thankfully accepted" by the Landessynode.

There were a few members of the committee who had begun studying the American Holocaust research, Eberhard Bethge and Edna Brocke. They and I met with the problem during our stay in the United States by the cooperation of my research center with Franklin H. Littell and the National Institute on the Holocaust in Philadelphia.[14] *All of us were increasingly conscious of the fact that the Holocaust was a turning point for the renewal of the relationship of our churches with the Jews.* Not until the Church faces the Holocaust will it be able legitimately to renew its relationship with the Jewish people.

The outstanding principle for this renewal was to be the following passage of the resolution:

We acknowledge Christian responsibility and guilt for the Holocaust [that is, the outlawing, persecution, and slaughter of Jews in the Third Reich. The confession] We confess that we are struck by the responsibility and guilt of the Christians in Germany for the Holocaust

has become the first sentence of the theological declaration of our church. Thesis I, devised by Eberhard

13. Hans-Joachim Barkenings was one of the first German theologians who asked for a radical renewal of the relationship between the Church and the Jewish people, at the same time renouncing Judenmission. *See* his paper "Die Stimme der anderen," in *Christen und Juden. Ihr Gegenüber vom Apostelkonzil bis zur Gegenwart*, ed. W. D. Marsch and K. Thieme. (Göttingen: Verlag Vandenhoeck & Ruprecht, 1961).

14. Eberhard Bethge gave an account of the proceedings in our committee in "Lessons of the Holocaust for Christians" presented to the International Theological Symposium on the Holocaust October 1978 (Philadelphia: Josephine Knopp, National Institute on the Holocaust, 1979), pp. 18–33. I gave a report on the "Inclusion of Lessons of the Holocaust" in the *Teaching and Textbooks of Schools in the Federal Republic of Germany* to the International Conference: *The Lessons of the Holocaust*, October 1978 (Philadelphia: Josephine Knopp, National Institute on the Holocaust, 1979), pp. 155–65.

Bethge and "thankfully accepted by the Synod," gives evidence that the Rheinische Kirche has unconditionally confronted the Holocaust as the first German Church and that it has been influenced therein by the Holocaust research in the United States.

Theses on the Renewal of the Relationship Between Christians And Jews: The Holocaust as a Turning Point

Leo Baeck, once the chief rabbi of Berlin, wrote:

Let there be peace among all men of evil will, an end to all revenge and to all talk of punishment and chastisement. . . . The deeds of abomination beggar description, they are beyond all limits of human comprehension, and there are so many martyrs. . . . Therefore o Lord, do not weigh their sufferings on the scales of justice, lest Thou might ascribe it to their executioners and call them to account, but let it be otherwise. Thou may rather allow for the murderers, informers, traitors, and all bad men and accredit them the courage and the strength of mind of the others, their modesty, their high-minded dignity, their silent exertions, their unconquered hope, their brave smile, that made their tears dry up, and all their sacrifices, their ardent love . . . all those tormented hearts, but all the same strong and always trustful, in the face of death and in the middle of death, yes, even the hours of their deepest weakness. . . . O Lord, let everything count before Thee as ransom for the forgiveness of guilt, for resurrection of justice—may all the good count and not the evil. And may we be no longer the victims in the memory of our enemies, nor their nightmare or their ghosts, but their help, that they may refrain from their fury. . . . Only this is asked of them—and that we, when everything is over, may be allowed to live as men among men, and that there may be peace on our poor earth for all

men of goodwill and for the others as well.[15]

We ask, Have his prayers for peace been realized?

Theses

Among the crises in which we live today the most menacing is that which has been produced by the Holocaust and which has produced the Holocaust. The Greek word "holocaust" means "totally burnt"; in the Bible it means "the sacrifice," which is totally burnt.[16] The Jewish writer Elie Wiesel uses the word to describe the slaughter of the Jews during the Third Reich. Six million people have been murdered by the heirs of Christendom for no other reason than the fact that they were Jews. The inscription on the memorial over the hill of ashes in Maidanek reads: "Men have done this unto their fellowmen." The Holocaust signifies the crisis of our civilization, our culture, our policy, and our religion:

Civilization: The universities developed and taught the knowledge that supplied the technical means for genocide.

Culture: Literature, art, and philosophy were to be cut from Jewish roots; all Jewish elements were to be extinguished.

Policy: The concept of a man exerting power over his fellowmen, controlling their lives, unmasked its worst aspects as aspects of ourselves, be it by active participation or by passive permission.

Religion: Every creed concerning the God of Abraham, Isaac, and Jacob, who elected this people, is

15. Leo Baeck in "Angst—Sicherung—Geborgenheit," Th. Bovet (Bielefeld: 1975).
16. Lev. 1:3.

made into a mockery because for the Christians the projected and executed extermination of God's Chosen People is accomplished blasphemy; and now their mouths have been silenced by their participation in this blasphemy. But if they yet open their mouths, their words of reconciliation and redemption are without any consequence.

Church leaders seek answers

Bonhoeffer wrote in 1940:

The Church confesses to having witnessed the arbitrary application of brute force, the physical and spiritual sufferings of innumerable innocents, oppression, hate, and murder without having raised its voice in their defence and without having found ways to come to their aid. It has become guilty, for it has wronged and taken the lives of the weakest and most defenceless brothers of Jesus Christ.[17]

John XXIII prayed: "We realize that the mark of Cain stands on our foreheads. . . . Forgive us for crucifying Thee a second time in their flesh. For we knew not what we did."[18]

Who is concerned in this monstrous event? The Jews are concerned, who after decades are trying to express in words what they have learned from the survivors of the Holocaust in the areas of civilization, culture, policy, and religion. And so are the Christians in Germany, who must live under the curse that Hitler's policy of *Judenreinheit* was nearly realized and, consequently, it might be possible to let bygones be bygones. But the abyss between the Jews' awareness of the crisis caused by the Holocaust and the suppression of events in our country must never be allowed to become greater. "Not until the Jews have forgotten may you forget!"

The theological significance of the crisis caused by the Holocaust is that the old problem of theodicy is put before us with a new acuteness. Jewish and non-Jewish writers have expressed it despairingly. The Church has remained silent up until now.

Elie Wiesel, having survived Auschwitz, writes 15 years later:

Never shall I forget that night, the first night in camp, which has turned my life into one long night, seven times cursed and seven times sealed. Never shall I forget this smoke. Never shall I forget the little faces of the children, whose bodies I saw turned into wreaths of smoke beneath a silent blue sky. Never shall I forget that nocturnal silence which deprived me for all eternity, of the desire to live. Never shall I forget those moments which murdered my God and my soul and turned my dreams to dust. Never shall I forget these things, even if I am condemned to live as long as God Himself. Never.[19]

The theodicy, that is, the question of the justification of God as being almighty, just, and loving, though always existing, is asked anew in three aspects. There is the common problem, How is it possible that God allows so much suffering to take place? He who is asking in this way thinks of God as an almighty being beyond the world of man, who ought to direct human destiny in a satisfying manner. It is out of the question that this ultramundane god himself should suffer from human suffering. But the Bible states, from Moses to Jesus, that God Himself is suffering with his creatures.

17. *Ethik* (München: 1953), p. 50.
18. P. Lapide, *Rom und die Juden* (Freiburg: 1967), p. 5.

19. Elie Wiesel, *The Night* (New York: 1960), pp. 44 ff.

Then there is the special problem, when man is in the situation of temptation, "My God, why hast Thou left me?"[20] In this case, God is a partner in dialogue who has addressed man and has to listen to man's questions, Where are you now? Why do you remain silent? God is understood as He who has promised His presence and who is now accused by the biblical worshipers, including Jesus: Why hast Thou left me? Then there is a last aggravation: why didn't God guard His chosen Israel like the apple of His eye?[21] What is it about the suffering of the chosen servant?[22] Has chosen been turned into rejection, the Messianic charge into the shame of being abandoned by God?

Scholars seek answers

There have been Jews and a few Christians as well who have started to ask questions about their painful experiences caused by the Holocaust. They have searched in three directions and have tried the following answers.

Richard Rubenstein refuses to understand the Holocaust as a punishment from God for the transgressions of Israel or as temptation like that of Job. "To see any purpose in the death camps, the traditional believer is forced to regard the most demonic, antihuman explosion in all history as a meaningful expression of God's purposes."[23] He therefore gives up the traditional image of God and acknowledges the nothing (nihil).

Roy Eckardt tries to adhere to the traditional image of God but expresses that God has become guilty like man in the Holocaust for the

simple reason that it is He who created the world and it is He who permits monstrous suffering to take place."[24] Now God is going to repent by giving back their land to Israel.

Emil Fackenheim writes:

I believe that whereas no redeeming voice is heard at Auschwitz a commanding voice is heard, and that it is being heard with increasing clarity: Jews are not permitted to hand Hitler posthumous victories. Jews are commanded to survive as Jews, lest their people perish. They are commanded to remember the victims of Auschwitz, lest their memory perish. They are forbidden to despair of God, lest Judaism perish. They are forbidden to despair of the world as the domain of God, lest the world be handed over to the forces of Auschwitz.[25]

Irving Greenberg states:

No attempt at learning lessons of the Holocaust can capture its meaning. Time and new events will refract new dimensions of the event and its normative significance for Jews and Christians. As understanding develops and repentance deepens, we will be open to new messages from it. Perhaps we can learn from the past models of Jewish and Christian tradition how to live with and draw insight from orientating events of such magnitude. Continual study, renewed encounter and reenactment of the event are necessary so that in "every generation a Jew should see himself as if he went out of Egypt," so that every Christian reexperiences the death and the resurrection of Jesus Christ. The same unremitting confrontation with the hell of Auschwitz is inescapable to religious and moral rehabilitation in our times. It takes courage and great risk to confront this ultimate agony.[26]

20. Ps. 22:2; Mark 15:34.
21. Deut. 32:10.
22. Isa. 41:8 ff, 50:4–9; 53:12.
23. Richard Rubenstein, *After Auschwitz* (New York: 1966), p. 153.

24. Roy Eckardt, "Is the Holocaust Unique?" *Worldview* XVII(9):34 (1974).
25. Emil Fackenheim, *Quest for Past and Future* (London: 1968), p. 20.
26. Irving Greenberg, Lecture: Lessons to be Learned from the Holocaust," Hamburg, 10 June 1975.

Abraham Heschel writes:

The State of Israel is not an atonement. It would be blasphemy to regard it as a compensation. However the existence of Israel reborn makes life less unendurable. It is a slight hinderer of hindrances to believing in God. . . . Is the State of Israel God's humble answer to Auschwitz? A sign of God's repentance for men's crime of Auschwitz?

No act is as holy as the act of saving human life. The Holy Land, having offered a haven to more than two million Jews—many of whom would not have been alive had they remained in Poland, Russia, Germany, and other countries—has attained a new sanctity. . . . And yet, there is no answer to Auschwitz. . . . To try to answer is to commit a supreme blasphemy. Israel enables us to bear the agony of Auschwitz without radical despair, to sense a ray of God's radiance in the jungles of history.[27]

Elie Wiesel, in spite of all his despair, nears the concept of the New Testament when answering in the face of the long-drawn-out execution of a Jewish child on a gallows in Auschwitz to the question, Where is God now? "Here He is—He is hanging here on this gallows."[28] Contrary to Rubenstein, he states: "To be a Jew means to have all the reasons in the world not to have faith in language, in singing, in prayers, and in God, but to go on telling the tale, to go on carrying on the dialogue, and to have my own silent prayers and quarrels with God."[29]

Franklin Sherman tries an explanation based on the cross of Jesus, "God participates in the sufferings of man, and man is called to participate in the sufferings of God."[30]

Irving Greenberg said that concerned Jews will continue to ask why the problem of theodicy is not a more severe challenge for Christians, and they invite us to seek an answer together with them however long the way of seeking may be. The question may be suppressed because it is thought of as blasphemous in the face of the monstrosity of the event. On the other side, it may be suppressed because people tend to forget in the cause of self-preservation. But the question will not be set aside.

Concerned Jews question

To seek an answer is very painful for Jews because of their own concern. They are right in refusing to comprehend the unthinkable and to express the ineffable by means of hasty consolation and thus deprive the martyrs of their death. Elie Wiesel gives expression to this thought in the prayer of a *tzaddik* (righteous):

I have never questioned Your justice, Your mercy, though their ways have often confounded me. I have submitted to everything, accepted everything, not with resignation but with love and gratitude. I have accepted punishments, absurdities, slaughters, I have even let pass under silence the death of one million children. In the shadow of the holocaust's unbearable mystery, I have strangled the outcry, the anger, the desire to be finished with You and myself once and for all. I have chosen prayer, devotion. I have tried to transform into a song the dagger You have so often plunged into my submissive heart. I did not strike my head against the wall, I did not tear my eyes out so as to see no more, nor my tongue so as to speak no more. I told myself: it is easy to die for You, easier than to live with You, for You, in this universe both blessed and cursed, in which malediction, like everything else, bears Your seal. I invented reasons, causes for rejoicing, to create a link to You and also to myself. But . . .

27. Abraham Heschel, *Israel, an Echo of Eternity* (New York: 1969), p. 113–15.

28. Wiesel, *The Night*, pp. 75 ff.

29. F. H. Littell and H. G. Glocke, eds., *The German Church Struggle and the Holocaust* (Detroit: 1974), p. 277.

30. Franklin Sherman, *Auschwitz in Speaking of God Today: Jews and Lutherans in Conversation* (Philadelphia: 1974), p. 157.

That's all over, . . . do You hear? It's all over, I tell You. I cannot go on. If this time again You desert Your people, if this time again You permit the slaughterer to murder Your children and besmirch their allegiance to the covenant, if this time You let Your promise become mockery, then know, O Master of all that breathes, know that You no longer deserve Your people's love and their passion to sanctify You, to justify You toward and against all, toward and against Yourself; if this time again the survivors are massacred and their deaths held up to ridicule, know that I shall resign my chair and my functions as guide, I shall fall to the ground, my forehead covered with ashes, and I shall weep as I have never wept in my life, and before dying I shall shout as no victim has ever shouted, and know that each of my tears and each of my shouts will tarnish Your glory, each of my gestures will negate You and will negate me as You have negated me, as You will have negated Your servants in their dazzling and ephemeral truth.[31]

It is difficult for Christians to answer because they are in danger of drawing back from their own participation in the events. This danger is imminent with a premature attempt to explain and give meaning to the events by a hasty and schematic theologia crucis, or by a cheap idea of resurrection without a long preceding repentance, or by a short-cut "nevertheless"[32] without a comparable situation of suffering.

Therefore the theological answer to the problem of theodicy must take care not to deprive God of the truth of His being God nor the slaughtered of the reality of their surrender. In the face of Holocaust, all general answers are without reason and conviction when confronted with genuine reality.

31. Elie Wiesel, *A Beggar in Jerusalem* (New York: 1978), pp. 140 ff.
32. Ps. 73.

Considering this situation, it may be justified to admit that we now have no answer whatever—indeed, that it is impossible to give an answer.

The silence in view of the question and the admittance that we cannot explain the inexplicable is different from the silence and dumbness that leaves victory to the Final Solution. The temporary answer which is theologically necessary would be to repent in deeds without words. Fackenheim states, "This fact doesn't call for an explanation but for a response."

RESPONSE?

With the Holocaust mocking all possible theological explanations, the power of death reaches out for us from Auschwitz, and what it proclaims is nothing but death. It tries to subdue us by its annihilation of speech, thereby forcing us continually to serve the victory of death. Therefore even the expression of our perplexity between Christians and, more so, between Christians and Jews will be a first step away from the thread of Auschwitz, especially if this expression takes the form of prayer.

The possible answers demanded of us will be manifold. In giving these answers we will enjoy the help of Jews. Not to respond is to give a negative answer, in other words to suppress, to forget, which is only possible by self-delusion, and to point to the guilt of others.

Positive answering starts with the confession of Franklin Littell: "In a mysterious and at the same time terrible way the Jews died for the truth, denied them by the Christians: namely that the Lord and Judge of history has been revealed to us from among the Jews. It is the tragic truth that most martyrs for Christ in this century have been Jews."[33]

The answer continues by listening to Irving Greenberg's proposal who, to the question of how it may be possible to speak of God after these events, has given the following answer: "There is only one testimony one can offer—it is the silent and most expressive testimony of re-creating the image of God by having a child or taking a human life which is degraded or besmirched and restoring the fullness of its image of God (e.g. its dignity, uniqueness and value)."[34]

Now the answers are divided into different tasks that seem, for the most part, to belong to a moral dimension but are based on theological principles:

cooperation in responsible control of our technocratic means, which in the meantime have been infinitely extended (*civilization*);

help in conquering the "terrible silence, passing through the thousand darknesses of deathbearing speech"[35] (*culture*);

critical resistance to any repetition of massing of power and to the deprivation of helpless social groups (*policy*); and

initiation of new conceptions of certain theological ideas which have hitherto burdened the Christian-Jewish relations (*religion*).

Then we may hope to spell out the "nevertheless" of Psalm 73 together with the Jews.

---

33. Quoted in P. Lapide, *Kirchenkampf und Völkermord* (Deutsches Pfarrerblatt: 1975), p. 793.

34. Greenberg, p. 10.

35. Paul Celan.

The Reparations Agreements:
A New Perspective

By LESLIE SEBBA

ABSTRACT: In the wake of the Holocaust, a series of agreements were reached between the Federal Republic of Germany and representatives of the Jewish people regarding compensation for the suffering inflicted during that terrible era.
The agreements had many unusual features to which insufficient attention has been devoted in the existing literature,
most of which is confined to specific issues of a legal, psychiatric, or economic nature. A more integrative approach
is presented here, through the perspective of a newly
developing field, namely, victimology. This approach provides a perspective for examining both the practical and the
ideological issues involved. It also raises the question as to
how far comparison may be made between genocide and more
"conventional" victimization processes.

*Leslie Sebba graduated from the Universities of Oxford and London before taking
his doctoral degree in Jurisprudence at the Hebrew University of Jerusalem, where
he now lectures at the Institute of Criminology in the Faculty of Law. In 1975–76
he was a Visiting Fellow at the Center for Studies in Criminology and Criminal Law
at the University of Pennsylvania.*

I
T IS perhaps a quirk of human
nature that enables two or more
parties who were recently locked in
internecine strife to seat themselves
around a conference table and negotiate the terms of a peace agreement.
Yet even allowing for this streak of
malleability in human conduct, it is
nevertheless remarkable, in view of
the untold misery and scientific destruction wrought upon the Jewish
people during the years 1933–45 by
one of the most pernicious regimes
in human history, that representatives of the persecuted race were
able to negotiate a financial settlement with their erstwhile oppressors
within the relatively short period of
seven years. How could the Jewish
people, who had seen two-thirds of
their number butchered into extinc-
tion, who were in the process of
developing a proud, independent
nationalism, and for whom everything German was total anathema,
resort to conventional modes of ne-
gotiation in order to translate such
unspeakable suffering into mere pe-
cuniary losses? This alone would
render the Reparations and Compensation Agreements concluded between the German government and
the representatives of the Jewish
people a topic of considerable interest, even apart from the many
other unusual features of these agreements, which will be described. Yet
the very enormity of the horrors
inflicted have inevitably caused scholars to focus their interests upon the
events of the Holocaust itself, rather
than on its aftermath. Thus the reparations agreements have attracted
less attention on the part of scholars,

or indeed of the public at large, than
their intrinsic interest would dictate.
This is not to say that there is a
total absence of serious writing on
this topic. A considerable literature
does exist, but by and large it has
been too limited in its orientation,
confined to the horizons of the discipline with which the particular
author is concerned. Thus jurists
have been immensely active in endeavoring to interpret and explain
the agreements and their implications for various categories of victims. In addition to a proliferation
of cases before the German and
Israeli courts, a special journal of
case summaries and commentaries
(*Rechtsprechung Zum Widergut-
machungsrecht*) is published in Germany. Such literature in other languages, however, is rare.[1] Further,
the international law aspects have
also been noted.[2] Physicians and
psychiatrists have been involved in
an ancillary way in this area as the
result of the need to elicit evidence
of physical and mental damage resulting from Holocaust-related trau-
mas. Many contributions to the professional literature of these disciplines have resulted but these are
mostly concerned with the pathol-
ogies of the victims as such, rather
than with the reparations issue.[3]

1. For a notable exception, *see* Kurt Schwerin, "German Compensation for Victims of
Nazi Persecution," *Northwestern University
Law Review* 67:479–527 (1972).
2. *See* Frederick Honig, "The Reparations
Agreement between Israel and the Federal
Republic of Germany," *Am. J. International
Law* 48:564–78 (1954).
3. An exception is Dr. Fink's paper delivered
at the First International Symposium on
Victimology in Jerusalem which dealt with
some psychopathological aspects of victim
compensation; *see* Klaus Fink, "Ambivalence
of Former Victims toward their Persecutors
at the Petition for Indemnification," in *Victimology: A New Focus, Vol. III: Crimes,
Victims and Justice*, I. Drapkin and E. Viano,

NOTE: The present article has developed
from a paper presented at the Third International Symposium on Victimology held in
Muenster in the Federal Republic of Germany in September, 1979.

Economists have been concerned with the effects of the reparations payments on the German and Israeli economies alike.[4] Moreover, one economist has effectively bridged the gap with political history since the study by Balabkins analyzed the dynamics of the negotiations leading to the agreements, as well as the economic repercussions thereof.[5] A number of autobiographies and memoirs were published by former statesmen who were involved in the negotiations, such as Konrad Adenauer, Felix Sinnar and Nahum Goldmann. There were also various publications by Nehemiah and Jacob Robinson.

It seems that the time is now ripe for a more comprehensive and integrated study of the agreements and their operation, taking advantage of the current interest in the Holocaust and of the greater perspective now available with the passage of time. Moreover, an innovative approach may be offered by analyzing the topic from the perspective of a newly developing discipline, if it may be so termed, namely, victimology.

EMERGENCE OF VICTIMOLOGY

Victimology, or the study of the victim, is an area of scientific research which has evolved rapidly during the past decade. The term was reputedly coined by the Rumanian-Jewish lawyer Beniamin Men-delsohn, who wished thereby to draw attention to the symbiotic relationship between offender and victim.[6] This theme was also developed by Hans von Hentig in his monograph The Criminal and His Victim.[7]

These early developments were followed by some pioneering empirical research, notably, by Marvin Wolfgang and Menachem Amir, on the phenomenology of certain types of crime, such as homicide and rape, with special reference to the respective roles of offender and victim.[8] This research is famous—infamous in the eyes of some—for its finding that some crime seems to be victim-precipitated but it also drew attention to the greater vulnerability of certain sections of the population to victimization. Moreover, a great deal of the most recent victimological literature has been concerned with victim welfare.

This interest in the plight of the victim has been prompted by an awareness that ever since the state's role came to predominate in the criminal justice system, the victim has become the " 'poor relation' of the criminal law,"[9] and his well-being—economic, social, and psychological—has been almost totally neglected. It may also be that recent interest in the victim has been spurred on by the prevailing disillusion

eds. (Lexington: Lexington Books, 1975), pp. 107–12.

4. See Michael Landsberger, Restitution Receipts, Household Savings and Consumption Behavior in Israel (Jerusalem: Bank of Israel, 1970).

5. Nicholas Balabkins, West German Reparations to Israel (New Brunswick, NJ: Rutgers University Press, 1971). A more specifically historical approach by Nana Sagi is currently being published in Jerusalem.

6. The term "victimology" appeared in the title of a paper circulated by Mendelsohn in 1946 but the theme had already been developed in an article he published in 1937; see "Pioneers in Victimology: Beniamin Mendelsohn," Victimology 1:211–15 (1976).

7. New Haven, 1948.

8. Marvin Wolfgang, Patterns in Criminal Homicide (New York: John Wiley & Sons, 1966); Menachem Amir, Patterns in Forcible Rape (Chicago: University of Chicago Press, 1971).

9. Stephen Schafer, The Victim and his Criminal (New York: Random House, 1968), p. 21.

regarding the possibility of rehabilitating the offender.

Against this background, initial steps were taken toward the academic organization of the field of victimology. In 1973, the First International Symposium on Victimology was held in Jerusalem; the second took place in Boston in 1976, and the third in Muenster in 1974.[10] The fourth is due to be held in Japan, where the first Institute for Victimology was established in 1969. These meetings have given considerable impetus to the study of the victim's needs and to the search for an optimal framework for ensuring his compensation.

Discussions have mainly been devoted in this context to assessing the practicality of the various solutions proposed and, occasionally—too rarely—to the conceptual issues involved. One of the main issues that arises under both headings is whether compensation to victims should be provided by the state or whether it should be forthcoming directly from the offender himself. In particular, what are the respective practical advantages and disadvantages for criminal and victim, after the guilt of the former has been determined, in reestablishing some form of contact between them, as implied in the concept of restitution? More mundane but no less important issues include the question of whether financial compensation for victims should be limited to direct material losses or whether they should also include indirect losses and compensation for the infliction of psychological harm and whether compensation is the personal right of the immediate victim or whether it should also be payable to indirect victims, heirs, and so forth.[11]

Can this developing victimological literature be of any relevance when considering the atrocities and suffering inflicted by the Holocaust? The crime of genocide, needless to say, is no ordinary crime, so that specific comparisons between the victimization process, or victim redress in this context, and the treatment of victims of conventional crimes must thus be proffered cautiously. Nonetheless, the emergence of victimology provides a point of departure for new perspectives on the topic of German reparations and for the raising of certain issues which have been neglected in the more specialized literature available hitherto on this topic.

A victimological approach draws attention to the moral, philosophical, and juridical aspects of the nature of the reparations payments and, in particular, to such questions as the interaction between the type of victimization and the form and extent of compensation and the significance of the payments for payer and payee, respectively. These issues are further complicated here by the diffuse structure of the reparations agreements, involving as they do the German government, the Israeli government, other Jewish representative organizations, individual benefici-

---

10. These meetings have at least symbolic significance in the context of this article. The relevance of Israel and Germany, locations of the First and Third Symposia, to the themes under discussion here does not need to be spelled out. As to the Boston Symposium, its organizer, the late Professor Stephen Schafer, survived persecution as a Jew in Hungary during World War II; see "Pioneers in Victimology: Stephen Schafer," *Victimology* 1:223–25 (1976).

11. Some of these issues were surveyed in Emil Meurer, Jr., "Violent Crime Losses: Their Impact on the Victim and Society," *Annals*, AAPSS, 443:54–62 (May 1979).

aries, and various secondary agencies via which the agreements have been implemented. Moreover, in addition to a consideration of these victimological issues on the theoretical level, there is also room for empirical study of selected phenomena. Indeed, unlike much of the discussion of victim compensation models that takes place on a speculative level, or at best is in its initial stages of implementation, the German reparations agreements constitute a reality that has already directly affected the lives of hundreds of thousands, even millions, of people.

The remainder of this article can attempt no more than to provide a background for the further exploration of these themes. For this purpose, the history and content of the agreements will be briefly described. This will be followed by a discussion of the fundamental moral dilemmas involved and reference to some of the specific issues that resulted from the special circumstances of the agreements. The final section will be devoted to an assessment of the contribution of a victimological perspective to the study of reparations for genocide, and vice versa.

THE REPARATIONS AGREEMENTS

The concept of a nation that has lost a war being obliged subsequently to pay indemnities to the other parties involved for the damage and costs attributed to that nation's policy is not a new one. It is a common feature of peace treaties. Suffice it to mention the Treaty of Versailles of 1919, reckoned by some to have been one of the incipient causes of World War II.

The reparations agreements discussed in this article, however, were of a totally anomalous character from the point of view of the history of

international law. This is because the payments were to be made, not to one of the nations which had defeated Nazi Germany in 1945—such reparations were agreed upon in Paris in the same year—but to a people (1) who were not formally a party to the war, (2) who had no recognized independent legal existence during the period of hostilities, and (3) of whose members many who were to be beneficiaries of the compensation were or had been citizens of the compensating nation. Moreover, the parties which negotiated the reparations agreements consisted of the Federal Republic of Germany, the state of Israel, which as indicated, had not been in existence at the time of the atrocities and with which the Federal Republic had at the time of the agreement no diplomatic relations at any level, and a body called the Conference on Jewish Material Claims against Germany, which was an amalgamation of various voluntary bodies representing the interests of Jews not residents of the state of Israel. That these three parties could legally enter into an internationally binding agreement, or would even purport to make such an agreement,[12] was a phenomenon explicable only in terms of the traumatic events of the preceding years, which shattered even the normative framework of international law.

The provisions of the reparations agreements—negotiated in Wassenaar in the Netherlands in March, 1952, and signed in Luxemburg in September of the same year because the idea that Jews would enter Germany or Germans enter Israel for this purpose was totally unthinkable—

12. Formally, the agreements to which the Claims Conference was a party were termed "Protocols."

were essentially as follows: First, the German government undertook to pay three billion deutsche marks (DM) to the state of Israel in recognition of the cost borne by that country in resettling and rehabilitating victims of the Holocaust. This is the agreement generally referred to as the "Shilumim" or Reparations Agreement. Second, a further 450 million DM, while transferred to the state of Israel, were earmarked for the Jewish organizations that took care of the welfare of Jews resident outside Israel. Third, the German government undertook to introduce legislation providing for the submission of compensation claims by all victims of Nazi persecution. The three agreements[13] thus corresponded with the three levels of beneficiary: (1) the Jewish state, (2) the Jewish organizations, and (3) the individual victims.

The agreements were naturally considerably more complex than indicated here. But in the present context it should be mentioned that one seemingly minor rider was incorporated in one of the accompanying letters,[14] which stated that Germany's obligation to the state of Israel under the Shilumim agreement exempted it in principle from the need to pay compensation or a

pension to the citizens of that country on an individual basis for medical damage suffered as a result of Nazi persecution. The significance of this provision for our present discussion will emerge subsequently.

The first two agreements did not give rise in principle to problems concerning their scope and interpretation since the sum involved—the transfer of 3.45 billion DM—was a liquidated sum, although there were, of course, provisions related to the rate of annual payment, the machinery for determining the goods to be purchased with these sums, and so forth. The provision for individual compensation, on the other hand, was more problematical, since here the obligation was open-ended; the scope of compensation would depend on the manner in which the appropriate legislation was drafted and on its subsequent interpretation as well as on the number of claimants who were forthcoming.

The legislation that provided for such compensation, the Federal Supplementary Law for the Compensation of Victims of National Socialist Persecution, was passed by the Bundestag in 1953. It was a supplementary law, since compensation had previously been provided for in the various zones of occupation by the Allied governments. The law was amended in 1956, and the Federal Compensation Terminal Law relating to this topic was passed in 1965. The provisions of these laws are highly complex, and the modifications are themselves indicative of continuing controversies regarding the scope of the law. Indeed, at the time of this writing, a new Final Compensation Law is under consideration by the Bundestag, its adoption opposed both by those who are against further payments and by those who object to their recogni-

13. "Reparations" is usually reserved for the payments made to the state of Israel whereas payments to individuals are termed either "compensation" or "restitution." For convenience, the three agreements are collectively referred to as "the reparations agreements." A fourth agreement dealt with compensation by Israel for property vested in the Israel government having previously been owned by German nationals; see *Documents Relating to the Agreement between the Government of Israel and the Government of the Federal Republic of Germany* (Jerusalem: Ministry for Foreign Affairs, 1953) (hereafter cited as *Documents*).

14. *Documents*, pp. 108–9.

tion as final. But these issues are beyond the scope of the present article.

In essence, the legislation provided for compensation for victims of Nazi persecution, defined as having been oppressed because of political opposition to national socialism, or because of race, religion, or ideology and who suffered in consequence loss of life, damage to limb or health, loss of liberty, property, or possessions, or harm to vocational or economic pursuits. Persons who suffered through identification with the plight of the persecuted also qualified for compensation. Finally, there were differentiations related to the extent of the entitlement according to whether the claimant was (1) a resident of Germany, (2) a member of the German cultural or linguistic group, (3) an Israeli, or (4) none of these.[15]

The far-reaching effects of the Luxemburg agreements have already been hinted at. According to the Israel Treasury Department dealing with this topic, some 100,000 Israeli residents receive social security payments from Germany while 46,000 Israelis receive compensation for permanent damage to health, in addition to some 136,000 non-Israelis. The total amount of compensation paid to individuals amounted by the year 1976 to $3.4 billion.[16] However, some three-fourths of the beneficiaries live in other countries. The additional sums transferred by way of Shilumim to the state of Israel were specified previously.

THE FUNDAMENTAL
MORAL DILEMMA

It is almost as difficult to re-create today the depth of the emotions

involved in the great debate that raged, primarily in the year 1952,[17] as to the morality of accepting monetary payment as reparation for the atrocities inflicted in the course of the Holocaust, as it is to grasp the horrors of the Holocaust itself. Balabkins[18] describes Germany's image following World War II as "a moral leper in the international community"; but this is to do no more than hint at the associations aroused in the minds of most Jews by the very words "German" or "Germany."

Thus the very idea of even negotiating with Germans was abhorrent to many. Indeed, descriptions of the negotiations indicate that such reserve was initially shared even by members of the negotiating team itself, despite their clear commitment in principle to the policy of accepting reparations. Further, the idea that any form of monetary compensation should be received in relation to the atrocities inflicted was seen to be an indication that Germany was to be allowed to pay off her moral debt and that forgiveness for the destruction of European Jewry was being solicited—and granted. Finally, the idea that individual citizens would receive specific sums related to their personal losses seemed to some to be adding personal sacrilege to the collective sacrilege involved in such an agreement. The surviving sons would be asked by their children: "How much did you get for Grandma and Grandpa?"

The main argument on the other side was that the Jews were merely claiming the minimum that was due to them. There was no possible justification for refusing to claim

---

15. For further elaboration of these categories, see Schwerin.

16. Y. Ortar, *Personal Compensation from Germany* (Jerusalem: Ministry of Finance, undated) (Hebrew).

17. Literature on this subject was published from the early years of the war, and already in 1945 Dr. Chaim Weizmann submitted a proposal to the Allied governments on this topic on behalf of the Jewish Agency for Palestine; *see Documents*, p. 9.

18. *See* supra, n. 5.

property abandoned or confiscated under racial laws and as the result of physical persecution. The often-quoted biblical verse was invoked, "You have murdered and also inherited?"[19] Depriving the murderer of his spoils could in no way be interpreted as forgiveness for the murder.

Naturally, there was a degree of selectivity in the arguments on both sides: opponents of the negotiations tended to ignore the specific property rights involved, whether restitution of specific property or indemnification for lost property, while supporters of the negotiations tended to ignore that, ultimately, individuals might be receiving payment for atrocities committed on themselves and their families. The emphasis, however, was on the state of Israel's collective claim and its entitlement to a minimum of assistance in building in a new society from the ashes of the Holocaust.

Notwithstanding the violence of the opposition, both intellectual and physical—street fighting broke out on the first day of the Knesset debate—Prime Minister Ben-Gurion managed to muster 61 votes out of a Knesset of 120[20] to support the continuation of the negotiations, which ultimately bore fruit: Ben-Gurion, like his counterpart Chancellor Adenauer, had made up his mind.

The macrodebate regarding compensation for the collective victimization of the Jewish people was thereby effectively concluded. There remained, however, innumerable microdebates calculated to rend the heart of every individual who qualified for compensation under the subsequent German legislation mentioned previously: To claim or not to claim? And if to claim, for

19. I Kings 21:19.
20. Fifty opposed; the remainder abstained or absented themselves.

what?—for property lost, for injuries inflicted, for loved ones? While the macrodebate echoed across Israel and among Jews the world over, the microdebates have gone unrecorded, and there is little systematic knowledge available as to how the issue was resolved and how the ultimate decision was rationalized.

SPECIFIC ISSUES

In addition to the fundamental moral issue relating to the acceptance of compensation, a number of more specific issues emerged, of which three will be briefly considered here.

The first problem to which I wish to allude is that of the falsification of particulars. The German compensation laws were enmeshed in a morass of qualifications, and legitimate victims of Nazi crimes frequently found themselves disbarred from claiming, although in many cases the categories of claimant were subsequently expanded to embrace them also. If an accidental detail, such as the geographical location of the claimant at a particular time, would stand between poverty and a minimal source of income, could not one apply a degree of flexibility in the recall of certain particulars? In formal terms, such conduct amounts to victimizing the offender by inducing him to pay a greater amount of compensation than the law demands. Yet in view of the horror of the crimes and the technical nature of the law, such conduct could perhaps on occasion be rationalized. It seems, however, that the authorities, including the Israeli criminal courts, reacted with severity in such cases, the latter taking the view that such practices, apart from their intrinsic immorality, would result in casting doubt on the authenticity of all claims and their outcomes would consequently be prejudiced.

The second and related problem is

that of the moral standpoint of the various agencies involved in the compensation-awarding machinery. What of the ethical standards of the Israeli advocates and other authorized representatives who assisted the victims in submitting their claims? It seems that it was frequently they who stimulated the prevarications mentioned previously. For this reason, as well as in recognition of the need for special expertize for these cases, the Israeli government introduced special legislation to ensure that the claims would only be handled by suitably qualified people. Moreover, the United Restitution Organization, which handled the cases of hundreds of thousands of claimants who had no private advocates, developed a close relationship with the German authorities that came to trust them.

A similar problem arises with the Israeli physicians who were accredited by the German authorities, on the recommendation of Israel's Ministry of Health, for the purpose of giving medical opinions as to compensation claimants, particularly in the face of doubt as to the causal connection between a particular pathological state and the traumatic events experienced by the claimant in the Nazi Era. In all these cases, the professional agent, by maintaining a strict level of professional ethics, may lay himself open to criticism by the victim for being on "the other side."

The third issue relates to the role of the Israeli government, which in this respect clearly crossed the Rubicon and became identified, for compensation purposes, with the victimizer. In a provision of the Luxemburg agreements alluded to earlier, the Israeli government waived the right of Israeli citizens to qualify for compensation from the German authorities in respect of certain categories of injuries to personal health. In order to prevent unfair discrimination against these Israeli victims, a law was enacted by the Knesset providing for equivalent compensation to be paid by the state of Israel. Some 16,000 Israelis receive payments under this law.[21] As a result, all claims and ensuing litigations, which seem to have been extensive, are directed against the Israeli government, which rejects claims it considers not to conform with the norms laid down in the Federal Republic of Germany and adopted in Israel. For this purpose there is total identity between the roles of the Israeli and the German governments vis-à-vis the victim.

THE REPARATIONS AGREEMENTS: TOWARD AN INTERNATIONAL VICTIMOLOGY

This survey of a few of the issues raised by the reparations agreements should suffice to convey the special fascination this topic holds for the victimologist and to indicate the type of contribution that may emerge from a victimological orientation. Closer studies of certain areas are called for, including a consideration of the specific provisions of the agreements, or the Compensation Laws which resulted therefrom, from a victimological point of view, case studies of the dynamics of the processing of claims by the relevant authorities, and, above all, the significance of the payments in the eyes of the recipients—as well as those who refused to claim.

Victimologists may, however, question the relevance of this topic beyond its own special circumstances and those of the Holocaust from which the reparations followed. Thus in addition to considering the

21. See Ortar.

question of the contribution of a victimological approach to the study of the reparations issue, it is equally important to consider the implications of reparations research to victimology in general.[22]

While the systematic and monolithic characteristics of genocide set this crime apart from "conventional" crimes, involving a qualitative rather than a merely quantitative difference, many of the individual acts involved in genocide resemble those committed as conventional crimes: robbery, maiming, sexual abuse, and so forth. Moreover, Cormier has coined the term "genocidal crime" to describe offenses committed in a conventional setting in which the selection of victim was only semi-specific."[23] This suggests a typological continuum extending from genocide to conventional crime. In any case, from the wealth of accumulated sources comprising both the juridical analyses of the provisions of the Federal Compensation Laws and the medical diagnoses which resulted from their implementation, surely some relevant material must have accrued which would be of value in considering the types of harm, as well as the machinery of proof, to be incorporated in provisions for regular victim compensation.

Similarly, some of the ideological issues involved in considering the victim's attitude to compensation payments—whether emanating from the state or from the offender—apply also to conventional crimes. A rape victim in particular may have difficulty in accepting a compensation payment for the assault on his or her personality, partly as a result of the continuing trauma involved and partly because of the risk of its being regarded as a "settlement of accounts." Thus some of these issues, too, are at least partially generalizable.

The negotiations between Germans and Jews may provide an interesting example of conflict resolution. The application of such techniques, applied initially in the sphere of international relations to reduce tension in the world, have lately been proposed as preferable to the conventional methods of dealing with criminals. To replace the current adversary system wherein the offender is stigmatized and the victim abandoned, a confrontation is suggested that would be to the mutual benefit of both parties. In this context it may be noted that the holding of the negotiations between German and Jewish leaders, irrespective of their outcomes, dramatically reduced the tensions between the leaders themselves and, subsequently, between those they represented. The relevance of this for conventional crimes may be considered.

Finally, the reparations agreements could prove to be a catalyst for the development of an "International Victimology."[24] For the victim has proved to be the "poor relation" of international law no

22. Cf. the view expressed by Elie Wiesel, who heads President Carter's Commission on the Holocaust, that historical interest alone did not justify the commission's activities unless some additional message resulted, such as a reduction of the probability of a second Holocaust.

23. Bruno Cormier, "Mass Murder, Multicide, and Collective Crime: The Doers and the Victims," in *Victimology: A New Focus, Vol. IV: Violence and its Victims*, I. Drapkin and E. Viano, eds. (Lexington: Lexington Books, 1975), pp. 71–90.

24. Cf. the plea for a "supra-national criminology" put forward by Professor Stanley Johnston at the First International Symposium on Victimology.

less than of municipal state law. Generally speaking, international law was in the past concerned exclusively with regulating relationships among states. Even where the rights of individual citizens were at issue, it was only the state of which he was a national that could take action on his behalf.

Some recognition of the obligation of states to pay compensation for misdeeds in wartime was included in the Hague Conventions of 1907. The Versailles treaty of 1919 went much further; not only were the rights of certain minorities and of individual citizens recognized, but individuals were themselves entitled to enter claims before the "Mixed Arbitral Tribunals." In one such case, a citizen was even able to bring a claim against his *own* state.[25] This precedent has far-reaching implications in the present context since genocide is frequently committed by a state against its own citizens.

More recently, in addition to the Convention on Prevention and Punishment of the Crime of Genocide of 1948, there has developed a body of so-called International Humanitarian Law, designed to protect the rights of individuals and minorities[26] in both peace and war situations. However, it is still rare for individual citizens to be able to pursue a claim on their own behalf under international law.[27] Moreover, progress toward ensuring the award of compensation to victims of war crimes has been negligible.[28]

The Geneva Conference on Reaffirmation and Development of International Humanitarian Law Applicable in Armed Conflicts produced the "Protocol Additional to the Geneva Conventions of 12th August 1949 and Relating to the Problem of Victims of International Armed Conflicts (Protocol I)."[29] Article 91 of this protocol specifies that "A party to the complaint which violates the provisions of the Conventions or of this Protocol shall, if the case demands, be liable to compensation." Such a nebulous provision is a far cry from the ultimate goal: the recognition of the victim's rights of compensation, or the rights of his group, against any oppressor, within his own state or beyond it. In this respect the reparations agreements remain a landmark for they guarantee the establishment of machinery for individual claims to be met, while cutting across national boundaries.

Thus it is not only state compensation schemes that can benefit from the experience accumulated in the course of implementing the reparations agreements between the West German government and the Jewish people. For if both the intricacies of these agreements and of the state compensation schemes are properly studied, the combined experience could generate a model compensation scheme for the aftermath of the horrors of genocide, insofar as mankind is to continue to be plagued with this phenomenon. It will be the task of the combined forces of International Humanitarian Law and International Victimology to ensure that the message of the reparations agreements will not be lost to history.

25. *Steiner & Gross v. Polish State* (1928), *Annual Digest of Public International Law Cases 1927–1928.*

26. The modern trend in international law is to protect minorities as such, rather than particular, named minorities.

27. *See* J. G. Starke, *Introduction to International Law*, 8th ed. (London: Butterworths, 1967), pp. 73–74.

28. For a discussion of this issue in the context of the war in Southeast Asia, *see* Benjamin Ferencz, "Compensating Victims

of the Crimes of War," *Virginia J. of International Law* 12:343–56 (1972).

29. Protocol II dealt with non-International Armed Conflicts.

Fundamentals in Holocaust Studies

By FRANKLIN H. LITTELL

ABSTRACT: Regular conferences on Holocaust Studies began in 1970. For serious study of the meanings of the Holocaust, certain ground rules are essential. Interfaith cooperation ensures that the event will not fall victim to Jewish preciousness or gentile banality. The Holocaust confronts Christianity with a massive credibility crisis that Christian preachers and teachers must work through. Interdisciplinary cooperation, essential to any aspect of studies in totalitarianism, is a second imperative. The death camps were planned, built, and operated by men and women of the modern university. The modern university, with its overwhelming commitment to technology and its scant attention to ethics and wisdom, is also called into question by the Holocaust. International cooperation—especially from programs involving Israelis, West Germans, and North Americans—has developed extensively with the passing of a generation and with the achievement of a certain distance from the anguish and trauma of the Holocaust. Nevertheless, the event confronts the individual as well as the society with a challenge that is total and not merely intellectual. In this it is an epochal event of the mass of the Exodus, Sinai, and the Destruction of the Temple.

Franklin H. Littell is a professor of religion, Temple University, and is a corresponding faculty member of the Institute of Contemporary Jewry, Hebrew University. He founded the Annual Scholars Conference on the Church Struggle and the Holocaust (1970) and the Annual Conference on Teaching the Holocaust (1975). He is chairman of the Board of the National Institute on the Holocaust and is a member of the International Council of Yad Vashem. Among his books are The German Phoenix, The German Church Struggle and the Holocaust, *and* The Crucifixion of the Jews.

THE FIRST conference on the Holocaust was held at Wayne State University, Detroit, in 1970. The official hosts were the president of the university and the governor of the state. The conference secretary was Dr. Hubert G. Locke, then director of religious affairs at Wayne State. I was the conference chairman and from 1958 on had been the consultant on Religion in Higher Education to the National Conference of Christians and Jews. The 1970 conference became the first in a series of Annual Scholars Conferences.[1]

The problems involved in a responsible and fruitful study of the Holocaust and its lessons showed up at the start. The fundamental rules to be observed, if the program were to have positive value to all concerned and not descend into morbid sentimentality, were also evident from the start.

NEED FOR UNDERSTANDING

At the beginning, the different anxieties of both Jews and Christians bobbed to the surface. For years, except for a few poets, novelists, and memoirists, neither Jews nor Christians could bear to talk about the event. For Jews, recollection of the Holocaust evoked memories of agony and abandonment by the so-called civilized world. For Christians, the Holocaust confronted believers with

1. The 1970 Conference Report was edited by Littell and Locke and published in *The German Church Struggle and the Holocaust* (Detroit: Wayne State University Press, 1974); it contains contributions by Eli Wiesel, Richard Rubenstein, Eberhard Bethge, John S. Conway, Arthur C. Cochrane, Wilhelm Niemoeller, Gordon Zahn, et al; in 1974, the Annual Scholars Conferences series was transferred to New York City and since then has been sponsored every March by the National Conference of Christians and Jews.

the guilt of apostasy and a crisis in credibility. The vast majority of the perpetrators of the crime, and almost all of the spectators, were baptized Christians. Adolf Hitler died a church-tax-paying Roman Catholic; Hermann Goering, a church-tax-paying Protestant. Neither was rebuked, let alone excommunicated. Few in number were the church officials who had the moral courage to admonish the faithless and rebuke the apostate, let alone follow church law in dealing with the perpetrators.

In dealing with the Holocaust, the easiest path for Jewish teachers was simply to subsume it under the ample rubric of "gentile persecutions and pogroms of the Jews." The easiest path for Christian or secular humanist teachers was to talk of genocide or "man's inhumanity to man" and to avoid confrontation with the Holocaust as a discrete event.

Most Marxists, like hard-line Nazis, simply denied the facts. The Marxist establishment used another escape mechanism: they tossed the sufferings of many peoples during World War II into the same cauldron, and, instead of confronting the significance of the martyrdom of the 6 million, they talked about the 11 million (total concentration camp dead), or the 22 million (total Russian dead), or the 42 million (estimated total losses of life in World War II). Of course, no Nazi sympathizers or Marxist officials came to the Annual Scholars Conferences. But those people who did participate were always aware that there was a mass of writing and political effort dedicated to eliminating all consideration of the meaning of the Church Struggle and the Holocaust. This awareness drew Jews and Christians of conscience into closer cooperation, both personal and professional.

From the start it was clear that study of the Holocaust and teaching of the lessons of the Holocaust must be interfaith, interdisciplinary, and international. Interfaith sponsorship averted the twin perils of Jewish preciousness and gentile abstraction. Moreover, it guaranteed, as the Philadelphia experience in launching the first system-wide instruction on the Holocaust in the high schools showed, a solid public support when American Nazis and their fellow travelers tried to block the program.

Interdisciplinary cooperation is imperative if the total resources of the modern university, which made the Holocaust technologically possible, are to be focused upon learning its lessons. By definition, totalitarianism encompasses all aspects of organized human life. All of the methodologies and idioms are needed to effectively penetrate its recesses and illuminate its repressive and genocidal potential. Furthermore, since men and women of the universities, not illiterate savages, designed and built the death camps and systematized the killing program, study of the Holocaust leads directly to study of the programs and the goals of modern higher education. Must technological objectives prevail?—or are the pursuit of wisdom and the commitment to life still recoverable goals of the university?

The credibility crisis of the modern university, with its blind devotion to *Techne* and its indifference to *Sophia*, is as acute as the credibility crisis of Christianity. What kind of a medical school trained a Mengele and his associates? What departments of anthropology prepared the staff of Strasbourg University's "Institute of Ancestral Heredity"? What teachers' colleges graduated those who prostituted their stewardship of young life to shape the *janizaries*

of *Hitlerjugend* and the *Bund Deutscher Maedel*? What theological faculties accredited the clergy who waffled the truth and developed an apologetic for heresy and murder? These are the kinds of questions which have in recent years, as the mass of the Holocaust becomes evident to a growing number of academics, exercised study groups of professors and students in professional schools as well as in the liberal arts. What lessons have been learned from the years of the Nazi assault upon civilization and its values, upon the Jewish people, and upon such Christians as stayed Christian? How are these lessons to be incorporated into changed structures of society?

DEVELOPMENT OF EDUCATIONAL PROGRAMS: 1975 TO PRESENT

How are these lessons to be transmitted to children and children's children? This was the concern which led to the launching in 1975 of the Annual Conferences on Teaching the Holocaust. Out of this series,[2] held every October under the sponsorship of the Philadelphia Metropolitan Christian Council, the Cardinal's Commission on Human Relations and the Jewish Community Relations Council, and directed by the interfaith Coordinating Council on the Holocaust, have emerged several continuing pedagogical programs:

1. the first system-wide teaching of the Holocaust at high-school level in the United States, developed under the Philadelphia Board of Education;

2. the National Institute on the

2. The Conference Reports are printed and are available from the National Institute on the Holocaust, Temple University, Philadelphia, PA 19122.

Holocaust, a service agency providing literature and professional assistance to adult education programs in Canada and the United States; and

3. a Ph.D. in Holocaust Studies at Temple University, operated in cooperation with the Institute of Contemporary Jewry, Hebrew University, Jerusalem.

Since the Philadelphia high-school program was launched, a number of city and state boards of education have introduced programs in teaching the Holocaust. The training of teachers had become an important responsibility. To meet this need a wide program of teacher training has been developed under the leadership of Professor Irene Shur at West Chester State College.[3]

Interfaith and interdisciplinary, scholars', and the pedagogical conferences have been concerned with education at all levels—from the lower schools through graduate and professional education to adult education. When the first series was started, there were not more than a dozen courses on the campuses in the United States; a 1978 survey reported over 700. The expansion at high-school level came later, but since the NBC television series, it has burgeoned.

The Holocaust conferences have also been international in participation. Perhaps the most widely attended event was the teaching conference of 1978, which was linked with an International Theological Symposium. There were registrants from Switzerland, Austria, East Germany, France, the Netherlands, Denmark, Czechoslovakia, and Hungary, as well as larger groups from Israel and the German Federal Republic. Consistently, the largest participation in both of the annual series from outside Canada and the United States has come from Israel and West Germany.

In Israel, the resources and publications of Yad Vashem have been preeminent for more than a decade, and the major academic personnel has been concentrated at the Department of Holocaust Studies of the Institute of Contemporary Jewry, Hebrew University.

In the German Federal Republic, outstanding work on the Holocaust and related issues, such as the Church Struggle, has been carried on for years by several institutions, notably, the Institut fuer Zeitgeschichte in Munich and the Institut zur Geschichte des Kirchenkampfes in Tuebingen. In terms of public education, the work of Arbeitsgruppe VI of the Deutscher Evangelischer Kirchentag—set up during the Eichmann trial, at the time of the Berlin, 1961, event—has been outstanding. Among adult education centers, Arnoldshain Evangelische Akademie, in the Taunus hills north of Frankfurt, concentrates on Christian-Jewish understanding and cooperation, with special attention to the two topics that have to do with Jewish survival: the Holocaust and Israel, and publishes excellent materials. In public high-school education, the work of a team at the University of Duisberg has been impressive. Under the chairmanship of Professor Heinz Kremers, and advised by Professor Chaim Schatzker of Hebrew University, the group has prepared four excellent textbooks mandated for the ninth and tenth grades of West

3. Among these are a Holocaust workshop, a certificate program (certificate granted after completion of six subjects) a committee that plans a yearly conference, and a State College Committee on the Holocaust comprised of professors from Pennsylvania's 14 state colleges. A summer seminar drawing participants from school districts all over the United States is being planned.

German gymnasien. At university level, the seminar taught by Dr. Erich Geldbach at Marburg should be mentioned.

The first high-school programs on the Holocaust in the United States, West Germany, and Israel began within a few months of each other. The question is sometimes asked why such a painful matter should be taken up so vigorously in the schools and congregations 35 years after the event. The question must be stood on its head: Why did a full generation have to pass before anyone, Jew or Christian—except for a few poets, novelists, solitary scholars, and devoted archivists—could face the implications of the Holocaust?

LEST WE FORGET

The uniqueness of the event and its massive moral, religious, and political impact upon human history could scarcely be comprehended by those who survived in its immediate shadow. The words which have come to be applied to it reveal the immensity of the event, and also the weight of the problem of interpreting its meaning: *novum*, unique, epochal, watershed, formative, shaping, primordial, and definitive. The conviction is more and more often expressed that the Holocaust is an event of the mass of the Exodus, the giving of the Law at Sinai, the Return from the First Exile, the Crucifixion of Jesus, and the Destruction of the Second Temple. This much can be said with certainty: among those who have plunged into its depths, no matter what their academic discipline and religious or aesthetic sensibilities, when they emerge to look around, nothing ever looks the same again.

The Teaching of the Holocaust: Dilemmas and Considerations

By CHAIM SCHATZKER

ABSTRACT: Education literature has failed to deal with the problem of teaching the Holocaust. Publications dealing with teaching the Holocaust begin appearing in the beginning of the sixties and in the late seventies in Israel, Germany, the United States, and elsewhere. Educators and students discovered that they were not prepared to confront the problems the Holocaust evoked. There are many educational approaches to the Holocaust but the educator needs the correct teaching aids, methods, and curriculum support. There is no clear-cut concept of the Holocaust. Rather, the problem is how to present the truth without traumatizing. Educators need to foster students' sensitivity to and involvement and identification with the Holocaust. To bring students to an honest confrontation with the phenomenon of antisemitism and with the murder of European Jewry while a silent world stood by is a universal objective.

Dr. Chaim Schatzker is a professor of education at Hebrew University, Jerusalem, Israel.

DURING the almost 20 years that followed the Holocaust, years in which the extent and results of the Holocaust were revealed and many thousands of books, witness reports, trial protocols, and sources of all kinds have been published, educational literature failed to deal with the problem of teaching the Holocaust. The topic was hardly broached in educational discussions and was almost nowhere integrated as a unique and clearly defined component in curricula and school systems.[1] It was only in the beginning of the sixties, due to a first outbreak of swastika paintings in Germany,[2] due to the Eichmann trial in Israel,[3] and, in the late seventies, due to the tensions and dangers of the Yom Kippur War, that we were witness to a wave of publications in Israel, Germany, the United States and elsewhere that dealt with the Holocaust as a didactic-educational problem.[4] Educators suddenly found themselves sharing in common the surprising discovery that their educational systems had not fulfilled their duty in teaching the Holocaust and had not been aware of the educational values and opportunities which might be implicated in this subject, thus leaving their students unprepared for the confrontation with the problems the Holocaust evokes.

It seems that new traumatic experiences, arising in times of stress and danger, brought about a spiritual readiness and an enhanced ability to deal with the overwhelming— and for a long time, repressed— traumatic experience of the Holocaust. Paradoxically, the further we get away from it, the more the Holocaust turns into a symbol which

1. See reports of George French, Harold Kessler, Margot Stern Strom, Roselle Chartok, Yaffa Eliach, Michael Berenbaum, Judy Muffs, and Josephine Knopp, United States; Herbert Steiner, Austria; Claire Huchet-Bishop, France; Heinz Kremers, Günther Neumann, and Herbert Jochum, Germany; and Arye Carmon and Chaim Schatzker, Israel; all in "International Conference, The Lesson of the Holocaust, October 1978," National Institute on the Holocaust, Philadelphia; see also Bernhard Blumenkranz, "How Holocaust History is (not) taught, Shortcomings of French Textbooks," in Patterns of Prejudice, I. J. A. Institute of Jewish Affairs 9(3) (May–June 1975) and Henry Friedlander, On the Holocaust, A Critique of the Treatment of the Holocaust in History Textbooks (New York: Anti-Defamation League of the B'nai B'rith, 1972 and 1973).

2. The resulting efforts on behalf of the German federal government, the "Länder," universities, research centers and various groups have been concentrated since then and until today mainly in the area of schoolbook revision. For the first systematic content analysis of German history textbooks regarding their treatment of Jewish history, Holocaust and the state of Israel see Saul B. Robinsohn and Chaim Shatzker, Jüdische Geschichte in deutschen Geschichtslehrbüchern (Braunschweig: Albert Limbach Verlag, 1963); another similar project was launched several years ago by Heinz Kremers from the University of Duisburg, BRD, on a broader and interdisciplinary basis.

3. See Chaim Schatzker, "Formation or Information: Trends in Holocaust Education in Israel," in Forum on the Jewish People, Zionism and Israel, pp. 135–41 (spring and summer 1978).

4. See Diane R. Roskies, Teaching the Holocaust to Children: A Review and Bibliography (Ktav Publishing House, 1975) and "Teaching the Holocaust: An Explanation of the Problem. Proceedings of a Colloquium" Stone-Sapirstein Center for Jewish Education (spring 1974); and Henry Friedlander, "Toward a Methodology of Teaching about the Holocaust," in Teachers College Record, Columbia University, 80(3) (Feb. 1979). At the college and university level in the United States, approximately 140 institutions offer courses in Holocaust studies. Holocaust centers have been set up in Philadelphia, St. Louis, Los Angeles, and Brooklyn. In other countries, with the exception of Israel, no centers exist; see The Current Status of Holocaust Education in the Diaspora (Institute of Contemporary Jewry–The Hebrew University of Jerusalem, 1979).

constitutes a reality in our lives and influences our consciousness and reactions in times of crisis, perplexity, and desolation. It is perhaps this *Condition humain* of our time, characterized by the Vietnam War, Biafra, Cambodia, the energy crisis, unsolved economic and social problems, and uncertainty and growing anxiousness regarding the future, that was responsible for the worldwide interest in and reactions to the television series on the Holocaust rather than the series' artistic qualities.[5] Since the present and its unsettled problems motivated this new interest in the Holocaust, there seems to be no other topic so saturated with unresolved emotions and spiritual conflicts, with self-accusation, accusation of others, and the necessity for defensiveness and apologetics that demands a willingness to either cope with or on the other hand, to repress the Holocaust.

DILEMMA OF TEACHING THE HOLOCAUST

In the absence of consensus regarding many aspects of the Holocaust, no final, clear-cut concept of it could or should be presented to students. Didactics can never reach beyond the framework of the society which they are supposed to serve, and teachers have no right to decide in matters upon which history and people have not yet delivered a final verdict.[6] For the same reason, curricula of the Holocaust are not transferable from one country to another. Every nation, every generation, and even every social and ideological group has its own problems of facing the Holocaust and its own way of integrating it into its life and into its educational system—since every educational system has its own set of aims, ways, and anticipation of results regarding the teaching of the Holocaust.

Consequently, we have to speak of dilemmas in teaching the Holocaust when facing a situation in which educational systems, curriculum makers, and teachers have to find their ways among various possibilities, arguments, views, and beliefs. It is the nature of dilemmas that whenever one takes one side or another and stretches it to its utmost limits, one is in danger of bringing his case *ad absurdum*. This is perhaps the tragic dimension of the term "dilemma": one cannot choose between two or more possibilities but has to consider them, knowing the limits and shortcomings of each of them. Guided by educational rather than by ideological deliberation, this consideration should be done, not by taking this side or another, but by reflecting on all possibilities and by considering their implications.

IMPORTANCE OF DEVELOPING A CORRECT APPROACH

Regarding the various alternatives and educational options in teaching the Holocaust, special care has to be

5. The action of President Carter in appointing the Presidential Commission to commemorate the Holocaust perhaps symbolized this development for the United States.

6. Several curricula have been published: Judah Pilch, ed., *The Jewish Catastrophe in Europe* (The American Association for Jewish Education, 1968); Spotts Leon, *Guide to Teachers* (New York: The National Curriculum Research Institute, 1968); Stadtler Bea, *The Holocaust* (March 1970) and *The Test* (Cleveland, OH: 1973); Sanders Beverly, "The Holocaust Resource Unit for High School Teachers," *New York Teachers Magazine*, 21 April 1974; The School Division of Philadelphia, "The Holocaust, A Teacher Resource," 1977; and Board of Education of New York City, Division of Curriculum & Instruction, "The Holocaust, A Study of Genocide," 1979; Chaim Schatzker, project director, "Antisemitism and Holocaust," 1977; Arye Carmon, "Teaching the Holocaust as an Education toward Values," 1979.

taken not to waste this newly aroused interest and not to let the former "conspiracy of silence" turn into a "conspiracy of banality."[7]

Educators have to find their way between reality and the limits of human cognition, between the whole scope of known facts and events, each of them more than enough to constitute a curriculum within the limited framework of the learning situation, by the natural limits of human perception, and by the learning processes of the students.

One might question the very possibility of studying or comprehending such a phenomenon, permeated with the ultimate in evil and human suffering, and lying beyond normal perception and apart from any human experience yet known in the history of mankind. While keeping these reservations in mind, one must not forget that the alternative to teaching the Holocaust would be to relegate it to oblivion for future generations. Our conceptual helplessness in the face of this phenomenon has led sometimes to the demonization of Holocaust operations and their executors, similar to the Middle Ages' conception of Satan, as the source and essence of all evil, an entity which man fears, rejects, hates, despises and constantly fights, but which remains beyond his comprehension and perception.

Obviously, this approach is not only at odds with scientific research, but poses an obstacle to our deriving any possible lessons or conclusions from the events of the period. Since one cannot draw an analogy between Satan and man, any demonization is in the nature of a fixation of evil in an external object instead of a search for it in the soul of man. One must understand the origins of evil and the atmosphere in which it thrives and acts so as to frustrate any such phenomenon in the future. If any lesson is to be learned from the Holocaust, there is no sense in attributing its execution to demonic monsters for then it becomes both impossible and irrelevant to underline a common human approach to their actions. Such a reading of Nazis out of the common human condition is precisely the obverse of the Nazis' attitude toward Jews.[8]

On the other hand, by trying to make the Holocaust understandable, to shape it in accordance with our own and our students' perceptive capabilities in order to explain it and to derive from it educational lessons, values, and directions, there is a danger that it will be dwarfed, diminished, and will lose its unique significance. Thus "Holocaust" and what it stands for would be simply explained away; instead of making students sensitive to the abnormalities of the Holocaust, they would get used to it and learn to regard it as one possible way of human and social behavior like others, leaving them wondering whether undergoing a special socialization process, becoming an SS mass murderer, would not have been the most natural thing to do.[9]

One possible way of overcoming this dilemma might be to break the

7. H. Klein, International Congress on Concentration Camps, Yad Vashem, Jerusalem, Jan. 1978; see also Hermann Glaser, "Unsere Geschichte mit dem Trivialen, Gedanken nach Holocaust," in Tribüne, Zeitschrift zum Verständnis des Judentums, 18. Jahrg., Heft 72, 1979.

8. The danger of a "demonizing" attitude toward the Holocaust and its educational shortcomings was mentioned first in Chaim Schatzker, "Didactical Considerations in Teaching the Holocaust" (1961) and recently in Arye Carmon, "Teaching the Holocaust as a Means of Fostering Values," in Curriculum Inquiry, 9(3):212 (1979) (hereafter cited as "Teaching the Holocaust").

9. This danger becomes evident in Arye Carmon, "Teaching the Holocaust as an Education towards Values," sect. I.

general and generalizing conception of the Holocaust into a series of limited human experiences that might be easier to approach and to identify with. This should be done, however, without losing the unique, inhuman dimensions of the phenomenon as a whole and without creating a neatly explained new Holocaust in the shape of the limited capabilities of human perception.[10] In any case, careful attention should be paid to the proper age of the students and to those contents with which he can be confronted without causing harm and without leading to a total rejection of the entire subject. The problem is how to present the truth without causing dangerous mental consequences—how to impress without traumatizing.

The Holocaust and its abstractions

Educators must also find their way between the uniqueness of this learning unit and the necessity of locating it amidst other disciplines, like history, political science, theology, moral education, psychology, and so forth.

It is understandable that a phenomenon like the Holocaust, has been focused upon by many disciplines, and one should consider whether this subject need not be taught in an interdisciplinary way. However, the danger exists that by being instrumentalized by the various disciplines for their own ends, the Holocaust would lose its substance and unique definition. The result in educational experience has been in many cases a highly abstracted teaching of the subject,

sometimes teaching the Holocaust without the Jews, sometimes even teaching the Holocaust without the Holocaust. Examples of this can be found in curricula and textbooks in Germany, the United States, and other countries where the policy has often approximated the following logic: Since you do not teach the Holocaust to tell the story, but to make the students aware of implicit structures and mechanisms, these aims could be acquired well and even better through more recent examples, like the case of contemporary minorities, the *Gastarbeiter*, and other socially deprived groups or in the case of other tragic events, like Vietnam, Biafra, and Cambodia. Since the scenario and the examples are interchangeable as long as you achieve through them special educational aims, one does not have to mention the Holocaust or the fate of the Jews anymore.[11]

This way of thinking was fostered by the discipline and the structure especially of the social sciences, which have in many cases replaced the discipline of history and have been adapted eagerly by groups and ideological streams, which, for reasons of their own, were and are not interested in stressing the Jewish component of the Holocaust and its historical consequences.[12]

The instrumental function of teaching the Holocaust

In addition, educators must be aware of the need to choose between the result of the relevant research

10. This way underlies the curriculum, "Antisemitism and Holocaust" (1977): "We intend to avoid any generalizing attitude to the 'Holocaust' "; *see also* "Antisemitism and Holocaust," Teachers Guide, p. 32 and "Teaching the Holocaust," p. 216.

11. *See* Walter A. Frank, "Das Soziale Vorurteil-zum Beispiel Antisemitismus," in *Juden, ein Beitrag zur Behandlung der Vorurteilsproblematik im Unterricht,* ed. Klaus Farbor and Heinz Kremers (Dortmund: W. Cruewell Verlag, 1974).

12. *See* Ernst Vogt, *Israel Kritik von Links. Dokumentation einer Entwicklung* (Wuppertal: P. Kommers, 1976).

and psychological, didactical, and educational intentions and considerations.

As in the case of the previously mentioned disciplines, there is not one educational objective that one would not be able to achieve through teaching the Holocaust. However, the question is whether one really needs such an enormous, tragic event in order to achieve some trivial educational objectives which could have been achieved just as well—in cases like moral education, certainly better—by any other, less tremendous event or patterns of human or social behavior.

The story of the Holocaust includes many moral dilemmas, some of them perhaps the most tragic that men ever had to face and to grapple with. Education should, of course, confront the student with those moral questions as well as with the danger in breaking away from personal moral standards by creating collective ethical standards that exempt the individual from his moral responsibility for his decisions and deeds.

There is indeed a moral message of the Holocaust to coming generations. The Holocaust has told us anew that in the last consequence there is nothing to stop man's complete deterioration but his ability to distinguish good from evil and his readiness to make his decisions out of inner moral determination.[13] But would it really be according to relevant theories of moral education to use the Holocaust only and alone as an example, as a coordinating net and an orientation point for moral dilemmas and moral solutions for adolescent students[14] instead

of looking for examples of moral education and moral behavior in situations that are more relevant to the students' experiences?[15] Is there not a message of the Holocaust that should not be wasted on commonplaces in the field of education?

The cognitive and affective approach

Educators must also be aware of subjectivity, that is, between extreme personal and emotional involvement and rational, cognitive, and analytical ways of thinking and presentation and between memorial ceremonies and sober learning processes.[16]

The various components of learning processes, such as cognition, perception, analysis, causalities connections, conceptualization, generalization, and deduction, differ from the psychological mechanism rooted in memorial days and ceremonies. By their very natures, the latter are not analytical processes. Their purpose is rather to induce a sense of sublimation amid the pain and the grief and to raise the pain and the mourning to a metaphysical experience, beyond time and place; all this is to enable man to come to terms with fate, often inexplicable and uncompromising, over which he has no control yet cannot but face and live with, aware of and wondering at the helplessness of his mere mortality.

15. Similar doubts have arisen in the field of political education; see Kenneth Prewitt, "Political Socialization Research in the United States: Can We get Where We Should be Going from Where We Have Been," in International J. Political Education, 1(2):118 (Feb. 1978).

16. See H. Klein and U. Last, "Cognitive and Emotional Aspects of the Attitudes of American and Jewish Youth Towards the Victims of the Holocaust," in Israeli Ann. Psychiatry and Related Disciplines, 12(2): 113–31 (June 1974).

13. See Chaim Schatzker, "Didactical Considerations in Teaching the Holocaust."

14. See Carmon, "Teaching the Holocaust," p. 213.

Both teaching processes and memorial ceremonies play essential parts in the life of men, societies, and nations, but they are not identical. To confuse these two trends would be to harm them both; one cannot be substituted for the other.

Jewish and universal elements

Educators have to decide the element they wish to stress—the Jewish uniqueness of the Holocaust or its universal human elements.

Whereas in Israel the main trend has been to regard the Holocaust as the culminating point of Jewish history, as a symbol of Jewish fate, Jewish interdependence, and Jewish identity, as one of the historic developments which led to the foundation of the state of Israel and as one of its justifications, curricula of other countries tend to stress the universal and human elements of the Holocaust. If one-sidedly overstressed and extracted from social context of time and place, both trends are in danger of losing the proportion between those two components of the Holocaust by distorting and bereaving it of its historic truth and human meaning.

By an oversimplification of the term "universal," by applying the term "Holocaust" to any other tragic event, or by including in it all atrocities by the Nazi regime[17] without differentiation, the real, historic Holocaust is emptied of all its inherent, unique meaning. Thus a decisive step in the direction of the "conspiracy of banality" has been taken that would either diminish the

seriousness and significance of the Holocaust or result in emotional and intellectual deception.

Teaching methods

Finally, educators have to find their way between frontal teaching methods and individual activity and between conventional and modern teaching methods.

Once we have decided to include the Holocaust into the school curriculum, the question of teaching methods, teaching aids, and selected sources according to different student age groups and levels arises in all its severity. As long as the teacher lacks these instruments, there will be no escape from arbitrary teaching of incidental events or from the entire nonteaching of this subject. The Holocaust differs from any normal experience, and conventional verbal presentation alone may leave a poor and insufficiently exhaustive exposure. Rational and factual analysis cannot, by its very nature, serve as an exclusive instrument in grasping and understanding those processes in which the irrational exceeds the rational. Therefore all relevant curricula will have to consider the use of teaching methods which might be able to strengthen the students' sensibilities to those existential human situations, to foster involvement and identification processes, and to shape attitudes. Here, too, the gliding into banality should be avoided, a danger which, for example, is inherent in the adaption of simulation methods regarding Holocaust topics.

Any simulation is based upon the assumption that there exists a fundamental similarity between the simulator and the subject of simulation. Affective simulation can be achieved only in the presence of such a basis

17. See Yehuda Bauer, "Right and Wrong Teaching of the Holocaust," in *The Lesson of the Holocaust* (Philadelphia: National Institute on the Holocaust, Oct. 1978), p. 3–5 (hereafter cited as "Right and Wrong Teaching").

of similarity—be it similarity of situation, of systems of thought, or of logic and rules of play—or the similarity arising from the fact that all men are human beings whose instincts and reactions bear a certain resemblance to one another. By its very definition, the term "Holocaust" cancels the possibility of simulation if the subject is outside the realm of one's experience and universe of discourse, imagination, and reason. Therefore every attempt to simulate another planet, possessing a logic and legitimacy of its own and a uniqueness born out of its deviation from norms accepted and recognized by the human race since time immemorial, seems to create oversimplicated attempts of imposing a nonexistent identity between simulation and reality. Ruling simulation out does not destroy the basis for any moral judgment but prevents the students from assuming the unjustifiable role of prosecutors, defenders, and judges of matters which are totally beyond their emphatic judgment and with which they cannot possibly identify.

IMPORTANCE OF WELL-ORGANIZED OBJECTIVES

In developing a special and unique message of the Holocaust for our generation, four main objectives should be mentioned which might help the teachers in deciding between the various alternatives:

1. Students should demand better information, especially regarding the dangers of wide-spreading neo-Nazi literature, which tries to diminish or even to deny the very existence of the Holocaust.[18] Al-though better information would not be helpful in the case of neo-Nazis, this demand seems to have become more relevant than it had been 20 years ago when the remembrance of the Holocaust was still alive in almost everyone. At present, many people do not really know even the most basic facts, and they might be the first to be the victims of that neo-Nazi literature.

2. Students should understand and be sensible to those structures and mechanisms that underlie illegitimate generalizations, conceptualizations, and stereotypings in the realm of human relations, prejudice, hatred, fear, and the drive to destroy. It is the reflective examination of those structures that should be regarded as the universal lesson of the Holocaust, relevant to every human being and to any system of education that derives its orientation from past mistakes and blunders. It is a lesson on the image of man and human nature which we have to learn through the Holocaust.

3. Students should be aware of the connection between those structures and mechanisms and the totalitarian regimes built according to them and, in turn, serving them. They should become conscious of the dangers of myths, mass hysteria, personality cults, and of breaking away from personal moral standards and personal responsibility by creating ethics either of the state or of racial teleology.

4. Students should be sensitive to the impact of blatant antisemitism.

---

18. See Hermann Langbein, "Literaturbericht, Überblick über neonazistische Literatur," in Zeitgeschichte, Juni/Juli 1975, Heft 9/10, Historisches Institut der Universität Salzburg; see also, Ino Arndt/Wolfgang Scheffler, "Organisierter Massenmord an Juden in nationalsozialistischen Vernichtungslager," in: aus politik und zeitgeschichte, B 19/76.

The persecution and mass murder of all Jews without any differentiation and exception has never been a marginal aspect of the Nazi ideology and the policy of the Third Reich. Jews were not just a by-product of the war and did not fall into the category of class struggle, policy toward minorities, war victims, or any other general term that tries to avoid the confrontation with the core of the so-called Holocaust.

To bring students to an honest existential confrontation with the phenomenon of antisemitism, its roots, history, and relevance, and with the murder of the European Jewry, not by an anonymous apparatus but by men, citizens, fathers, husbands, and sons, with the silent consensus of many millions and a whole world standing aside, would be perhaps a universal, not just Jewish, objective.[19] This, regardless of the ideological and political conclusions, may differ from country to country or from group to group.

19. *See* Bauer, "Right and Wrong Teaching," p. 6.

ANNALS, AAPSS, **450**, July 1980

Problems in Coping with the Holocaust: Experiences with Students in a Multinational Program

By ARYE CARMON

ABSTRACT: Ever since the end of the Holocaust we have been forced to confront the penetrating question, Does pedagogy have a special and unique task in the education of man in the world after Auschwitz? The program "Teaching the Holocaust as Education Toward Values" has been developed over the past three years in various educational settings in three different countries: the United States, Germany, and Israel. In order to overcome the problems in coping with this unique theme in the classroom, we have used as a guiding principle the placing of adolescents at the focal point of the educational process. Beyond the differences in the cultural backgrounds and emotional attachments, students in all three countries underwent a similar process: giving up preconceived judgments and stereotypes and replacing them with an effort toward critical thinking. As one of the students expressed: "Auschwitz is the furthest end of a human continuum. I am obliged to do everything I can to prevent the human degeneration toward it."

Arye Carmon is presently a senior lecturer in the Department of Education at Ben Gurion University of the Negev and is fellow researcher at the Van Leer Jerusalem Foundation. He was born in Jerusalem in 1943 and obtained his Ph.D. in history at the University of Wisconsin. He is currently directing the final stages of a cross-cultural study on the effects of a Holocaust curriculum in three countries, is coeditor of a forthcoming account on education in Israel, and is the author of various articles on the role of German higher learning during the Nazi Era and on the educational means of coping with the Holocaust.

IN 1945 the crematoria of the un-precedented, horrific factory of death had just ceased to burn when Carl Jung concluded his article "Nach der Katastrophe" with the following sentences:

. . . We must all open our eyes to the shadow who looms behind contemporary man. We have no need to hold up the devil's mask before the Germans. . . .

Everything possible has been done for the outside world: science has been refined to an unimaginable extent, technical achievement has reached an almost uncanny degree of perfection. But what of man, who is expected to administer all these blessings in a reasonable way? He has simply been taken for granted. No one has stopped to consider that neither morally nor psychologically is he in any way adapted to such changes. As blithely as any child of nature he sets about enjoying these dangerous playthings, completely oblivious to the shadow lurking behind him, ready to seize them in its greedy grasp and turn them against a still infantile and unconscious humanity. . . . The question remains: How am I to live with this shadow? What attitude is required if I am to be able to live in spite of evil? In order to find valid answers to these questions a complete spiritual renewal is needed. And this cannot be given gratis, each man must strive to achieve it for himself.[1]

THE EDUCATIONAL CHALLENGE OF COPING WITH THE HOLOCAUST

Ever since the end of the Holocaust we have been forced to confront the penetrating question, Does pedagogy have a special and unique task in the education of man in the world after Auschwitz? The first generation of the aftermath has made many efforts to answer this ques-

tion, however minute their efforts may be vis-à-vis the magnitude of the challenge. Lately such efforts—along with a spate of attempts to deny that the Holocaust ever happened—have reached a peak. The educational programs and/or Holocaust units that are sprouting in various frameworks have now joined the broad spectrum of attempts to confront the phenomenon of the Holocaust, which has recently included even a commercial television production. This display of current interest sharpens the urgency of a few fundamental questions and dilemmas that must be met primarily by those engaged in the field of education.

1. What are the educational objectives in grappling with the phenomenon?

2. Should it be taught as a mere historical event? Is it a mere historical event?

3. How do we cope with the insoluble dilemma of the unique and the universal? The Holocaust with its magnitude and evil, being hitherto the only attempt at the systematic murder of a people, is by its very nature unique. The quest to seriously draw meaningful moral lessons in a world that had witnessed such a phenomenon in its midst forces its universal nature. Are we then to divorce the unique from the universal or learn to cope with the inseparable?

4. Finally, how can any educational objectives be achieved without running the risk of vulgarizing attitudes toward this subject?

Now, one generation after Auschwitz, there is a feeling—so it appears—that we are living in a transitional era: a transformation from simply knowing to being aware of. As the tragedy is further removed each day, and as the physical fades

1. Carl Jung, "Nach der Katastrophe" in *Neue Schweizer Rundschau*, n.s. XIII (Zurich), pp. 67–88.

into the metaphysical, the impossibility of comprehending the facts is turning into the possibility of fostering the awareness of their implications.

The program "Teaching the Holocaust as Education Toward Values" has emerged from the assumptions inherent in such reflections. Our guideline in developing this program has been values education. By this we mean aiding the individual student in formulating a set of moral rules for himself through a meaningful confrontation with the Holocaust. The student thus deals with the Holocaust through a series of moral dilemmas.

THE VALUES EDUCATION APPROACH

The guiding principle for the entire educational program has been to place the adolescent student at the focal point of the educational process. It is the student for whom the phenomenon should have meaning and implications; it is the student who in his future life, it is hoped, will be able to draw upon the lessons of the Holocaust. In other words, throughout the entire learning process of our program the student is meant to ask himself, whether directly or indirectly, What does this mean to me?

The concept for this pedagogical principle is based on the following Eriksonian argument:

In youth, the life history intersects with history; here individuals are confirmed in their identities and societies regenerated in their life style, historical processes have already entered the individual's core of childhood. Past history survives in the ideal and evil prototypes. . . . Historians on the whole make little of this; they account only for the content of autonomous historical ideas and are unconcerned with the fact

that these ideas reach down into the lives of generations and re-emerge through the daily awakening and training of historical consciousness in young individuals. . . . To enter history, each generation of youth must find an identity consonant with its own childhood and consonant with an ideological promise in the perceptible historical process. But in youth the tables of childhood dependence begin slowly to turn: no longer is it merely for the old to teach the young the meaning of life. It is the young who, by their responses and actions, tell the old whether life as represented to them has some vital promise, and it is the young who carry in them the power to confirm those who confirm them, to renew and regenerate, to disavow what is rotten, to reform and rebel.[2]

This principle generated the more specific educational objectives of our program. These are divided into the program's two main dimensions: the Universal Dimension and the Jewish Dimension.

The objectives: Universal and Jewish Dimensions

"The major objective of the Universal Dimension is to heighten the student's awareness of the critical function of individual responsibility in a democratic society."[3] This objective is to be achieved through fostering the student's awareness of the human tendency toward stereotyping, prejudice, ethnocentrism, and obeying authority and thus escaping responsibility, in short, through fostering critical thinking. Thus "The attainment of this objective is a dynamic process in which the utilization of critical thinking is fundamental. Critical thinking is thus re-

2. Erik Erikson, *Identity, Youth and Crisis* (New York: W. W. Norton, 1968), pp. 257–58.
3. Arye Carmon, "The Teaching of the Holocaust as Education Toward Values," unpublished pamphlet, (Van Leer Jerusalem Foundation, 1977).

garded as a skill essential to the internalization of the value of individual responsibility. Critical thinking is also regarded as the necessary mode of treatment for the entire educational process."[4]

"The various units of the Jewish Dimension are designed to assist and heighten the development of Jewish identity in the Jewish adolescent. Along with the development of Jewish identity, the objective of this part is to foster the acceptance of the Jewish value of individual responsibility to community as well as participation in the collective responsibility that binds the Jewish people 'Arevut Hadadit.' "[5] This objective is to be achieved through the understanding of the following: (1) the special nature of the relationship between the individual and his community in the Jewish tradition; (2) the nature of coping with existential problems in the Jewish tradition, both on the physical and the spiritual level; and (3) the implications of being a minority.

The method

The method of the program is a combination of learning by inquiry and working in groups. Each of the program's units is divided into several subunits and the class is divided into workshops, each dealing with one subunit. Thus three concentric circles emerge: individual work, workshops, and integrative discussions. In other words, in the inner circle each individual student deals with one specific document; in the middle circle a small and intimate group of students is able to exchange feelings and opinions; and finally, in the outer circle, the entire class completes the discussions of the topic at hand. This method, when coupled with the contents of the program, realizes what we call a dialectic confluence:

The students' first task is to familiarize themselves with the content. This is a classic, intellectual task and places the student's task in the cognitive domain. But dealing with the content implies coming into contact with material that arouses a sense of familiarity in the student. The content in the first units is not alien to the students and they cannot remain apathetic to it. Thus, the factors contained in the content are meant to generate a transition from the intellectual-abstract to the affective-concrete. In the affective realm, the students face questions and moral dilemmas that are relevant to their own lives. Elucidating these moral dilemmas means coming to terms with the relevance that the material holds for the student. This elucidation manifests itself in the dialogue between the students and their own conscience, and between students and their colleagues, that is repeated in all the units. It is meant to be carried out within a framework synthesized from both the cognitive and affective domains as the highest phase of this dialectic confluence. In other words, "social experience" is generated by a thought process in which a constant balance is maintained between the cognitive and the affective.[6]

The program

The following is an outline of the program. The first two parts form the Universal Dimension, the following two form the Jewish Dimension, and the fifth part relates to both.

4. Ibid.
5. Ibid.

6. Arye Carmon, "Teaching the Holocaust as a Means of Fostering Values," *Curriculum Inquiry* 9(3):225 (1979).

Part I. The meaning of life in the irrational entity
Unit 1: The roots; Unit 2: The captive youth; Unit 3: Fostering the antirational; Unit 4: The "us" versus the "them"
Part II. The executors of the murder
Unit 5: The social conditioning of the SS man; Unit 6: The murder of a people
Part III. The way of life of a Jewish community in the pre-Holocaust Era
Unit 7: A model of a Jewish community; Unit 8: Various answers to existential questions
Part IV. Moral dilemmas of groups and individuals during the Holocaust
Unit 9: Annihilation of a community; Unit 10: Dehumanization
Part V. Moral challenges after the Holocaust

THE PROJECT: A THREE-COUNTRY REPORT

The program has been experimented with in a series of trial runs in three different countries: the United States, Germany, and Israel. At this point in the development of the program, educational institutions in two additional countries are exploring the possibility of joining the project: Holland and England. Dealing with a variety of student populations with different cultural backgrounds and different emotional relationships to the Holocaust and studying in different educational systems, challenged us to adjust the program accordingly. The modular manner in which the program has been structured enabled us to omit and add units as the necessity arose.

Israel

The country on which the Holocaust left its most dramatic and traumatic imprint on the collective level is Israel. It appears that this impact generates not only the emotionally filled attitude and behavior of those individuals who are closely related to it—children of survivors, relatives, and so forth—but it has much wider implications as well, such as influencing, even if indirectly, political judgments. The role of the Holocaust as a component in the national consciousness over the last three decades is an intriguing theme still open for research. The problematic role of the Holocaust in Israel must be reflected on the educational level.

The powerful impact of the phenomenon in Israel and the implications that evolved from its uniqueness as a phenomenon incomprehensible to the human mind were a dangerous base for the emergence of generalities, myths, rationalizations, and stereotypic attitudes. For many years the German appeared as part of the so-called syndrome of the "other planet." That is, Auschwitz, an inconceivable phenomenon, could only have been created by beasts of another world. Solving the problem by relegating it to another world, however, is not coping with it but escaping from it. Such a solution excludes any possibility of a significant value judgment.

Ironically, the Israeli image of the Jewish victim is also comprised of negative stereotypes. A survey conducted at the outset of the project among Israeli high school students exposed the shocking fact that many adolescents hold stereotypes of the Jews as strong as any to be found in *Der Stürmer*. This attitude to the Diaspora Jew is rooted in one of the themes of Zionist ideology: the negation of the Diaspora. Thus the student in Israel, ever since the pre-State era and even before the Holocaust, has been confronted in his textbooks with negative aspects of Jewish life in exile. This attitude is strengthened by the continuous emphasis on the active resistance of the few thereby implying the passive submission of the masses.

Stereotyped views and generalized axioms create—at least superficially—a paradoxical symmetry between the victim and the murderer. For example, the assertion that "the creation of Auschwitz is an act rooted in the German mentality" perpetuates the negative image of the Germans, while the question, "Why did they go off like sheep to the slaughter?" nurtures the negative image of the Jews.[7]

In Israel the teaching of the Holocaust became a compulsory 30-hour unit for senior high school classes only in 1979. Up until then it was included in history and literature classes as the teacher saw fit. As we have argued previously, it seems reasonable that the explanation for this delay is the impossibility of dealing with facts when we are too close to the event.

Our project is at an advanced stage. In the spring of 1980, the Department of Curriculum of the Ministry of Education published the program in two volumes. This year we have 40 classes participating in the project. The project has completed its first stage: the designing and adjusting of the program to the Israeli scene. It is now in its second stage, the main purpose of which is evaluating the achievements of the program's declared objectives.

An integral part of the development of the program is the teacher's training. The teacher's role in leading a values education program differs from that of a conventional teacher. For values education, the teacher should develop an aware-

ness of his own attitudes before attempting to guide others. In our specific case, a precondition to implementing the project in the classroom has been to confront the teachers with their own preconceived judgments and stereotypes.

The teacher's training is based on two methods: (1) the teacher experiencing the program in a simulated classroom situation. When the teacher plays the role of his students, he confronts his own stereotypes. Once having faced his stereotypes, he is able to perceive his role in the classroom in a different light. (2) The teacher's training continues throughout the program. He is thus able to discuss his experiences with those of his colleagues as the program progresses.

Along with this year's experiment, we are developing a comprehensive teacher's guide that, in the future, should replace the training sessions.

Germany

Europe singles out Germany as the land and the people that are enveloped in a cloud of guilt, for the horror happened in Germany and its perpetrators were Germans. No German can deny this, any more than a European or a Christian can deny that the most monstrous crime of all ages was committed in his house.[8]

Experimenting with the program "Teaching the Holocaust as Education Toward Values" in Germany has in many respects been our most challenging experience. It has attempted to free the individual German student from the influences of tendencies prevalent in Germany for over a generation—to collectively repress the Nazi past. Through the

7. Ibid., p. 211.

8. Ibid.

students' confrontation with specific events that are embarrassing for them, they are aided in formulating universal, moral rules necessary for a member of the post-Holocaust human race and a future citizen of a democratic society.

External symptoms of the repression included the prohibition to utilize primary sources from the Nazi Era, such as excerpts from *Mein Kampf*, and authentic Nazi films. More significant symptoms, however, were exposed in the classroom in the initial stages of the program when students had difficulty in dealing with the subject matter. Our approach, that of placing the student at the very heart of the program, has helped to overcome this problem. The main thrust of the program has been the meaning of the subject matter for the student rather than the subject matter itself. Other sources of assistance in overcoming difficulties in Germany have been the involvement of one of the most important educators in Germany today[9] as well as the readiness and openness of the teachers who have participated in the project. The teachers are in their thirties, hold similar liberal political and pedagogical views, and are committed to the project.

At the outset of the trial runs in Germany we defined our objectives in the following way:

. . . to confront the student with the contemporary tendency to deny the phenomenon of the Holocaust and/or the avoidance of dealing with the valuable significance this theme contains for the German people, to foster the awareness of the possible development of an irrational entity within a society which contributed tremendously to Western thought and culture.

In any and all of the above categories the focus of the educational process is the student, and the orientation is toward the future.[10]

In Germany, as in Israel, the project is now in its second stage. Currently we have 10 classes in Tübingen. They include mostly eleventh-grade classes, a few classes in the final year of high school, and a few tenth-grade classes, all in comprehensive schools and gymnasien and 15 classes in Berlin, only in gymnasien. The teacher's training in Germany has been conducted in the same way as in Israel. While simulated classroom situations in Israel exposed teachers to their own stereotypes, in Germany they helped the teachers face their inhibitions in dealing with the subject. Both in Israel and in Germany the concept of final examinations (*Bagrut* and *Abitur*) dominates the instructors' pedagogical attitudes. This, coupled with the fact that the timetable does not include values education as a teaching area, reenforces the necessity for the teacher to redefine his role in the classroom.

Teachers' involvement in the adjustment of the program to the German scene exceeded what we had expected. It included many detailed reports on almost every unit and included several suggestions for the German edition of the textbook. In addition, we had the benefit of the evaluation of university students who sat in some of the classrooms as outside observers.

The most interesting parts of the reports that we received from Germany were the reactions of the students. These included their tendency

---

9. Professor Hellmut Becker, Director of the Max Planck Institute for Bildungsforschung in Berlin.

10. Carmon, "The Teaching of the Holocaust as Education Toward Values."

to talk about themselves and to draw analogies to present situations. One of the reactions in an advanced stage of the program was the question, Why did not the Jews resist? This question might be an indication of the students' ability to free themselves from their own past. Another sign of the deep involvement of the students in one specific class was their suggestion to use their parents' schoolbooks as the basis for the discussion on indoctrination in the schools. Another reaction, albeit exceptional, was the initiative of one of the classes to conclude the course by traveling to the concentration camp Theresienstadt in Czechoslovakia.

In the final analysis, the overall reaction of the German students did not much differ from their peers' in other countries. As elsewhere, the most important thing was the students' ability to responsibly draw moral conclusions.

The United States

The many attempts in the last few years to develop teaching units and curricula about the Holocaust in the United States is another indication of the ever-growing awareness of the Holocaust. Endeavors in the United States are of a large variety. They include many Jewish educational settings and pioneering breakthroughs in public schools, such as those in Philadelphia, followed by those in New York City and Brookline, Massachusetts, to name only a few. This large variety of locations raises the question about the role of the Holocaust in the collective consciousness of the world's largest democracy and about how this role reflects the changes realized on its values scale. This discussion, however, exceeds the bounds of this article. We can

nevertheless assess these background factors that were exposed throughout our trial runs in as far as they influenced the process of adjusting our program to the American scene.

Our experiments took place in Los Angeles and they were divided into two categories: classes in various Jewish educational settings and in public schools. As far as the former are concerned, it is interesting to compare the emotional reactions which are prevalent among Jewish parents in the United States with those which exist in Israel. We have argued that in Israel the paths of relating to the Holocaust are saturated with negative stereotypes. We have also argued that this trend and the tendency to rationalize and generalize stem from distress and ambivalency, which prevail in the Israeli collective consciousness. What we found in our classes is that whereas the stereotypic image of the German is the same for both the Israeli and the American Jew, the image of the Eastern European Jew is not. In Israel, the prominent view of the Eastern European Jew is that of one who passively went to the slaughter; in America, the image of the Eastern European Jew is one of a martyr. However, in both cases Jewish students were reluctant to identify with the Nazi victims.

In Jewish school classes, but much more prominently in American public school classes, the problematic interaction between the unique and the universal emerged. The tendency toward universalization of the phenomenon was exposed through analogies with discrimination toward American minorities. It has been our opinion that whereas these analogies are legitimate in part, they must follow from the whole process of learning but they should by no means be a point of departure in dealing with the Holocaust. The latter case is one of the roots of the vulgarization of the phenomenon.

Our work in Los Angeles was one of the first trial runs. The workshop with the teachers, including the ongoing contact with the teachers in the first year of the project, formed the concept of teachers' training in all the three countries. In Los Angeles we also experimented with the integration of informal settings in the program. Students were involved with the topic of the Holocaust for either a full day or an entire weekend outside the classroom. During these sessions they were given the chance to read texts, have discussions with Holocaust survivors, and view authentic films and slides. Most importantly, they could conduct informal discussions among themselves regarding the implications of the material, without being limited either by the framework of a classroom or by time.

AN INTERIM CONCLUSION

During the years of experimentation we have recorded many unexpected reactions among the students in the three countries. In retrospect these have formed other pedagogical challenges resulting from a significant confrontation with the Holocaust as subject matter in the classroom.

Beyond the specific reactions, it seems feasible, based on our experiences, to carefully analyze what happened to the students who were confronted with the Holocaust through a values education approach.

In all the classes in which the program was tested, the students had already had some previous knowledge of the Holocaust; the differences were quantitative only. In all

cases, the students had ambivalent feelings at the outset of the program. While they were reluctant to deal with the subject, they strongly wished to be given explanations and answers. During the first stages of the program the reluctance toward the subject increased. Students tended to resist giving up their protection, whether in the form of stereotypic attitudes or of repression. Their struggle was directed against the program's stand that Auschwitz was established on this earth and by human beings. This assertion, which is the precondition for reaching a significant value judgment, neutralizes those defense mechanisms that differentiate between the "us" and the "them." Gradually, however, this resistance began to fade, only to be replaced by a feeling of helplessness. At this point, when the student had thrown away his crutch, he opened himself to the possibility of critical thinking and moral judgment. "Auschwitz," as one of the students expressed, "is the furthest end of a human continuum. I am obliged to do everything I can to prevent the human degeneration toward it."

Against this background we can cautiously attempt to formulate the universal rule of confronting moral dilemmas. In most of the cases, when the unavoidable question, How would I have behaved if I had been in this situation? arises, the student finds himself in a cul-du-sac and must answer, "I don't know." Nevertheless, this dead end forces the student to examine the human motivation behind the behavior he is confronted with. Through the clarification of this motivation, the universal question can be asked: How should I have behaved? Thus, for instance, when the student begins to empathize with his peer in the Third Reich and begins to understand the indoctrination methods that were used to prevent his free thinking, he can begin to apply the answer to the question for moral behavior. On the other hand, when at another point in the program he is faced with the terrible dilemma of the Jewish *Judenrat* (Jewish Council), he can again ask himself what moral behavior in this case means.

In the final analysis, placing the student at the focus of the educational process when the subject matter is the Holocaust has enabled the realization of the ineffectual manner in which we have related to the phenomenon until now. It has stimulated the confrontation with significant moral rules. It has opened up the possibility of perceiving a personal ability to cope with ambiguous situations. It has shown that, in dealing with the Holocaust, formulating questions is more important than providing answers. And beyond all this, it has reenforced the need to grapple with a problematic theme of which only the tip of the iceberg has been exposed in the classroom.

ANNALS, AAPSS, 450, July 1980

The Holocaust: Rescue and Relief
Documentation in the National Archives

By JOHN MENDELSOHN

ABSTRACT: The National Archives is a major center for the study of the Holocaust. Records on the subject are scattered throughout its vast holdings in several locations and no general finding aid exists. Researchers have explored the records of the killing and the destruction of nearly six million Jews in some detail, but have neglected records dealing with rescue and relief attempts. Hence this article focuses on the latter topic by delineating where in the National Archives one may find such documentation. Foremost are the records of the War Refugee Board, which was created in early 1944 to provide avenues of rescue and relief to the Jews in Nazi-controlled Europe. Other records concern the emigration of Jews from Nazi Germany, the Evian Conference and the subsequent Schacht-Rublee negotiations, the Haavara agreements on emigration to Palestine, and the trip to Havana and return of the S.S. *St. Louis*. There are many other records, including those on the deals the SS was willing to make by trading Jewish lives for needed commodities. More articles that present overviews of significant segments of Holocaust records in the National Archives are needed for a comprehensive introduction of these holdings to researchers.

John Mendelsohn was born in Berlin, Germany, and has lived in the United States over 25 years. He received his Ph.D. from the University of Maryland in 1974 and wrote his dissertation about the documentation of the Nuremberg trials. He has taught in various institutions including the American University in Washington, D.C. At present he is the archivist in charge of war crimes records in the National Archives. He has prepared many archival publications dealing with war crimes and related topics. Among these have been the microfilm pamphlets United States of America v. Karl Brandt et al., Erhard Milch, *and* Oswald Pohl et al., *and the Nuernberg NM Prosecution Document Series.*

NONE OF the many collections of records in the National Archives and Records Service in Washington, D.C., pertains exclusively to the Holocaust, that unique event which not only constitutes the most terrifying phenomenon in human history but which also has grown into a distinct and separate field of scholarly endeavor. Nonetheless, the documents dealing with the episode and deposited in the institution amount to far over a million pages.

HOLDINGS OF THE NATIONAL ARCHIVES

By virtue of these large holdings alone, the National Archives has become one of the world's major centers of scholarly activities and sources for the Holocaust. Most of these sources are records of the perpetrators but they also include documentation of observers and victims.

Trial records

The Nuremberg trial records, for example, occupy an important place among this Holocaust documentation.[1] An indispensable guide, prepared by the cooperative effort of Yad Vashem in Jerusalem and Yivo in New York, describes these records that include many of the standard reports so well known and so often used by researchers and students of the Holocaust.[2] They contain

the notorious pictorial report on the destruction of the Warsaw ghetto by SS Brigadier General Jürgen Stroop, edited and published recently by Sybil Milton of the Leo Baeck Institute in New York. The report documents not only the terrible plight of the ghetto dwellers, but also the military effort of the SS in the destruction of the ghetto and the utilization of Ukrainian auxiliaries in the brutal endeavor.[3] A transcribed copy with handwritten outline notes of Reichsleader of the SS Heinrich Himmler's infamous speech to the SS generals at Posen in October, 1943, in which he quite openly referred to the meaning of the Final Solution, complements this collection. The chief exterminator praised his generals who had all seen mountains of dead Jews but who had remained "decent and loyal" to the Final Solution at the same time.[4]

Other Nuremberg trial records include the report by Hermann Friedrich Graebe, an engineer who managed a German construction firm in the Ukraine, which describes in graphic detail the murderous activities of an SS Einsatzkommando.[5] A number of Nuremberg documents demonstrate how Nazi racism went to the extreme of killing 112 Jews for the sole purpose of obtaining

1. John Mendelsohn, "The Holocaust in War Crimes Trials Documentation" (Unpublished paper presented to the 1976 Annual Scholars Conference on the Church Struggle and the Holocaust in New York City).
2. Jacob Robinson and Henry Sachs, The Holocaust The Nuernberg Evidence Part I Documents (Jerusalem: Yad Vashem and Yivo, 1976).

3. Nuernberg Prosecution Document 1061PS, "The Warsaw Ghetto is No More," report by SS and Police Leader Warsaw District, 16 May 1943, National Archives and Records Service, Record Group 238, National Archives Collection of World War II War Crimes Records (hereafter cited as NARG 238).
4. Nuernberg Prosecution Document 1919PS, speech by Heinrich Himmler in Posen to SS Generals, 4 Oct. 1943, NARG 238.
5. Nuernberg Prosecution Document 2992PS, Two Affidavits by Hermann Friedrich Gräbe on Massacre of Jews in Rovno and Dubno, 10 Nov. 1945, NARG 238.

their skeletons for a collection at the University of Strassbourg.[6]

The Nuremberg records amount to many thousand documents of which over 18,000 alone served as prosecution exhibits in the 13 proceedings against war criminals there.[7] These documents form the core of the Holocaust records in the National Archives. They have many good additional finding aids and indexes, for example, *Special List No. 42* which represents a one-volume, item-by-item description of the records of the *Einsatzgruppen* case in which 22 members of these mobile murder commandos who killed nearly a million Jews in the Soviet Union stood trial.[8]

Records of the Office of Military Government for Germany (United States)

Yet the Nuremberg records do not constitute the only source of Holocaust documents in the National Archives. There are many other important collections of records dealing with the Holocaust, for example, the OMGUS records, the records of the Office of Military Government for Germany (United States). They contain pawnshop tickets from the official pawn office in Berlin for bags with gold, silver, plate, jewelry,

and other valuables.[9] The SS had taken these from the wretched Jews before gassing or shooting them and had deposited the jewelry at the official pawn office in Berlin in order to convert it eventually into cash on national or neutral markets.[10]

SS Captain Bruno Mellmer delivered other valuables and dental gold removed from the jaws of dead Jews to the *Reichsbank* to credit the proceeds to the account of one Max Heiliger, a totally fictitious person.[11] A team of German archivists and historians described these records on data sheets at the General Archives Division in Suitland, Maryland, and the National Archives produced additional descriptive inventories.

Heinrich Himmler's official files, microfilmed at Alexandria, Virginia, are replete with documentation on the ill treatment and destruction the SS visited on Europe's Jews. Several guides from the captured records series constitute excellent finding aids for these records. Another collection, the records of the German foreign ministry contain many items on the final solution to the Jewish question. The killing of Jewish children and the only extant copy of the Wannsee Protocol, which welded together efforts of many Nazi governmental agencies in order to make possible the extermination of the Jews or their possible shipment to Madagascar,

---

6. Nuernberg Prosecution Documents NO 085 to NO 091, File pertaining to Skeleton Collection at the University of Strassbourg, 5 Feb. 1942 to October 1944, NARG 238.

7. John Mendelsohn, "Trial by Document: The Problem of Due Process for War Criminals at Nuernberg," *Prologue* (Winter 1975), p. 228.

8. *Nuernberg War Crimes Trials Records of Case 9: United States of America v. Otto Ohlendorf et al. Special List No. 42*, comp. John Mendelsohn, National Archives and Records Service, (hereafter cited as NARS), General Services Administration [GSA], 1978).

9. Official Pawnbroker tickets, Berlin, various dates, Records of the Finance Division of the Office of Military Government for Germany (U.S.) (OMGUS) NARG 260, Records of the United States Occupation Headquarters, World War II.

10. Raul Hilberg, *The Destruction of the European Jews* (Chicago: Quadrangle Books, 1979), pp. 616–17.

11. Ibid.

are included in the holocaustal part of this collection.[12] The well-known Kent Catalog, a four-volume compendium, indexes these documents.[13]

U.S. Army

Finally, the records of the U.S. Army commands include 10 folders with records collected by the U.S. Army in connection with the extradition of about two dozen war crimes suspects from the U. S. Zone of Occupation in Germany to Poland to stand trial there for crimes committed at the Auschwitz Concentration Camp. Among the documents are files recommending camp staff for the war Merit Cross, including Dr. Mengele, the "Angel of Death," for his "exemplary medical work."[14] This record group has no published finding aids or indexes.

As the records cited so far represent just the barest sampling of the National Archives' Holocaust holdings, it becomes clear that a short article cannot do justice to listing and describing all the records. It appears necessary therefore to concentrate on one specific area of the Holocaust only. As the records concerned with attempts to rescue individuals from extermination and to relieve their suffering do not seem as fully explored and utilized as, for example, those dealing with the

actual extermination processes, this article will henceforth concentrate on the former. Rescue includes both attempts by the suffering Jews themselves through emigration and the efforts of other countries or agencies to relieve their plight. Despite the reduction in scope, the size of the various collections and the variety of records contained therein necessitate that this article can only highlight the more important areas.

War Refugee Board

The National Archives' Franklin D. Roosevelt Library in New York's beautiful Hudson Valley houses the records of the War Refugee Board that constitutes the central, but by no means the only, collection of documents pertaining to rescue. The War Refugee Board evolved as a response to many pressures. These encompassed a more detailed knowledge by U.S. authorities of the extent of the Nazi extermination program, cries for help from the American Jewish community, humanitarian considerations, and the desire to take the lead in aiding the victims so that other nations would follow suit without the United States alone having to accept hundreds of thousands of helpless, demoralized survivors. On the whole, the administration acted slowly in forming the board, and their fears of resurrecting the old taint, "Jew Deal," impeded its creation.[15]

When formally established in January, 1944, the War Refugee Board embodied nonetheless the secretaries of state, the Treasury Department, and the War Department as policymakers. During the

12. Wannsee Protocol and related Records, National Archives Microfilm Publication T120, Records of the German Foreign Ministry, Serial K797, Frames k210398-499.

13. *A Catalog of Files and Microfilms of the German Foreign Ministry Archives 1920–1945*, comp. and ed. George O. Kent, 4 vols. (Stanford: Hoover Institution, 1962–1972).

14. Investigative Records of Auschwitz Concentration Camp Personnel, various dates, European Command War Crimes Records, National Archives and Record Group 338, Records of the United States Army Commands 1942–.

15. Henry L. Feingold, *The Politics of Rescue: The Roosevelt Administration and the Holocaust 1938–1945* (New Brunswick: Rutgers University Press, 1970), p. 9.

first year of its existence, John W. Pehle, assistant secretary of the Treasury, directed the board's activities whereas Brigadier General William O'Dwyer did so until the dissolution of the board in the fall of 1945. The board acted through attachés for refugees accredited with diplomatic status to U.S. embassies and legations in strategic areas in foreign countries, such as neutral nations, recently conquered areas, and Allied countries.

The board's main concerns focused on arriving at effective means for rescue of victims of Nazi oppression and the establishment of refugee camps and temporary safe havens. The board cooperated in these endeavors not only with other governments but also with private individuals and organizations and the Vatican. It established a safe haven in Oswego, New York, for 1,000 refugees outside the quotas to which immigration laws restricted the acceptance of refugees in this country.[16]

In view of the massive genocide perpetrated by the Nazis, one must sum up the board's effectiveness as being too little and too late. Nonetheless, the records of the War Refugee Board, amounting to about 45 linear feet, document both the failures and the successes of the agency. The central files of the board, known as general correspondence, make up about a quarter of the records in this collection. They include correspondence with agencies concerned with relief and rescue, for example, the American Jewish Committee, the World Jewish Congress, and the American Jewish Joint Distribution Committee, especially relating to the evacuation of Jewish children from France.

Other records deal with con-

16. Ibid., p. 263.

centration camps and the issue of licenses to relief organizations pursuant to relief recommendations of the War Refugee Board, relief and rescue efforts for Hungarian Jews, media output on rescue, requests for specific aid, and many other items.

A file almost as large as the general correspondence is the projects and documents file. These records deal with cooperative efforts of the United States at relief and rescue with other nations, particularly neutral European countries including Spain, Sweden, Switzerland, Turkey, and Latin American states. Other records concern attempts to halt further persecution, especially in Hungary, by such means as issuing visas or other national identification to persecutees or by negotiations with the oppressors.

The records further delineate Red Cross aid to concentration camps, relief channeled through Switzerland, and relief to Jews in Holland. They document evacuation of Jews through Spain and Portugal and transfer of Jews from Tansnistria and elsewhere to Turkey and Switzerland.

Other relief and rescue programs documented include the establishment of temporary havens in North Africa, the United States, and elsewhere and the permanent settlement of Jews in Palestine, Mexico, and the United States.

In addition to the general correspondence and project and document files, the records contain a personal papers file of Roswell D. McClelland, the board's special representative in Bern, dealing with various aspects of the plight of European Jews and the many attempts at relief and rescue. Other files pertain to the admission of refugees to the United States outside the quota system; the abortive proposal by Joel Brand, a Hungarian Jew, to trade 10,000 trucks and other materials to be used by the Nazis on the eastern front for the lives of Hungarian Jews; financial records; a history of the War Refugee Board; and other subjects. A published inventory and a very useful shelf list facilitate intelligent research. Especially helpful to this end, too, are available indexes.[17]

The records of the War Relocation Authority, which ran various camps with luckless Japanese-American inmates and also administered the Refugee Shelter at Oswego, New York, and of the War Refugee Board are mixed together. They contain documentation on the inception of the idea of free ports or temporary havens for Jews in the United States and the establishment and operation of the Oswego Shelter.[18]

Others: documents and relief attempts

The remaining records on relief and rescue in the National Archives deal with a very large variety of topics. Some of the major events documented concern the emigration of Jews from Nazi Germany during the prewar era, including such topics as the Evian Conference and the subsequent Schacht-Rublee negotiations, the Haavara agreements on emigration to Palestine, and the trip to Havana and the return of the S.S. St. Louis. Other documents inform

of the attempts by various countries and individuals to alleviate the suffering of the Hungarian Jews, by enabling some to emigrate, and of deals the SS was willing to make by trading Jewish lives for needed commodities. Attempts to rescue Jewish children and to stop the carnage by bombing railroad centers leading to Auschwitz and the slaughterhouse itself constitute frightening additions to the record of man's inhumanity to man.

Evian-les-Bains Conference

As the persecution of Jews in Germany accelerated, pressures in the United States increased to extend help to the sufferers. Responding to this pressure, President Roosevelt called for an international conference in the spring of 1938 for the purpose of facilitating the emigration of Jews from Nazi Germany. The conference took place later in the summer in Evian-les-Bains in France. Several of the participating nations accepted Roosevelt's call only conditionally. Great Britain did not wish the Palestine question discussed, France wanted prior consultation, and other countries expressed their reluctance to accept additional refugees. Italy refused to attend the conference and Germany received no invitation.[19]

Since the Nazis forced Jewish emigrants to leave their financial assets behind, most countries refused to accept penniless Jews. As a consequence, the conference did not produce many positive results. In fact, Adolf Hitler and Nazi propaganda minister Joseph Goebbels taunted the nations attending the Evian Conference for talking with

17. These finding aids consist essentially of *National Archives Preliminary Inventory No. 43, Records of the War Refugee Board,* comps. Henry T. Ulasek and Ira N. Kellogg, Jr. (Washington: NARS, 1952) and a 61-page shelf list of the Franklin D. Roosevelt Library for the Records of the War Refugee Board.

18. *National Archives Preliminary Inventory No. 77, Records of the War Relocatin Authority,* Record Group 210 (Washington, DC: NARS, 1945), p. 28.

19. Arthur D. Morse, *While Six Million Died: A Chronicle of American Apathy* (New York: Random House, 1967), p. 207.

great sympathy about the suffering Jews but refusing to extend any substantial aid to them.

The records of the Evian Conference are scattered among several collections in the National Archives in Washington, D.C., and in the Franklin D. Roosevelt Library in Hyde Park, New York. The president's secretary's file on refugees in the Franklin D. Roosevelt Library has some good sources on the origin of the conference, the motives of the president in calling it, and United States' reactions during the conference.[20] The papers of Myron C. Taylor, the chairman of the U.S. delegation, also contain a considerable number of important records on the Evian Conference, including transcripts of proceedings, resolutions, reports, and many other items.[21]

The records of the Department of State in the National Archives also provide a good deal of detail concerning happenings at the conference. Essentially in the central decimal files, many records deal with U.S. contacts with other nations, conference proceedings, reluctance of receiving nations to accept Jewish refugees, and the German reaction to the conference.[22] Purport lists constitute finding aids to these documents.[23] In addition, several of the documents in these files are also printed in the *Foreign Relations of*

the *United States* series.[24] A number of German foreign ministry documents deal mainly with the German reaction to the conference.[25] Also a few Nuremberg trials records portray Foreign Minister Joachim von Ribbentrop's refusal to cooperate with the conference and German emigration plans for the Jews.[26] There are also some records on the conference in the official files of *Reichleader* SS Himmler.[27] A few of the German diplomatic records on this topic are printed in the *Documents on German Foreign Policy 1918–1945* series[28] and there are many records in several files of U.S. diplomatic and consular posts, for example, the Havana file.[29]

One of the accomplishments of the Evian Conference was the establishment of an intergovernmental committee for the purpose of finding ways and means to enable Jews from

24. *Foreign Relations of the United States*, I:740–57, 1938.

25. The major serials of Microfilm Publication T120 which concern the Evian Conference include 3496, 2134, 1125, and 7051.

26. Particularly Nuernberg Prosecution Documents NG 3702 documenting Foreign Minister von Ribbentrop's refusal to cooperate with the Evian Conference and NG 5764 dealing with Nazi emigration plans for Jews.

27. Records of the *Reichsleader* of the SS and chief of the German police, National Archives Microfilm Publication T175, roll 410, beginning at frame 2934577, pertains to the meetings of the Evian Conference. Guide No. 39 of the Guides to German Records microfilmed at Alexandria VA (Washington, DC: NARS, 1963), p. 107, describe this file.

28. Several of the records from the German foreign ministry pertaining to the Evian Conference are printed in *Documents on German Foreign Policy* 1918–1945, ser. D, V:894–96.

29. *See* Havana Post File, 1938, vol. 14, Decimal 848, Accession Number 55A354, National Archives, Record Group 84, Records of the Foreign Service Posts of the Department of State.

20. Franklin Delano Roosevelt Library, Official File; File 3186 particularly contains correspondence on the president's motives.

21. There is a good finding aid for the papers of Myron C. Taylor as chairman of the U.S. Delegation to the Evian Conference in the Franklin D. Roosevelt Library.

22. The decimal pertaining to the Evian Conference is 840.48/Refugees and the records are scattered throughout the decimal for the 1938 period.

23. Purport lists are bound in volumes; they constitute an index and refer to document number within a certain decimal.

Germany and Austria to leave these Nazi-controlled countries. The difficulty the committee had to cope with lay in the German refusal to let the Jews take their capital out of the country and in providing for the emigration of penniless Jews.

George Rublee, an official of the Department of State, directed the work of the intergovernmental committee. During 1938 and 1939, Rublee conducted negotiations with Hjalmar Schacht, president of the *Reichsbank*, and acquitted of war crimes by the International Military Tribunal at Nuremberg. After Schacht's dismissal as negotiator, Rublee continued with Helmuth Wohlthat, a foreign exchange expert.[30] They reluctantly agreed on emigration; however, the agreement had little chance of implementation because of the outbreak of World War II in September, 1939. Nonetheless, a large number of Jews managed to leave Germany during and after the negotiations.[31]

Rublee-Schacht negotiations

The records of the Rublee-Schacht negotiations are scattered throughout several records collections in the National Archives. The papers of Myron C. Taylor in the Franklin D. Roosevelt Library contain a good many records on the subject, including Roosevelt's personal comments on the Rublee negotiations.[32]

The president's press conferences[33] and the diaries of Henry Morgenthau, Jr., contain many records and comments on the negotiations.[34] In addition, the records of the Department of State document the talks fairly thoroughly. Especially noteworthy are Schacht's proposals and Rublee's reports and assessments of the situation.[35] Most of these documents are part of the refugee decimal of the central decimal file, well indexed in the purport books.

The German foreign ministry records constitute an especially rich source of the reluctant German reaction to negotiating Jewish emigration. State Secretary Ernst von Weizsaecker, later tried and convicted in case 11 by a U.S. military tribunal at Nuremberg, for example, saw no need for the negotiations for he believed that no country was willing to accept penniless Jews, especially not 600,000.[36] Other records in this collection deal with passport restrictions, emigration of Jews to Switzerland, German reluctance to let Rublee come to Berlin, Schacht's visit to England, and the impact of the *Kristallnacht* pogrom on emigration.[37]

The German foreign ministry records are indexed in the Kent

---

30. Feingold, p. 49.
31. Ibid., p. 67.
32. *See* papers of Myron C. Taylor as chairman of the U.S. Delegation to and President of the Intergovernmental Committee on Political Refugees, Evian, France, July 1958, London and elsewhere 1938–54, in the Franklin D. Roosevelt Library, particularly boxes 2 through 5.

33. Among the finding aids in the Franklin D. Roosevelt Library there is a good index to the president's press conferences arranged by subject. All the materials of interest here are arranged under the word "Refugee."
34. The index to the so called Morgenthau Diaries contains good information particularly on the Rublee-Schacht negotiations.
35. These are again in Decimal 840.48/ refugees for the year 1938, particularly document numbers following 1000.
36. *See* especially Microfilm Publication T120 Serials 1125, 2959, 7051, and 7062.
37. Ibid.

Catalog. They are reproduced on microfilm, subdivided into serials with a descriptive data sheet preceding the serial.[38] The Nuremberg trial records duplicate several of these documents, but this collection also contains other records on these negotiations including a report by Rublee that Jews could not take property out of Germany, British views on the Rublee negotiations, Schacht's summary on the talks, and other items.[39] As noted previously, the best finding aid for these records is the Yad Vashem/Yivo Guide supplemented by staff analyses fashioned by analysts working for the prosecution staff at Nuremberg.

More successful than the Schacht-Rublee agreement, the earlier Haavara agreements enabled Jews to emigrate to Palestine and to take some of their capital out of Germany. The Nazis and the Jewish Agency for Palestine agreed to pay a German exporter from blocked Jewish accounts for goods exported to Palestine. The Jewish Agency would compensate the refugee in Palestinian currency.[40] In this fashion, indirect capital transfers took place.

The records of the Haavara agreements center mainly on the reluctance with which the German foreign ministry, particularly the Nazi Party Abroad Organization, dealt with the agreements because they provided advantages for Jews and the Jewish

Agency in Palestine as well as for the Nazi economy. The Arabs, too, strongly opposed the agreements, particularly the Grand Mufti of Jerusalem who did not take kindly to Jewish emigration from Germany and resettlement of the Jews in Palestine. Most of the records are in the Department of State's central decimal file as well as in the mission and post files,[41] the microfilm of the German foreign ministry records,[42] and some are printed in the *Documents on German Foreign Policy 1914–1945* series.[43]

S.S. St. Louis *affair*

The central file documenting one of the most dramatic and highly publicized incidents of Jewish flight from Germany, made into a motion picture later, the S.S. *St. Louis* affair, is the central decimal file of the Department of State in the National Archives.[44] In the spring of 1939, the Nazi effort to make Germany *Judenrein* accelerated. Subsequently, the number of those lucky Jewish refugees possessing visas or landing permits increased measurably. The Cuban director of immigration, Colonel Manuel Benitez, had sold many landing permits wholesale to the Hamburg-America passengership line. The line resold the permits to individual Jews at $150.00 per permit. The line failed to inform the 930 permit holders who sailed on the S.S. *St. Louis* bound for Havana

38. The arrangement of these indexes requires cross-reference to the National Archives Microfilm Publication roll number list toward the closing pages of each *Catalog* volume.

39. *See* especially Nuernberg prosecution documents PS3319, NG 1521, 1522, 1524, and 1537; *documents on German Foreign Policy 1918–1945*, ser. D, V: 900–12, 919–26.

40. Hilberg, p. 95.

41. Decimal 840.48/Refugees.

42. Noteworthy are Serials 64, 73, and 495 of Microfilm Publication T120.

43. *Documents on German Foreign Policy* 1918–1945, ser. D, V:746–815.

44. Particularly Decimal 837.55 J contains rich documentation.

that the Cuban government had revoked the permits.

Upon arrival in Havana in May, 1939, the Cuban authorities remained adamant in their refusal to let the refugees land despite a dramatic suicide. The S.S. *St. Louis* consequently was forced to return to Europe where a terrible fate seemed to await the emigrants in Nazi Germany.[45] Fortunately, however, after days of intense drama, England, France, Holland, and Belgium decided to provide asylum for the refugees. Many of those who stayed in the last three countries eventually died in Auschwitz after these nations were overrun by the Nazis.[46] Other ships faced similar problems.[47]

The records of the S.S. *St. Louis* affair in the Department of State's files deal with citizens requesting President Roosevelt to accept the S.S. *St. Louis* refugees and the Department of State's denying these requests in stereotyped replies, reports on the situation in Cuba by various individuals, especially the U.S. consul in Havana, attempts to get back the money paid by refugees, the landing of the S.S. *St. Louis* in Europe, and the distribution of refugees in Belgium and Holland.[48] Also the Morgenthau Diaries in the Franklin D. Roosevelt Library record the secretary of the treasury's concern over the refugees aboard the vessel and how they could receive aid.[49] Many records on the S.S. *St. Louis* affair are part of the diplomatic and consular post files. They include a good deal of information not in the central Department of State files, such as reports and memoranda on the changing situation in Cuba.[50]

Although the priorities assigned to rescue and relief by Allied and neutral countries alike never seemed very high, after the outbreak of hostilities in 1939, they sank to an even lower level. With the United States entering the war in late 1941, the Nazis continued on the road toward extermination of the Jewish people with impunity because now reasonable possibilities for Jewish resettlement had altogether disappeared.

When the extent and the brutality of the Nazi extermination program became subject to wider publicity in early 1943, pressure to do something about impeding or stopping this program began to mount.[51] As a consequence, Anglo-American authorities called a conference to deal with the problem of Jewish and other refugees and their possible resettlement..This was the Bermuda Conference in mid-1943. In the final analysis, the conference failed to accelerate rescue and did not show any tangible results.[52]

Bermuda Conference

The records of the Bermuda Conference are among those deposited by the Department of State in the National Archives and are among the holdings of the Franklin D. Roosevelt Library, particularly the War Refugee Board documents.[53] A

45. Feingold, pp. 65–66.
46. Ibid.
47. Ibid.
48. Decimal 837.55 J.
49. Particularly card No. 194 of the Morgenthau Diaries index in the Franklin D. Roosevelt Library under the category "Refugees" describes noteworthy records.

50. *See* Havana Post File, 1939, Decimal 848, Accession Number 55A354, NARG 84.
51. Feingold, p. 208.
52. Morse, p. 59.
53. Particularly the General Correspondence File of the War Refugee Board in the Franklin D. Roosevelt Library.

few documents are part of the German foreign ministry microfilm, and some are published in the *Foreign Relations of the United States* series.[54]

Others

Despite the difficulties and failures encountered, the rescue attempts continued and met with occasional positive results. Particularly strong efforts exerted in the rescue of Jewish children resulted in some success. Despite constant pressure by the SS and German foreign ministry officials to place obstacles in the way of various groups in Balkan countries endeavoring to provide for the emigration of Jewish children to Palestine, the records of the German foreign ministry document occasional success for the proponents of rescue. For example, one report indicates that over a quarter of nearly 300 children from Hungary arrived safely in Palestine.[55]

For the most part, on instructions from von Ribbentrop, the German foreign ministry played along with rescue attempts, including a British offer to accept 5,000 Jewish children, without ever really intending to let large numbers of Jewish children escape.[56] Otto Ohlendorf, the chief of *Einsatzgruppe D*, explained and attempted to justify the killing of Jewish children at his trial at Nuremberg. He felt that if they were left alive, they would grow up to visit vengeance on the murderers of their parents. He expressed thus the views of the highest echelon of the Nazi extermination machinery.[57]

As the war progressed, rescue attempts accelerated. The terrible plight of the Hungarian Jews in 1944 made this particularly apparent. After the German occupation of Hungary had resulted in the deportation of over 400,000 Jews to the extermination camps, the SS began to meet with Jewish leaders and neutrals in earnest in order to obtain scarce goods and foreign exchange in return for Jewish lives. These attempts received official Nazi sanction because they might be turned into a tool useful to drive a wedge between the unity of the Allies.

Joel Brand, an officer of the Assistance and Rescue Committee in Budapest, figured prominently in these blood-for-goods negotiations. Before the slaughter of the Hungarian Jews by the Nazis began, Brand went to Istanbul with a Nazi offer to spare their lives for a payment in goods including 10,000 trucks to be used on the eastern front only. British authorities arrested him as he entered Syria from Turkey and detained him there. They also publicly denounced the truck deal. While he was held by the British, the extermination of the Hungarian Jews proceeded.[58]

Other blood-for-goods negotiations of the Nazis met with greater success than the truck deal. Some resulted in the shipment of Jews to Bergen-Belsen instead of Auschwitz and from there eventually to Switzerland. These negotiations and their

54 *Foreign Relations of the United States*, I:134–49, 1943; the decimals involved are 840.48/Refugees for 1943, particularly documents in the 3600 Series and Decimal 548.J1.

55. Report by Legations Councilor Rademacher to Ambassador von Killinger, 11 March 1943, Nuernberg Prosecution Document NG 2184.

56. Particularly Nuernberg Prosecution Document NG 5049 and NG 5138.

57. *Transcript United States v. Otto Ohlendorf et al.*, 2: 475–543 8 Oct. 1947, NARG 238.

58. Feingold, p. 271.

results as well as the efforts by Raoul Wallenberg, a Swedish diplomat, and by members of the diplomatic corps from other neutral countries who successfully extended to a sizable number of Hungarian Jews the protection of their countries, are documented in the records of the War Refugee Board and in those of the Nuremberg trials, particularly a number of affidavits by Rudolf Kastner, the vice-president of the Assistance and Rescue Committee, and Dieter Wisliceny and Kurt Becher, both SS officers.[59] Others are in the files of the Department of State, the German foreign ministry microfilm, as well as in the official files of Heinrich Himmler,[60] and some records are published in the *Foreign Relations of the United States* series.[61]

The attempts of a number of wealthy industrialists' families in Hungary to buy their freedom by ceding their holdings to the SS met with more success than did, for example, the Brand negotiations. These included the Weiss, Kornfeld, and Chorin families who were able to leave Hungary for Switzerland and Portugal together with some other families.[62] There are a good many records on these negotiations and emigration, especially in the official files of Heinrich Himmler, including lists of names of all the individuals

involved.[63] These records are also among the reports of the Office of Strategic Services.[64] Other negotiations involving Walter Schellenberg, the SS intelligence chief, and Jean Marie Musy, a former Swiss federal councillor, lead to the leaving of a trainload with 1,200 Jews from the Theresienstadt Concentration Camp and their safe arrival in Switzerland.[65] The Musy affair is best documented in the Nuremberg trial records.[66]

A desperate attempt to interrupt and delay the seemingly inexorable exodus of Jews from Hungary to the extermination camps envisioned the aerial bombardment of Kashan, the only railroad center leading from Hungary to Auschwitz, and eventually the bombing of the killing facilities themselves.[67] Requests by Rabbi Wise for such bombings from the armed forces resulted in none of the desired actions. In fact, a letter by John J. McCloy, assistant secretary of war, to John W. Pehle, director of the War Refugee Board, suggested that such bombing could not be given a priority and was impractical. Nonetheless, the army air force bombed the I. G. Farben

---

59. Also among the interrogations for both the International Military Tribunal at Nuremberg and the 12 U.S. military tribunals there.

60. Of particular interest are the War Refugee Board General Correspondence File, Microfilm Publication T175, roll 59, and Microfilm Publication T120, Serial 324/.

61. *Foreign Relations of the United States, 1944,* I:1044–60, mainly decimal 840.48/ Refugees.

62. Mario D. Fenyo, *Hitler, Horthy and Hungary: German-Hungarian Relations, 1941– 1945* (New Haven: Yale University Press, 1972), p. 193.

63. Microfilm Publication T 175 roll 59.

64. Three Office of Strategic Services (OSS) Reports pertain to the emigration of the Hungarian industrialists: OSS104280, 21 Nov. 1944 pertains to the holdings of the Weiss Konzern; OSS107062 deals with the Weiss, Kornfeld, Chorin, and Mauthner families; and OSS109833, 6 Jan. 1945 also pertains to the families.

65. Feingold, p. 279.

66. Especially Nuernberg Prosecution Documents NG 5230 and Affidavit by SS Colonel Kurt Becher and NO 5762 and Affidavit by SS General Walter Schellenberg; *see also* Microfilm Publication T175 roll 118 including Heinrich Himmler's correspondence and notes on his negotiations with Musy on behalf of the orthodox Rabbis of the United States and Canada.

67. Feingold, 256–57.

Buna plant at Auschwitz adjacent to the killing facility.

The records documenting the abortive attempts of bombing the extermination facilities out of existence and thereby putting an end to the extermination of Jews there lie scattered in many collections, including the War Refugee Board, the Office of Strategic Services, the United States Strategic Bombing Survey, the Joint Chiefs of Staff, the War Department, the assistant secretary of war, and many others.[68]

The documents discussed in the preceding pages represent the major holdings of the National Archives and Records Service on the subject of rescue and relief of Jewish suffering during the Nazi Era. The size and the complexity of these records preclude listing them all, but those discussed will often provide leads to those not mentioned. The drama of rescue and relief continues beyond the scope of this article into the post–World War II Era. Pertinent records in the National Archives include such topics as treatment of the survivors of the Holocaust, return to their countries of origin or to new ones, their stay in displaced persons camps, and the restitution of property to them. These records were created by United States military agencies, such as the Office of Military Government for Germany and Army commands, particularly headquarters of Seventh and Third U.S. Armies, and later civilian agencies, especially the Office of the United States High Commissioner for Germany.

NEEDED: THE POOLING OF RESOURCES

The researcher of rescue and relief records and the diplomatic historian often face the same dilemma: in order to delineate a less-biased history, they must consult records in many depositories. And, indeed, many depositories in the United States and elsewhere have collected rescue and relief records. Foremost are Yivo and the Leo Baeck Institute in New York City; The Hoover Institution on War, Revolution, and Peace in Stanford, California; Yad Vashem in Israel; the Centre de Documentation Juive Contemporaine in Paris; the Rijksinstitut voor Orlogsdocumentatie in Amsterdam; the Wiener Library in London; and many others.

The availability of records pertaining to rescue and relief in many depositories underlines the need to know the extent of the holdings in each in order to perform comprehensive research. In addition to articles such as this one, which introduces researchers to the holdings of a particular archive, a more comprehensive finding aid must be produced. Only the cooperation of all the archives that hold pertinent records can accomplish such an objective by pooling their resources to produce a computer-assisted index of finding aids as the first step in this direction. Such an index would greatly facilitate shedding light on some unknown territory and could become the forerunner of a general index to records on the Holocaust; it would help us also to move to a better understanding of the Holocaust.

---

68. A file in the Modern Military Branch, entitled Auschwitz, contains a conglomerate of records on the bombing of Auschwitz and Kashan. Particularly noteworthy are recent photo interpretations by the Central Intelligence Agency which clearly identify the killing facilities.

The Holocaust: A Never-Ending Agony

By FRED ROBERTS CRAWFORD

ABSTRACT: How long does a severe traumatic experience remain in the memory and affect behavior? Many years later, in interviewing American soldiers who encountered Nazi concentration camps during World War II, we quickly learned that their responses in at least 40 percent of these interviews revealed severe emotional stress as they described the tragic details that they had seen as eyewitnesses. They frequently had kept the photographs taken during these experiences and also shared official army booklets, films, and military orders all pertaining to the concentration camps and those victims. From an original goal of 10 oral histories, our project titled "Witness to the Holocaust" has expanded to almost 400 known GI witnesses and has completed interviews with 80. The truths which these men and some women nurses, Red Cross workers, and United Nations Refugee Relief Agency (UNRRA) workers have shared verify beyond question the terrible nature of the concentration camp system and its impact on Jews and non-Jews during World War II. Now sociologists, psychiatrists, and historians are analyzing the interview data confirming, among other things, that many of these witnesses still suffer from the awful experience of liberating or even seeing a camp after liberation. This agony seems never to end.

Fred Roberts Crawford is an eyewitness of the Holocaust, having been placed in a concentration camp in Hungary during June, 1944, after being shot down while flying with the USAAF's 52nd Fighter Group. He was mistaken for a Jew but was later identified and then sent to a prisoner-of-war camp in Germany. On 30 April 1945, he saw Dachau. He has served as director, Center for Research in Social Change, Emory University, and as professor of sociology there since 1966. He also directs the "Witness to the Holocaust" project, has produced a television series on this subject, and has spoken at professional meetings on the project.

HOW LONG does a severe traumatic experience remain in the memory and affect behavior? In our research, we are learning that time does not heal all things. Over the passing years, details may become blurred and emotions may become less acute but memory of the Holocaust persists and the emotional impact still causes pain, depression, anger, and grief. Perhaps it would be no surprise if the subjects of our study were Holocaust survivors but they are not. The men and women who are sharing with us their experiences pertaining to the Holocaust are American and Allied soldiers, nurses, Red Cross workers, United Nations Refugee Relief Agency (UNRRA) workers, and others who came into contact with concentration camps and Holocaust victims during the spring and summer of 1945. It is their traumatic experiences resulting from involvement with the concentration camps and survivors which we are now documenting and analyzing.

INTRODUCING THE HOLOCAUST

NBC's Holocaust series, shown in the spring of 1978, has done more than any other source to make the public in America and Europe aware anew of the terrible tragedy which the Nazis perpetrated against civilians during World War II. In the concentration camps, in the labor camps, and to a lesser degree in the death camps, civilians who opposed Hitler or who simply were defined as enemies of the state, were arrested, stripped of their civil rights, and incarcerated to be dealt with as "undesirables." Possibly as many as five million from all of the Nazi-occupied nations are of this type, including Gypsies, Jehovah's

Witnesses, thousands of Roman Catholic priests and nuns, Lutheran and other Free and Land church ministers and members, and on and on. They were enemies of the Nazi state, criminals according to the Nazi regulations.

However, the Jews of Europe had not opposed Hitler. They had not broken the laws of the nations in which they lived. Their only fault was in the fact that they were Jews and, by Hitler's definition, "inferior humans" who could have but one end under the Third Reich: death. Thus six million were systematically identified, stripped of human linkages, separated, deported, and destroyed by forced labor, starvation, torture, bullets, and gas.

The Holocaust is still present—in many ways—as we are learning. We know of its presence by omissions: the one million missing adults with all of their creative abilities who would be alive, contributing members of the European world today if they had not been murdered as children during the Holocaust; the missing generations of those who survived—grandparents, uncles, aunts, cousins, all who died in the Holocaust; and the absence of Jews in modern Europe.

The Holocaust is still present because of its commissions—the guilt and retribution manifest in the Federal Republic of Germany but peculiarly, not in East Germany, Hungary, Poland, and the other Nazi-cooperating nations who were directly involved in deporting and/or killing Jews. We still see the Holocaust in the lives of survivors. And we now are finding the effects of Holocaust reflected in the words and actions of those World War II soldiers and support persons who, while pursuing the remnants of the

Nazi armies, encountered the prison camps. These are our prime witnesses.

IMPORTANCE OF THE STUDY

My own World War II experiences placed me in a concentration camp collection center for Jews in Hungary in June, 1944, (although I was a U.S. army officer/pilot and a Christian) and at Dachau on 30 April 1945 (the day after it was liberated, as I also had been at Stalag Luft VII A). More recently, WSB television officials— NBC in Atlanta—who knew something of my experiences invited me to discuss the television series immediately after the final episode, which I did. By the next day, telephone calls and letters were arriving at the station and my office questioning the truth of the Holocaust and the accuracy of my own eyewitness testimony. Two characteristics dominated the criticisms: strong anti-semitism and/or ignorance. I quickly learned that the American television public did not—would not—believe the truth from Jewish sources which had prevailed in dealing with the Holocaust since the 1930s and now could not accept my brief testimony. I asked, "What evidence will they accept?"

I then realized that the predisposition of most Americans was to believe a relative, someone they knew—a father, grandfather, husband, or son. Thus if we at the Center for Research in Social Change could locate and interview 10 or a dozen such eyewitnesses and then publish their actual accounts, *the impact on the non-Jewish American public would be vital*. So we started out seeking 10 such persons who, while serving in the U.S. Army, came into contact with a concentration camp during the closing weeks of World War II.

On our own campus we quickly located several witnesses, including a retired major general. Reporters for local newspapers did features, as did radio reporters and television newscasters, including a national reference over CBS's evening news program. Contacts poured in from Atlanta, Georgia, and more than 25 states until we had the names of more than 300 witnesses. Caught in this same concern were the unexpected—an UNRRA social worker who had written her autobiography of the months in Europe immediately after V-E day; an army nurse who had helped survivors in two camps; survivors themselves who had never told their stories to anyone and now wished to do so; one of the Nuremberg trial judges' daughters who had sat through every session of the trial and knew most of the Allied figures personally; and on and on. We were overwhelmed, but we started using volunteers. In fact, we were all volunteers since there was no funding for this research.

Some initial findings

Interviews with Atlanta witnesses taught other truths to us about the Holocaust. During the second interview, a witness broke down and began to cry while describing what he had seen at Buchenwald. Every effort was made to restore him to stability, and the interview was completed. The interpretation of this case was that it was unique, related to the particular personality of this individual. However, within the first 10 interviews, four had revealed intense emotional responses as they described their experiences pertaining to concentration camps and survivors. Now we realized that the behavior we were observing was not unique to an individual but possibly linked to the Holocaust experience. This became a major hypothesis in our study.

As the interviewing continued, we prepared our volunteer interviewers to observe the respondent's body language. Clenched fists, tears in eyes, whiteness in facial skin, rapid, shallow breathing, and so on were behavioral characteristics commonly reported by the interviewers. We hope and intend to continue our research into these phenomena in the future.

Of primary importance to our original purpose was the accumulation of specific details about many concentration camps and murder sites as reported by our witnesses. Those who had taken photographs and had managed to keep them over these past 34 years brought this evidence to us. We copied their photos and returned the originals. One of our first witnesses brought an old copy of a booklet entitled *The Seventy-First Came . . . to Gunskirchen Lager.* This document, with its foreword by Major General Willard G. Wyman who commanded the 71st Division, was printed during the summer of 1945, because as General Wyman wrote:

The damning evidence against the Nazi war criminals found at Gunskirchen Lager [which was six kilometers north of Lambach, Austria and a sub-unit of Mauthausen] is being recorded in this booklet in the hope that the lessons learned in Germany will not soon be forgotten by the democratic nations or the individual men who fought to wipe out a government built on hate, greed, race myths and murder. This is a true record. I saw Gunskirchen Lager myself before the 71st Division had initiated its merciful task of liberation. The horror of Gunskirchen must not be repeated. A permanent, honest record of the crimes committed there will serve to remind all of us in future years that the freedom we enjoy in a democratic nation must be jealously guarded and protected.

During the past 18 months, we have found only one other witness who had a copy of this booklet. With its photographs of the dead and surviving, the camp and its condition, with its sketches by Pfc. Norman Nichols of the camp and its tragic inmates, and with the verbal descriptions of key witnesses, the booklet carries an impact of unusual degree. We decided the booklet coud speak for itself and arranged to have it photocopied, printing 1,000 replicas for distribution to interested persons and agencies.

Additional developments

Some funding came in. IBM's local agency donated funds to assist in purchasing tape recorders and copiers. The Center for Research in Social Change at Emory used what funds it had. Emory's President James Laney contacted a division of the United Methodist church, and the project received a grant of $3,000 from this source. Student interns were permitted to register for training in research as part of the staff on this project. One of these, Francine Chase, is the daughter of a survivor, Sally Chase.

As our efforts to present this new evidence to the public increased, the opportunity arose to produce a television series of eight 30-minute episodes, "Witness to the Holocaust." Through the cooperation of CBS affiliate WAGA in Atlanta as part of its public broadcasting service, these programs were developed, taped, and shown several times in Atlanta over WAGA and also the local PBS station. One of these programs is built around an interview Francine conducts with her mother as the interviewee. All who have responded to viewing this show stress its tremendous impact on their own knowledge and emotions.

Other episodes presented the major general; the contributor of *Gunskirchen Lager;* three Buchenwald witnesses; three Dachau witnesses; a dialogue between a survivor who wound up in Buchenwald after suffering for years in various camps, and a black GI who helped liberate that camp and took photographs of it; and other related topics and witnesses. Copies of these programs were requested and sent to a dozen U.S. cities, to Israel, and to West Germany.

Other documents and memorabilia were being contributed with the passing weeks and months. A second crucial booklet, *Dachau,* was donated and photocopied with 1,000 replicas again being produced and shared with interested sources. Three others are in the files of the project but lack of funding has precluded their being copied thus far. We have received a manuscript autobiography from an army major who was responsible for a displaced persons' camp during the summer of 1945, a manuscript autobiography from a survivor who is now in Ecuador; 8-mm movie films taken at Ohrdruf Concentration Camp by an officer, and so on.

The interview data are revealing many new—not present in current literature—facts about the camps at the time of liberation, treatment of German guards still at the camps, information about smaller camps not usually mentioned or described,

and also the reaction of the GIs involved. These interviews are currently being transcribed and will be published in the future as funds permit.

CURRENT PURPOSES OF THE PROJECT

The original intent has been expanded into these five areas: (1) to collect and add to the existing historical evidence pertaining to Nazi concentration camps the testimony of eyewitnesses, the GIs, Red Cross workers, UNRRA workers, and others who came into contact with camps at the close of World War II; (2) to collect and share all other evidence, such as photographs, documents, and military reports, which clarify the conditions of the camps and the behavior of the inmates and liberators and Germans at the time of liberation and thereafter; (3) to identify as many witnesses as possible and to offer them the opportunity to tell their personal experiences; we are finding now that known witnesses are nominating other witnesses so that we have not just a self-selected pool of those who contacted us, but also some who are cooperating because we contacted them; (4) to study, where the witness is willing, the possible presence of long-range effects from the experience of coming into contact with a Nazi concentration camp and its victims at the close of the war; these effects may include physiological reactions, psychological responses, interactional patterns including familial, and orientations to participation in civil rights and possibly even antiwar movements; and (5) to study the societal processes reflected by the testimony as these clarify response patterns of survivors, of military personnel to the camps and survivors; to methods of social control activated by the military upon liberation and thereafter; the interaction of military, survivors and Germans, military and civilian; and between Allied military and civilian workers and agencies as the postwar summer developed.

Early in the interviewing as the body language of respondents was recognized as being of importance, videotapes were taken on an experimental basis. Such evidence recorded in this form is of great importance. Videotaping future interviews will represent yet another innovation in Holocaust-related research.

Our "Witness to the Holocaust" project has become interdisciplinary, involving sociologists, psychiatrists, political scientists, and historians as well as communication specialists and journalists. Our volunteer interviewers usually are professionals in social work, counseling, or other public contact occupations. We are training capable students to interview also.

Each week, additional witnesses are identified for the project. Although only a third of the known witnesses have thus far been interviewed, the objective is to reach every one because each personal account is unique, conveys new information, and also assists in establishing the accuracy and completeness of the episodes developing around the historical locations and times of this study. Cooperation has been offered and accepted from the Oral History Association, the Minnesota Center for Social Research, the Department of Sociology of the University of Texas at El Paso, of several other colleges, and by individuals from Savannah to San Diego and from Miami to New York.

One of the four originators of our project, Sylvia Becker, served as a member of the Expert Advisory Panel for President Carter's Holocaust Commission. The second, Kaethe Solomon, is chairperson of Emory's Cantor Isaac Goodfriend Holocaust Collection. Dr. David Blumenthal, who holds the Jay and Leslie Cohen Professor of Judaic Studies Chair at Emory in its Department of Religion, is the third originator, while the fourth is myself.

We sincerely solicit inquiries and nominations of possible witnesses for our study. The Holocaust is still very much with us and new generations must be exposed to this truth.

EPILOGUE

The articles in this issue of THE ANNALS have been presented to the readers as products of scholarly thinking and writing. At one level, they are the kind of thing readers of THE ANNALS have come to expect of every issue. At another level, they have presented an event which is a challenge to every thinking and feeling person—to his conscience, to his religious integrity, to his understanding of university ethos and professional ethics, and to his perception of the misery and grandeur of the human condition. At this level, they are a reminder that we were human persons before we became members of the *universitas fidelium* and that one of the lessons of the Holocaust is that we must remain human persons afterward as well.

FRANKLIN H. LITTELL

INDEX